*"To tell the truth,
there is no fraud or deceit in the world
which yields greater gain and profit
than that of counterfeiting gems."*

From the *37th Book of Historie of the World*
by the Roman historian, C. Plinius Secundus

Published in the year 77 A.D.

GEM
IDENTIFICATION
MADE EASY
5th Edition

A HANDS-ON GUIDE TO MORE
CONFIDENT BUYING & SELLING

ANTOINETTE MATLINS, PG, FGA
&
A.C. BONANNO, FGA, ASA, MGA

GEMSTONE PRESS
Woodstock, Vermont

Gem Identification Made Easy, 5th Edition:
A Hands-On Guide to More Confident Buying & Selling

2014 Fifth Edition, Hardcover, Second Printing

For information regarding permission to reprint material from this book, please mail or fax your request in writing to GemStone Press, Permissions Department, at the address / fax number listed below, or email your request to permissions@gemstonepress.com.

Library of Congress Cataloging-in-Publication Data

Matlins, Antoinette Leonard.
Gem identification made easy : a hands-on guide to more confident buying & selling.
—5th edition.
    pages cm
Written by Antoinette Matlins and A.C. Bonanno.
Includes bibliographical references and index.
ISBN 978-0-943763-90-3 (hc)
1. Precious stones—Identification. I. Bonanno, Antonio C. II. Title.
QE392.M33 2013
553.8028'7—dc23
                                            2012050758
ISBN 978-0-943763-93-4 (eBook)

Jacket Photographs: Emeralds courtesy of Robert Weldon
Jacket Design: Stefan Killen and Bridgett Taylor
Text Design: James F. Brisson
Illustrations: Kathleen Robinson

Some of the material in this book appeared originally as articles in *National Jeweler.*

10 9 8 7 6 5 4 3 2

Manufactured in the United States of America

Published by GemStone Press
A Division of LongHill Partners, Inc.
Sunset Farm Offices, Rte. 4, P.O. Box 237
Woodstock, VT 05091
Tel: (802) 457-4000   Fax: (802) 457-4004
www.gemstonepress.com

A SPECIAL THANKS

To each of you who participated in our
pocket instrument workshops across the country,
whose excitement and delight with each discovery
affirmed our belief in the need for this book
… and gave us the extra support and
encouragement to make it
a reality.

To Ruth Bonanno,
who since our writing of
Jewelry & Gems: The Buying Guide
still has nothing—and everything—
to do with it

and
Stuart M. Matlins,
without whose confidence, support,
encouragement, and endurance
this book would not have been written

Contents

List of Tables

List of Color Plates *(FOLLOWING PAGE 234)*

Preface to the Fifth Edition

Gem Identification Made Easy was first published in response to requests from students in our gem identification workshops. Increasingly, the people who attended our workshops were not so much interested in becoming "gemologists" as they were in learning specific skills that could help them spot a treasure in a flea market or protect themselves from the growing numbers of imitations, synthetics, or treated gems in the marketplace. They needed information that was simple and practical, and tools that were inexpensive and portable. Thus, *Gem Identification Made Easy* was born.

Previous editions of this book have focused on meeting the needs of collectors, connoisseurs, and hobbyists from all walks of life—with or without gemological or scientific backgrounds—as well as the needs of retailers, jewelry designers, bench jewelers, and diamond and gemstone dealers. Experienced gemologists have also come to realize that simple tests can be huge time-savers and also, more importantly, that the tools on which they rely so heavily in the lab are of little or no help in the field or at major trade shows. Gemologists now see that traditional gemology courses offer little information or instruction on simple, portable, inexpensive tools that can be especially useful to the experienced gemologist.

Following the publication of the first edition in 1989, *Gem Identification Made Easy* was a finalist for the American Bookseller's Association's "Benjamin Franklin Award for the Best How-To Book of the Year." This award gave me and my coauthor father, Antonio Bonanno, a wonderful feeling of satisfaction, and made us feel that perhaps all the work that went into writing it was really "worth it."

But we also knew that the true test of its merit could only be measured by you, our *readers*. Did the book do what it was intended to do: simplify the subject and provide a practical approach to help you develop the skills you need to recognize an opportunity or protect yourself from a costly mistake? For us, your letters and personal feedback are the most important measures of success, so we really appreciate the many wonderful letters we have received, and the conversations we've had with those of you we've had the pleasure of meeting.

My father died just prior to the publication of the third edition of this book, but with each new edition, I know we are keeping alive his view of the world: that people from every walk of life can be successful in this field—especially those who fear it might be too difficult, or take too much time, or cost too much for the right tools. He focused on making the field *accessible* to a wide audience, and this gave him, as it now gives me, a sense of great personal satisfaction. Today, with greater and greater focus on high-tech equipment and the need to turn to major gem-testing labs, the necessity to keep gemology accessible is stronger than ever. And once again, this book continues to demonstrate the value—even in a high-tech world—of basic, practical gemology.

Of particular importance in this edition is the information we provide on a new *type* of imitation, which entered the market after the publication of the last edition of this book and is being misrepresented as genuine ruby and sapphire. This new type of composite, involving the infusion of *lead*-glass into low-quality stones, is *even fooling some gemologists and appraisers.*

The extent to which they are misrepresented—even by honest retailers—and the degree of confusion about what these new imitations really are is unprecedented. For this reason, and in light of the threat they pose to everyone who loves rubies and sapphires, this edition focuses special attention on these imitations throughout the book. We have also added an entire new chapter dedicated to explaining what these imitations are and how they differ from "treated" rubies and sapphires (Chapter 18).

This new fifth edition of *Gem Identification Made Easy* follows our original philosophy and the approach is the same—keep it simple, affordable, relevant, and interesting, and *anyone* can identify most gems. The instruments and basic techniques that we recommended in earlier editions, and most of the information that was covered in those editions, are as viable today as ever and continue to be accurate and reliable. In addition to focusing on lead-glass infused corundum imitations, this edition also includes information on:

- Several new, easy-to-use, portable instruments—for spotting new treatments, synthetics, and look-alikes—and how to use them
- "HPHT-treated" diamonds—what HPHT is, and easy ways to screen for it
- Cobalt-coated "blue" sapphires and tanzanite, coated "fancy-color" and "colorless" diamonds, and many other "coated" gemstones—what they are and how to spot them
- Tanzanite imitations flooding the market—and easy, fast ways to separate them
- The latest in synthetic gems, including diamonds—and simple, affordable identification techniques
- And more ...

The trend in recent years within the gemological community has been away from simple instruments, to ever-more-complicated, expensive laboratory equipment. In the wave of technological and scientific advancement, simple techniques and their application to gemstone identification have been overlooked and forgotten. Total dependence on highly sophisticated instruments and training, however, is not practical in the real world of buying and selling. Most of us, even gemologists, don't have the luxury of always having access to a complete laboratory, nor the time to subject every stone or piece of jewelry to sophisticated testing. And many who aren't gemologists can't afford the time or financial commitment to become gemologists. One of our goals in writing the first edition of *Gem Identification Made Easy* in 1989 was to remind people how valuable—and how reliable—*simple* techniques can be. Indeed, in many cases they are all one really needs. And today, so many years later, this is perhaps truer than ever before.

As always, our emphasis is on simple techniques that are easily learned and applicable when away from a laboratory. This is why we named the book *Gem Identification Made Easy* and we still think it best describes what we provide in the book. With each passing year, and the introduction of more and more treatments and new types of imitations into the marketplace, I continue to find our techniques effective, reliable, convenient, and efficient.

It is not our intent, nor has it ever been, to oversimplify the science of gemology. As we state repeatedly throughout the book, there are new synthetics and treatments that can only be detected with the most sophisticated training and equipment, and we stress the importance of seeking the services of a professional gemologist or gem testing laboratory. We applaud the work done around the world by laboratories and schools such as American Gemological Laboratories, The Gemological Institute of America, HRD Institute of Gemmology in Antwerp, SSEF (The Swiss Gemmological Institute) in Basel, The Gemmological Institute of Thailand (GIT) in Bangkok, The Gemmological Association of Great Britain, and other associations and schools. We certainly recognize the importance of extensive gemological training and the value of costly sophisticated equipment, and take particular delight in hearing from readers who tell us that our book helped them take the "first step" and that they are now enrolled in a gemology course at one of the major institutions! But we also realize that there is much that can be done using simpler, less-sophisticated procedures. Feedback from our readers and students confirms the need for this information, and affirms its validity.

We think it is important—perhaps essential—to recognize that you do not need to be a gemologist to know enough to protect yourself from many costly mistakes. In our opinion, the well-being of this entire field depends increasingly on people becoming more aware of what they *can do*. We think that gaining a level of proficiency in gem identification is important for *everyone* who loves gems and jewelry. *Gem Identification Made Easy* reflects this belief and opens the door to everyone.

For those who already have an earlier edition of *Gem Identification Made Easy*, I hope you will find this new edition a welcome addition to your library. For those who are just venturing into this fascinating field, I hope *Gem Identification Made Easy*, Fifth Edition, will lead to many "sparkling" and "brilliant" discoveries, and give you greater confidence and appreciation for all your future gem and jewelry purchases.

Antoinette Matlins

Acknowledgments

All of the charts that appear here were specifically designed and executed for use in this book; however, in some cases, charts from other publications were used as inspiration and reference. Grateful acknowledgment is given to the following for use of their charts as references, and for photographs and other invaluable contributions:

Accredited Gemologists Association (AGA)
American Gem Society (AGS)
American Gem Trade Association (AGTA)
American Gemological Laboratories, Inc. (AGL)
American Society of Appraisers (ASA)
Asian Institute of Gemological Sciences (AIGS)
Eickhorst & Company
Gem-A (The Gemmological Association of Great Britain)
Gemological Institute of America (GIA)
Hoge Raad Voor Diamant Institute of Gemmology (HRD)
Kassoy
Orwin Products Ltd. (OPL)
Meiji Techno America
National Jeweler Magazine
Swiss Gemmological Institute (SSEF)
Robert Weldon

Special acknowledgment is also given to:

William Pluckrose and Eric Bruton of the Gemmological Association of Great Britain, for their confidence in our work and special support;

The late Robert Kammerling, General Manager Technical Development and Dona Dirlam, Head Resource Librarian of GIA; Rodger Bucy, Columbia School of Gemology; C.R. Beesley, AGL; and Elisha Morgan for special photographic assistance;

Kathryn Bonanno-Patrizzi, FGA; Kenneth E. Bonanno, FGA; and Karen Ford DeHaas, FGA, for their technical gemological contributions;

Steve Liesman and Rosemary Wellner Mills for their editorial assistance;

Monica Wilson for her unrelenting persistence and superb organization, and Seth C. Matlins, whose marketing talent helped make this possible.

C.R. Beesley and Christopher Smith of American Gemological Laboratories, New York City, for the information they provided on detection of new colored gemstone treatments, especially epoxy-resin treated emerald, fracture-filled rubies, and surface-coated tanzanite and blue sapphire; and for sharing findings from field work and research conducted by GemCore on the Kashmir ruby deposits and identifying characteristics; and a special thank you for his enthusiastic support and encouragement of my work over the years.

Kenneth Scarratt of AGTA Gem Trade Laboratory, New York City; Mark Van Bockstael of HRD Institute of Gemmology, Antwerp, Belgium; Dr. H.A. Hanni and Jean Pierre Challain of Swiss Gemmological Institute (SSEF), Basel, Switzerland for providing information and photographs on synthetic diamonds, epoxy resin treatment of emeralds, fracture-filled rubies, diffusion-treated corundum, and HPHT-treated diamonds; and Charles Meyer, Bellataire, Inc., for candidly sharing his knowledge regarding the HPHT process and the diamonds produced by Bellataire.

Ron Yehuda of Yehuda Diamond Co., New York City, for diagnostic information and photographs of fracture-filled diamonds.

Introduction

The great transition of gemology from an art to a science is little more than 50 years old. "Exotic" tools, such as the microscope and refractometer, were both unknown to jewelers and unused in jewelry stores just a few decades ago. Merchants tended to take the word of salespeople and jewelry suppliers about a gemstone's species or quality. Common distinctions, such as a species (a division that indicates a single mineral) and a variety (different colors and types within a species) were unknown to those merchants. Identification and quality grading was based on the personal and primitive investigations of a few, the superstitions of some, and the ancient customs and beliefs of many.

As with all new concepts in any field, gemology as a science has been a slow and difficult one to take hold. In ancient times, some of the gemstones we wear today, such as tanzanite and tsavorite, were unknown. Had they been known, tanzanite would probably have been called sapphire and tsavorite, emerald. It was generally held that if a stone were blue it was sapphire, if it were red it was ruby, if green, it was emerald, and so on. The primary criteria used to identify stones were hardness and color. And since the hardness test was a "destructive" test (putting a scratch on the gem would certainly mar its beauty), color was relied on almost exclusively where jewelry was concerned.

Furthermore, imagine if you will how baubles, bangles, and beads were traded and regarded in ancient times. It was of little consequence if the gemstones were imitation or precious. Imitation lapis-lazuli was known and used in ancient Egyptian times and regarded with as much devotion as the genuine material. It was, after all, the color that was the most profound reason for owning a stone. Color had a deep personal and emotional impact on the psyche and most ancient people ascribed both magical and medicinal powers to gemstones based on their colors. Color, the ancient tradesman understood, was the way to separate one gem from another and any technology that might aid in such separation was left to the alchemists.

Innumerable mistakes resulting from identification based on color alone have been made throughout history, even into the 20th century. Bearing witness to this is the Black Prince's Ruby set in the Imperial State Crown of England. This jewel, according to jewelry historians, found its way to England and into the hands of the Black Prince in the 14th century. It was later worn by Henry V on his helmet when he crushed the French forces at Agincourt in 1415 and later by Richard III. It was lost in the disposal of the Crown Jewels by the Puritans. As fate would decree, the Black Prince's Ruby was bought by a jeweler for a mere £15, and later sold to Charles II after the Restoration of the Stuarts in 1660. For centuries, that matchless stone was believed to be a priceless ruby, until modern technology made separation and exact identity possible. It was found that the Black Prince's Ruby is not a ruby, but, instead, a large ruby-colored spinel of great beauty. A red spinel is another lovely red stone, often indeed a true "gem." But it is not a ruby. Given its size and beauty, were the Black Prince's Ruby truly a ruby, its value would be beyond imagining.

The story has its parallel in today's antique jewelry, lovingly carried to a jeweler for appraisal and sometimes repair. Often the stones set in antique jewelry are not what the owner thinks they are. Unfortunately, when the owner learns that the stone is an imitation such as glass, a doublet, a synthetic, or some altogether different gemstone, the jeweler's skill and honesty are questioned because the owner doesn't know whom to believe. For after all, didn't this belong to grandmother or great-grandmother?

Credibility problems often arise because few within the jewelry trade or among the general public are aware of the many types of imitations that exist, or that imitations have been made for thousands of years. Even synthetic stones have been around for almost 100 years! In 1885, near Geneva, Switzerland, small pieces of synthetic corundum of good ruby color were fused together into larger stones. Between 1885 and 1903, these "Geneva Rubies" were often sold as natural rubies. Some of these stones may well have been set in jewelry and reached the showcases of fine American jewelry firms. At that time, jewelers knew very little about gemstones and relied on their suppliers, wholesalers, and manufacturers for factual information. Relying on erroneous information themselves, they might easily have *mistakenly* sold them as natural ruby.

Information was so scant and technology so new that almost anyone's advice on testing was considered scientific. The following was written by an author known only as Charubel and comes from his book *Psychology of Botany,* published in 1906. The advice is for testing a genuine ruby:

> Get a round goblet glass free from cuts or marks of any kind. Place your stone within the bottom of the glass, at the centre. Then fill the glass with clear water; allow the daylight to fall on the glass, and keep it clear of the shades of outside things. Also, keep clear of direct sunshine. Your stone will now be magnified so as to enable you to see such marks in it as you could not see otherwise, as the magnifying power will be equal at all points. If you find your stone laminated, and a haze at some point, you may infer it to be the true Ruby. The paste [glass] one cannot be made to contain these characteristics; consequently the paste will appear more brilliant than the true stone, but, more glassy.

The world of gemology in the United States remained largely rooted in primitive techniques until 1930 when a young visionary named Robert Morrill Shipley began to teach and call for professionalism in the jewelry trade. Mr. Shipley, with an encyclopedic knowledge of gemology and newly graduated from the National Association of Goldsmiths in London (now called the Gemmological Association of Great Britain) and Paris, went to California in 1931 and founded what became the Gemological Institute of America. After Shipley decided that he would learn how to detect fake and fraudulent gems and distinguish them from natural ones, he became the evangelist who brought the gemological gospel to the jewelers of America.

Over the past 50 years, the creation of gemstone synthetics has accelerated concurrently with gemological technology. It has been stated by experts that every gemstone—except garnet and peridot—has now been synthesized and is available in the marketplace. This includes lapis-lazuli, malachite, coral, and turquoise. Even a limited number of small "fancy" yellow diamond synthetics and some gem-quality white diamonds are being produced.

With every step forward in the advancement of gem synthesis and treatment techniques, the jeweler and gem enthusiast have required more and better laboratory equipment and training. Scientists immersed in gemology continue to develop new methods and instruments for detection that play a major role in helping to minimize the opportunity for misrepresentation.

Science, gems, and jewelry are inextricably woven together today. And this worries some. Does it mean the romance will fade from buying, owning, and wearing gemstones and jewelry? Hardly. Quite apart from science is the deep human desire for beauty and self-adornment; the love of brilliant colors; the thrill of seeing sparkling white light from a diamond. These are motivations for buying and owning gems. In each of us who loves and appreciates beautiful gemstones is an inner knowledge that every gemstone has a magical charm of its own and is, in its own way, precious. And in each individual gem or piece of jewelry there lies a special aesthetic value and emotional appeal that resists all efforts to be scientifically measured.

In this world of investigative reporters, media probes, and industry scandals, it will be the professional gemologists and gem connoisseurs who labor to know more about the identity of each gemstone, and insure that each is properly and accurately described, who will uphold and maintain the integrity of this exciting field. And, in so doing, they are the ones who will ultimately sustain the magic, excitement, and pleasure found in the jewels we love so much!

Anna M. Miller, GG, RMV
Author of *Gems and Jewelry Appraising:
Techniques of Professional Practice* and
*The Illustrated Guide to Jewelry Appraising:
Antique, Period, Modern*

PART 1
BEFORE BEGINNING

1 / Before beginning

Today, knowing your gems, being absolutely sure about what you are buying and selling, is essential. Major changes in the gem world—new synthetic stones, new treatments to enhance and conceal, new gems, and more stones available in every hue and tone of color—make accurate gem identification more important than ever to both buyers and sellers.

Whether you are the owner of a large retail jewelry chain or small family-run business, someone who enjoys collecting or acquiring gems for personal pleasure, or a serious investor, insufficient knowledge can be costly. It can result in a bad purchase, damage to a reputation, and, equally significant, failure to recognize an opportunity.

Recently, in one of my classes, a student learned how costly incorrect identification can be. An avid jewelry lover, she read about an upcoming jewelry auction to be held in a hotel at which—according to the promotional material—many pieces had been "seized by law enforcement officials." She eagerly went to view the pieces in hope of discovering a treasure that she could acquire at a great price.

She spotted a very lovely ruby and diamond necklace, which contained a large oval ruby of exceptional color and brightness surrounded by numerous diamonds. It had a "laboratory report" *and* "appraisal," from a legitimate-sounding Los Angeles company which also had a professional-looking website. This should have been the first red flag. One should always be dubious about "accompanying documents" where a "laboratory" issues a "certificate" *and* a valuation. GIA, for example, issues lab reports but does not provide any "valuation." When buying in such a venue, misleading

3

documents—paid for by the seller—are often used to increase the price that the piece will bring.

In this case, the appraisal identified the center stone as a genuine ruby, noting it was "treated," and that it had an appraised retail value of $22,100. Since she thought the piece was really beautiful and didn't care that it was "treated"—she knew most rubies sold today are also treated—she decided to bid on it. She was thrilled when she succeeded in getting it for only about $10,000 in total (after paying the buyer's premium—the percentage that buyers pay to the auction house on top of the "hammer price"—and the local sales tax).

She then took the pendant to a jewelry store, at which she'd been a long-time customer, for an independent appraisal. She was even more pleased when it was appraised for $25,000! All was well ... until about a year later, when she participated in the annual 3-day course I give in Woodstock, Vermont ... and where she discovered what she really had!

One of the things covered in the class was a new type of *imitation* ruby flooding the market that is being misrepresented as genuine and sold at highly inflated prices. This imitation is a composition—a blend—of two very different substances: tinted lead-glass and very low-quality corundum (the mineral we know as "ruby" only when it occurs in a transparent red variety, which is rare).

Because of the presence of corundum and the use of *lead*-glass, which gives a reading that matches "ruby" on certain tests gemologists use, superficial testing may indicate "ruby" even though the stone is not ruby. The presence of the lead-glass causes problems, however, never associated with ruby. Unlike ruby, which is very tough and durable, this product is very fragile and can be easily damaged in the normal course of wear. Even worse, for bench jewelers—those who actually make jewelry, or resize, repair, or remount stones—they have become a nightmare. When doing any work involving these "rubies," they are quickly—and irreparably—damaged by techniques that have been used on real ruby for centuries! Then the innocent jeweler is accused of damaging the customer's stone, when the fault is not the jewelers' but the stone itself, because it is *not* a genuine ruby.

Now, back to the students. Several lead-glass composites were passed around for everyone to see, and one small ruby was put in a capful of freshly squeezed lemon juice. Everyone agreed how easy it would be to mistake these great looking lead-glass composites for genuine ruby; they look more like ruby than glass or other types of ruby imitations. Suddenly the students were worried about making a mistake themselves. Fortunately in the case of lead-glass composites, they are actually very easy to spot once you know what to look for (see Chapter 18), and everyone quickly mastered the techniques to recognize them.

Later in the day, I removed the one "ruby" that had been placed in the lemon juice, and everyone gasped when they saw the whitish etch lines across the entire stone ... from just being in lemon juice for about 5 hours! The acid from something as common as lemon juice was enough to etch the lead-glass wherever it reached the surface of the stone.

At that point, it was clear that the student who'd purchased the ruby pendant was very upset. She explained that she had brought her ruby pendant with her to class and, after learning how to spot these imitations, she was eager to examine her own ruby. But she was confused because she thought she was seeing the telltale signs that her ruby was one of these imposters. She knew this couldn't be the case since the appraiser had confirmed it was genuine and worth a lot more money than she'd paid. But when she saw what happened to the little ruby after something so minor as putting it in lemon juice, she was really worried. She asked me what she was doing wrong. Unfortunately, she was doing nothing wrong! She was seeing the telltale indicators that her ruby was not genuine.

It was all terribly distressing to her, and rightly so. In this particular situation, she wisely sought to verify the purchase *immediately,* and certainly had expected that the appraiser was reliable. But reliability requires that any gemologist keep up to date in terms of what is in the market, and he had not done so. Even worse, and as hard as it is to believe, he sent a letter stating that he *"assumed that the value given by the company that sold it to [her] was fair for the piece as identified by the seller and [he] based [his] 'replacement value' on the purchase price [she] paid."* This type of "appraisal" is all too common.

The irresponsible action of the appraiser deprived her of legal recourse while there was still time to do something about it. She had paid with a credit card, and the auction was taking place over several days and was still going on, so had it been properly identified at that time, she may have had legal recourse, or recourse through the credit card company. But by the time she found out what she really had—during my class over a year later—there was nothing she could do.

This story is not only sad in terms of how this student was exploited by an unscrupulous seller, but it also underscores why it's so important to know what credentials to look for in an appraiser or gemologist to whom you might turn for assistance in confirming what you have, or to help you master the techniques and skills we discuss here. To help ensure you find someone competent, be sure to refer to the International List of Gem Testing Laboratories and Gemologists in the appendix.

My student didn't find a treasure. But she is not alone in searching for one, hoping to discover something of value that others don't recognize. Each of us yearns to make such a discovery. And we might. There are such treasures still out there, waiting to be found. The key to discovery lies in our ability to recognize a treasure when we see it, and it can happen to you as easily as to anyone else.

Several years ago a former student of my father went into a midwestern pawnshop to kill some time. While there, she discovered a beautiful ring that appeared to contain diamonds and an emerald. The pawnbroker told her the diamonds were unusually fine, which her examination confirmed. The ring was also beautifully designed, with outstanding workmanship. The green stone posed the problem. Was it an emerald or some other less expensive green stone? And, if examination confirmed emerald, was it *natural* or *synthetic*?

She examined the stone carefully with three simple pocket-size instruments as she learned in my father's class, and concluded that the material was emerald. The only remaining question was whether it was natural or synthetic. The price being asked—$500—suggested that the pawnbroker believed the stone was synthetic.

While viewing the stone with the loupe, however, she thought she saw an inclusion indicative of natural. While she didn't have the necessary equipment to see the inclusion clearly enough to be sure, she decided to buy the ring because she liked it and the price was right, assuming the emerald was synthetic. But she could hardly contain her excitement. She really thought she might have a genuine, natural emerald of very fine quality. As soon as she returned to Washington, the ring was examined at our lab. It contained a fine, genuine natural emerald, with a value of nearly $50,000 at that time!

Unfortunately, few have the knowledge to know for sure what they are getting, and many make costly mistakes buying from pawnshops, auctions, flea markets, and private estates. But for the knowledgeable, such places can be very profitable.

The key to avoiding costly mistakes and recognizing profitable opportunities is knowing both what to *look for* and what to *look out for.*

In today's gem market one must contend with more gemstone materials than ever before. There are not only the old-type synthetics, which are relatively easy to identify, but new ones spawned by modern, sophisticated technology that are extremely difficult to distinguish from their natural counterparts.

Mother Nature has further compounded the difficulties by creating colored stones that closely resemble one another so look-alikes abound—tanzanite can look like sapphire, tsavorite (a green variety of garnet) can look like emerald, red spinel can look like ruby, and so on.

No matter what color you choose, there are at least three different gems readily available in that color. There are also many new imitations (simulants), and, as more and more venture into the exciting realm of antique jewelry, the oldest forms of imitation and reproduction are resurfacing, sometimes with a modern twist.

What all of this means is that jewelers and gem enthusiasts are more vulnerable. The risk is greater than ever. The need to depend more on your own skill, and less on someone else's, is paramount.

This is why we've written this book.

We recognize that not everyone is inclined to be a professional gemologist, nor are we suggesting it. Yet, many would like to know more about how to identify gems and, until now, there has been very little available to help those who fall into this category. The choice has been either to become a professional gemologist or to remain virtually in the dark.

It doesn't have to be this way. With minimal effort and a nominal investment in several instruments, almost anyone can venture into the

world of gemology and begin to experience the thrill and fun of discovery—learning just what a particular stone really is. You can learn
to separate real from imitation, one look-alike from another, dyed
from natural, and so on. Sometimes just a basic knowledge of how
to use a simple instrument is all that is needed to avoid an expensive
mistake or recognize a profitable opportunity.

Our experience teaching gem identification has shown us that
people from every walk of life can master it—English teachers,
auctioneers, homemakers. One doesn't need a scientific or technical
aptitude to be competent at most basic gem identification and becoming familiar with the use of certain instruments is not difficult. It only
requires patience, persistence, and practice. It can also be great fun
and offer personal challenge.

The purpose of this book is to open up the world of gem identification to everyone who has an interest in learning about it, regardless of
background or profession. It is meant for those who have little or no
scientific background or inclination, for those who have no gemology
course available to them in their location, for those who can't stop
what they are doing to go to school, and for those who just aren't sure
this is anything they really want to spend time and money to learn.

We have tried to make this a practical guide, explaining what instruments you will need to do the job, how to use them, and what to look
for, stone by stone. We do not delve into scientific explanations of
what you will see. (For those interested in scientific explanations, see
our recommended reading list in the Appendix.)

Please *use* the book. We have left blank pages at the end of each
chapter so you can make personal notes, especially of your own
observations as you practice with each instrument. While years
of training and experience are necessary to become qualified as a
professional gemologist, with practice and a little hands-on work,
you will find it takes surprisingly little time before you will feel more
confident about what you are buying and selling.

Before you become *too confident*, however, we hope this book will
do one more important thing. In addition to giving you the skill to
identify many stones, detect certain treatments, and spot certain fakes,
we hope it will help you appreciate the importance of the professional
gemologist and gem-testing laboratory. As important as developing

your own skill is the need for you to know when your own skill is insufficient—when the help of a professional gemologist or lab should be sought. As a general rule, whenever there is doubt, seek the professional. (See Appendix for list.)

We also hope this book will be a launching pad for some of you, merely the beginning of the pursuit of gemological knowledge. We would like to encourage you to keep up with changes in the industry by subscribing to gemological journals and attending lectures and workshops whenever possible. One thing that never changes in this fascinating field is that something is always changing.

And finally, we wish to encourage each of you who finds this book interesting and helpful to continue what you have learned here by enrolling in a gemology course. In the Appendix we have provided a list of schools and institutions offering courses in gemology.

In summary, it is our sincere hope that *Gem Identification Made Easy* will make the subject of gem identification fun and interesting, rather than tedious. We hope it will help you:

- Open your eyes to the types of imitations, synthetics, look-alikes, and fakes that can be encountered in today's gem and jewelry world.
- Learn how to tell the difference between them.
- Recognize the limitations of your own skill and when to employ the services of a professional gemologist or lab.
- Become more professional in your business or hobby.

Most of all, we hope it will help each of you become less dependent on what you're *told* … and more dependent on *your own gem knowledge*.

Antoinette Matlins

PART 2
GETTING READY

2 / Setting up the lab

Contrary to what many people believe, it isn't necessary to spend $100,000 (or more) for elaborate gem-testing equipment. An investment of less than $3,500 is sufficient to be a successful gemological detective and accurately identify most gems. Or, for less than $200, one can begin with just three "pocket instruments": the loupe, Chelsea filter, and dichroscope. Used together, these three simple, portable instruments can enable one to properly identify almost 80% of the colored gemstone materials encountered today as well as diamonds and most diamond look-alikes. Once you've mastered these three, you can then add other instruments to help you identify the remaining gemstone material and confirm identification made with the pocket instruments. Some of these other instruments also make identification faster and often easier.

We recommend six instruments as essential for setting up a useful lab: the loupe, Chelsea filter, dichroscope, refractometer, ultraviolet lamp, and microscope. We also recommend several optional pieces of equipment, depending on the type of gemstones you will be handling: the spectroscope (when working with fancy-color diamonds, it is not optional but essential), the polariscope, the synthetic emerald filter, and immersion cell. And for anyone handling diamonds, even in *old* jewelry, we strongly recommend an electronic "dual" diamond tester—one that measures both thermal conductivity *and* electrical conductivity—in order to avoid mistaking synthetic moissanite for diamond; a dark-field loupe, for faster and easier detection of *fracture-filled diamonds* and *lead-glass filled rubies and sapphires;* the SSEF Diamond-Type Spotter, to screen

13

for diamonds that may have been *treated by HPHT techniques;* and a rare-earth magnet, to aid in the detection of *synthetic diamonds* and in *identifying colored gemstones.*

Personal Preference and Practice

When selecting your own instruments, make sure they have the necessary features for gem identification that we describe in the following pages, but the final choice is largely one of personal preference. For example, while it is easier to focus critically with a small loupe, some prefer a larger loupe because they find it easier to handle. When it comes to choosing a dichroscope, most prefer a model with large, rectangular windows because they find it easier to see subtle color differences over a larger viewing area, but others prefer overlapping circular windows.

The most important thing is getting used to the instruments you buy. Practice with them until you feel comfortable. Carry your own instruments with you, whenever possible, because being comfortable with the instrument you are using can affect your proficiency. Some people never leave home without their credit cards—we never leave home without our loupe, dichroscope, Chelsea filter, and synthetic emerald filter.

While any one of these instruments alone is usually insufficient to make a conclusive identification, a combination of two or more will often be enough to tell you what you really have. The key, of course, is knowing how to use them and what to look for.

THE ESSENTIAL INSTRUMENTS

These instruments will be discussed individually in the following chapters, where you will learn in detail how to use them and what they will show. Most are available at major jewelry supply houses (see Appendix). Or you may order directly from GemStone Press, using the order form provided at the end of this book. Here is a brief overview of each, what they are, how much they cost, their primary use, and types or models we recommend. **Note that prices shown are for reference and comparison, and reflect quotes provided prior to publication. For current prices, check with suppliers.**

Note: Wearing glasses or contact lenses will not impair your ability to identify gems. The only requirement is that you have good vision in at least one eye, with or without the aid of glasses. My father was blind in one eye, and wore glasses since his early youth, but this didn't stand in the way of his becoming a skilled gemologist. All instruments described here work just as well for the person who wears glasses and require no special techniques. If glasses or contact lenses are normally worn for close work, they should not be removed.

10X Triplet-Type Loupe

($30–$90). This is a hand-held magnifier, sometimes called the jeweler's loupe, used essentially to detect chips, cracks, scratches, symmetry in cutting, sharpness of facet edges, and the presence and type of flaws. There are many manufacturers making fine

A 10X triplet loupe with black housing

loupes, and we don't feel the brand name is important. However, for gem identification purposes it is essential that the loupe you buy be a *10 power (10X) triplet-type with a black casing* (never purchase a chrome or gold-plated loupe).

Dark-Field Loupe

($60–$200). The dark-field loupe is a small cylinder-shaped instrument that gives you standard or 10 power magnification in combination with a specially constructed area for viewing the stone against a *black* background with strong *lateral* illumination. This is called *dark-field illumination,* hence "dark-field loupe." This type of loupe is larger than the standard loupe, approximately 2 3/4 inches high by 1 1/8 inch in diameter. The magnification is housed in the upper portion of the instrument, the dark-field is provided in the

Dark-field loupe with maglite

lower portion, and the area in between enables you to manipulate the stone or piece of jewelry being examined. For illumination, the dark-field loupe is simply placed on top of a small maglite, and you're ready to examine the stone.

Viewing a stone against a black background using lateral illumination—light coming from the *side* rather than being transmitted through the bottom of the stone or coming from above the stone— makes it easier to see inclusions and to determine more precisely what they are.

The dark-field loupe has always been popular with colored gemstone buyers and gemologists because inclusions play such an important role in identifying a gem, and in detecting treatments; anything that makes it easier can be an invaluable tool. Today the dark-field loupe has also become an *essential* tool for anyone buying diamonds or diamond jewelry because it enables even beginners to spot fracture-filled diamonds, quickly and easily.

There are several dark-field loupes now available, but some are not true "dark-field" loupes and provide lateral lighting that is too weak to enable you to see telltale indicators you would see readily with a true dark-field loupe. We like the dark-field loupe that is found in the RosGem Gem Analyzer™ ($285, including a portable polariscope and immersion cell) or the Diamond View™ ($60). GIA also makes a good dark-field loupe ($195, with maglite), but it was designed for use with unmounted stones and cannot be used to examine stones mounted in most rings or other jewelry.

Chelsea Filter

($45). The Chelsea filter (sometimes called an emerald filter) is a pocket-sized color filter. Today it is used primarily to spot

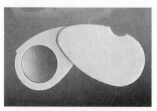
A Chelsea color filter

fakes mixed in with natural stones in colored stone parcels and jewelry, and to differentiate emerald from emerald look-alikes, sapphire from sapphire look-alikes, aquamarine from aquamarine look-alikes, and *dyed* green jadeite jade from fine *natural* green jadeite. There are other types of color filters, ranging in price from $25 to $80, some for use with all stones, some only for red, or blue, or green. Some of the most popular include the Walton filter ($80) made in France, the Hanneman four filter Bead Buyer and Parcel Picker set ($25), which includes four filters, and the "Gem Filter" by Gepe of Sweden. The new Hodgkinson-Hanneman *Synthetic emerald* filter set ($35) is a very important tool—used in conjunction with the Chelsea filter—*to separate natural emerald from most synthetics.*

Synthetic Emerald Filter Set

($35). A new pocket-size two-filter set introduced in the mid-1990s by the Scottish gemologist Alan Hodgkinson and American William Hanneman. The filters—used in conjunction with the Chelsea filter—can quickly separate most natural emerald from synthetic and are essential for anyone buying and selling emeralds. One filter is used to separate flux-grown synthetic emeralds from natural chromium-rich emeralds; the other is used to separate hydrothermal synthetic emeralds from natural non-chromium-rich emeralds such as those coming from India or Zambia.

Hanneman-Hodgkinson
Synthetic Emerald Filter

Calcite-Type Dichroscope

($115–$150). This is a small, pocket-sized tubular instrument used for transparent colored gemstones, to differentiate stones of the same color from one another. It is one of the handiest and most useful instruments for anyone buying colored gemstones. It is one of the quickest and easiest ways to separate stones such as sapphire-blue color *synthetic spinel* from genuine sapphire, or for separating green garnet from chrome tourmaline or emerald. However, it will not separate natural gemstones from their synthetic counterparts (synthetic emerald from natural emerald or synthetic sapphire from natural sapphire). It will enable you to easily separate single-refracting colored gemstones from those that are double-refracting, and thus make many important distinctions among look-alikes and imitations.

EZ View dichroscope by Gem-A Instruments and a RosGem dichroscope

Another important benefit is that it can be used with gemstones that are still "in the rough," that is, have not been cut or polished. It is also very useful in cases where cut stones have such a low polish that other instruments (such as the refractometer) can't be used, or for jewelry pieces in which stones have been set in a way that prohibits the use of other instruments. Among the best calcite dichroscopes are those made by RosGem, GIA, and Gem-A Instruments.

Refractometer

($435–$900). This is a small instrument available in either portable or desk models. It enables you to get what is called an R.I. measurement (generally, the higher the R.I., the more brilliant the stone). Since the R.I. differs for every stone, the measurement provided by the refractometer provides the identity of most stones, although it won't distinguish between natural gemstones and their synthetic counterparts. It is used most easily with stones that have at least one flat, polished surface (a "spot" method can be used for cabochons, but this is a little more difficult).

The GIA *Duplex II* refractometer with utility lamp

The RosGem refractometer, complete with carrying case, R.I. liquid, polarizing filter and both monochromatic and white light capability

The major shortcoming of most refractometers is that they will not work for stones with a very high R.I., such as diamond, certain diamond imitations, and certain varieties of garnet. In addition, the stone must have a good polish; you cannot use a refractometer to identify rough stones or stones that are badly worn and lack a good polish.

The GIA *Duplex II* desktop model ($595) is probably the most widely used in the United States (optional light source required for operation, approximately $475; the total cost is $1,070). The RosGem ($625, with light source) is rapidly gaining popularity; it has a more precise scale (for improved accuracy) than most refractometers, including the GIA model, and it provides monochromatic *and* white light. Its compact design and sturdy construction give it portability. One important advantage of the RosGem is that it doesn't require a special light and operates with a simple

Eickhorst model 3

Rayner Dialdex refractometer

inexpensive maglite ($15). We also like the Rayner Dialdex refractometer by Gem-A Instruments ($580), and the Eickhorst brand, which is available in several models ($435–$1,000).

Ultraviolet (UV) Lamp

($85–$425). This is an amazingly useful instrument often overlooked by gemologists (portable and desktop models are available)! It is used to detect the presence or absence of fluorescence—a stone's ability to exhibit color when viewed under ultraviolet light, color not visible in ordinary light. For gem identification purposes we recommend a hand-held type that provides both longwave and shortwave light, controlled by individual buttons (so you view the

Portable "mini" longwave/shortwave lamp by Ultra-Violet Products

An ultraviolet lamp and viewing cabinet from GIA

stone under longwave *or* shortwave, but never under both wavelengths simultaneously). We like Ultra-Violet Products, Inc. models
#UVGL-25 ($200) and #UVGL-58 6-watt model ($400), and their
portable *mini* longwave/shortwave model #UVSL-14P ($75) that
is very reliable and great for anyone on the go! GIA also offers a
shortwave/longwave ultraviolet lamp ($350), and there are other
models, such as those made by Raytech or Spectroline, which are also
very good and a little less expensive.

We also recommend getting a viewing cabinet for your UV lamp,
to create a miniature "darkroom" (necessary to see fluorescence).
Such cabinets are available from the manufacturers and prices range
from about $125–$200. Or, just turn off the lights before turning on
the UV lamp (if it's daylight, go into a closet and turn off the lights!).

Microscope

($990 and up). This is a desk or countertop instrument used primarily
for magnification. Many models are also portable. The microscope
can be used to observe more clearly the same items observed with the
loupe, but its capability for much higher magnification is especially
critical in differentiating natural gems from today's synthetics.

For gem identification, you must have a *binocular* microscope
that offers both dark-field and bright-field illumination, and a light
source at the top of the instrument to *reflect* light from the stone being
examined. If you are planning to use the microscope to identify current new-type synthetics, you must have a magnification capability
up to 60X. If not, then magnification up to 30X is all you need for
other gem identification. Just remember, however, that if you have
a gem that appears to be unusually fine, especially "flaw-wise," it
could be synthetic. If you lack the proper equipment to see the telltale
inclusions, you must verify genuineness with a skilled gemologist or
gem-testing laboratory. A "zoom" capability—increasing the power
without changing eyepieces—is a very convenient feature but is not
necessary in a microscope being used for gem-identification purposes.
It is important, however, if you are planning to use it to determine
diamond proportioning and measurements such as the table "spread."
The zoom feature will add significantly to the cost of the microscope.

We like the following microscopes:

Meiji GemZ-5   Eickhorst Gemmoscope E   GIA's GemoLite Super
                                                    60 Zoom Mark X

- Meiji Techno GM5-Z ($2,420) which has all of the essential features we recommend for gem identification (with dark-field attachment), magnification up to 90X, and includes 10X and 20X super wide-field eyepieces; Techno GEMT-2 ($2,460) with built-in dark-field illumination, magnification to 60X, fluorescent box illuminator, and gem clamp; and the GEMZ-5 Zoom ($3,075) with all of the essential features, including built-in dark-field illumination, magnification from 7X to 90X, swivel base, and inclusion pointer.
- GIA "GemoLite Super 60 Zoom Mark X" ($3,850)—has all of the essential features, with a magnification range of 10X to 60X.
- Kassoy Leica Microscope GMK775300 ($3,495) has essential features, magnification to 64X, plus optional doubler lens for 128X ($200), built-in fiber optic light, 360° rotation and tilt, and flush-mounted stone holder.

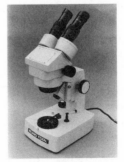

Kassoy   Eurotool
Leica Microscope   Zoomscope
GMK775300   5MIC300

- Eurotool Zoomscope #MIC300 ($990) has essential features plus zoom feature, providing magnification to 45X.
- Eickhorst Gemmoscope E ($2,190) has essential features plus zoom feature, providing magnification to 40X.

OPTIONAL INSTRUMENTS

In addition to the instruments we've just discussed, you may wish to add some optional pieces of equipment. We do not consider them essential for the beginner, but they do have specific uses that can make identification of certain types of stones faster and more definitive. In some cases, they are the only instruments that will tell you what you need to know.

The best way to determine whether to buy them is to read the chapters describing each one and see if they deal with situations you think you'll encounter. And, of course, there is no need to rush out and buy all these instruments at once. You might work with a few for six months and then determine you need additional equipment. For example, if you find you are frequently working with fancy-color diamonds, especially yellow diamonds, you might find that a spectroscope—essential for differentiating *natural* fancy-color diamonds from those that obtained their color by irradiation—is something that could save you a lot of time and help you feel more secure about your conclusions. Or if you are concerned about HPHT-treated diamonds (see Chapter 12), having a SSEF Diamond-Type Spotter may be essential, not optional. If you think other instruments might be useful to you, you can always purchase them as your skill—and needs—change.

Spectroscope

($225–$5,000). There are two types of spectroscope in common use for gem identification, the prism type and diffraction-grating type. The standard diffraction type is less expensive, but the prism type has two advantages—it admits more light into the instrument, and it is easier to read in the dark blue end of the spectral display. There are also several new diffraction models with fiber optic lighting and digital readouts that eliminate the problems found in standard diffraction models, but they are more expensive. Whether you buy a diffraction type or prism type, we recommend models that come as a unit, complete with light and stand, because we think they allow better control of both the instrument and the light intensity and direction necessary for successful use. Models that can be inserted into a microscope in place of an eyepiece also work well (but not without the microscope). The OPL hand-held model can be very useful in the field especially when used with the handy, portable stand/stone holder unit made by Hanneman. This makes it much easier to handle the stone and control the light in order to see the absorption bands in the spectrum.

Photo: C. Winter, OPL

OPL spectroscope and stand

Eickhorst spectroscope

Wavelength prism spectroscope by Beck

OPL portable diffraction-grating spectroscope

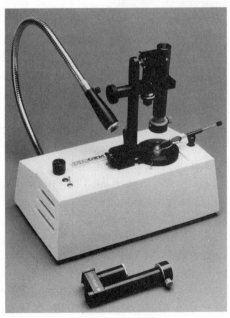

GIA prism 1000

The spectroscope shows a complete color spectrum, exhibiting vertical black lines or bars at certain points of the spectrum that indicate the specific gemstone identity. Its most important uses, gemologically, are to distinguish natural fancy-color diamonds from diamonds that have obtained their color by irradiation; to separate naturally green jadeite jade from dyed and impregnated jadeite; and to separate natural blue sapphire from most synthetic blue sapphire. Some prefer the spectroscope to other instruments for much broader gemstone identification.

Spectroscopes we like include GIA's Prism 1000 ($4,950, mounted) and Beck's prism spectroscope ($3,800). They are easy to read and very precise. Standard diffraction grating spectroscopes such as the OPL portable model sell for as little as $90, but, as we've mentioned, many are less reliable and more difficult to use than other types. We prefer the OPL "standard" spectroscope, with stand, which is larger but easier to use ($225).

Polariscope

($175–$400). The polariscope is a desktop instrument used to detect optical properties of gemstones. For gem identification, we think the best polariscopes are the GIA Illuminator Polariscope ($295), the Rayner ($340) and the portable polariscope/immersion cell combination that is part of the RosGem "Gem Analyzer" ($285). Whatever polariscope you select, we also recommend using it with an immersion cell ($30), a liquid called benzyl benzoate ($15), which is essential for amethyst, and rubbing alcohol, so you can also examine stones using immersion techniques.

GIA Gem Instruments'
Illuminator Polariscope

The polariscope is used to determine quickly and easily whether a stone is single- or double-refracting, the presence of strain in diamonds and other gems, and it is being used increasingly today because of its value in separating synthetic amethyst from genuine. This is the only affordable instrument currently available that can

Rayner Polariscope

make this separation. Because of the wide circulation of synthetic amethyst, often represented as genuine, this instrument meets an important
need. It can also be used for other gem-identification purposes.

SSEF Diamond-Type Spotter and SSEF Blue Diamond Tester

($150). Anyone buying fine diamonds
today, whether colorless or fancy-color,
must be concerned about whether the color
is natural or the result of high-pressure/high-
temperature annealing techniques (referred
to as HPHT techniques). Fortunately, not all
diamonds can be improved by this method;
only certain rare diamond "types" respond
(see Chapter 12). However, experts estimate that significant numbers of diamonds

SSEF Diamond-Type
Spotter and
Portable Illuminator
(photo: Prof. H. Hänni,
SSEF)

over three carats with high clarity grades (VS or better) are among
the types that are candidates for HPHT alteration. While there are no
published figures, there is concern that this number may exceed 20%.

The Swiss Gemmological Institute (SSEF) noted that the rare diamond types that can become colorless, near-colorless, pink, or blue
as a result of HPHT techniques *transmit shortwave ultraviolet radiation*. With this knowledge, SSEF developed a simple, portable tool
with which *anyone* can quickly and easily determine whether or not
a diamond is one of these types and, thus, whether or not it poses a
risk or, if a brown diamond, an opportunity! (See Chapter 12.) This
tool may be optional for many, but it is essential for diamond buyers
seeking to reduce the risk of inadvertently buying or selling an HPHT
color-enhanced diamond or identifying brown diamonds that can
be improved by HPHT techniques. In the case of brown diamonds,
if the Diamond-Type Spotter indicates the stone is a type that can
be improved, the SSEF Blue Diamond Tester—a portable electrical
conductivity meter—will tell you whether the resulting HPHT-treated
color will be *blue* (cost: $695).

The SSEF Diamond-Type Spotter is available for $150. In addition
to the spotter, you will need a lamp that provides shortwave ultraviolet

light, such as the standard or portable longwave/shortwave ultraviolet lamp, or a high intensity shortwave lamp specially designed for use with the spotter (SSEF Shortwave Illuminator, $450, portable model, $300). We also recommend the use of ultraviolet-protective safety glasses or goggles when working with shortwave ultraviolet ($25).

Immersion Cell with Diffused Light Unit

($120–$285). Immersing stones in liquid using diffused light facilitates seeing important identifying characteristics. Invaluable with the polariscope, microscope, or untrained eye. Makes spotting traditional "doublets" fast and easy, and is essential to detect diffusion-treated sapphire. Several portable models are available, but you can also use any clear glass beaker, juice glass, etc., held over a diffused light source.

Electronic Diamond Testers

($150–$800). Diamond testers are available in both portable and desktop models. They are very easy to use and most work simply by pressing a metal point against one of the stone's facets. The tester will then

DiamondNite Dual Tester

give a signal indicating if the stone is a real diamond or not. They have become very popular because they require no gemological skill and make diamond testing both fast and easy. They are also helpful for small, mounted stones that can be difficult to examine with other instruments. The diamond tester can also be used to assure another party that their stone is, or is not, a diamond. However, most will only tell you that and cannot identify what the stone is.

A word of caution: Many people rely totally on electronic diamond testers. While very reliable in separating diamond from most imitations, such as CZ, electronic diamond testers are not foolproof. The major shortcoming in many of these instruments is that they may provide a false *positive*; that is, indicate that a stone *is* diamond when it is not. This is the case with colorless corundum (sapphire) and the new diamond imitation, synthetic moissanite; with both of these stones, many diamond testers now available give a false "positive" indicating that they *are* diamond. Today, electronic diamond testers that measure thermal conductivity alone are considered obsolete. Most people prefer a "dual tester," one that conducts two tests—thermal conductivity *and* electrical conductivity—in a matter of seconds in order to distinguish moissanite from diamond.

When using an electronic diamond tester, we recommend not relying on the diamond tester alone when the result is positive. As we have said previously, be careful about making any identification based on the results of a single test. In the case of colorless corundum or synthetic moissanite, both can be quickly distinguished from diamond using other simple instruments, such as the polariscope. In the case of corundum, a standard refractometer or ultraviolet lamp (which we recommend as a "companion" to the electronic diamond tester) will quickly distinguish it from diamond (see Chapters 8 and 14).

Popular models include:

- GIA's Pocket Diamond Tester (portable)—$150.
- Ceres' Czeck Point (portable)—$170.
- Diamond Star (portable)—$110.
- Diamond Beam II (portable)—$170.
- DiamondNite Dual Tester (portable)—$270.

Synthetic Diamond Testers

Synthetic gem-quality colorless diamonds are not yet in wide circulation, but there have been significant scientific advances and colorless to near-colorless synthetic diamonds in sizes over one-carat, and even as large as two-carats, are now available. Production and availability of larger sizes is also increasing. Fancy-color synthetic diamonds are now readily available in yellow, orangy yellow, greenish yellow, yellowish green, deep green, pastel blue, and even red.

Major gem-testing laboratories can distinguish natural diamond from all of the synthetic diamonds now produced. Several very sophisticated instruments that can check large quantities of stones very quickly are also available today, but the cost of these instruments and lack of portability make them impractical for most people. Fortunately, several very simple, inexpensive tools are also proving very effective in detecting many synthetic diamonds now in the marketplace.

Many synthetic diamonds can be easily detected today using routine tests, often with simple, portable instruments such as the longwave-shortwave ultraviolet lamp and, occasionally, a simple 10X loupe. These will be discussed later in greater detail. While not 100% effective, they are reliable in the *positive;* that is, when they indicate a diamond *is* synthetic, then it is. If they give no response or a response indicating natural diamond, then you must test further or submit the diamond to a laboratory.

One of the simplest and most reliable tests is checking for magnetism with a special rare-earth magnet. Synthetic diamonds often have some degree of magnetism resulting from the metal flux used in the process to create them, so they will be drawn to a strong magnet while the natural diamond will not. If a diamond is drawn to the rare-earth magnet, you know it is synthetic. However, if it is *not* drawn to the magnet, it may be natural or it may be a synthetic diamond that lacks sufficient flux residue to create magnetism. You must perform additional tests to know for sure.

A rare-earth magnet is not your normal magnet. It is a neodymium boron iron magnet, a remarkably strong magnet. Because of its magnetic strength, you need only a very tiny magnet, which also makes it very inexpensive. Hanneman's Magnetic Synthetic Diamond Wand is essentially a wooden stick (slightly larger than a match stick) with a rare-earth magnet attached to one end, and it sells for under $15. This simple magnetic wand can be an invaluable tool in separating natural from synthetic diamonds when used properly (see Chapter 15).

Tools for determining whether or not a diamond is Type I or Type II are invaluable for pre-screening colorless and near-colorless diamonds from their synthetic or treated counterparts. We use the SSEF Diamond-Type Spotter in conjunction with a portable longwave-shortwave lamp. I never leave home without them! (See Chapter 12)

WARNING: THE MAGNETIC STRENGTH OF SUCH TOOLS CAN INTERFERE WITH THE OPERATION OF PACEMAKERS AND SIMILAR LIFESAVING DEVICES. THEY SHOULD NOT BE USED BY, OR AROUND, ANYONE WHO USES A PACEMAKER OR SIMILAR DEVICE. DO NOT USE AROUND COMPUTERS OR ELECTRONIC EQUIPMENT.

For more information on magnetism and gemstones, visit www. gemstonemagnetism.com.

Carbide Scriber

($15–$25). There are many types of scribers on the market, including stainless steel scribers, but for gemological purposes the scriber *must* have a *tungsten carbide point*. The carbide scriber has become an essential tool for anyone buying diamonds, to aid in detecting surface coatings applied to diamonds to create "colorless" and "fancy colors" from off-color stones.

Carbide scribers come in several models and with tips in varying sizes; we recommend using a scriber with a medium tip because the scratch that will indicate the presence of a coating will be easier to see (see page 237 on how to use the scriber). We also prefer models that allow you to store several different tips within the shaft so you can choose the size and shape that will make it easiest to use. It is also wise to store whatever tip you are using in between uses rather than leaving it exposed; carbide is very hard, but it is also brittle and can break if you drop it and the point strikes the floor at just the right angle. We like the deluxe carbide scriber available from the Accredited Gemologists Association (www.accreditedgemologists. org). It comes with two points and provides storage within its penlike shaft. The points are also replaceable if damaged.

By selecting carefully, as you can see, one can buy all the essential instruments for under $2,200, and add most of the optional instruments for about $800 more. Also, note that most instruments are small enough to take along with you when you travel.

Loupe (pocket size)	$30
Chelsea filter (pocket size)	45
Synthetic emerald filter set	35
Calcite dichroscope (pocket size)	120
Refractometer (portable model, with light)	625
Ultraviolet lamp (small model)	75
Microscope	1,200
	$2,130

Optional Instruments

Polariscope/dark-field loupe/immersion cell— portable combo	$285
Portable electronic dual diamond tester	270
Diffraction-grating spectroscope—pocket size	90
SSEF Diamond-Type Spotter	150
SSEF Blue Diamond Tester	695
Carbide Scriber	20
	$1,510

A CHECKLIST OF INCIDENTALS YOU MAY NEED

Before you get started, here is a quick checklist of other useful items.

- *Good light* (see Chapter 3). You will need two types of light—a source for *incandescent* light, such as the light from an ordinary light bulb in a household lamp; and *daylight* light, or light from a lighting unit or fixture that has Daylight-Type fluorescent tubes. We recommend a desk-type lamp that provides both, ideally with a flexible arm attached to the base. We also like the Eickhorst Dialite Flip lamp ($70), which is very compact and takes up very little desk space.
- *Portable penlight or flashlight.* This can come in very handy, especially for colored stones, and can be purchased at many places, including the drugstore. Jewelry supply houses sell them from $5 to $20.
- *A pair of locking tweezers.* We recommend a medium point tweezer with a self-locking feature ($15–$30).
- *Retractable prong tweezers.* These make it easier to hold unmounted stones. Push the end (like a ballpoint pen) to release a 3-prong or 4-prong tweezer to snugly grip the stone you wish to examine. Prongs retract when finished ($5–$10).
- *Bottle of rubbing alcohol* ($1).

- *Bottle of clear* acetone-*based nail polish remover*, without *conditioners* ($2).
- *Can of compressed air*. This can be obtained from any photo or jewelry supply house. Any brand will do. "Dust Off-II" has a special formulation for jewelry and costs about $45 including the trigger valve; refills are $15; pocket size, $10. "No Dust" (available at photo supply houses) costs $20; refills are $5.
- *Liquids:*
  Methylene iodide—a liquid with many uses. $50 for 30 ml bottle.
  Refractive Index (R.I.) Liquid—necessary for most refractometers, preferably with an R.I. of 1.81 for use with a wider range of gemstones. $70 (10 g).
  Benzyl Benzoate—a liquid used with the polariscope when examining amethyst. $20 (30 ml).
- A magnifying headpiece such as the OptiVISOR ($25–$30) or VigorVISOR ($15). Available in various powers of magnification. It can be particularly helpful when you need both hands free.
- *A roll of white toilet tissue* (a coarse, lint-free brand) serves a variety of purposes.

OptiVISOR magnifying headpiece (other manufacturers such as Vigor also make a similar product). Particularly useful when you need both hands free.

A Word about Specific Gravity Liquids

In this book we limit our discussion to *instruments* we consider important for gem identification. We do not include gem-testing *liquids*. However, using liquids can be an easy and quick aid for determining the identity of many stones and spotting look-alikes.

Of particular importance are "specific gravity" liquids used to determine the specific gravity of gemstone substances. Some don't consider a lab complete without a set of these liquids. We will briefly discuss such liquids, but anyone interested in using liquids should learn more about them and how to use them before you begin. We recommend starting with Richard T. Liddicoat's *Handbook of Gem Identification*,

12th Edition (GIA, Carlsbad, CA), or Robert Webster's *Practical Gemmology*, 6th Edition (N.A.G. Press, London).

What Is Specific Gravity (S.G.)?

The specific gravity of a substance is a measurement indicating how heavy (dense) that substance is—it shows the ratio of the weight of the substance compared to the weight of an equal volume of water.

Let's use cubic zirconia (CZ) and diamond to explain specific gravity. The specific gravity of CZ is 5.65. That means it will weigh 5.65 times more than an equal volume of water. By comparison, diamond has a specific gravity of 3.52. That means diamond weighs 3.52 times more than an equal volume of water. CZ has a specific gravity almost 1.6 times more than diamond. In other words, CZ is 1.6 times *heavier* than diamond.

What does this really mean? Let's take an unmounted CZ and an unmounted diamond that appear to be the same size—round, brilliant-cut stones, measuring 6.5 millimeters in diameter. We know that a 6.5 millimeter round diamond will weigh approximately one carat on a diamond scale. If CZ and diamond had the same density (weight), the same specific gravity, then the CZ would also weigh approximately one carat. But when we weigh the CZ, we find out it weighs much more. The scale will show almost 1 3/4 carats! Even though they look as if they're the same size, the carat weight will be different because the density of cubic zirconia is greater than the density of diamond.

The higher the specific gravity, the heavier the substance; the lower the specific gravity, the lighter the substance. If you compare a CZ that actually does weigh one carat with a diamond that weighs one carat, the CZ will look *smaller* than the diamond since it is a heavier substance. For the same reason, a one-carat ruby (S.G. 4.0, which is higher than diamond) may look smaller than a one-carat diamond; and a one-carat emerald (S.G. 2.72, which is lower than diamond) may look larger than a one-carat diamond.

Since each stone has a different specific gravity, by immersing it in a liquid with a specific gravity close to that of the stone you suspect it to be, one can easily approximate the stone's specific gravity—by observing whether it sinks or floats; if it floats, how buoyant it is in the liquid; or, if it sinks, how quickly or slowly.

Knowing a stone's specific gravity provides an important aid in identification. While liquids are usually not precise enough to give a positive identity if used alone, when used in conjunction with the refractometer or other instruments, they are often all that is needed to confirm identity.

For those interested in using liquids, the following can be very useful:

- *Methylene iodide* (diiodomethane). This is the liquid we consider the most important. We have already recommended it because of its many uses.
- *Benzyl benzoate.* This liquid, and other liquids made by mixing benzyl benzoate with methylene iodide, are useful for determining an unset stone's density or specific gravity.
- *Tetrabromoethane* (acetylene tetrabromide). This liquid is also used to help determine specific gravity. It is also important in helping to separate jadeite from nephrite jade.

GIA sells a *Specific Gravity Liquid Set* ($195) which contains five of the most useful liquids.

WARNING: THESE LIQUIDS CAN BE HARMFUL IF INHALED, SWALLOWED, OR ALLOWED TO HAVE PROLONGED CONTACT WITH SKIN. EXERCISE CAUTION WHEN WORKING WITH ANY CHEMICAL.

The Value of a Good Library

In addition to the instruments and incidentals listed in the preceding pages, we want to stress the importance of having a reliable library for reference and assistance. We have provided a list of books in the Appendix that we think you will find particularly useful. While you may not be able to acquire all the books we recommend at one time, for gem-identification purposes we recommend especially Richard Liddicoat's *Handbook of Gem Identification*, Robert Webster's *Practical Gemmology*, Peter G. Read's *Gemmology*, Gubelin/ Koivula's *Photoatlas of Inclusions in Gemstones,* and Ted Themelis' *The Heat Treatment of Ruby and Sapphire;* for diamonds, Eric Bruton's *Diamonds*, and Verena Pagel-Theisen's *Diamond Grading ABC*; and for general information about buying gems, our books *Jewelry & Gems: The Buying Guide*; *Colored Gemstones: The Antoinette Matlins Buying Guide; Diamonds: The Antoinette Matlins Buying Guide;* and *The Pearl Book: The Definitive Buying Guide.* In light of worldwide problems related to a new type of composite stone imitating ruby and sapphire—and the high number of such stones being misrepresented as genuine—I highly recommend Craig Lynch's booklet, *Is It Really a Ruby?*, which is filled with excellent photos of the telltale indications that can be seen with simple tools. It is available directly from the author (see Chapter 18).

In addition to books, you should subscribe to at least one of the journals on gemology listed in the Appendix, and online software such as *GT Pro* from www.gemologytools.com can be very helpful. It is essential to keep up to date on new developments in treatment and synthesis. As we have pointed out repeatedly, this field is ever-changing. In fact, there could be changes taking place even now, as this book goes to press. Your only protection against change is keeping yourself informed. We especially recommend *Gems & Gemology,* published by the Gemological Institute of America (GIA), and the *Journal of Gemmology,* published by Gem-A (The Gemmological Association of Great Britain).

NOTES

3 / Proper lighting for gem identification

As you begin to explore the world of gems, you will undoubtedly encounter some words or terms that will be new and sometimes complicated-sounding. As you will see, most are really not complicated at all. There is one very important area, however, that requires an understanding of very specific terms. Before we begin, it's important to understand them.

One of the most important tools of gem identification is usually taken for granted by beginners—the "light" they use as they work. Gem identification employs one sense above all else—the sense of sight. Even the most expensive instruments will do us little good if they are used with incorrect light because the lighting itself influences what we see. Improper lighting can result in a more difficult or even an incorrect identification.

We want to make sure you understand the need for proper lighting and what it is and will briefly explain the different types of light needed with each instrument. Before starting to use any instrument, check the chapter describing it to learn special lighting instructions.

When it comes to lighting, you must think about three things as you examine stones:

1. **Intensity**—Is the light source bright enough for you to see what you need to see, or is it so weak you have to strain?
2. **Position of light source**—Is the light coming from over the stone, from behind or underneath it, or from the side?
3. **Type of light**—Is the light *incandescent* or *natural daylight*? Or *fluorescent*? *Monochromatic* or *white* light?

INTENSITY OF LIGHT

Intensity describes simply the strength or brightness of light. Intensity
can be increased or decreased, for example, simply by taking a lamp
shade on or off. Some lamps, and even some penlights, have a feature
allowing you to change the intensity.

For gem identification, "normal" light, light that isn't too bright or
too weak, is usually sufficient. When working with some instruments,
a small utility lamp such as those sold by GIA often comes in handy.
A utility lamp makes it easy to direct light where you really need it
while working. We also recommend the Eickhorst high intensity fiber
optic lamp with its flexible neck and pinpoint beam.

Never examine a stone if the light is very weak. We are always
amazed when friends ask us, for example, to evaluate a piece of jewelry while dining in a lovely candlelit restaurant. When we tell them
there isn't enough light to see, they don't understand. As you will
realize when we discuss the loupe and other instruments, examining a
stone with insufficient light, or with a very dark background, reduces
your ability to see flaws or inclusions that may be present. Working
in poor conditions—especially bad lighting—increases chances for
making errors.

POSITIONING OF LIGHT

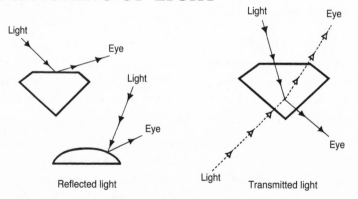

Knowing the direction from which the light should be coming as you
examine a stone is very important. Light can come from overhead,
from under the stone, or through any of its sides.

Reflected Light

Reflected light refers to light shining on the surface of the stone. When reflected light is called for, you must have light coming from *overhead* while tilting the stone at a slight angle so that the light will bounce back off the surface rather than continue through the stone. An example of looking at something in reflected light can be easily found at a lake. When you look out at just the right angle, you will often see a spot on a lake that looks very shiny, almost like a mirror. That mirror-like illusion is created by light being *reflected* from the surface. You are looking at a section of the lake with "reflected light."

Using reflected light is especially important when examining colored gems. It can help you spot a "garnet-topped doublet" (an ingenious fake we'll discuss later, often found in antique jewelry), a dangerous crack that breaks the surface of the stone, or, possibly— when you've become very experienced—a glass-filled cavity (a technique used to fill a crack and enhance color in gems such as ruby).

Transmitted Light

If you're examining a stone with transmitted light, this means you are examining it as light travels *through* the stone.

The light can be coming from any direction—overhead, behind, or from the side. The light travels through the stone and illuminates its interior. Sometimes it is helpful to use a flat white business card to reflect light from the card into the stone. This often reduces glare and enables you to see into the stone more clearly.

With the loupe you will use both transmitted and reflected light. The majority of examinations will be done using transmitted light, but reflected light will sometimes help you spot certain inclusions, or notice differences in reflection off certain facets—a definite red flag.

With the dichroscope, you must use transmitted light. A penlight works especially well with this instrument to give transmitted light. A small utility lamp such as the one sold by GIA, on *top* of which you set the stone being examined, also provides transmitted light and eliminates reflected light. Both the penlight and the utility lamp offer the added benefit of stronger light since the stone can be held close to the light source.

You can also examine a stone with the dichroscope using light coming from a ceiling fixture. Just hold the stone and dichroscope up, looking into the light, with the light coming through the back of the stone.

TYPES OF LIGHT

As we discuss the various instruments and how to use them for gem identification, you will repeatedly encounter four terms referring to types of light: incandescent, daylight, fluorescent, and monochromatic.

When we talk about light, what usually comes to mind is "visible" light—the light we can actually see. But few people really understand light, and a full understanding involves some fairly complex scientific principles. We will try to explain only what you need to know, as simply as possible.

First one must understand that there is both *visible* light and *invisible* light. Light travels in waves, and the length of the wave determines whether or not we see it. It also determines what *color* the light will be when we see it.

The longest wavelength we are able to see produces RED; the shortest produces VIOLET. The visible colors, sometimes called the visible spectrum of light, include (starting with the longest wavelengths visible to our naked eye and proceeding to the shortest) red, orange, yellow, green, blue, indigo and violet.

White Light and Monochromatic Light

When *all* the colors of the visible spectrum are blended together, we get white light. We use *white* light with most gem ID instruments.

Sometimes, however, we want to use "monochromatic" light. Monochromatic light is light composed of only *one* of the colors of the spectrum. In monochromatic light, six of the seven colors in the visible spectrum are filtered out, and only one (mono) color (chromatic) remains. A yellow monochromatic light is normally used with refractometers. Many utility lamps such as those sold by GIA provide both white light or yellow monochromatic light. However, if you don't have a yellow monochromatic light, you can make a filter to produce a good substitute by simply covering your light with several pieces of yellow cellophane (such as a candy wrapper).

Incandescent Light

Incandescent light is white light. It has all the colors of the *visible* spectrum blended together. The word "incandescent" means "to grow hot" or "to glow" and is used when referring to light produced by the glowing or heating of an object—candlelight is incandescent light; an ordinary household lamp, which contains an ordinary light bulb (which "glows" from a heated filament inside) gives incandescent light.

Natural Daylight

Both visible and invisible wavelengths are present in natural daylight. As a result, the color we see in gems can sometimes look different in daylight than in incandescent light. For example, alexandrite, a color-change stone, is green/blue-green in natural daylight, but raspberry red in incandescent light. It's no wonder that when it was discovered—outside, in daylight—it was thought to be an emerald. What a shock someone must have had when they looked at the stone again that evening in the glow of a lantern or candlelight!

In many instances, one can use either daylight or incandescent light. However, where we specify "fluorescent" or "daylight-type fluorescent" light, we mean incandescent light should *not* be used. Or, if we specify incandescent, then *fluorescent* light should not be used. For example, we specify using incandescent light when using the Chelsea filter. While natural daylight is also acceptable, fluorescent light is *not*. It will not produce the same effect.

Fluorescent Light

Two types of fluorescent light are commonly encountered in homes and offices, both in desk lamps and ceiling fixtures—"cool white" and "daylight" type. Fluorescent lights produce wavelengths that go beyond our visible spectrum to include some degree of "ultraviolet"— a wavelength beyond visible "violet." In daylight-type fluorescent light, there is a greater concentration of ultraviolet rays than in "cool white." Normally, where we specify fluorescent light, we will be specifying daylight type. We should point out here that we use daylight type for gem identification and most color grading. However, for color grading diamonds, using this type of light may result in error (we explain why in the chapter on ultraviolet lamps).

For the gem identifier's purpose, you need to recognize that fluorescent light is produced by those long frosted glass tubes mounted in ceilings (sometimes recessed and often behind diffusers, which create the worst possible light for viewing jewelry—all jewelry in these lights looks "deadish").

What you must find out, however, is whether those tubes are producing "cool white" or "daylight" type light. If you don't know, it is written on one end of the tube. If you can't reach the tube, you might be able to tell by the type of light you are seeing—"daylight type" has a much stronger white with a bluish tint, while "cool white" has a faint yellowish tint.

We recommend using a desk-type lamp with "daylight" fluorescent tubes (if the lamp you are using does not have such tubes, simply change them). If you don't have a fluorescent lamp and are going to buy one, we recommend one of the circular models that combine both fluorescent lighting with incandescent lighting (approximately $100). We like the type with a flexible extension arm attached to the base. However, the circular fluorescent tube that normally comes with these lamps is usually "cool white" *so you must replace it with a daylight-type tube that you can obtain from an electrical supply house*. We also like the Dialite Flip Lamp ($70), a fluorescent lamp made by Eickhorst, because it provides a diffused light source with a fuller daylight color spectrum than other lamps (producing color equivalent to natural daylight of 6000 kelvin).

Invisible Light—Ultraviolet

As we mentioned earlier, there is both visible and invisible light. We have talked about visible light. Now we will take a moment to describe invisible light. For our purposes, the only type of invisible light one needs to know about is "ultraviolet light." Ultraviolet light is invisible because its wavelengths are much shorter than what the human eye can see. On one end of the visible spectrum we have violet, which has the shortest visible wavelength. Ultraviolet goes beyond this—"beyond violet."

One of the most important instruments the gem identifier uses, the ultraviolet lamp, is a special lamp that provides *only* ultraviolet light. Gemologists use a lamp that supplies two different wavelengths of ultraviolet light—longwave and shortwave. Some gems will reveal a distinctive color when viewed with longwave or shortwave ultraviolet light, color that is *not seen* when the stone is viewed in ordinary light. These stones are exhibiting a property we call fluorescence. Fluorescence is easily seen with the proper use of the ultraviolet lamp. Some stones exhibit color only when viewed with shortwave light, some only when viewed with longwave light, and others will show color under both waves. The colors revealed, and the wavelengths under which they are revealed, provide important clues to the identity of many gems. This property is discussed in greater detail in the chapter on the ultraviolet lamp.

Invisible Light—X-ray

X-ray light is a type of invisible light similar to ultraviolet light and can be used to observe many similar phenomena. However, X-ray light is very dangerous and we do not recommend its use for gem identification.

Suggested Lighting for Gem Identification Instruments

	Incandescent	Fluorescent	Transmitted	Reflected	Special Comments
Loupe	Yes	Yes	Yes	Yes	
Chelsea FIlter	Yes	No	No	Yes	When examining *rough* material (uncut), transmitted light may also be used.
Dichroscope	Yes	Yes	Yes	No	
Refractometer	Yes	No	Yes	No	Many stones show a clearer reading with *monochromatic (yellow) light*. Some refractometers, such as the RosGem, provide monochromatic light. Lamps such as the GIA utility lamp also provide it, or you can make a filter for your light with several sheets of yellow cellophane.
Ultraviolet Lamp	No	No	No	No	This instrument provides a special type of light. A "darkroom" or darkened viewing cabinet is required for proper use.
Microscope	Yes	Yes	Yes	Yes	
Spectroscope	Light source is usually self-contained.				
Polariscope	Light source is usually self-contained.				
Electronic Diamond Tester	Not applicable.				
"Syn. Diamond Detectors	Not applicable.				
Immersion Cell	Yes	Yes	Yes	No	Diffused light often useful.
Dark-field Loupe	Yes	No	No	No	Provides strong *lateral* light.
Syn. Emerald Filter	Yes	No	No	Yes	

NOTES

PART 3

THE ESSENTIAL INSTRUMENTS— WHAT THEY ARE AND HOW TO USE THEM

4 / The loupe and dark-field loupe

WHAT IS A LOUPE?

The loupe is the most widely used and most familiar gem-identification instrument. It is the first of the three most essential pocket instruments, which, just as they sound, are small enough to be carried in a pocket.

The loupe is simply a special type of magnifier. Loupes come in various powers of magnification: 6X, 10X, 14X, 20X, and 24X. A 6X loupe, for example, presents an image six times larger than what is being viewed. For gem identification, the loupe must be a Hastings triplet-type in a black housing—not gold or chrome-plated. We recommend 10X power for reasons we explain below.

The triplet-type loupe is essential because it has been made specially to correct two problems other types of magnifiers have—the presence of traces of color (chromatic aberration) normally found at the outer edges of the lens; and visual distortion (spherical aberration), also usually at the outer edges of the lens.

Eliminating the traces of color present at the edges of an uncorrected lens is particularly important when you use the loupe to color grade diamonds. Even the slightest trace of color that may be present in a non-triplet type can cause improper grading of diamond color. The Federal Trade Commission in the United States requires that the observation of diamonds for grading purposes be made only with the 10X triplet-type magnifier (10X specifically for determining the clarity [flaw] grade—if it isn't visible with 10X magnification, it doesn't exist for clarity grading purposes).

Correction for visual distortion in the triplet-type creates what we call flatness of field. If we were to look at a gem with a magnifier that was not a triplet-type, any flaw seen at an outer edge of the magnifying lens would be distorted, more or less so depending on how close the flaw is to the edge of the viewing lens. This impairs one's ability to see the flaw clearly, and may result in improper identification of the flaw, and, hence, improper identification of the stone.

We recommend a black housing (casing) because it eliminates distracting glare. Gold or chrome-plated loupes are not recommended because they can throw white or yellow color into stones being examined, especially diamonds. Some jewelers use watchmaker-type loupes, which allow freedom of the hands. If you prefer this type, be sure it is a triplet since most are not. We also recommend the new *dark-field* type since dark-field illumination facilitates detection of fillers and certain internal characteristics.

A Word about Magnification— Higher Power Can Make It Harder to See

Most people think that the higher the magnification, the easier it is to see whatever you are looking at, especially inclusions (flaws). However, this is not exactly true. Unless you understand how magnification works and know how to focus properly, using high-power magnification can be *more difficult* and result in major errors.

It's true that when you have an inclusion in view under higher-power magnification, it's easier to see it clearly, and determine what type it is. However, when you're looking for inclusions, the higher the magnification, the more difficult it may be to spot them. This is because as magnification increases, the focal distance—the distance to point of sharpest focus—decreases, and the depth of focus—the area that appears to be in focus—also decreases, so you have less latitude in the area that will be in focus at a given point, making it much harder to focus critically. An inexperienced person can easily miss small inclusions with a higher-power loupe. The loupe might be in focus just in front of, or behind, an inclusion—but not at the very point where the inclusion actually is, causing one to miss it altogether!

Here's why. With a 10X loupe you have a one-inch focal distance. This means that anything present in a stone at a distance of one inch from the end of the loupe will be in focus. In addition, with a 10X loupe you also have a little latitude in terms of the area in focus, which means that something present at a distance of only 3/4 of an inch, or 1 1/4 inch, will also be seen. It may not be clear, or in focus, but you will see that something is there and can then move the loupe accordingly to focus it more sharply. This is not the case with higher power magnification. A 20X loupe, for example, has only a 1/2 inch focal distance, *and extremely little latitude in front of or behind the 1/2 inch*. Therefore, if there is something just in front of the exact point that is in focus, or just beyond it, you will not see it. There have been cases where gems examined with a 20X loupe have been called flawless, when they clearly were not. With a 10X loupe one would have seen the flaws that were missed with the 20X!

Some unethical jewelers and dealers who understand the difficulty of focusing at higher magnification have developed a very clever ploy to use with customers. They immediately offer a 20X or 24X loupe to use to "take a closer look." They are well aware that the novice will probably see little or nothing at such high-power magnification, but the unsuspecting novice thinks more highly of this dealer for giving them every possible opportunity to really know what they are buying.

We recommend using nothing higher than 10X. If you wish, you may add a 14X or 20X loupe to your store of gem instruments to observe more clearly what you see with the 10X.

The loupe can help determine whether a stone is natural, synthetic, glass, or a doublet (stones that consist of two parts glued or fused together to simulate any gem desired). It can help identify characteristic inclusions, blemishes, cracks, chips, scratches, and bubbles. And, at the very least, the loupe can help determine the workmanship that went into the cutting of the stone, such as symmetry, proportioning, alignment of facet edges, etc.

HOW TO USE THE LOUPE

Before you begin to examine jewelry, practice with the loupe. Learn to see through it clearly. A 10X loupe, while easier to use than a higher powered one, is difficult to focus initially. With a little practice, it will become simple. Practice on any object that is difficult to see—the pores in your skin, the root of a strand of hair, a pinhead. Play with the item being examined. Rotate it slowly, tilt it, move it back and forth while rotating it, look at it from different angles and different directions. Focus holding the loupe at different distances from the object being examined. It won't take long before you are able to focus easily on anything you wish to examine. When you feel comfortable with familiar things, you're ready to begin looking at jewelry.

The first step is to make sure the stone is clean. A thorough cleaning is mandatory before examination. Steam-cleaning is very good for most gems. Another safe method is to stroke the stone gently with a fine-pointed artist's brush dipped in clean isopropyl rubbing alcohol. This method usually removes bits of dust, fingerprints, grease, and often dislodges embedded dirt wedged under prongs. If you are examining a stone under a microscope, you may be surprised to see how many "flaws" wash off when brushed with alcohol.

Holding an unmounted stone with tweezers, or a piece of jewelry by the metal setting, dip it in a small glass of clean alcohol. Stroke it gently with the brush. When you are finished cleaning it, remove it and dry with a clean cloth, paper towel, or toilet tissue. Blow off any remaining lint, which may have been left while drying the piece, with compressed air, such as Dust Off.

Ultrasonic cleaning is recommended only for diamonds. It should never be used for opals, pearls, emeralds, or any gemstone that is heavily flawed. Ultrasonic cleaning can seriously damage these stones.

If no other means is available to clean the stone, breathe on it in a huffing manner to steam it with your breath. Then, wipe it with a clean cloth, such as a handkerchief or shirt. This will at least remove any superficial grease film.

When the stone is clean you are ready to use the loupe. You shouldn't have any problem if you follow these steps.

Key Steps to Using the Loupe

1. Hold the loupe between your thumb and forefinger. Hold the stone or piece of jewelry being examined similarly in the other hand. If examining a loose stone held in a tweezer, hold the tweezer near the tip for greater security.

2. Bring the loupe close to your eye. To prevent movement or shaking, brace the hand that is holding it against the cheek, nose, or any part of your face that is comfortable. The loupe should be as close to the eye as possible (it is not necessary to remove eyeglasses).

3. Now, bring the object being examined *to the loupe*. The hand that is holding the object must also be braced to prevent movement during examination. Hold your hands together so that the fleshy parts just below the thumbs are pushed together and braced by the lower portion of each hand just above the wrists. The wrist must be free to act as a pivotal point when moving the stone to view it from different angles.

4. Find a sturdy, three-point position. With your hands still braced together, and resting against your cheek or nose, place both elbows firmly on a desk, table, or countertop. If nothing else is available, brace your arms against your chest or rib cage. This is the only way to have a really steady hand, and with gems it's very important to have steady hands to insure proper focus.

Examining a stone with the loupe, using tweezers

How to hold a loupe when examining a stone

5. If you are examining an unmounted stone, hold it so that the fingers touch only the girdle of the stone. Putting your fingers on the table (top of the stone) and/or pavilion (bottom) will leave traces of oil. The careful use of tweezers instead of fingers is recommended.

6. Rotate the stone and slowly tilt it back and forth to view it from different angles. This is important because, as we mentioned earlier, your eye may be clearly focused on one area of the stone, but can be completely out of focus in the area immediately adjacent—causing you to miss a nearby flaw altogether. By slowly turning and tilting the stone, you will be more likely to focus in on all areas.

7. Focus the loupe both on the surface of the stone and into the interior. To focus into the interior, start at the surface and then slowly move the stone closer to the loupe so that you are changing the distance between the loupe and each area within the stone; pause and look carefully; now slowly move it closer to the loupe again and look carefully, etc. Now repeat this, looking through the sides. And so on. If you focus on the surface of the stone only, or from the top of the stone only, you will not see what is in the interior of the stone.

8. If you are looking for inclusions, wiggle a finger up and down behind the gemstone. This will cause a shadowing and brightening effect inside the stone, which will highlight any inclusions and make them more definitive in shape, color, and size. We call this the Bonanno-Wiggly-Finger Technique and students have found it very helpful for over 50 years.

LIGHTING AND THE LOUPE

Using Transmitted and Reflected Light

You will first want to hold the stone so that the light is being transmitted through it, from behind, travelling toward your eye. This is easiest if the light is situated at about the same height as your head; just hold the stone up, in front of the light, and examine with loupe. If you are using an overhead light source, hold the stone so that the light is entering from the top, and hold a white business card behind the stone. As the light leaves the stone, the white card will reflect it back into the stone. This technique will also reduce glare, enabling you to see more clearly into the stone.

Sometimes it is also useful to illuminate the stone from behind with a maglite or penlight, but you must be careful to avoid too much glare. To reduce glare, or to create a softer, diffused light, we often take a piece of white paper, such as a napkin or tissue, and simply lay it over the top of the light; the paper serves as a diffuser, and provides instant "diffused" light. Diffused light is often helpful in seeing certain types of inclusions such as the "curved striae" indicating synthetic ruby or sapphire (see page 62).

Most examinations will be done using transmitted light, but it is sometimes helpful to view the stone with reflected light (see Chapter 3). Therefore, also practice with the light shining down on top of the stone, viewing it with the loupe while tilting and turning the polished facets so that light is reflected off the top of each facet.

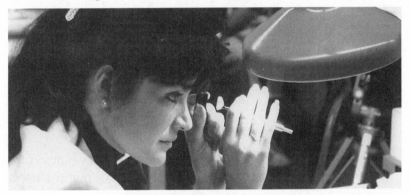

Using loupe with transmitted light,
incorporating our *Bonanno-wiggly-finger* technique

In this way, it is sometimes possible to see scratches or worn edges, certain types of inclusions, or to pick up differences in the "shine" of the upper facets (produced by the light reflection) that would be present in some doublets frequently seen in antique jewelry prior to the production of good synthetics.

It is important to practice using the loupe and focusing it. Practice on things you are already familiar with. Use the wiggly-finger technique. Practice with different light sources—coming from different directions and at different strengths. *Dark-field loupes* (see pages 15 and 16) are especially useful in detecting certain types of inclusions and the flash-effect in filled diamonds.

WHAT THE LOUPE CAN SHOW YOU

With practice and experience a loupe can tell even the amateur a great deal. It can help determine whether a stone is natural, synthetic, glass, or a doublet; it can help identify characteristic inclusions, blemishes, or cracks; it can reveal important cutting or wear faults. This section will cover what you can see with the loupe generally, and will then discuss in detail diamond and colored gemstone imperfections.

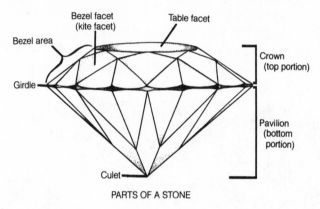

PARTS OF A STONE

Here are some of the first things you'll be able to spot.

- *The workmanship that went into the cutting.* For example, is the symmetry of the stone balanced? Does it have the proper number of facets for its cut? Is the proportioning good? Herein lies an important clue to a stone's genuineness since few cutters put the same time and care into cutting glass as they do into a diamond.
- *Spotting chips, cracks, or scratches on facet edges, facet planes, or table.* While zircon, for example, looks very much like diamond because of its pronounced brilliance and relative hardness, it chips easily. Therefore, careful examination of a zircon will often show chipping, especially around the table edges and the girdle. Glass, which is very soft, will often show scratches. Also, checking around the prongs of a ring setting will often reveal where a setter may have chipped or scratched it while simply working the prongs to hold the stone.
- *Spotting surface crazing* in the new type of composite rubies and sapphires (see Chapter 18).

- In stones such as emerald, the loupe can also help you determine whether or not any natural cracks are really serious—how close they are to the surface, how deep they run, and whether or not they make the stone more vulnerable to breakage as a result.
- *Sharpness of the facet edges.* Harder stones will have a sharp edge, or sharper boundaries between adjoining planes or facets. Many imitations are softer and under the loupe the edges between the facets will appear less sharp—they will have a more rounded appearance. With the loupe it is also possible to spot the rounded edges characteristic of molded plastic.
- *Surface texture differences* that help separate real pearls from fake pearls. Because simulated pearls have a painted surface coating, one may see a pebbly veneer when examining a fake pearl with the loupe, rather than the smooth skin that is characteristic of the real pearl (natural or cultured). A simple comparison under the loupe of pearls you know to be real as compared to those that are fake will teach you the difference immediately.
- *Inclusions and blemishes* (also called flaws). Many inclusions (internal features *included* within the stone, such as cracks, crystals, gas bubbles, etc., that reveal the conditions under which the stone formed) and blemishes (external characteristics such as chips and scratches) that cannot be seen with the naked eye can be viewed with the loupe. With minimal experience, you can learn to spot the characteristic bubbles and swirl marks associated with glass. But remember, most inclusions are not easily seen unless you have experience with the loupe. This is the most difficult area of gem identification to master. It requires lots of patience—taking it one step at a time. Try focusing on just one type of inclusion, or types of inclusions found in one particular gem, such as sapphire. It is helpful to seek professional guidance if possible until you feel confident about what you should be seeing. Don't be afraid to keep reference books and pictures of different types of inclusions on hand. For excellent photographs and additional information, we recommend obtaining a copy of *Internal World of Gemstones* by Edward Gubelin, or *Photoatlas of Inclusions in Gemstones* by Edward Gubelin and John Koivula.

- *Laboratory report ID numbers.* Many labs today inscribe the number of their report on the girdle of the diamond. GIA, for example, inscribes the number of the report on all "Dossier" documents (done for smaller diamonds). This provides an excellent means to make sure you have the diamond for which the Dossier report was issued.

Just learning to focus the loupe so that you are able to spot inclusions that may be present in a stone is an accomplishment that should give you pride. Once you can do this, you should be able to identify what you are seeing simply by referring to the photos provided in this book or in one of those mentioned above.

When examining a colored gem, remember that flawlessness in colored stones is perhaps even rarer than in diamonds. In colored gems, the *type* and *placement* are more important considerations than the presence of flaws in and of themselves. Unlike diamonds, normally they don't significantly reduce the value of the stone. They often provide the necessary key to positive identification, help determine whether or not a stone is natural or synthetic, and possibly indicate the country of origin, such as Burma or Colombia, which may *increase* the value of the stone.

NOTE: See the color section at the center of the book for photographic illustrations of the inclusions described below.

DIAMOND INCLUSIONS AND BLEMISHES

When describing diamond characteristics, we refer to them as *inclusions* when internal and *blemishes* when external. Below we describe various inclusions and blemishes you might see.

Inclusions

Bearding or Girdle Fringes. These are usually the result of hastiness on the part of the cutter while rounding out the diamond. The girdle portion becomes overheated and develops cracks that resemble small whiskers going into the diamond from the girdle edge. Sometimes the bearding amounts to minimal "peach fuzz" and can be removed with slight repolishing. Sometimes the bearding must be removed by faceting the girdle. A lightly bearded stone can still be classified IF, Internally Flawless.

Cleavage. A cleavage is a crack that has a flat plane which, if struck severely, could cause the diamond to split.

Colorless Crystal. This is often a small crystal of diamond, although it may be another mineral. Sometimes it appears very small, sometimes large enough to substantially lower the flaw grade. A group of colorless crystals can lower the flaw grade considerably.

Dark Spot. A small crystal inclusion or a thin, flat mirror-like or metallic reflective inclusion.

Feather. This is another name for a crack. A feather is not dangerous if it is small and does not break through a facet. Thermoshock, which is exposing a gem to extreme temperature changes, or ultrasonic cleaners, can enlarge it (see *Flash Effect*).

Flash Effect. This refers to the appearance of an orange or pinkish zone that "flashes" to violet or blue as you tilt or rock the stone while examining it with the loupe, and indicates the presence of a man-made *filler* forced into cracks to conceal them. It can be seen most easily using a dark-field loupe. (See page 63.)

Growth or Grain Lines. These can only be seen when examining the diamond while rotating it. They appear and disappear usually instantaneously. They will appear in a group of two, three, or four pale brown lines. If they cannot be seen from the crown side of the diamond and are small, they will not affect the grade adversely.

Knaat. This is a comet-shaped ridge that can appear anywhere on a diamond's surface, usually on the table. It's actually part of a small diamond crystal that is invisible to the cutter until it suddenly appears during polishing.

Laser Line. Laser treatment is used to make flaws less visible, and thus improve a stone's appearance. For example, a black inclusion can be vaporized with a laser beam and practically disappear. The laser holes can be seen with a 10X loupe. They look like fine, *straight* white threads extending from the facet surface down to the area containing the vaporized inclusion.

Photo: R. Bucy, Columbia School of Gemology

Laser drill holes
seen with a loupe

Pinpoint. This is a small, usually whitish dot (although it can be dark) that is difficult to see with a 10X loupe. There can be a number of pinpoints (a cluster) or a "cloud" of pinpoints (often hazy in appearance and difficult to see).

External Blemishes

Abraded or Rough Culet. In a modern-cut stone, the culet is a very small facet, nearly a point. An abraded or rough culet has been chipped or poorly finished and will look larger. This is usually a minor flaw.

Girdle Roughness. This blemish appears as crisscrossed lines, brighter and duller finishing, or minute chipping. It can be corrected by faceting or repolishing the girdle.

Knaat or Twin Lines. These appear as very small raised ridges, often having some type of geometrical outline. They are the result of two diamonds having grown together (twin crystals). They are difficult to see and usually can only be seen if light is reflected off the facets.

Natural. A natural is a remnant of the original diamond skin. It is often

Photo: GIA

Natural on the girdle

Photo: GIA

Nick or chip on girdle

left on the girdle in order to cut the largest possible stone from the rough. Naturals usually occur on the girdle and look like rough, unpolished scratch lines. Some exhibit small triangles, called trigons. If the natural is no wider than the normal width of the girdle and does not disrupt the circumference of the stone, some do not consider it a flaw. Naturals are often polished and resemble an extra facet, especially if they occur below the girdle edge.

Nick. This is a small chip, usually on the girdle, and can be caused by wear, especially in diamonds with thin girdles. Sometimes a nick or chip can be seen at a point where two facet edges meet (making a "bruised corner"). If small, the bruised corner can be polished, creating an extra facet. These usually occur on the crown.

Pits or Cavities. These are little holes, usually on the table facet. If deep, they will quickly lower the flaw grade of the stone. Removing the pits involves recutting the whole top of the stone, with a resulting loss in carat weight and a shrinkage in the stone's diameter. Recutting will also affect the symmetry.

Polishing Lines. Many diamonds exhibit polishing lines. If they appear on the pavilion side and aren't too obvious, they do not lower the value. However, in some small diamonds these scratch lines can be obvious, and are usually the result of a badly maintained polishing wheel.

Scratch. A scratch is usually a minor defect that can be removed with simple repolishing.

If you are planning to repolish a stone to remove an external blemish, remember that it must be removed from its setting and reset after polishing.

INCLUSIONS AND SURFACE FEATURES IN COLORED GEMS

Numerous types of inclusions are found in colored gems. Since certain ones are found in some gems and not in others, they provide an important means of positive gem ID—especially in combination with other test results. Types of flaws to look for include the following:

Bubbles. These inclusions look like little bubbles and occur in various shapes and sizes. Round bubbles usually indicate glass or synthetic, although they can be found in natural amber. In synthetic ruby or sapphire they can be round, profilated (a string of bubbles with a large bubble at the center and progressively smaller bubbles on each side), pear-shaped, or tadpole-shaped. In the last two, the tail always points in the same direction. When numerous bubbles are seen, you are probably seeing air bubbles in glass. However, if you see only a few, higher magnification is required to determine whether what you are seeing is truly a bubble or a *small crystal* that may *look like a bubble when viewed with only 10X magnification.*

Cleavage Fault. This is a type of break in the stone rather than an actual inclusion. It is observed in topaz, diamond, feldspar, kunzite, hiddenite. It is a plane- or sheet-like type crack and can weaken the stone if it is exposed to extreme temperature change (thermoshock). If struck with a severe blow, the stone may break apart. Also, a cleavage crack may become larger in ultrasonic cleaning.

Curved Striae. These are concentric curved lines that appear in old-type synthetic sapphires and rubies. Sometimes the curvature is very pronounced; sometimes the lines are slightly curved and appear almost straight. They are difficult to see in light-colored stones, such as pale synthetic pink sapphire. They are most easily observed with a microscope, using diffused or weak light.

Dark Ball-like Inclusions. These are found exclusively in Thai rubies. They appear as dark, opaque balls surrounded by an irregularly shaped, wispy, brown cloudlike formation. They are never seen in Burmese stones, which often contain needlelike inclusions not seen in Thai stones. This type of inclusion will confirm beyond doubt the identity of a genuine Thai ruby.

Feather. A crack that can either be inside the stone or breaking the surface. A large crack that is near the surface, or breaks it, can weaken the stone and make it more vulnerable to damage. One must be particularly careful to check for such cracks when examining emerald, since the oiling of emerald may make cracks more difficult to see. Examining an emerald with the loupe *using reflected light* will reveal cracks that break the surface. Such a crack will appear in reflected light like a little hair or thread on the facet plane and will not disappear after cleaning.

Cracks with a "rusty" look usually indicate a stone is genuine.

Numerous cracks arranged in a web-like or fishnet pattern when seen on the surface of a green stone that appears to be emerald proves the stone is a Lechleitner synthetic.

Fingerprint. These are small crystal inclusions that are arranged in curved rows in such a way as to resemble a fingerprint. They can be seen in the quartz family (amethyst, citrine, etc.) and in topaz. They closely resemble the liquid-filled healing feathers seen in sapphires.

Flash Effect. In emeralds this is the appearance of a flash of yellow or orange that turns blue as you tilt the stone or rock it back and forth. This indicates the presence of an epoxy-resin filler. A flash effect can also be seen in other gems (but the colors of the flash vary) and indicates the presence of a filler.

Halo or Disc-like Inclusions. Many pastel colored Ceylon (Sri Lanka) sapphires contain flat, disc-like inclusions referred to as halos. These are small fractures that result from the growth of zircon crystals inside the host stone. The small crystal is sometimes visible, or may appear as a small dot at the center of the disc, often extending above it. Halos can also be seen in other gems such as garnet.

Internal Growth Patterns. Distinctive internal growth patterns often provide the key to detecting synthetics. Some hydrothermally grown synthetic emeralds exhibit a growth pattern that resembles a mountain range with very pointed peaks.

Liquid-Filled or Healing Feather. This type of inclusion is found in the corundum family (sapphire and ruby) and is more frequently observed in sapphires than in rubies. It resembles a maze of slightly curved little tubes lying next to one another with each tube separated by a space. The overall appearance often resembles a maze or fingerprint.

Needlelike or Fiberlike Inclusions. These look like fine needles or fibers and are sometimes called silk. This type of inclusion can be found in almandine garnet, sapphire, ruby, and aquamarine.

Pavilion Iridescence Indicating Surface Coating on Pavilion. A distinctive pattern of iridescent colors seen in stones that have been color-enhanced by applying a coating to the pavilion only. The colors are seen reflecting off the pavilion facets, resulting from light interference between the coating and surface of the stone.

Some think it's best seen when rocking the stone back and forth beneath a strong light source, while others see it more easily using a diffused light source. The intensity of the iridescence varies depending upon the stone and manufacturer; it is usually very easy to see on coated topaz and beryl, but very subtle and difficult to detect on cobalt-coated sapphire and tanzanite.

Rain. These are dashed lines that resemble rain. They are seen in flux grown synthetic rubies such as the Kashan synthetic.

Surface Crazing. Surface crazing looks like a network of lines resembling scratches across the surface of the stone. They can appear on any part of the stone or over the entire stone. These are an

indicator of a new type of lead-glass and corundum composite now imitating ruby and sapphire and being misrepresented as genuine (see Chapter 18). These lines are not scratches, but surface-reaching glass, revealing the extent of glass present alongside the corundum. They actually penetrate into the stone, but due to the high R.I. of the lead-glass—which is almost identical to that of corundum—it is difficult to see this; they seem to go out of focus or simply "disappear" as you examine them with your loupe.

Surface crazing on table of lead-glass ruby composite.

Photo: Craig Lynch

Swirl Marks. These are found in glass. They are curved, sometimes snake-like, and resemble the swirl marks made when slowly stirring a jar of honey.

Three-Phase Inclusions. These look like irregularly shaped pea pods, usually pointed at both ends, containing a bubble and a cube-shaped or rhomboid-shaped solid that is adjacent to the bubble. The three-phase inclusion is liquid, solid, and gas. These are found in genuine Colombian emeralds and sometimes in Afghanistan emeralds, and verify the emerald's genuineness and country of origin.

Tube-like Inclusions. These look like long, thin tubes. Sometimes they are filled. They are seen in Sandewana and Zambian emeralds, and synthetic spinel.

Twinning Planes. These are found in rubies and sapphires and occasionally in some of the feldspar gems, such as moonstone. They have the appearance of parallel cracks that resemble panes of glass lying in parallel planes. In rubies and sapphires, these can often be found to crisscross at 60 and 120 degrees. These types of inclusions can prove the genuineness of a ruby or sapphire, but if too numerous they can both weaken the stone and diminish its brilliance.

Two-Phase Inclusions. This is an inclusion that usually has a "frankfurter" outline with an enclosed bubble—which may or may not move as the "frank" is tilted from end to end. These can be observed in topaz, quartz, genuine and synthetic emeralds, and sometimes tourmaline.

Photo: Robert Weldon

Two-phase inclusions and liquid-filled fissures in North Carolina emerald

Veils. These are small bubblelike inclusions arranged in a layer-like formation that can be flat or curvaceous, broad or narrow, long or short. They may be easily observed in some synthetic emeralds.

If inclusions weaken the stone's durability, affect the color seen, are too easily noticeable or too numerous, they will significantly reduce price. Otherwise, they may not influence price to any great extent. In some cases, if they provide positive identification and proof of origin, they may actually increase the price (as with Burmese rubies or Colombian emeralds). It is also true that flawless colored stones are rare, and so may bring a disproportionately higher price per carat. However, with today's new synthetics we are immediately suspicious of any flawless colored stone and would urge examination by a professional gem lab.

The loupe can be an invaluable aid to today's jeweler. Whether you plan to use it to observe some of the simpler things, such as scratches and chips on a stone, or to begin learning how to spot some of the flaws or inclusions to determine a gem's ID, the extent to which you will feel confident using it depends on the amount of practice you give it.

SURFACE CHARACTERISTICS SEEN WHEN EXAMINING PEARLS

A simple 10X loupe can be very useful when examining pearls, revealing characteristics indicative of imitation, evidence of dyeing, and other treatments.

Swirl Marks. Random swirls on or under the surface are an indication of imitation pearls.

Color Concentration at Drill Holes. A layer(s) or zone of concentrated color at the drill hole is an indication of dye. It is often seen in "white-rosé" cultured pearls; the pink dye is absorbed by the porous conchiolin layer indicating that the color is not the color of the "nacre" but, rather, the result of dye.

Uneven Color Zones and Mottled Color in Various Areas Around the Surface of the Pearl. Indicates some form of treatment to alter color. Often seen in black pearls, and increasingly in other pastel colors, including "golden" pearls.

Small Spots of Concentrated Color. The presence of small spots of concentrated color, *within* surface blemishes (pits or blisters), indicates treatment to alter color. Treated-color "golden" pearls have been found to have *reddish spots within "whitish" surface blemishes;* they can sometimes be seen with a loupe, but if you are not sure whether or not this is what you are seeing, confirmation can be made using a microscope at 15X–20X magnification.

Fillings and Surface Cracks. Pearls, especially natural pearls, may have surface-reaching cracks or cracks just beneath the surface, making the pearl more vulnerable to damage and reducing its value. Serious pearl blemishes, such as a deep pit, can also be repaired using a filler of some type, and an oddly placed drill hole can be filled to conceal it. Careful examination with a loupe will reveal these cracks and repairs; often the material used to make the repair has a different reflectivity than the pearl's own lustrous character, and this difference in reflectivity can be immediately detected with the loupe.

WHAT IS A DARK-FIELD LOUPE?

The dark-field loupe is a small instrument that provides 10X magnification as in a standard loupe, with an important added feature: it is combined with a specially constructed area that enables you to view a gem against a *black* background with strong *lateral* lighting. This is called *dark-field illumination*, which is why this instrument is called a "dark-field loupe." The magnification is housed in the upper portion of the instrument; the dark-field is provided in the lower portion; the area in between enables you to manipulate the stone or piece of jewelry being examined. To use the dark-field loupe, all that is required is a simple maglite, on top of which the dark-field loupe is placed prior to examining the stone.

What Does the Dark-Field Loupe Do That a Standard Loupe Doesn't Do?

The dark-field loupe provides a "dark-field" environment for examining a stone, a special type of lighting environment that a standard loupe does not provide (although you may be able to improvise one in certain situations). A special "well" has been constructed so you view the stone against a *black* background (if you look at the bottom of the dark-field loupe, you'll see it's black) with light coming from the *side* rather than being transmitted through the bottom of the stone or coming from above. This is called lateral illumination.

Dark-field loupe and maglite
with which it is used

This type of lighting environment makes it easier to see certain types of inclusions and to determine more precisely what they are. For this reason it is especially valuable for colored gemstone buyers because seeing inclusions clearly plays an important role in separating one colored stone from another. Inclusions are also a key to knowing whether or not a stone has been treated in some way. Today, most good microscopes provide dark-field illumination, but the dark-field loupe provides an invaluable benefit for anyone who must travel or identify gemstones when away from a laboratory: portability.

What the Dark-Field Loupe Will Show

The dark-field loupe is very useful for examining inclusions in colored gems. Viewing the inclusions against the dark background provided by the dark-field construction, combined with strong lateral lighting, makes it easier to see the inclusions, and better distinguish what they are. We have found it especially useful in seeing curved striae in synthetic sapphires and rubies, and also in seeing telltale "flux" inclusions in flux-grown synthetic gems. As you gain experience using the dark-field loupe to examine colored gems, you will find that many different types of inclusions are easier to identify with dark-field illumination.

As important as the dark-field loupe can be when examining colored gemstones, today it is also an *essential* tool for anyone buying diamonds or diamond jewelry because there are so many "fracture-filled" diamonds in circulation worldwide. Using the dark-field loupe is the easiest way for most people to spot fracture-filled diamonds, and even among those who are proficient using the standard loupe or microscope, most find the dark-field loupe much faster.

What Is a Fracture-Filled Diamond? A fracture-filled diamond, also called a *clarity enhanced* diamond, is a diamond which contains a crack or cracks that have been filled with a glass-like substance to improve the overall appearance of the stone. Prior to being filled, a crack interferes with light travelling through the stone—it blocks the light from continuing through the stone as it should—causing "dead" or flat areas, and an overall reduction in the diamond's brilliance and liveliness. After the filling process, the cracks no longer block the light because the filler provides a medium through which the light can continue to travel and be reflected back. In effect, the cracks seem to disappear, and the stone becomes much more brilliant, much more beautiful and desirable.

We have been aware of filled diamonds in the marketplace for the past decade. Numerous companies are now engaged in filling diamonds, each closely guarding the "secret" of their exact process. We do know, however, that the fillers differ; some are more durable than others and can withstand most jewelry-making or repair techniques, including high heat, while others cannot. When exposed to heat—such as one might encounter in resizing or repairing a piece of diamond jewelry—some fillers *evaporate*, causing the stone to revert to its "pre-treatment" appearance. While it can always be re-filled and restored to a more attractive appearance (most manufacturers give a lifetime warranty), whether you are buying, selling, or repairing a piece of diamond jewelry, it is easy to see why it is important to know—in advance—whether or not the diamond is fracture-filled.

There is nothing wrong with anyone buying or selling a fracture-filled diamond as long as they understand what they are buying and pay the right price (about $1/2$ the cost of one that isn't filled). Fracture-filled diamonds offer an attractive and affordable alternative to many people. For years, however, many people in the trade didn't know how to spot filled diamonds, so many were bought and sold without disclosure. This situation continues today. Many people who have them *don't know* they have them.

Fortunately, discovering how easy it is to spot most fracture-filled diamonds with the dark-field loupe has removed a lot of the fear, but it is necessary to check *all* diamonds and diamond jewelry carefully; filled diamonds are popping up even in antique and estate pieces, and they have been found in all types of jewelry, in pawnshops, flea markets, and even big-name auction houses.

It should also be mentioned that the dark-field loupe can be especially valuable to retail jewelers, or anyone taking in jewelry for resizing, repair or remounting. Since, as we said earlier, most people don't *know* their diamond is fracture-filled, jewelers must check carefully before taking in any piece of diamond jewelry, for any reason. And they must check before the customer leaves the store. The dark-field loupe gives one the ability to do this, right at the counter, quickly and easily. And, if the stone *is* filled, the customer can even use the dark-field loupe to see for themselves!

HOW TO USE THE DARK-FIELD LOUPE

The dark-field loupe is constructed to fit over the end of a standard maglite. Place the instrument over the light, and be sure the battery is strong.

Notice that there is a well in the center of the instrument. Hold the stone or piece of jewelry over the center of the well. If unmounted, use tweezers to hold the stone. If mounted, hold it by its setting. Just be sure to hold it so that the diamond is sitting in the well and the light is entering through the sides of the stone. Now, simply bring your eye to the eyepiece at the top of the instrument and look at the diamond.

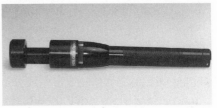

While looking at it, *rock the stone back and forth and tilt it up and down*. This is essential: you must tilt or rock the stone back and forth, while looking at it, and as you turn it, be sure to keep rocking or tilting it. Be sure the stone is going back and forth *into the well* to make sure it is properly lighted.

The dark-field 10X loupe simply attaches to a standard maglite. Dark-field illumination facilitates detection of the flash-effect in filled diamonds and emeralds with epoxy-resin fillers, as well as other internal characteristics in gemstones.

As with a standard loupe, examine the diamond from the top, from the back and the sides, through the girdle. When examining through the girdle, be sure to rotate the stone a full 360°, or if it's not round, from every side. As you examine it, be sure to tilt and rock the stone, keeping it well lit. If using tweezers, be sure to examine the stone through the girdle, from the side profile, by grasping the girdle with the tip of the tweezers. Use the side of the tweezers to hold the girdle when examining from the tip through the table, or from the back, through the culet.

How to Spot Fracture-Filled Diamonds with the Dark-Field Loupe

In fracture-filled diamonds, the dark-field illumination provided by this type of loupe quickly reveals the presence of a *"flash effect"* that is seen in *all* fracture-filled diamonds—a broad "flash" of color, usually bright pink or orange, purplish, blue or green—that suddenly appears as you rock or tilt the stone while viewing it through the dark-field loupe. As you rock or tilt the stone while examining it, the orange or pinkish color can "flash" to violet or blue, and back again.

It is really not difficult to understand why a fracture-filled diamond exhibits a flash-effect, and why the dark-field loupe makes it easy to see.

A diamond with a large crack is not as beautiful as one without a crack because the crack causes the light to stop as it travels through the diamond. While you may not actually see the crack, you see the result: the stone seems to have a flat or "dead" spot; or many such spots! When the crack is filled with the right filler—something with a refractive index close to that of diamond—*the filler provides a medium through which the light can continue to travel and be reflected back, rather than being stopped by the crack.* Thus, we no longer "see" it (or, more correctly, the result of its presence).

The filler is not diamond, however, so it has a different refractive index than diamond (see page 126). Therefore, as the light is travelling through diamond, it will be travelling in a particular way; when it passes through the filler, however, it will change its path. This is why we can see a "flash effect"—a flash of color—in the area of the crack.

We would see a very different effect if the crack were *unfilled*. Diamonds with unfilled cracks can show *interference colors*, but these look very different from the flash effect. Interference colors look like mini-rainbows, very similar to an oil slick on water.

This is not what we are talking about when we say "flash effect"; the term "flash effect" refers to a flash of predominantly *one color*, possibly with a slightly different shade of that color at the edges. The

Examining a diamond ring using a dark-field loupe

The dark-field loupe is placed on top of the maglite and the diamond held over the well at the center; the ring is tilted, rocked, and turned while being viewed through the 10X eyepiece at the top of the instrument. *Notice that the instrument is brought to the eye,* as with a standard loupe.

This model has an important feature not found in most other dark-field loupes; it has been designed with a much greater distance between the upper portion and lower portion, making it possible to examine stones set in jewelry as well as those that are unmounted.

colors typically seen are a bright pinkish orange, purplish pink, and green; as you tilt or rock the stone, the color may "flash" between blue and green, or between pink and purple, but you are seeing predominantly one broad flash of color in a given area.

Dark-field illumination makes it much easier to see the flash effect; the dark background against which you are viewing the diamond makes it easier to see the color, and the strong lateral lighting increases the likelihood of the light being caught at just the right angle to cause the color flash. Using a microscope with dark-field illumination does the same thing. The primary benefit of the dark-field loupe, however, is its portability and the ease with which it can be used, anywhere, and by anyone. It is also much faster, and, in many cases, in the time that it would take you to set up the microscope and piece of jewelry to be examined, the dark-field loupe could already have told you what you want to know.

The only shortcoming of the dark-field loupe is that some mountings, or some unusually large jewelry pieces, may not fit properly in the opening and thus prevent proper positioning of the diamond over the well. For this reason we recommend developing a good standard loupe technique as well. When using the standard loupe, however, try to improvise a "dark field" by using a strong light and directing the light through the sides of the stone; be sure to tilt the diamond back and forth, roll it around your finger, and so on, as you would using the dark-field loupe; and if possible, see if you can find something dark to hold behind the stone.

We recommend that you go to workshops, visit the booths of companies selling fracture-filled diamonds at various shows, or simply contact one of the distributors of filled diamonds to obtain some study stones. Most are very happy to be helpful and make stones available for study purposes.

For practice, observe several stones that you know to be filled (ask for a stone in which it is *easy* to see the flash effect, one that is *more difficult*, and one that is *very difficult*) and examine them first with the dark-field loupe, then with a standard loupe. You'll see how easy it is with the dark-field loupe, and once you see the telltale "flash effect" you won't confuse it with anything else. NOTE: The Gemological Institute of America (GIA), the American Gemological Laboratory

(AGL), and most other recognized gem testing laboratories will not issue a diamond grading report on any diamond that is fracture-filled. When in doubt, get a laboratory report.

Using the Dark-Field Loupe to Examine Emeralds and Rubies

The dark-field loupe can also be a valuable tool in examining emeralds and rubies. Emeralds are now being routinely treated with epoxy resins to fill fractures, and fractures in rubies are being filled with glass fillers.

One of the best-known substances used in emerald is called "Opticon," but several different types of epoxy resin fillers are being used, and their properties vary somewhat. Palm oil is an epoxy resin. While some people think that this type of treatment is better than the traditional practice of using oil because it is more permanent, there is some evidence that this type of treatment can make it more difficult to determine the true clarity of the stone and result in greater breakage during normal wear or by jewelers performing routine repair. There is also evidence that green tinted fillers are being used to artificially enhance the color as well as the clarity, making it even more difficult to determine the true quality and value of the stone. Until there is a better understanding of the short- and long-term effects of epoxy resin fillers, some people prefer to avoid emeralds treated with "Opticon" or similar fillers so it is important to know whether or not the emerald is treated in this manner.

While the presence of an epoxy resin used to fill emerald fractures may be difficult to detect, *many exhibit a flash effect* that can be most easily seen when viewed with dark-field illumination. Glass fillers in ruby also exhibit a flash effect that is easier to see with dark-field illumination. To see the flash effect, examine the stone with the dark-field loupe in the same manner you would examine a diamond; epoxy resin fillers often exhibit a flash of *blue, yellow, or orangey-yellow*. Glass fillers used in ruby usually exhibit a *blue* flash effect. When you see the blue flash, this provides positive confirmation that the stone *is* filled with an epoxy resin (in the case of emerald) or glass (in the case of ruby). The presence of a blue or strong orangey-yellow flash is positive confirmation in emerald that it is filled with epoxy resin filler, but be careful not to confuse a "yellow" flash with the yellowish residue that sometimes remains in a fracture when the oil has come out. The presence of a blue or strong orangey-yellow flash-effect is positive confirmation that the emerald is filled with Opticon or a similar epoxy resin filler, but if you are unable to detect a flash-effect, or if you see only a yellow flash and are not sure whether or not it is residue from oil, other testing is recommended to know for sure.

NOTES

5 / The Chelsea filter and synthetic emerald filter

WHAT IS THE CHELSEA FILTER?

During the past 50 years, a number of optical filters for gem identification have been introduced to the gemologist. The most popular is the Chelsea filter, developed in the early 1930s from a formula worked out by B.W. Anderson and C.J. Payne while teaching at the Chelsea College of Science and Technology in London—hence the name. We like it because it is affordable, widely available, and offers in a single filter what it can take several other types of filter to do.

The Chelsea filter is used for colored gemstone materials, both transparent and opaque. It first came to be called the emerald filter since its original use was to differentiate genuine emeralds from their green look-alikes—green sapphire, tourmaline, peridot, and glass. Emerald would appear pink to red when viewed through the Chelsea filter, while these other stones would not. Unfortunately, in the case of emeralds today, positive identification based on what is seen through the Chelsea filter is no longer an adequate test when used alone. There are genuine emeralds being mined that may not appear red or pink under the filter and synthetics that do. Other, more recently discovered gemstones, such as tsavorite, also show a red reaction to the Chelsea filter. So, while it's still an important aid in the identification of emerald, it must be used in conjunction with the loupe and other instruments.

New uses for the Chelsea filter have renewed its importance. The Chelsea filter proves very helpful in detecting certain dyed and treated stones, and in separating some gems from their common imitations. It offers an effective means for differentiating sapphire-colored synthetic spinel from genuine sapphire, aquamarine-colored synthetic spinel from genuine aquamarine, and natural-colored green jadeite jade from much dyed jadeite. These are all frequently encountered and often confused.

We recently viewed a pair of jadeite earrings that were going to be auctioned by a well-known auction house. The earrings were estimated to fetch $10,000 to $15,000. They looked like exceptionally fine jade, truly "imperial" quality. The first thing we did was pull out a Chelsea filter. And were we surprised! In less than 15 seconds we knew that they were dyed. The earrings were genuine jadeite, but not the magnificent quality they appeared to be. They were inexpensive dyed jade, worth a fraction of the estimate.

The Chelsea filter is really quite a simple instrument. It is a color filter, designed to allow only two wavelengths of light to be transmitted—red and green. Therefore, a stone can only appear some shade of red, green, or a mixture of the two, when viewed through the filter. The particular chemical and other physical properties of the stone being viewed determine which color you see.

The Chelsea filter costs about $45 and can be obtained at many of the supply houses listed in the Appendix in the back of the book.

HOW TO USE THE CHELSEA FILTER

The Chelsea filter is the easiest and fastest of all instruments. One simply holds a stone in a good light, looks at it through the filter, and notes what color the stone appears. Normally, the depth of color in the stone being examined determines the depth of color seen when viewed with the filter. For example, a pale green emerald will appear pinkish when viewed through the filter while a deep green emerald will appear red. And so on. When this is not the case, one should be suspicious. The color the stone appears when viewed through the filter—red, green, or some combination of these two—provides an important clue to identity.

As simple as the instrument is, however, many people use it improperly and get incorrect results. Let's take a moment to explain how to use it properly.

1. *Use a strong WHITE light source for viewing the stone.* Incandescent light such as that provided by an ordinary 60- or 100-watt light bulb is excellent. Natural daylight light may also be used. However, *do not use fluorescent light.* Fluorescent light has less of the red wavelength present than white light and will alter what you see with the filter. For example, when one views a nice, rich green Colombian emerald through the Chelsea filter using proper light, it will look RED. However, if viewed using fluorescent light, in some cases you might not see red at all, or the red may appear much weaker than it should. If you concluded, therefore, that the stone wasn't Colombian, you would be wrong.

2. *Place the stone or jewelry directly UNDER the light source so that the light is being reflected from the surface of the stone into the filter.* Place the stone or jewelry as close to the light as possible. *Note:* If examining rough gemstones (i.e., uncut), you might need to illuminate from behind the stone. With polished gems, however, the light should always come from above, as described here.

3. *Hold the filter as close as possible to the eye.* It is also helpful to close the other eye when using the filter.

4. *Bring your eye/filter to the piece being examined.* If you must get closer to the piece you are examining to be sure what you are seeing, remember that the piece you are examining must remain close to the light source. DO NOT MOVE THE STONE AWAY FROM THE LIGHT; MOVE YOUR HEAD! In most cases, if the stone is close to a strong light you can see the color reaction from several feet away and it is not necessary to get close to it (you can get quite a backache at a big show if you are always bending over to look closely!). However, sometimes interference from incidental light might cause difficulty in being sure what you are seeing. Ideally one should try to view the stone at a distance of about 10 inches, or less. Protect yourself from the glare of the lamp by keeping the housing from the light source between you and the object being viewed.

5. *Try to cover any metal or diamonds near the stone being examined.* We have found that reflections from yellow gold, from the mounting in which a stone is set, can sometimes create a "pinkish" impression making it appear that the *stone* is showing a pink

Examining a stone with a Chelsea filter. Notice that the gem being examined is held close to a strong light, but that the filter is held close to the eye.

reaction when it is not. Diamonds can do the same thing; they often show reddish flashes that can create an impression that the colored stone it is near is exhibiting a reddish reaction. When possible, especially when looking at smaller gemstones, try to cover or conceal the diamonds or metal from view (we sometimes cover the whole piece of jewelry with a piece of white napkin, tissue or handkerchief, leaving just a small area of the stone showing).

You may find that a piece of black cardboard placed behind the gemstone is helpful for observing any coloration seen through the filter. A piece of white cardboard or flat white business card will work even better. Whether you are using a white or black background, be sure it doesn't have a shiny surface.

WHAT THE CHELSEA FILTER WILL SHOW

As we mentioned, the Chelsea filter was originally designed for the examination of emeralds and emerald look-alikes. Colombian and Siberian emeralds appeared red when examined with the filter while other green gems did not, and, therefore, could not have been emeralds. However, today this no longer holds true because emeralds mined in places other than Colombia and Siberia often do not appear red, and most synthetic emeralds do. We have also come to learn that gemstones such as the rare chrome tourmaline, which obtains its green body color naturally from the presence of chromium, will exhibit a red color through the Chelsea filter.

The most important uses for the filter today include: detecting certain types of dyed-green jadeite; separating fine blue sapphire from blue synthetic spinel; separating aquamarine from aqua-colored synthetic spinel; and separating pink sapphire from pink tourmaline. It is also a very useful tool to detect the mixing of fakes in with parcels of natural stones, in beads and in jewelry containing many stones.

We have found the Chelsea filter invaluable in checking parcels of stones for imitators that have been mixed in with natural stones. The Chelsea filter is now the first tool I use when examining *any* parcel of colored stones. In parcels of "Paraiba" tourmaline, the beautiful—and very costly—neon colored tourmalines discovered a few years ago in Paraiba, Brazil, we have discovered "Paraiba-colored" apatite (an inexpensive, softer natural stone that makes a great look-alike) and a new imitation "Paraiba-colored" YAG using only the Chelsea filter. While the filter alone could not tell us what we had, these stones popped out of the parcel because their color reaction through the filter was noticeably different from the reaction of the tourmaline: the tourmaline was yellowish/green, the YAG was bright pink, and the apatite was grayish/ yellow. We've also found sapphire-colored blue synthetic spinel mixed in with genuine sapphire (the synthetic blue spinel looks bright red through the filter, while sapphire remains blackish/green), and even spotted synthetic ruby mixed in with genuine ruby because the synthetic appears much brighter red than the natural ruby! Today there are also several imitation tanzanites that pose risks to the tanzanite buyer. One type, a tanzanite-colored YAG, will appear intense red through the Chelsea filter and should easily stand out in a parcel (some natural tanzanite will also appear reddish through the filter, but the intensity of the YAG is much greater, so it should still stand out from the rest; if in doubt, use the ultraviolet lamp for an instant confirmation (see page 123).

Dyed versus Natural Color Green Jadeite

Let's take a look at green jadeite as an example of how useful the Chelsea filter can be. The Chelsea filter is invaluable for detecting certain types of *color-enhanced* jadeite, poor quality jadeite that has been dyed to get its rich, deep green color.

Fine green jadeite jade derives its color naturally from chromium, as does chrome tourmaline and Colombian emerald. Normally when chromium is present, it causes whatever gem is being examined to appear *red* when viewed through the Chelsea filter. This is why Colombian emerald and chrome tourmaline always appear red with the filter.

Curiously enough, this is not the case with green jadeite. In fact, with green jadeite we see just the opposite of what we would expect— natural color green jadeite does not appear red when viewed with the Chelsea filter. It remains greenish. It shows no reddish or pinkish reaction. Certain types of *dyed* jadeite, however, will show a reddish coloration (ranging from a weak orange-brown to a pale pink, to red). This coloration is easily seen when the specimen is held against a black cardboard background. *With jadeite, whenever the stone appears REDDISH through the Chelsea filter, you have positive proof it has been treated.* This certainly is simple enough. The presence of red indicates the color has been enhanced, that it is not natural. For those who love jade, the Chelsea filter is invaluable just for its ability to detect such stones, and many a costly mistake has been prevented with it.

But beware. The converse is not true. There are also treated stones which, like natural green jadeite, remain the same color. You must be careful not to draw an erroneous conclusion. If the jadeite is inert when viewed with the Chelsea filter, other tests are necessary before you can be sure whether or not the color is natural. The spectroscope can be very useful in making a positive determination here (see Chapter 10). Just remember, *the presence of red is conclusive* evidence of color alteration, but *the absence of red is inconclusive.*

Aquamarine versus Synthetic Spinel

Now let's look at aquamarine. Today synthetic aquamarine-colored spinel is often misrepresented as genuine aquamarine. The Chelsea filter can tell you immediately if you have synthetic spinel. Synthetic spinel gets its color from the element cobalt, as does much blue glass. When cobalt is present, one will see a reddish reaction with the filter. If the color is light blue, you will see a pinkish color; if dark blue, you will see red. Aquamarine on the other hand will never show pink or red. It appears greenish through the filter. As you can see, while light blue synthetic spinel can easily pass for aquamarine to the naked eye, it is quickly detected with the filter since the synthetic spinel will show a pink tint and genuine aquamarine will show a greenish tint; a pink reaction tells you immediately that you do not have aquamarine, and other tests will quickly help you identify the stone as synthetic spinel.

Pink Sapphire versus Pink Tourmaline

Pink tourmaline is a very popular stone today that can be mistaken for pink sapphire. However, once again, the Chelsea filter can be of great assistance. Pink tourmaline will retain its pink color when viewed with the filter, while pink sapphire, the more expensive of the two gems, will appear a stronger red.

Blue Sapphire versus Cobalt-Coated "Blue" Sapphire

The gem trade was recently surprised by the arrival of "blue" sapphires that were found to be off-color sapphires altered to appear rich blue in color following surface treatment using a cobalt coating.

Where the color is the result of cobalt-treatment, the particular hue may provide the experienced gemologist or sapphire buyer with a visual indicator—the cobalt-coated stones lack the intense, rich blue color of fine sapphires and typically have a violet component to the blue.

The fastest and easiest test to screen blue sapphires for cobalt treatment is to use the Chelsea filter. This is especially practical when checking parcels that might have had cobalt-treated stones mixed in. *All cobalt-treated blue sapphires will show a pronounced pink or red color (depending upon the thickness of the coating and resulting depth of blue) when viewed with the Chelsea filter.* With the exception of "color-change" sapphires (which show a blue color in daylight and a purplish color in incandescent light), blue sapphires do not show a reddish or pinkish reaction when viewed through the Chelsea filter. (Note: Cobalt-treated blue sapphires are *not* color-change sapphires. Also, the red reaction through the filter is much stronger with cobalt-treated stones than what is seen with color-change sapphires.) Whenever you get a reddish reaction through the Chelsea filter when examining a "blue sapphire," you know there is something wrong and will need to check further with other instruments for confirmation as to what you really have.

REACTIONS OF POPULAR GEMS TO THE CHELSEA FILTER

It is very helpful to take the Chelsea filter and use it to look at stones whose identity you already know, making a note of what you see. It takes practice and, as you will see, several stones of the same color may also react similarly under the Chelsea filter. However, by narrowing the possibilities, and then viewing them also with the loupe and the dichroscope, one can positively identify approximately 85% of the colored gemstone materials encountered today.

A brief tabulation of reactions of gems when viewed through the filter follows. Keep your own notes at the end of the chapter, especially when new gemstones are discovered or new synthetics or imitations enter the market. We like to find someone selling any new material and request sample "study stones" or simply visit them at one of the gem shows where we can use our instruments to see what they will show.

Green Stones

Emerald. Most Colombian and Siberian emeralds and emeralds from the recent find in Hiddenite, North Carolina, as well as most synthetics, exhibit a good red. The depth of the green will determine the depth of the red when viewed under the filter. However, Chatham, Linde, and Regency synthetic emeralds possess such a strong red that it is usually an immediate giveaway, and should make one instantly suspicious.

Indian and African Emerald. Indian emeralds and most African emeralds do not exhibit any red or pink. Some from Sandewana, however, do show a red color.

Afghan Emerald. These usually exhibit a reddish reaction.

Brazilian Emerald. These may be inert, but they can also show a reaction that varies from a brownish red to a strong red similar to Colombian stones.

Emerald-Colored Soudé-Type Doublets. This is an imitation gem fabricated from two pieces of material (often colorless synthetic spinel) that have been cemented together with emerald-green colored glue. It is inert when viewed with the filter (continues to look green). This type of doublet can readily be detected by submerging it in methylene iodide and examining it through the girdle while tilting it back and forth in the liquid. The methylene iodide will enable you to see that the top and bottom are colorless, and will reveal the plane of colored glue.

Demantoid Garnet. Fine green demantoid garnet will appear reddish with the filter; yellowish-green stones may not.

Diopside. Although sold as "chrome" diopside, does *not* show reddish reaction. It is "inert" (doesn't change color) because the reaction is blocked by the presence of iron.

Tsavorite Garnet. Will appear red.

Green Zircon. Most will appear reddish.

Green Chrome Chalcedony. Strong red reaction. (Dyed green chalcedony may also show reddish if dye contains chromium.)

Dyed Green Jadeite. Sometimes dyed jadeite will exhibit a reddish or pinkish tint (occasionally appearing orangish or brownish). When it does, you have conclusive proof of color alteration. However, the absence of a reddish coloration does not prove that the color is natural. If jadeite is inert (shows no color change) when viewed with the filter, other tests are necessary to determine whether or not its color is natural.

Green Glass. Usually remains green; may appear reddish if it gets its coloring from chromium enhancement.

Green Tourmaline. Most green tourmaline, including the copper-bearing type often called "Paraiba" or "Paraiba-type," remains green. However, the rare *chrome* tourmaline will show red, and *must* show red, or it is *not* the costly chrome variety. We wish to stress this because chrome tourmaline costs about ten times more than other green tourmalines and we have had students buy what they thought was "chrome" tourmaline, and pay the price for chrome tourmaline, only to find out that it was not. One student actually returned her Chelsea filter to us because she thought her *filter* was broken since the tourmaline didn't show a red reaction! Since she knew the dealer and had been buying gemstones from him for years, she couldn't imagine that he had misrepresented it, or had made a mistake. In fact, he had not only made a mistake in what he had sold her, but when she returned it and he checked his entire parcel (fancy-cut stones from a well-known cutter in Idar Oberstein, Germany, a premier cutting center for colored stones), he discovered that only half of his parcel were chrome tourmaline, and *he* had also paid for chrome!

Green Fluorite. This will exhibit red. *Note*: Not only will green fluorite exhibit red, as does Colombian emerald, but it may also contain three-phase inclusions, which are also seen in Colombian emeralds. A three-phase inclusion is one that encompasses all three states of matter—gas, solid, and liquid. It typically consists of a liquid pocket, inside of which will be a bubble (gas) and a tiny, often rectangular crystal (solid). In cases where three-phase inclusions are observed with the loupe and red is exhibited with the Chelsea filter, other tests are necessary to positively identify the stones.

Green Quartz. Irradiated green quartz will appear red with the Chelsea filter, while prasiolite remains greenish (prasiolite is usually the result of heating amethyst from some sources, but it also occurs naturally).

Alexandrite. Will show a strong red in natural daylight and a stronger red in incandescent light.

Greenish Aquamarine. Will appear greenish.

Hiddenite (Spodumene). Varieties from North Carolina appear reddish; other varieties appear green.

Peridot. Will appear greenish.

Green Sapphire. Will appear greenish.

Green Tanzanite. Although often sold as "chrome" tanzanite, will remain greenish.

Synthetic Green Sapphire. Will appear red.

Synthetic Green Spinel. Will usually appear green but can appear red.

Synthetic Green YAG (diamond simulant). Will show strong to moderate red.

Red and Pink Stones

Garnet. Red varieties will remain red.

Glass. Remains red.

Doublets. Remain red.

Red Beryl (also called red *emerald*). Usually inert, but may exhibit slightly stronger red.

Ruby. Both natural and synthetic ruby will exhibit a strong red, redder than it will appear without the filter; synthetic ruby usually exhibits an even stronger red than natural ruby and, when mixed with the natural in parcels, the color difference may enable you to quickly spot the synthetics (the stronger red shown by the synthetic sometimes just "pops out" from the natural).

Spinel. Both natural and synthetic spinel will exhibit red, but usually a weaker red than ruby.

Pink Sapphire. Will appear pinkish-to-red, but not as strong as ruby.

Tourmaline. Remains pinkish or reddish.

Blue Stones

Spinel. This usually remains a dark greenish but the rare natural "cobalt" spinel exhibits a red reaction.

Synthetic Spinel. Will exhibit a reddish reaction resulting from the presence of added cobalt, which acts as a coloring agent. Deep blue synthetic spinel will appear red; light blue synthetic spinel may appear pink or orangish.

Aquamarine. Will appear greenish.

Blue Topaz. Most will appear green; "electric" blue may appear pinkish, but a distinctly different shade from synthetic spinel.

Blue Tourmaline. Indicolite (dark blue) tourmaline will appear dark, sometimes almost black; Paraiba or Paraiba-type blue tourmalines (which get their particular color from the trace element copper) have a greenish reaction, sometimes silvery-green or blue-green.

Blue Zircon. Will appear greenish.

Sapphire. Will appear very dark green, often black.
   Cobalt-treated sapphire in which the blue color results from cobalt-treatment will have a pink or red reaction.

Blue Glass. May appear pink to strong red if the blue coloration results from the use of cobalt. Otherwise, inert or, if pale blue, sometimes greenish.

Blue Tanzanite. Usually appears reddish, but can also be inert (the stronger the violet overtone, the redder; gray-blue tanzanite is usually inert—remains greenish).

SEPARATING SYNTHETIC *FROM* NATURAL *EMERALD* *WITH COLOR FILTERS*

One of the most exciting recent developments in gem testing has been the introduction of a new set of color filters to be used in conjunction with the Chelsea filter: the Synthetic Emerald Filter Set. With the Chelsea filter and the synthetic emerald filters it is now very easy to spot many synthetic emeralds that would have been very difficult to detect using other methods, especially for anyone who isn't a highly trained gemologist. These filters are inexpensive and simple to use, so we highly recommend them to anyone who buys emeralds.

   The synthetic emerald filter set contains two filters. You must first use the Chelsea filter to determine which of the synthetic emerald filters to use. Some emeralds, both natural and synthetic, contain chromium and some do not, so you must use the Chelsea filter first to determine whether there is chromium. Once you know this, you will know which filter to use—the "synthetic emerald filter" or the "support filter"—to determine whether you have natural or synthetic. The synthetic emerald filter is very effective in spotting flux-grown synthetic emeralds, and the support filter is helpful in detecting many hydrothermal synthetic emeralds. Prior to using them, however, you must be sure that the material you are checking is, in fact, *emerald* and not some other green material such as glass, or chrome tourmaline (you will learn more about how to do this as you continue reading!).

To use the synthetic emerald filters, just follow this simple procedure:

1. Check the response of the emerald with the *Chelsea filter,* following the steps we've already discussed. Be sure to hold the Chelsea filter close to the eye (as you would a loupe) while placing the emerald as close as possible to a strong incandescent light (don't forget to place the stone against a flat white background, and when possible, cover the metal from the mounting, or any diamonds or other sidestones as we suggest on page 79). Note the reaction of the stone with the Chelsea filter.

2. After noting the color the stone appears when viewed through the Chelsea filter, put the Chelsea filter down. Now move the stone SEVERAL INCHES AWAY FROM THE LIGHT (you don't want the stone as close to the light when you use the synthetic emerald filters as you do with the Chelsea filter).

3. Now examine the emerald again, this time using one of the synthetic emerald filters rather than the Chelsea filter. If the emerald appeared *pink or red* through the Chelsea filter, now examine it using the synthetic emerald filter; if it remained green using the Chelsea filter, now use the support filter. Note: In most cases you will use one *or* the other (see exception below), based on the response through the Chelsea filter. Do not use both.

4. Note the color seen when viewed through the synthetic or support filter:

Synthetic Emerald Filter
(use when emerald appears pink or red through Chelsea filter)
Red or pink: the emerald is *synthetic*
Greenish: the emerald is *natural* (see exception below)

Support Filter
(use when emerald remains green through Chelsea filter)
Lilac or pink: *synthetic*
Greeny-blue or bluish-green: *synthetic*
Green: may be natural or synthetic; check with loupe for telltale inclusions; most hydrothermal synthetics look very different from the natural.

Important exception: there is a synthetic emerald now on the market that will appear reddish with the Chelsea filter and then appear greenish using the synthetic emerald filter, leading one to conclude that the emerald may be natural when it is not. However, the color it appears with the Chelsea filter is a *purplish* red, a shade that is very different from the color seen with a chromium-type natural emerald. In this case—and in this case only, when the stone appears purplish red through the Chelsea filter and greenish with the synthetic emerald filter—use the support filter. The synthetic will NOW look greenish through the support filter, while the chromium-type *natural* emerald will look *reddish*. Also, the appearance of these synthetic emeralds through the loupe is very different from the natural; they are much too clean and free of typical inclusions seen in chromium-type or other natural emeralds.

It is important to note that new synthetic materials continue to be introduced, and it is possible that a synthetic emerald could be produced which will show the same color as a natural emerald when viewed through these filters. However, ANY emerald that appears *PINKISH OR REDDISH through the Chelsea filter and then appears pinkish or reddish through the synthetic emerald filter IS SYNTHETIC.* When this is the case, the reactions to the filters are conclusive for determining that it is synthetic, and you do not have to administer any other test. If the reaction through the Chelsea filter is red, and then the reaction through the synthetic emerald filter remains greenish, other instruments may be required to confirm whether the emerald is synthetic or natural. If the emerald does *not* show a reddish reaction through the Chelsea filter, indicating the use of the support filter, and then shows a reddish or pinkish reaction through the support filter, the emerald *is synthetic* and the use of the filters is conclusive and no other tests are required. When in doubt, submit it to a gem-testing lab.

What You Will See Using a Chelsea Filter and Synthetic Emerald Filters

NATURAL EMERALDS	SYNTHETIC EMERALDS
Chromium type (such as Colombian or Russian)	**Chromium type** (flux grown)
Chelsea filter response: pink or red	*Chelsea filter* response: pink or red
Synthetic emerald filter response: greenish	*Synthetic emerald filter* response: pink or red*
Vanadium type (such as Zambian or Indian)	**Hydrothermal type** (not flux grown, no chromium)
Chelsea filter response: greenish	*Chelsea filter* response: greenish
Support filter response: greenish	*Support filter* response: see chart**
* There is a synthetic emerald now on the market that will appear greenish. See the important exception on page 90. ** Provided on package insert	

NOTES

6 / The dichroscope

WHAT IS A DICHROSCOPE?

The dichroscope is one of the most important pocket instruments. As we mentioned earlier, armed with only the loupe, Chelsea filter, and dichroscope, a competent gemologist can positively identify approximately 85% of all colored gemstones. While it takes years to develop professional-level skill, knowing how to use these three instruments will start you on your way.

Like the Chelsea filter, the dichroscope is very easy to use. It is used *only* for transparent colored stones and not for colored opaque stones, or amber and opal.

The dichroscope provides one of the easiest and fastest ways for differentiating transparent stones of the same color from one another. The jeweler who knows how to use this instrument can easily distinguish, for example, a ruby from a red garnet or a red spinel (one of the popular "new" stones seen with increasing frequency); a blue sapphire from fine tanzanite or blue spinel; an amethyst from purple glass; or an emerald from many of its imitations or look-alikes.

The dichroscope we recommend is a *calcite-type* (not a polarizing type). It is a small tubular-shaped instrument that is approximately 2 inches long and ¹/₂ inch in diameter. In most models, the tube has a small round opening at one end, and a rectangular opening on the other (in these models, look through the *round* opening). Some models have two round openings, one slightly larger. Look into the dichroscope without any stone or piece of jewelry. Just hold the instrument up to the light, and look through it. Do you see two small rectangular windows at the opposite end? If not, look through the other end. The important thing is to be sure that when you look through the opening, you are looking through the end that allows you to see a pair of rectangular windows at the opposite end.

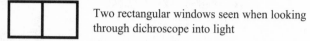

Two rectangular windows seen when looking through dichroscope into light

When colored stones are viewed with the dichroscope, some will show the same color in both rectangular windows while other stones will show two colors, or two different tones or shades of the same color. For example, you might see blue in one window and yellow in the other. Or, you might see pink in one window, and red in the other. In either case, the colors you see would be considered "two" colors, even though pink is really a lighter shade of the color red. If you were to see orangey-red in one window and violet-red in the other, this would also be considered seeing two colors, even though they are really different shades of the same color.

One can successfully use the dichroscope without understanding why only one color is seen with some stones and more than one with others. You simply need to know how to use the instrument properly, and what to look for, stone by stone. However, we think it is interesting to understand why, so we will take a moment to explain it in very simple terms.

When a ray of light enters a colored gemstone, depending on the particular properties of that stone, it will either continue travelling through as a *single* ray, or divide into *two rays*. Stones through which it continues as a single ray are said to be "single refracting"; stones through which it splits and travels as two rays are "double refracting." If you look at an object through a strongly double refracting stone such as calcite, you will actually see two images. Try it. Write your name on a piece of paper and then read it through a piece of calcite—you'll see double.

Single refracting stones are those that will always show *the same color* in both rectangular windows of the dichroscope. Only a few gemstone materials are single refracting—diamond, garnet, spinel, glass, colored YAG, colored CZ, and plastic. Therefore, if you have a stone that only exhibits one color, identity can be fairly quick, since there are so few possibilities.

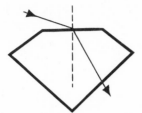

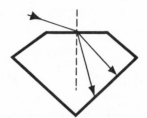

Single refraction: A ray of light enters the material and continues travelling through it as a *single* ray.

Double refraction: A ray of light enters the material and *splits* into *two rays*, each travelling at a different angle and speed.

Most gems are double refracting and will show *two colors*, one color in one rectangular window of the dichroscope, and a different color or distinctly different *shade* of color in the second window. We call these stones "dichroic" (di = 2; chro = color). When a ray of light enters the stone and splits into two rays (as it does with all double-refracting stones), each of the two rays will travel through the stone *at a different angle and speed*. The angle and speed at which light travels determine the color we see. So, if we could separate the rays and see each one individually, we would see a different color for each. This is what the dichroscope does. It separates each of the two rays so we can see both colors.

Some stones show *three colors* when viewed with the dichroscope. We call these stones *trichroic* (tri = 3; chro = color). These stones are also double refracting, but when light enters from certain directions we get one pair of rays (travelling at certain angles and speeds), and when it enters from another direction, we get a *different* pair. In the second pair, one of the two rays will travel at an angle and speed different from either of the two rays in the first pair. Thus the third color. We get two colors (one in each rectangular window) in certain directions, and two colors from another direction, but not the same two colors. One of the colors in the second pair will be different from the colors seen in the first pair.

Same color seen in both rectangular boxes of dichroscope in single-refracting stones.

Different colors, or shades of same color, seen with dichroscope in double-refracting stones.

The specific color or shades of color seen through the dichroscope present a very important clue to the identity of a stone. Let's take two red stones that are approximately the same color red—ruby and red spinel—and view them through the dichroscope. We would be able to identify the ruby immediately because two distinctly different shades of color would appear, one in each of the two small rectangular windows: a strong orange-red would show up in one, and a strong purple-red in the other. However, the red spinel would exhibit the same color in both windows—there would be no difference in tone or shade of red, but exactly the same red. (*Note:* the dichroscope can separate stones that look like one another in color—ruby from glass, sapphire from spinel, and so on—but cannot separate *natural* from *synthetic*. Additional tests are required for that.)

The particular colors observed may also help you determine whether or not the color of the gem is *natural*. Such is the case with the popular, strongly trichroic blue gem called "tanzanite," a member of the zoisite family. Zoisite occurs naturally in a wide range of colors from brownish or greenish-yellow to lavender, to violet-blue or deep sapphire-blue. The lovely blue colors that are so desirable, however, are rare; most blue tanzanite is *brownish* zoisite that has been *heated*. When heated, the brownish color changes to a much prettier blue color. But heating changes more than just the body color seen; it changes the trichroic colors seen with the dichroscope. Natural color blue tanzanite exhibits three distinct, *different* colors: a pronounced blue, purple, and green are typically seen. Sometimes the purple color is very reddish, and sometimes yellow is present rather than green, but the important thing to note is that you will observe three *different* colors. "Heated" blue tanzanite, however, usually exhibits two colors—purple and blue—but you will see two different *shades* of blue, one distinctly lighter than the other, so it is still considered a "trichroic" gem. What is important to note is that the green/yellow color is usually absent in heated blue tanzanite. **When checking tanzanite with the dichroscope, the presence of green or yellow in the trichroic colors seen may indicate that the stone's blue color is *natural*; the absence of green or yellow usually indicates *heat-induced* color.**

HOW TO USE THE DICHROSCOPE

Although the dichroscope is simple to use, it is important to make sure you have proper light and that you rotate the dichroscope as we will describe below. You must also remember to view the stone from five different directions. Keeping these points in mind, proceed as follows.

1. Hold the dichroscope between your thumb and forefinger, gently resting it against the stone being examined.

Using the dichroscope. Notice that the dichroscope is held very close to the stone and the eye. Holding the tube between the thumb and the forefinger allows easy rotation of the dichroscope as you view the stone. The light is being *transmitted* through the stone.

2. Place the eye as close as possible to the end of the dichroscope. Be sure you are looking through the end that allows you to see a pair of rectangular windows at the opposite end.
3. View the stone with strong light that is *transmitted through the stone*. A small high-intensity utility lamp is a good source for transmitted light (these lamps offer the added benefit of stronger light since the stone can be held close to the light source). A strong penlight also provides good light to use with the dichroscope. Or, use light coming from a ceiling fixture (hold the stone and dichroscope up, looking into the light, with the light coming through the back of the stone).
4. To view the stone with the dichroscope, hold the dichroscope as close as possible to the stone, even touching it (be sure a strong light is coming through the stone, from behind it).
5. Look into the dichroscope. While looking through it, slowly rotate the *dichroscope* (not the stone) at least 180 degrees. Does a second color appear in either of the windows as you rotate it?

For example, while looking at ruby you may see the same color in both windows as you begin, possibly an orange-red color. Then, as you turn the dichroscope, you will see a second color appear. You will still see the orange-red color you've seen all along in one window, but in the second window the color may change to violet-red. If there is no apparent change of color in one of the windows, continue rotating the dichroscope until you have turned it a full 360 degrees. If you still don't see a second color, change the direction through which you are viewing the stone.

6. Following exactly the same procedure described above, examine the stone from another direction. You must examine the stone from *five* different directions to be sure that there is, or is not, a second (and sometimes a third) color. The five directions are: top to bottom; side to side; front to back; on a diagonal to one of those directions; on a diagonal to the other direction.

Using the ruby again as an example, if we viewed it from only one direction, even though we rotate the dichroscope, we might only see a single color in the two boxes. If we stopped here, we could draw

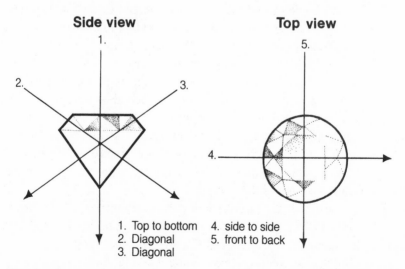

Examine the stone from five directions: top-to-bottom, side-to-side, front-to-back, and from two different diagonals.

a false conclusion that a genuine ruby were a garnet or spinel. If we do not detect more than one color in the first direction, we must repeat the examination from a second direction, and again from a third direction, and so on, until we have examined it from all five directions.

REMEMBER: AS YOU VIEW THE STONE IN EACH DIRECTION, YOU MUST ROTATE THE DICHROSCOPE.

7. Note the color seen in each window, in each direction. You may see only one color; or two colors (in which case you are observing *dichroism*); or, in some stones, three colors *(trichroism)*.

In the case of trichroic stones, you will see one pair of colors in the rectangular windows when viewed from one direction, and a second pair when viewed from a different direction. One color will be the same in both pairs.

Andalusite provides a good example of trichroism. When it is viewed with the dichroscope in one direction, you may see yellow in one window and green in the other. Then, when viewing it from another direction, you might see the same yellow you saw in the first pair of colors and, in addition, a reddish-brown in the other window.

The specific colors seen in the rectangular windows, as well as the number of colors seen (two or three), can help you make a positive identification of most colored stones. But remember, you must observe the stone from at least five different directions. A second color will often fail to show up when viewed from only one direction. And, of course, a third color, which would indicate a trichroic stone, might be present. If you think a stone might be one that exhibits trichroism, you must not stop after seeing a second color, but continue through all five directions until you have, or have not, detected the third. This can be especially important in gem identification since far fewer stones are trichroic and, therefore, the test would give positive ID on the spot.

While the dichroscope is an easy instrument to master, we recommend having someone who is already familiar with it assist you the first time. This will help insure that you are holding it properly and have the proper lighting. It shouldn't take more than 15 minutes to get the hang of it.

WHAT THE DICHROSCOPE WILL SHOW

Once you feel comfortable handling the dichroscope, you are ready to start viewing stones. If only one color is observed with the dichroscope, it usually indicates that you have a "non-dichroic" material. You can see from the following list that there are only a few gemstones in this category. If you see two colors, you have a "dichroic" (di = two; chro = color) material; if you pick up a third color, a "trichroic" (tri = three; chro = color) material.

In the following pages we have provided lists showing, both by color and by gemstone family, the colors you should see when looking at the popular gemstones with the dichroscope. Such tables are also provided in standard gemology textbooks (see "Tables on Pleochroism").

Once you note the colors you see with the dichroscope, check the chart to see which stone(s) would show those colors. If there is only one, you can now make a positive identification. If there is more than one, you may need to use the Chelsea filter, loupe or other instrument.

REMEMBER: The dichroscope can separate stones that look like one another in color—ruby from glass, sapphire from spinel, and so on—but cannot separate *natural* from *synthetic*. Additional tests are required for that.

LEARN TO USE THE THREE POCKET INSTRUMENTS TOGETHER

Sometimes a gemstone that should show dichroism doesn't. Two stones that demonstrate how checking for dichroism alone may be inconclusive for gem ID are peridot and green zircon. These exceptions offer excellent examples of how useful the loupe, Chelsea filter, and dichroscope can be in assuring accurate gem ID *when used together*.

Peridot and green zircon can resemble each other. There is also green glass that can look like both of them. The dichroic colors of green zircon will differentiate it from peridot and glass (and vice versa) when you can detect them, but sometimes they are too weak to detect. And sometimes green zircon just doesn't exhibit dichroism. Here's where using another one of our three pocket instruments can be useful.

If you examine a green zircon with a Chelsea filter you will see a reddish coloration, which you will not see with peridot (peridot remains green when viewed with the filter). However, it could still be green glass.

Now your loupe will come to the rescue. First, the loupe may reveal "doubling." This is an optical effect that makes you think you are "seeing double." To observe doubling, look through the stone (check from several different directions). If the edges of the back facets appear double, as if you have double vision, you are seeing "doubling" (sometimes the facet edge, instead of looking like a single line, will resemble a narrow set of railroad tracks).

Zircon will exhibit doubling (peridot will also show doubling of the back facets, but we eliminated it with the Chelsea filter—since it showed reddish, it can't be peridot. Peridot would have remained green). Glass is still a possibility. However, glass will not show any doubling. Zircon does. So, by checking with the loupe to see if we can observe doubling, we can determine the identity of the stone. If we see doubling, we now know we have zircon.

If you are not sure whether or not you see doubling, the loupe will still aid you. It will tell you from the presence and type of inclusions whether it is glass or zircon. Now we will know for sure that we have zircon.

Next let's take a look at peridot. If you are able to detect trichroism, you will have no question as to the stone's identity being peridot. But peridot often shows only two colors and might be confused with green zircon. To further complicate matters, there are three types of zircon, all of which may occur in some shade of green: "low" (also called "metamict"), "intermediate," and "high." The crystalline structure of zircon has been broken down as a result of naturally occurring exposure to radiation and may exhibit virtually no double refraction, no dichroism, and no doubling; intermediate zircon has had a less severe breakdown of the crystal structure than the "low" type so it *will* exhibit double-refraction, weak dichroism, and doubling (but less strong than peridot); "high" zircon has strong double refraction, and will exhibit good dichroism and very strong doubling, even greater than peridot. *Usually* green zircon is either "low" or "intermediate" so seeing strong doubling would lead us to conclude the stone is peridot. Furthermore, "high" zircon is also typically light green, while peridot can be medium to deep green. So if the color is a deeper green, strong doubling might lead us to conclude the stone is peridot. Peridot is also encountered far more frequently than green zircon. Nonetheless, in this example, you might not be able to make a positive determination with just the loupe and dichroscope. Here again, using another instrument, in this case the Chelsea filter, will give you the answer. If the stone is peridot, it will remain greenish when viewed through the filter, but if it is green zircon it will look *reddish* through the filter.

Another important use of the dichroscope is for separating tanzanite from its imitations. Many imitations are single-refracting and exhibit no dichroism, while tanzanite is trichroic. Synthetic corundum (sapphire) is produced in tanzanite colors, but it is dichroic and produces different dichroic colors from tanzanite. Synthetic forsterite could be mistaken for tanzanite, but it is also dichroic, not trichroic. However, one of the colors seen in forsterite (purplish pink) might suggest tanzanite, especially if mounted in a way to prevent checking from multiple directions. In such cases, examination with an ultraviolet lamp (Chapter 7) or refractometer (Chapter 8) will instantly indicate whether or not it is tanzanite.

Practice using these three pocket instruments together. Within a surprisingly short period of time, you'll become much more confident, and begin to enjoy the rewards of accurate gem ID.

COLORS EXHIBITED BY POPULAR DICHROIC AND TRICHROIC GEMS—BY GEM COLOR

2-Dichroic 3-Trichroic		S-Strong D-Distinct W-Weak	
Note: Light-colored stones exhibit weak dichroism—hard to detect			
Gemstone	Dichroic or Trichroic	Intensity of Color	Colors Seen
PURPLE OR VIOLET GEMS			
CHRYSOBERYL			
Alexandrite	3	S in deep colors	In natural light: emerald-green/ yellowish/reddish In artificial light: emerald-green/ reddish-yellow/red
Synthetic Alexandrite (corundum-type)	2	S in deep colors	In natural light: brownish-green/ mauve In artificial light: brownish-yellow/mauve
CORUNDUM			
Violet Sapphire	2	S	yellowish-red/violet; or pale gray/ green
QUARTZ			
Amethyst	2	D to W	purple/reddish-purple; or purple/ blue
SPODUMENE			
Kunzite (lavender)	3	S	colorless/pink/violet
TOURMALINE			
Purple/Violet	2	S	purple/light purple
ZOISITE			
Tanzanite	3	S	blue/purplish or reddish/green or yellow; or blue/lighter blue/purplish or reddish [Note: the presence of *green* or *yellow* may indicate *natural* color.]
BLUE GEMS			
BENITOITE	2	S	colorless/indigo-blue (or greenish-blue)
BERYL			
Aquamarine	2	S to W	Blue variety: blue/colorless Blue-green variety: pale blue-green/pale yellow-green to colorless
CORUNDUM			
Blue Sapphire	2	S	greenish-blue/deep blue

104

FORSTERITE			
(Synthetic)	2	S	blue/purplish pink
IOLITE			
(Dichroite)	3	S	pale blue/pale straw-yellow/ dark violet-blue
TOPAZ			
Blue	3	S to D	colorless/pale blue/pale pink (Note: pink usually is imperceptible.)
TOURMALINE			
Indicolite (blue)	2	S	light blue/dark blue
Blue-Green	2	S	light blue-green/dark blue-green
ZIRCON			
Blue	2	D	colorless/blue
ZOISITE			
(Tanzanite)	3	S	blue/purplish or reddish/green or yellow; or blue/lighter blue/purplish or reddish [Note: the presence of *green* or *yellow* may indicate *natural* color.]

GREEN GEMS

ANDALUSITE (green)	3	S	brownish-green/olive-green/ flesh-red
BERYL			
Emerald	2	S to W	yellowish-green/bluish-green
CHRYSOBERYL			
Alexandrite	3	S in deep colors	In natural light: emerald green/ yellowish/reddish In artificial light: emerald-green/ reddish-yellow/red
Synthetic Alexandrite (Corundum-type)	2	S in deep colors	In natural light: brownish-green/ mauve In artificial light: brownish-yellow/mauve
CORUNDUM			
Green Sapphire	2	S	yellowish-green/green
PERIDOT	3	D to W	yellow-green/green/yellowish [Note: It often is difficult to detect two colors; the third usually is imperceptible.]
SPODUMENE			
Hiddenite (green)	3	S	bluish-green/grass-green/ yellowish-green or colorless
TOURMALINE			
Green	2	S	pale green/ strong green; or brownish-green/dark green [Note: If you see *red* through Chelsea filter, it's Chrome Tourmaline.]

ZIRCON	2	W	brownish-green/green (or colorless)

YELLOW GEMS

BERYL			
Heliodor (yellow)	2	S to W	pale yellow-green/ pale bluish-green
CHRYSOBERYL			
Yellow	3	S in deep colors	colorless/pale yellow/ lemon-yellow
CORUNDUM			
Yellow sapphire	2	D to W	very weak yellowish tints
QUARTZ			
Citrine	2	D to W	yellow/paler yellow (or colorless)
SPODUMENE			
Yellow	3	S	yellow/pale yellow/deep yellow
TOPAZ			
Yellow	3	S to D	honey-yellow/straw-yellow/ pinkish-yellow [Note: In topaz, a third color seldom is seen.]
TOURMALINE			
Yellow	2	S	light yellow/dark yellow
ZIRCON			
Yellow	2	W	brownish-yellow/yellow

BROWN OR ORANGE GEMS

CORUNDUM Sapphire	2	S	yellowish-brown to orange/ colorless
QUARTZ Smoky	2	D to W	brownish/reddish-brown [clear differentiation]
TOPAZ			
Brown/Orange	3	D	colorless/yellow-brown/brown
TOURMALINE Brown/Orange	2	S	yellow-brown/deep brown; or brownish-green/dark green
ZIRCON			
Brown	2	W	yellow-brown/reddish brown

RED/PINK GEMS

BERYL			
Morganite (pink)	2	S to W	pale rose/bluish-rose
Red (red "emerald")	2	S	orange-red/purple-red
CHRYSOBERYL			
Alexandrite	3	S in deep colors	In natural light: emerald-green/yellowish/reddish In artificial light: emerald-green/ reddish-yellow/red
Synthetic Alexandrite (Corundum-type)	2	S in deep colors	In natural light: brownish-green/ mauve In artificial light: brownish-yellow/mauve

CORUNDUM			
Ruby	2	S	orangish-red/purple-red
Pink Sapphire	2	S to W	Two slightly different shades of pink; often difficult, if not impossible, to detect in pale stones.
DIASPORE (color-change "Zultanite")	3	S	bluish, greenish, yellowish (easiest to see third color when viewed in diffused, full-spectrum daylight such as found outdoors on a sunny day, away from direct sunlight)
QUARTZ Rose	2	D to W	pink/pale pink [clear differentiation]
TOPAZ Pink	2	S to W	colorless/very pale pink/pink
TOURMALINE Rubellite (Red)	2	S	pink/dark red (or magenta)
ZIRCON Red	2	W	clove-brown/reddish-brown

Popular Gems' Usual Dichroic or Trichroic Colors by Gem Family

2-Dichroic 3-Trichroic		S-Strong D-Distinct W-Weak	
Note: Light-colored stones exhibit weak dichroism—hard to detect			
Gemstone	Dichroic or Trichroic	Intensity of Color	Colors Seen
ANDALUSITE (green)	3	S	brownish-green/olive-green/ flesh-red
BENITOITE	2	S	colorless/indigo-blue (or greenish-blue)
BERYL			
Emerald	2	S to W	yellowish-green/bluish-green
Aquamarine	2	S to W	Blue variety: blue/colorless Blue-green variety: pale blue-green/pale yellow-green (or colorless)
Morganite (pink)	2	S to W	pale rose/bluish-rose
Red ("red emerald")	2	S	orange-red/purple-red
Heliodor (yellow)	2	S to W	pale yellow-green/ pale bluish-green

CHRYSOBERYL			
Yellow	3	S in deep colors	colorless/pale yellow/ lemon-yellow
Alexandrite	3	S in deep colors	In natural light: emerald-green/ yellowish/reddish In artificial light: emerald-green/ reddish-yellow/red
Synthetic Alexandrite (Corundum-type)	2	S in deep colors	In natural light: brownish-green/ mauve In artificial light: brownish-yellow/mauve
CORUNDUM			
Ruby	2	S	orangish-red/purple-red
Blue Sapphire	2	S	greenish-blue/deep-blue
Green Sapphire	2	S	yellowish-green/green
Orange/Brown Sapphire	2	S	yellowish-brown to orange/colorless
Pink Sapphire	2	S	two slightly different shades of pink; often difficult, if not impossible, to detect in pale stones
Violet Sapphire	2	S	yellowish-red/violet; or pale gray/green
Yellow Sapphire	2	D to W	very weak yellowish tints
DIASPORE (color-change "Zultanite")	3	S	bluish, greenish, yellowish
IOLITE (Dichroite)	3	S	pale blue/pale straw-yellow/ dark violet-blue
PERIDOT	3	D to W	yellow-green/green/yellowish [Note: it often is difficult to detect two colors; the third usually is imperceptible.]
QUARTZ			
Amethyst	2	D to W	purple/reddish-purple; or purple/blue
Citrine	2	D to W	yellow/paler yellow (or colorless)
Rose	2	D to W	pink/pale pink [clear differentiation]
Smoky	2	D to W	brownish/reddish-brown [clear differentiation]
SPODUMENE			
Kunzite (lavender)	3	S	colorless/pink/violet
Hiddenite (green)	3	S	bluish-green/grass-green/ yellowish-green (or colorless)
Yellow	3	S	yellow/pale yellow/deep yellow

TOPAZ			
Blue	3	S to D	colorless/pale blue/pale pink [Note: pink usually is imperceptible]
Brown/Orange	3	D	colorless/yellow-brown/brown
Pink	3	S to D	colorless/very pale pink/pink
Yellow	3	S to D	honey-yellow/straw-yellow/ pinkish-yellow [Note: in topaz, a third color seldom is seen.]
TOURMALINE			
Blue-Green	2	S	light blue-green/dark blue-green
Brown/Orange	2	S	yellow-brown/deep brown (or brown-black or greenish-brown)
Green	2	S	pale green/strong green; or brownish-green/dark green [Note: If *red* through Chelsea filter, it's Chrome Tourmaline.]
Indicolite (blue)	2	S	light blue/dark blue
Purple/Violet	2	S	purple/light purple
Rubellite (red)	2	S	pink/dark red (or magenta)
ZIRCON			
Blue	2	D	colorless/blue
Brown	2	W	yellow-brown/reddish-brown
Green	2	W	brownish-green/green (or colorless)
Red	2	W	clove-brown/reddish-brown
Yellow	2	W	brownish-yellow/yellow
ZOISITE (Tanzanite)	3	S	blue/purplish or reddish/green or yellow; or blue/lighter blue/purplish or reddish [Note: the presence of *green* or *yellow* usually indicates *natural* color.]

"Gems" That Show No Dichroism

Garnet
Spinel & Synthetic Spinel
Colored Diamond
Colored Diamond Simulants (CZ, YAG, etc.)
Glass
Plastic

NOTES

7 / The ultraviolet lamp

Ultraviolet lamp and
viewing box

WHAT IS AN ULTRAVIOLET LAMP?

An ultraviolet lamp is a small lamp, very simple to use. It can be an invaluable aid in gem identification, and also for detecting some types of treatment.

The ultraviolet lamp, also called a UV lamp, produces a special type of light (actually radiation) called *ultraviolet.* These lamps are used to reveal the presence or absence of *fluorescence* in gems. Fluorescence refers to whether or not a stone produces a color reaction when exposed to ultraviolet radiation—color that is not visible in ordinary light—a color seen *only* when the stone is viewed under ultraviolet radiation. For example, when we say a *white* diamond "fluoresces" *blue,* we mean that it will appear blue when viewed under the ultraviolet lamp (which produces ultraviolet radiation), but it is really a white diamond, and will look white in normal light.

The ultraviolet lamp serves many purposes for the gem identifier. By viewing gems with an ultraviolet lamp in a blackened environment, we are able to see different reactions depending on the gem and, in some cases, an ultraviolet lamp is all we need to determine whether a stone is genuine, an imitation, synthetic, or has been treated. The use of longwave ultraviolet radiation has proven especially useful for testing emeralds and indicating whether or not they've been oiled. It is also very useful for separating synthetic white spinel and colorless synthetic sapphire from diamond, and in helping to distinguish between natural blue sapphire, heated blue sapphire, and the older Verneuil synthetic blue sapphire. Testing for fluorescence in diamonds is also critical when color grading them, as we discuss later, to insure proper grading. Shortwave radiation is also very important, and today it is the fastest and easiest way to separate tanzanite from all of the tanzanite imitations currently available.

There are several types of ultraviolet lamp, but for gemological purposes you must have a lamp that independently produces both *longwave* and *shortwave* ultraviolet radiation. Several manufacturers produce ultraviolet lamps. We recommend hand-held models such as #UVGL-58 6-watt unit by Ultra-Violet Products, Inc., GIA Gem Instruments' longwave/shortwave ultraviolet lamp, Spectroline's #ENF240, or Raytech's #LC-6. These models also provide separate control buttons so you can use shortwave when needed or, simply by pushing another button, longwave (but never both wavelengths simultaneously). We also like the inexpensive, lightweight, *battery-operated, portable* unit made by Ultra-Violet Products, #UVSL-14P. It provides both longwave and shortwave capability in a very compact unit. Some lamps provide only shortwave; others only longwave. Be sure the model you select provides both (see Chapter 2).

It is also important to be sure the lamp has the proper *intensity* to ensure reliable results. When looking at specifications, be sure to check the intensity. For example, the intensity at 3 inches on the UVGL-25 is 720/760; on the 6-watt UVGL-58, 1200/1350; on the mini UVSL-14P, the intensity at 3 inches drops to 68/113. This means that you must examine the stone at much closer range when using the mini. More importantly, when examining stones that typically show weak fluorescence, you may not detect it using the mini; in such cases, you cannot be sure without using a lamp with greater intensity. The mini has an intensity that is adequate for many stones and it is an invaluable tool because of its portability. But some lamps, mini models and desk-top alike, have such a weak intensity that they will not reveal the ultraviolet reaction and may lead you to an erroneous conclusion. If you fail to see any reaction using a portable lamp, double-check with a stronger one.

In addition to the lamp, we recommend a "black box"—a viewing box or cabinet specially designed for hand-held lamps. This will allow you to view the stone or jewelry in a totally dark environment and enable you to observe the presence of fluorescence and, possibly, phosphorescence more easily. You can easily make a basic black box by painting a cardboard box with flat black paint and cutting out a small viewing window at the top and an opening to accommodate the lamp. Some equipment supply houses and ultraviolet light manufacturers sell viewing cabinets. If you wish to purchase one, we recommend those with protective eyepieces. They range in price from about $150 to $230.

UNDERSTANDING ULTRAVIOLET LIGHT AND FLUORESCENCE

Ultraviolet light and fluorescence are not really difficult to understand. In fact, fluorescence is one of nature's most interesting mysteries to observe. You simply need to know that there is visible light and invisible light all around us. Light travels in waves, and the length of those waves determines whether they are *visible* or *invisible*, and what color we actually see. Some light waves are too short to be visible to humans; some are too long to be visible. The colors we see, such as red, blue, or green, have wavelengths that occur in a range visible to the human eye. Ultraviolet has wavelengths that go beyond what we are able to see, and so they are invisible to us.

The ultraviolet lamp emits ultraviolet light rays. These rays are too short to be visible to the human eye. However, when they strike certain gems, properties within those gems *change the length of the invisible wavelengths into longer wavelengths so that they become visible.* When this happens, colors appear that were not visible before viewing with the ultraviolet lamp. When a gem material produces colors when viewed with the ultraviolet lamp, colors not seen without it, we say it *fluoresces* or it has *fluorescence.* The ultraviolet lamp enables us to know whether or not a stone fluoresces and, if so, the color of the fluorescence.

Some stones also *phosphoresce.* This means that they will continue to glow for a period of time after turning *off* the lamp. The phosphorescence (the continued glow) may be weak or strong. It may last only a split second or it may last for several hours.

FLUORESCENCE AND GEM IDENTIFICATION

The ultraviolet lamp enables us to observe fluorescence. Under its ultraviolet rays, fluorescent substances glow with color that can't be seen in normal light. Even stones that appear drab brown, black, or gray in normal light may exhibit a brilliantly glowing blue, red, or green under ultraviolet light—where invisible ultraviolet rays have been converted to visible wavelengths. If your local museum has a fluorescent gem or mineral display, make a trip to see it. It can be quite a treat!

The precise color seen under ultraviolet light will be determined by the properties of the substance being viewed. Certain stones will glow one color, while others will glow a different color; some fluoresce under longwave, others under shortwave, and some under both long- and shortwave.

The information provided by the ultraviolet lamp can be an important clue in gem identification. It will immediately show you whether or not the stone fluoresces or phosphoresces and, if so, whether the reaction is produced under longwave, shortwave, or both (this is why you must have an ultraviolet lamp that produces both long- and shortwave light). While it is seldom a conclusive test, it can be a fast and easy way to confirm your diagnosis when used in conjunction with other tests.

HOW TO USE THE ULTRAVIOLET LAMP

Before beginning our discussion, we want to stress that SHORTWAVE ULTRAVIOLET CAN BE DANGEROUS IF USED CARELESSLY. *Caution must be exercised when using shortwave ultraviolet.*

- *Never look into any ultraviolet light.* Keep it turned away from your eyes at all times. Shortwave ultraviolet light can cause serious eye injury. You may wish to use a pair of special goggles that can be obtained from equipment suppliers listed in the Appendix, or wear eyeglasses with glass lenses (shortwave radiation will not go through glass).
- *Avoid continuous exposure to skin.* Don't expose your skin to its rays for longer than necessary. Shortwave rays can cause serious skin burns after only minutes of exposure.
- Do not turn on the lamp until everything is in proper position. This will help avoid unnecessary exposure.
- Whenever possible, use protective goggles or glasses.

1. *Clean both the stone being examined and the mounting in which it may be set.* Substances such as skin oils, lint, or dirt under a prong may fluoresce and distort your conclusions.
2. *Put the stone or piece of jewelry being examined in a nonreflective darkened environment.* It's important to examine the piece in as dark an environment as possible. Use a special viewing cabinet designed for ultraviolet examination, or black box such as we've described earlier in the chapter. Place what you are examining on a flat black background (a piece of black construction paper will do in a pinch). If you don't have a proper viewing box, go into a room without windows (such as a closet) and view the piece in the dark. Just remember to keep the lamp turned away from your eyes.
3. *Hold the lamp directly over the item being examined, WITHOUT TURNING IT ON.* Direct the light down onto the item, *holding the lamp as close to it as possible.* Remember, the closer the stone is to the lamp, the easier it will be to see any reaction to the ultraviolet radiation. Also, be sure you use a lamp with adequate intensity.
4. *NOW turn the lamp on.* First depress the longwave button. Press only one button at a time.

   View the stone under longwave. Note whether or not the stone fluoresces and, if so, what color, and the intensity. If it doesn't fluo-resce, note that it is inert (which means it shows no change).

   View the stone under shortwave. Repeat the step above, depressing the shortwave button. Again, note whether or not there is any fluorescence, and, if so, its color and intensity.
5. *View the stone from several different directions.* Remember to keep the stone as close as possible to the lamp. Be sure not to mistake the purplish glow from the lamp itself (being reflected from the stone's facets) for weak fluorescence. The stone must glow from within.
6. *Turn off the lamp.* Note whether or not the stone continues to glow. If it does, it's exhibiting phosphorescence. Note the color and duration.
7. *Remove the item from the viewing area.*

Remember: *While using the ultraviolet lamp, always keep it turned away from your eyes and never look into it.*

What the Ultraviolet Lamp Will Show

As we've already mentioned, the ultraviolet lamp will reveal the presence of fluorescence in gems and thus aid in gem ID. At the end of this chapter we have provided charts that show the colors gemstones may exhibit under long- and shortwave UV-light, and how ultraviolet examination can help separate look-alikes. There is also a list of phosphorescent gemstones. However, note that not all stones fluoresce. Furthermore, it is important to be aware that in some gem families, stones that are found in certain places may fluoresce while stones from other places will not. Also, if there are traces of iron in a gemstone (such as we find in rubies from Thailand), fluorescence may be very weak or not exhibited at all.

Before you begin to use the charts, however, we'd like to make a few general comments.

Separating Natural Diamond from Synthetic Diamond.

One of the most important uses for the ultraviolet lamp today is separating natural from synthetic "gem" diamond ("gem" to distinguish this from the "industrial" quality synthetic diamonds which are in wide circulation).

While synthetic colorless gem diamonds are not yet in wide circulation, this is changing. Colorless (as opposed to "fancy-color") stones are now available in sizes over one carat, some exceeding 2 carats, and production is rapidly increasing. Synthetic diamonds in fancy colors, such as blue, yellow, and even red and deep green, are being encountered with increasing frequency. Several very sophisticated instruments have been developed that offer great promise for quickly separating synthetics from natural, especially for anyone who must frequently check large quantities of stones, but for most people such equipment is too costly and lack of portability makes them impractical.

All synthetic diamonds now being produced can be separated by major gem-testing labs, and many can be detected by experienced gemologists with routine gemological tests. These include examination with the loupe and microscope for distinctive inclusions such as whitish "bread crumb" inclusions and unusual intersecting graining or growth features. Often, simple tests are all that are required, using instruments that can be easily and quickly learned. Of these, one of the most reliable is ultraviolet examination.

When exposed to ultraviolet radiation, natural diamond may exhibit no fluorescence at all, or it may fluoresce one of many colors, the most common being blue or yellow. When examined under both longwave and shortwave radiation, you will note that natural diamonds that *do* fluoresce normally fluoresce *stronger* under *longwave* radiation. This is important to keep in mind because it is just the *reverse* of what typically occurs with synthetic diamonds. In the case of synthetic diamonds, fluorescence is usually observed under *shortwave* examination, and may be much weaker, or "inert," under longwave. This is the first thing to check. (NOTE: Both the Cullinan I and II exhibit no fluorescence under longwave radiation yet show a weak greenish gray under shortwave. The Cullinan II also phosphoresced briefly. These reactions, however, are not typical for diamonds.)

While some synthetic diamonds may not fluoresce, all of the synthetic diamonds we have recently seen *do* fluoresce. When they do fluoresce, one of the most distinguishing characteristics of the synthetic diamond is a weak-to-moderate yellow, greenish-yellow, or strong green fluorescence that is more noticeable under *shortwave*. Some synthetic diamonds also exhibit a yellow *phosphorescence;* that is, they continue to glow in the dark for a time after the ultraviolet light is turned off. Extremely long-lasting yellowish or greenish phosphorescence—sometimes a minute or longer—is positive confirmation of synthetic.

Some charts listing identifying characteristics of synthetic diamonds indicate that yellow phosphorescence is always indicative of synthetic diamond. This is NOT TRUE. Natural "chameleon" diamonds (diamonds that change color when exposed to heat, and which tend to become more yellow when left in the dark for a period of time) also exhibit a similar yellow phosphorescence. If a diamond phosphoresces yellow, double-check to make sure it is not a chameleon-type diamond. NOTE: If the phosphorescent color a diamond exhibits is different from its fluorescent color, the diamond is a natural diamond but one that has been specially treated to imitate a chameleon-type diamond.

Ultraviolet examination is especially useful with *blue* diamonds. Synthetic blue diamonds are quickly identified because they exhibit a distinctive chalky yellow fluorescence to shortwave radiation and very long-lasting phosphorescence. Natural blue diamonds are usually inert to both longwave and shortwave ultraviolet radiation although the Hope diamond exhibits a distinctive red phosphorescence.

Another distinguishing characteristic can be found in the distribution of the fluorescent color seen; in natural diamond the fluorescence is evenly distributed across the stone. In the synthetic, however, this is normally not the case; in the synthetic, the fluorescence is often *zoned*, sometimes creating a triangular pattern, or a cross-shaped pattern (somewhat like a Maltese cross). When this distinctive zoning is observed in the fluorescence, seen under shortwave, it provides immediate confirmation that the diamond is synthetic. (See Color Section.)

To sum up, when testing a diamond, whether colorless or fancy-color, stronger fluorescence under *shortwave,* combined with *phosphorescence,* usually indicates synthetic. Distinctive zoning patterns also indicate synthetic. While several new techniques for synthesizing diamond produce stones that do not exhibit fluorescent patterns or behaviors described here, when diamonds *do* exhibit these patterns or behaviors to ultraviolet, you can conclude they *are* synthetic. If unsure, use magnification to check for metallic inclusions or cross-like color zoning; the presence of either confirms synthetic.

Testing Emeralds. Longwave ultraviolet examination has proven especially useful in testing emeralds. Natural emeralds, whether Colombian, Zambian, Pakistani, Brazilian, or Afghan, very seldom fluoresce under longwave (in other words, they seldom show any color change). However, synthetic emeralds often do. Those produced by hydrothermal and flux-melt techniques fluoresce very strongly—they turn intense red under longwave UV light. Also, the Linde-type synthetic emerald being produced by Regency fluoresces a very strong red. The Chatham and Gilson synthetics also fluoresce strongly (although some of the older Gilson synthetics did not)—the Chatham turns an intense red, and the Gilson turns orange-red or olive-brown.

Ultraviolet examination of emeralds is also important for another reason. Many natural emeralds are soaked in oil. While oiling may improve the color and overall appearance of the stone, and even strengthen it in some respects, the procedure actually reduces the visibility of cracks that would otherwise be readily visible. In emeralds that have been oiled, ultraviolet examination will reveal what the oiling process has concealed.

When examined under the ultraviolet lamp, the *oil* that has been used usually *fluoresces,* thereby revealing the presence of treatment by oil as well as the presence of the cracks. Here, since the ultraviolet lamp enables you to see them, it can assist you in determining whether or not the cracks present make the stone unusually vulnerable to breakage—by revealing whether or not there are too many; whether or not any are abnormally large; whether or not they penetrate the stone too deeply; and whether or not they are positioned in a part of the stone, that might be more susceptible to an accidental blow (such as a corner or under the table facet).

Ultraviolet examination is also an important test when confirming the origin of emeralds from Hiddenite, North Carolina. All the material mined there since 1998 exhibits a fluorescence rarely seen in emerald, a faint yellowish or chalky bluish fluorescence under *shortwave.* Such fluorescence has not been seen in emeralds from most other locations. To see it, you must examine the stone on a flat, black surface in a dark room, holding the lamp *very* close to the stone.

Testing Blue Sapphire. The ultraviolet lamp also has an important use today in distinguishing the older Verneuil-type synthetic blue sapphire from natural blue sapphire, and some natural-color blue sapphire from sapphire that has been heated to enhance its color.

The Verneuil-type synthetic blue sapphire appears frequently in old jewelry made after 1910. Such sapphires used to be easy to spot because they always contained certain telltale signs, concentric curved lines called curved striae (see color insert). Today this is no longer the case. These telltale signs *can be removed by treatment,* and one might mistake the synthetic for natural. When viewed under *shortwave* ultraviolet, however, the synthetic will show a blue-white fluorescence. Natural blue sapphire will not.

The ultraviolet lamp is also useful to help spot some sapphires that have been heated to improve their color, and in many cases, those that have been diffusion treated (colorless sapphire heated in combination with a coating of titanium oxide to obtain a blue color on the surface only). Not only will Verneuil-type synthetic sapphires show a blue-white fluorescence, but so will some heated blue sapphires. If you see blue-white fluorescence, you should be immediately suspicious. You either have a Verneuil-type synthetic, or you have a genuine sapphire, but one that has been heated to enhance color. In this case you must use your loupe or microscope; the presence of disk-like inclusions (see color insert) which are often present in heated sapphire would confirm natural, *heated* sapphire because such inclusions are not present in synthetic.

Blue sapphires exhibiting *greenish* fluorescence should be immediately suspect: some of the more recent "lab-created" synthetic sapphires exhibit a greenish fluorescence, as do many deep-diffusion treated sapphires. Fluorescence is especially helpful in confirming "deep diffused" sapphires that are often difficult to confirm with simple immersion techniques. Strong green fluorescence may also indicate diffusion treated, *synthetic* sapphire. Greenish fluorescence combined with inclusions typical of natural (such as healing feathers or halos) is positive confirmation of diffusion treated, natural sapphire.

A Few Additional Comments

Separating Synthetic White Spinel and Colorless Corundum from Diamond.
Another important use of the ultraviolet lamp is to separate synthetic white spinel from diamond. Spinel is often seen in older jewelry in place of diamonds. Even today, small melee-size (usually under $15/100$ths carat) stones used in jewelry sometimes turn out to be synthetic white spinel rather than diamond. The ultraviolet light, however, can help you spot these imposters. When viewed under longwave ultraviolet light, synthetic spinel and colorless corundum exhibit *no* fluorescence yet exhibit *strong* fluorescence under shortwave. Synthetic spinel fluoresces a strong milky white under shortwave; colorless corundum fluoresces a strong blue or greenish-blue under shortwave. Natural diamonds that show no fluorescence under longwave typically show *no* fluorescence under shortwave. Natural diamonds also seldom fluoresce white, but when they do, will *never* fluoresce under shortwave.

Accurate Color Grading of Diamond. Diamonds should *always be examined for fluorescence prior to color grading to ensure accuracy.* Testing for fluorescence not only helps separate diamond from its imposters, but it is very important in the color grading of diamonds. Some diamonds fluoresce and others do not. Of those we have personally examined, about 50% have shown fluorescence. Usually, if a diamond fluoresces, it will show blue, yellow, or chartreuse (a pale yellowish-green color).

If a diamond fluoresces, one can make a mistake when color grading the stone if a UV-emitting daylight-type fluorescent light is being used. Most fluorescent lights emit ultraviolet wavelengths similar to a UV lamp, but to a less intense degree. The closer a diamond is held to a fluorescent light, the stronger its fluorescent reaction will be, and the greater the effect on its *perceived* color. For example, a diamond that fluoresces "strong blue" will appear much whiter when it is held within a few inches of a fluorescent light; it will appear less white when held only a foot away from the light, and much less white at normal "people distance" from the light (at about four feet or more from the source). Depending upon the strength of a diamond's fluorescent reaction, and the grading distance from the light, a diamond can show a 3- to 4-grade range! Diamonds with blue fluorescence will always look much whiter in *outdoor* daylight where UV wavelengths are *much* stronger than what is found in "daylight-*type*" fluorescent light.

In the same way, if a diamond fluoresces yellow, the stone will exhibit more yellow in the body color when viewed only a few inches from a standard daylight-type fluorescent light, and appear much less white than its true body color, which could result in a lower color grade than it deserves.

We might mention here that, in our opinion, diamonds that fluoresce blue offer a little extra to the purchaser. Whatever the actual body color of the stone, when worn outside in daylight where it will be exposed to the ultraviolet rays of the sun, or indoors directly under a fluorescent light, the color may appear better than it actually is. Grandmother's "blue-white" diamond was probably a stone that exhibited a very strong blue fluorescence!

It is important to note that at one time major gem testing laboratories used a special UV-*filtered* daylight-type fluorescent light that eliminated the impact of ultraviolet wavelengths on the diamond's color. This was done in order to more accurately grade the color typically seen in any lighting except outdoors, in natural daylight. By so doing, a fluorescent diamond was graded in its "steady" state, that is, without triggering any fluorescent reaction caused by exposure to UV wavelengths, which would affect its color. By using this type of light, the grader could most accurately determine the diamond's color—its *inherent body color*—which is the color normally seen in *any* type of *indoor* lighting.

It is important to understand that while there are UV wavelengths in fluorescent light, the farther these wavelengths travel from the immediate source, the weaker they become, and at normal "people distance" (about 4 feet or more) there are insufficient UV wavelengths to trigger any noticeable fluorescent reaction. The color seen indoors is the color seen when the diamond is in its "steady" state (when it is not fluorescing). When diamonds were graded using a UV-filtered light, the color and strength of the fluorescence were noted on reports, and "blue" fluorescence was seen as a unique *benefit*, a little something *extra*.

At some point, however, laboratories changed this procedure and began to grade with unfiltered fluorescent light, thereby grading a fluorescent diamond when in its *excited state*, that is, while fluorescing. If a diamond has *medium, strong*, or *very strong* fluorescence, the grade shown on a report may indicate a color that is different from the color normally seen (except outdoors, in *natural* daylight). When graded while the fluorescence is excited, the color seen is not the inherent body color, but its fluorescent color, and the color grade may be inflated 1–4 grades above the color most often seen. With the grade thus inflated, the price might also be inflated.

We don't know exactly when laboratories changed their color-grading techniques, but some are now reconsidering the validity of this decision. In the meantime, it is important to judge the color and intensity of any diamond's fluorescent reaction and make your own decision regarding the accuracy of the grade and the stone's value.

If properly graded, we think fluorescent diamonds are an excellent choice; fluorescent diamonds are unique and offer unique benefits. But the key to enjoying these properties is proper grading and pricing.

Detecting Tanzanite Imitations. Tanzanite does not fluoresce, but all of the known imitations at this time *do* fluoresce. Typically they exhibit a weak chalky blue-white or orange color under long-wave and a very strong blue-white or orange under shortwave. The latest imitation, synthetic forsterite, exhibits a muddy green or yellowish green under both long and shortwave, but it is difficult to see except in a darkened environment.

Detecting Polymer-Impregnated Jade. Much jade today is bleached and then coated or filled with some type of polymer such as wax or opticon. When exposed to longwave ultraviolet radiation, the presence of a bluish-white to yellowish-green fluorescence indicates that it *has* been treated in this way.

Detecting Treated-Color Black Pearls. Natural-color black pearls have become very popular. Not all black pearls, however, are black naturally. *Natural*-color black nacre (the pearl coating) *fluoresces* brownish or reddish under *longwave* ultraviolet radiation. The *absence* of fluorescence—or the presence of a chalky *yellowish* fluorescence—is usually indicative of *treatment*, but may also be natural, so additional testing will be necessary *if* they do *not* show any reddish or reddish brown. Beware: treated color "chocolate" pearls *will* show a pinkish reaction.

Detecting Treated-Color Yellow Pearls. Under longwave ultraviolet radiation, some yellow cultured pearls have been found to exhibit an unusual fluorescence that indicates the color has been treated. They show yellow-green fluorescence for the most part, but reveal areas that fluoresce yellowish white, with inert centers. When such a reaction is present, magnification of the whitish areas will reveal a non-nacreous character, with isolated bright red spots or red rims in openings, an immediate indication of treatment.

Natural versus Synthetic Opal. Natural opal will phosphoresce while synthetic opals will *not*.

Other Uses for the Ultraviolet Lamp

The ultraviolet lamp is also helpful in distinguishing the following stones from one another: pink topaz, pink sapphire, and pink tourmaline; lapis and dyed jasper ("Swiss lapis"); reddish-brown amber and plastic look-alikes; blue zircon and aquamarine; natural black pearls and dyed black pearls; natural black opal from sugar-treated black opal; and new imitations from their natural counterparts, such as tanzanite from tanzanite-colored YAG.

And, finally, fluorescence—or its absence—is important to note when doing appraisals. When appraising jewelry, particularly jewelry set with diamonds, indicating whether any of the diamonds fluoresce, where they are located in the piece, and what color they show, can be of particular value in cases involving stolen property or in instances where there is any question of stone switching.

Examination of stones or jewelry by ultraviolet lamp may be one of the quickest and simplest tests available today.

Even when inconclusive alone, in combination with other instruments such as the loupe, dichroscope, or Chelsea filter, this test may be all you need for a positive ID. Properly used, the ultraviolet lamp can be a real friend to the gem enthusiast.

Fluorescent Gemstone Chart

Gemstone	*Short*wave	*Long*wave
Alexandrite**	red	red
Alexandrite-type synthetic corundum (sapphire)	red; orange (usually)	reddish
Amber	white, yellow, orange	same as shortwave
Amethyst, natural	usually inert; deep blue	same as shortwave
Amethyst, synthetic	inert	inert
Aquamarine	inert	inert
Irradiated maxixe-type	moderate yellow-green	moderate green
Benitoite**	strong blue	inert
Cubic Zirconia (colorless)	strong orange or yellow (new material may be inert)	same as shortwave but weaker
Chrysoberyl		
Chartreuse tint	yellow-green	inert
Alexandrite**	red	red
Yellow, dull green and brown varieties	inert	inert
Diamond	weak colors; usually inert	weak to strong blue orange, chartreuse, yellow or inert
natural fancy blue	inert	usually inert

(Diamonds can fluoresce all colors except violet. General fluorescence is weak to strong blue; yellow also is fairly common. BLUE fluorescence confirms NATURAL diamond.)

Synthetic diamond (see pp. 116–118)	weak to moderately strong yellow, chalky yellow, or greenish yellow	weak yellow or greenish-yellow; or inert
GGG diamond simulant (colorless)	moderate to strong, orange, chartreuse, or inert	same as shortwave but weaker
Emerald		
Natural	usually inert or reddish	same as shortwave
Synthetic	usually weak red	usually strong red
Gilson-type synthetic	weak red or inert	strong red or inert
Jade		
Natural lavender	weak brownish-red	same as shortwave
Dyed lavender	weak brownish-orange to brownish-red	strong to very strong orange
Kunzite**	weak orange-pink	strong orange-pink
Moonstone**	strong to weak reddish	greenish to yellow
Opal**	white, green, yellow	blue, white

(Opal often exhibits phosphorescence also; synthetic opal will not phosphoresce.)

Pearl		
Cultured white**	weak whitish	strong bluish-white (Some old cultured may show "tannish" as in the natural pearls)
Natural white	usually inert	strong to weak white or tan
Natural black	inert	red or brownish
Cultured, dyed black	inert	inert to greenish, chalky yellowish-white
Cultured, treated "chocolate"	greenish	pinkish
Cultured, natural black	inert to weak white	red or brownish, usually (see page 123)
Cultured, natural black, from Mexico	weak	always pinkish

Gemstone	*Short*wave	*Long*wave
Cultured, natural yellow	usually inert	yellow to yellow-green or greenish-brown to brown
Cultured, treated yellow	usually inert	yellow-green with yellowish white areas with inert centers
Cultured, freshwater golden *treated*	usually inert	orangey-yellow sometimes mottled with blue; pink with an uneven orange mottling
Peridot	inert	sometimes reddish
Ruby		
Natural	strong red	very strong red
(some dark stones, such as some Thai rubies, may be weak to inert)		
Synthetic	strong red	stronger red than shortwave
Synthetic Ramora	chalky yellow or weak bluish "bloom"	
Sapphire		
Natural blue	usually inert	inert
Ceylon-blue** (the light blue variety seen in older jewelry)	weak orange or reddish	usually moderate to strong red to yellow-orange
Ceylon-yellow**	orange-yellow	strong orange
Colorless	strong bluish or greenish-blue	inert
Blue, diffusion-treated	greenish	usually inert
Blue, heat-treated	milky bluish-white	inert
Blue, synthetic	milky bluish-white or green	usually inert
Orange, synthetic	red	red
Pink, natural	strong red	strong red
Spinel		
Natural red	moderate to strong red	strong red
Natural mauve	yellow	yellow-green
Synthetic white**	strong white	inert
Tanzanite	inert	inert
Imitation (YAG)	strong orange	weaker orange
Imitation (synthetic corundum)	strong milky blue-white	weaker milky blue-white
Imitation (synthetic forsterite)	moderate to dull yellow, greenish, or brownish with green "bloom"	very weak
Topaz, pink	weaker reddish	strong pink-reddish
Surface-coated	inert	inert
Tourmaline		
Deep red	medium bluish/lavender	inert
Yellow (Tanzanian)**	pale yellow	orange
Turquoise, composite	weak to inert	distinct patchy, strong fluorescence; color varies with color of turquoise
YAG (diamond simulant)	weak red to inert	inert
YAG (tanzanite simulant)	intense orange	weak to moderate orange
YAG (Paraiba tourmaline simulant)	moderate greenish	weak to moderate greenish
Zircon		
Colorless	yellow to orange or inert	weak to strong yellow, mustard yellow or inert
Blue	yellow to orange or inert	weak to strong yellow, mustard yellow or inert

** Gemstone always fluoresces

Use of Ultraviolet Examination for Separating "Look-Alikes"

Gemstone	*Long*wave	*Short*wave	Comments
Diamond vs Cubic Zirconia vs.	orange / weaker orange	*weaker orange* / orange	Some diamonds show orange fluorescence under longwave light and a *weaker* orange under shortwave. Cubic zirconia (CZ) OFTEN shows orange fluorescence, but IN REVERSE ORDER. This reversal is a sure test for diamond versus CZ.
Colorless corundum vs.	inert	strong bluish or greenish-blue	
Synthetic colorless spinel vs.	inert	strong milky white	
Synthetic Diamond (see pp. 116–118)	inert or weak yellow to greenish yellow or chalky yellow	moderate to strong yellow or greenish yellow sometimes showing irregular zoning or triangular or Maltese cross shaped patterns (note *reversa* from natural diamond, which normally has to *longwave*).	BLUE fluorescence confirms *natural* diamond. Strong long lasting phosphorescence indicates synthetic diamond.
Natural Ruby vs.	red to strong red	red to strong red	Thai stones are inert to weak red.
Synthetic Ruby vs.	very strong red, usually stronger than natural	very strong red, usually stronger than natural	Often much stronger than natural. Kashan weaker than Verneuil type synthetic, but stronger than natural.
Red Spinel vs.	weaker red than ruby	weaker red than ruby	NO DICHROISM
Red Garnets vs.	inert	inert	NO DICHROISM
Red Glass	usually inert	usually inert	NO DICHROISM
Natural Blue Sapphire vs.	inert to moderate red	inert to moderate red; some show whitish to light green glow.	Inclusions will identify.
Syn. Blue Sapphire vs.	usually inert	bluish-white to yellowish-green	Heated natural blue sapphires may also fluoresce pale bluish-white. Types of inclusions will distinguish.

Gemstone	*Long*wave	*Short*wave	Comments
Nat. Blue Spinel vs.	usually inert; some show greenish	inert	NO DICHROISM. Strong red with Chelsea filter (not seen in sapphire).
Syn. Blue Spinel vs.	red or pink	orangish, reddish, or bluish white, sometimes mottled	NO DICHROISM. Strong red with Chelsea filter (not seen in sapphire).
Benitoite	inert	*strong* blue	DICHROISM—blue and colorless.
Natural Emerald vs.	inert/weak red	inert	May show yellow-green fluorescence if dye used in the oiling process.
Nat. Emerald from North Carolina vs.	inert	faint yellowish or chalky blue	Such fluoresence has not been seen in emeralds from other locations.
Syn. Chatham vs.	red	red	Inclusions differ from natural.
Syn. Gilson vs.	inert, orange-red or olive-brown	inert or weak orange	Inclusions similar to Chatham but cleaner.
Syn. Linde (Regency)	very strong red	weaker red	Inclusions differ from natural/other synthetic.
Black Opal vs.	bluish-white	bluish-white	
Sugar-treated "Black Opal"	usually inert	usually inert	Examination with loupe will reveal fine pinpoints on polished surfaces.
Nat. Black Pearl vs.	light red or brownish	inert	Velvety appearance under longwave.
Dyed Black Pearl vs.	inert	inert	
Dyed Black Cultured vs.	inert or greenish or chalky yellow-white	inert	
Natural Yellow Cultured Pearl vs.	yellow-green	weak or inert	
Treated-Yellow	yellow-green with areas fluoresc- ing yellow-white with inert center		Examination at 15X magnification reveals red spots.
Pink Sapphire vs.	strong orange-red	weak orange-red	
Pink Topaz (natural color) vs.	greenish	dark greenish	Pink topaz from Ouro Preto (Brazil) and Katlang, Pakistan may fluoresce red-orange (longwave), sometimes unevenly; weaker under shortwave.
Pink Topaz (heated) vs.	(same as natural)	moderate to strong whitish-green	
Pink Tourmaline	inert	inert	

Gemstone	*Long*wave	*Short*wave	Comments
Blue Zircon vs.	mustard-yellow or inert	inert or weaker mustard-yellow	Dichroism in both is the same. However, zircon shows strong *doubling* of black facets.
Aquamarine	inert	inert	
Citrine Quartz vs.	inert	inert	
Yellow Topaz vs.	weak orangey-yellow to orange	inert	
Yellow Beryl vs.	usually inert	usually inert	
Yellow Scapolite	red	inert	
Lapis Lazuli vs.	light red spots (due to inclusions)	whitish-green	No "red spots" seen in fine Afghanistan materia
"Gilson" imitation lapis vs.	inert	inert	
"Swiss Lapis" (dyed jasper)	inert	inert	
Tanzanite vs.	inert	inert	Trichroism confirms tanzanite.
YAG vs.	orange	very strong orange	No dichroism.
Syn. Corundum vs.	chalky blue-white	very strong blue-white	Dichroic, not trichroic.
Syn. Forsterite	weak brownish-green	moderate brownish-green	Dichroic, not trichroic.

Phosphorescent Gemstone Chart

Gemstone Family	Phosphorescent Color
Beryl (colorless-Goshenite)	blue-white
Beryl (pink-Morganite)	pink
Diamond	blue
Diamond, Blue	under shortwave, strong red or very weak to weak blue or yellow, of short duration
Synthetic Blue	strong yellowish under shortwave, of *very* long duration
Diamond, Chameleon-type	yellow (If the fluorescent color differs from phosphorescent color, the diamond is *natural*, but *treated to imitate a Chameleon*)
Synthetic diamond	yellow, greenish yellow, or chalky yellow (often very long-lasting)
Opal	white (often seen)
Kunzite	orange (often seen)
Topaz	"cream" (rare)
Zircon	blue-white

NOTES

8 / The refractometer

WHAT IS A REFRACTOMETER?

The refractometer is considered by some to be the most important of all gem-testing instruments. It is a fairly small, portable instrument, almost rectangular in shape, approximately 6 inches long by 3 inches high by 1 1/2 inches wide. It measures the angle at which light rays bend (refract) as they travel through a substance, and provides a numerical reading from a scale you see when you look through the eyepiece. The cost of a good refractometer runs from $435 to $895 (see Chapter 2).

When we discussed the dichroscope (Chapter 6) you learned that as light rays strike a transparent stone, the speed at which they travel is altered, causing the rays to bend (refract) as they travel through it. In some stones the ray travels through as a single ray (single refracting substance); in others the light ray splits into two rays (double refracting). Whether or not a stone is single or double refracting depends on its particular physical characteristics. As you will remember, certain gems show single refraction (such as diamond, spinel, garnet) and others exhibit double refraction (such as emerald, zircon, sapphire).

The refractometer also can be used to determine whether or not a stone is single or double refracting (you will get only one reading on its scale if it is single refracting, and two readings if it is double refracting). But the refractometer does much more. It is of particular importance because it is one of the few instruments that can give you information for *opaque* stones (stones you cannot see through, such as lapis) as well as transparent or translucent stones.

The primary use of the refractometer is to measure the angle at which light travelling through the stone is bent or refracted. This measurement is called the Refractive Index (R.I.). Since the Refractive Index usually differs from gem species to gem species, this provides an invaluable clue for accurate gem ID.

Finally, the refractometer will give you another important piece of information. For stones that are doubly refracting, simply by computing the difference between the two R.I. readings you obtain from the refractometer, you will be able to compute the strength of the stone's double refraction. This is called birefringence. Birefringence also differs from gem to gem, and so it, too, offers an important gem identification aid.

Many types of refractometers are used for numerous industrial purposes. Some are very sophisticated and expensive, but for gem identification adequate refractometers are available for under $600 (see Chapter 2). The GIA *Duplex II* is popular, and the Eickhorst and RosGem are getting outstanding reviews. Rayner, Topcan, and Krauss also make fine refractometers.

As with most of the gem-identification instruments you are learning to use, the refractometer is both fast and easy to handle. Once you understand how to use it, the refractometer *alone* can often supply enough information for positive identification of many stones.

Use a utility lamp such as that pictured here with the *Duplex II* refractometer, or a light such as the GIA *Fiberlight.*

The GIA *Duplex II* refractometer with utility lamp

HOW TO USE THE REFRACTOMETER

Before you begin, the first step is to have a proper light source. You will need both a white light source (such as a halogen lamp) and a monochromatic yellow light source that filters out all colors of the spectrum except yellow (see Chapter 3). If you don't already have one, you may find it useful to invest in a utility lamp such as the one made by GIA that furnishes both white and monochromatic yellow light, depending upon which you need.

Now we are ready to begin. As we mentioned earlier, the information obtained with the refractometer results from its ability to measure the degree of bending or refraction that takes place when a light ray strikes a stone. When the stone is properly examined with the refractometer, you can observe a "shadow edge" or green line (depending on the type of light used with the refractometer) imposed on a scale that you see through the eye piece. But the key to seeing this line and obtaining the correct reading (its Refractive Index reading, R.I.) is proper use of the instrument.

The refractometer has a scale that shows the R.I. of a stone. The scale can show R.I.s as low as 1.35 or as high as 1.80. The R.I. of most gems falls well within this range, so the reading provided by the refractometer will tell you what most gems are.

An important advantage of the refractometer for gem identification is that it can provide an R.I. reading on any stone that has a good polish. It makes no difference whether the stone has a flat or curved surface, or whether it's transparent, translucent, or opaque. Therefore,

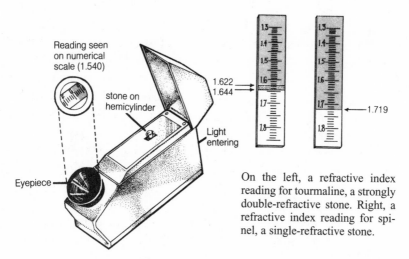

On the left, a refractive index reading for tourmaline, a strongly double-refractive stone. Right, a refractive index reading for spinel, a single-refractive stone.

The reading shown on a refractometer

it can even be used for stones such as jade, opal, and lapis. The only requirement is that the stone have a good polish. The better the stone's polish, the clearer the reading you will get with the refractometer. However, if the stone has a poor polish, as you may find when examining softer stones such as malachite or rhodochrosite, it may be very difficult—if not impossible—to get the R.I. reading.

The major weakness of most refractometers is that they *cannot give readings for stones that have an R.I. higher than 1.80.* The instrument simply doesn't have the capability to provide such high readings. This means they are ineffective for stones such as diamond, diamond look-alikes such as zircon, and certain varieties of garnet, to name a few. The Jemeter, however, does not have this problem and has an advantage over traditional refractometers because it is effective for stones with R.I.s higher than 1.80.

For purposes of convenience, we will be using a GIA *Duplex II* refractometer. If you have a different type, there may be minor differences, but the basic procedures still apply.

The technique you will use with the refractometer differs slightly depending on the stone's surface and degree of polish. We will first describe the technique for examining stones with flat surfaces and a good polish (stones such as faceted sapphires or rubies).

Familiarize yourself with the refractometer. As you look at the instrument, you will notice it has a lift-up cover on top. Lift it and you'll see a flat working surface about 2^1/$_2$ inches long by 1^1/$_2$ inches wide. A small rectangular-shaped piece of glass is set into the center of this working surface. This piece of glass is called the hemicylinder. It's important to exercise care when taking the stone on and off the hemicylinder because the glass is soft and can scratch easily if you're careless. If badly scratched, it can prevent your getting a reading on the refractometer.

Next, look at the front of the refractometer and notice the opening. This is where light enters the instrument. Be sure to position your light *in front of this opening.* Also, be sure your light source provides both white and monochromatic yellow light.

Check the eyepiece. Notice that it has a polarizing filter that rotates. We will explain how this is used later in the chapter.

Determining the R.I. of a Stone with a Flat Surface

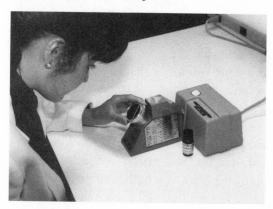

Using the refractometer—Notice the light is positioned in front of the slit at the end of the instrument, and the gemologist is rotating the polaroid filter.

1. *Carefully place a small drop of refractive index liquid on the hemicylinder.* Included with your refractometer is a small bottle of refractive index liquid supplied by the manufacturer (if not, contact the manufacturer or instrument supplier). Place a small drop of this liquid at the center of the hemicylinder. This liquid eliminates air between the stone and glass so that optical contact is established between the two surfaces. Such contact is necessary to obtain a reading from the instrument. Refractive index liquid can be obtained for about $45 a bottle from the manufacturer or supplier.

2. *Place the stone on the hemicylinder.* Find the largest facet with the best polish (usually the table facet). Make sure it's clean (rub it on a chamois, soft cloth, or piece of paper to remove dust and dirt). Carefully place the stone on the glass so that this facet is making contact with the drop of liquid you've just placed there. Some find it easier to place the drop of liquid on the metal surface beside the hemicylinder, dip the facet in the liquid, then gently place or slide it onto the glass. If the stone is set in jewelry, be sure the prongs aren't in the way of the facet making contact with the liquid *and* the glass. The prongs should rest *below* the facet surface to ensure optical contact between liquid and stone.

3. *Place a white light in front of the refractometer.* At the front of
the refractometer you will see an opening through which light
enters the instrument. Place a white light in front of this opening
(the utility lamp we recommended earlier works well here).

4. *Look through the eyepiece.* Look into the instrument, keeping
your head about 6 inches from the eyepiece. Move your head
back and forth slowly until you see a shaded or shadowy area
that does *not* move. Notice that at the end of this shaded area is
a green line. It may be necessary to move the stone forward or
backward gently to see it. (*If you must move the stone, use your
fingers. Never use tweezers because they can scratch the hemicylinder glass.*) The shaded area will extend from a low numerical reading at the top of the scale to a higher numerical reading
further down. The numerical reading you see at the green line is
the approximate refractive index of the stone. Take the reading to
the nearest thousandth (0.000) and write it down.

5. *Repeat the procedure using a monochromatic yellow light.* When
using monochromatic yellow light, you will not see a *green* line.
You get the refractive index from the reading at the *base of the
shaded area.* The monochromatic light sharpens the base of the
shaded area so it is easier to read. Again, note the R.I. to the nearest thousandth (0.000).

6. *Slowly rotate the polarizing filter.* The refractometer has a polarizing filter that fits over the eyepiece. Slowly turn this filter 180
degrees and note if the shaded edge moves. If not, turn the *stone*
45 degrees and rotate the filter again. Note whether or not the
shaded edge moves. Move the stone another 45 degrees, and
repeat the process. Continue with two more rotations of the stone
(until you have rotated the stone a full 180 degrees), turning the
polarizing filter each time.

*If the shaded edge does not move, you have a SINGLE REFRACTING
stone.* Note the R.I. reading on the scale, check the R.I. Table for
Single Refracting Stones at the end of this chapter, and you will probably know the identity of the stone.

One word of caution. If you are looking at a transparent, faceted
stone with an R.I. that falls between 1.45 and 1.65 it is probably glass.
There are many different types of glass, each with a different R.I.,

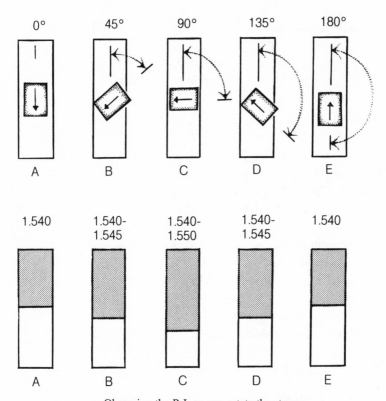

Observing the R.I. as you rotate the stone

but seldom lower than 1.45 or higher than 1.65. Amber is the only transparent gemstone material that falls within this R.I. range (1.54). Chalcedony also has a R.I. of 1.54, but is translucent or opaque rather than transparent.

If the shadow edge DOES move, you have a DOUBLE REFRACTING stone. Rotate the *filter* 180 degrees and write down the number you see on the scale at the shadow edge. Rotate the *stone* 45 degrees and turn the filter again, noting the number you see on the scale. Keep repeating this process until you have turned the stone 180 degrees (halfway around) in small increments, rotating the filter each time and noting the R.I. readings you see. Now, write down the highest and lowest reading you were able to obtain.

For example, in the first viewing the readings may have been 1.644 and 1.624; in another viewing the readings may have been 1.643 and

1.624. The highest reading of the four would be 1.644; the lowest of the four would be 1.624. Therefore, the R.I.s for the stone would be 1.644 and 1.624. Using the *highest* and *lowest* readings, check the Refractive Index Table in the Appendix for corresponding readings to determine what stone you have—in this case you'll find that the stone is tourmaline.

Caution: If the reading is 1.80, use other tests to verify identity. If you use a standard refractometer to try to identify a stone that has an R.I. of 1.80 or higher, you will not be able to get a reliable reading. As we mentioned earlier, standard refractometers are only useful for stones with R.I.s lower than 1.80 (the Jemeter is an exception and can give reliable readings for stones with much higher R.I.s). If the stone you are examining has an R.I. of 1.80 or more, the shadow edge will go right into the 1.80 portion of the scale, but this is not the stone's R.I. Instead you are actually reading the CONTACT LIQUID. The liquid itself has an R.I. of 1.80. Do not confuse this reading with that of the stone. Since there are few stones with R.I.s over 1.80, other tests can usually determine identity easily and quickly.

Determining Birefringence

Birefringence indicates the strength of a stone's double refraction. The higher the birefringence, the stronger the double refraction. The stronger the double refraction, the easier it will be to see doubling of the back facet edges with the loupe (see page 93).

Once you know you have a double refracting stone and have determined its two R.I.s from the highest and lowest readings, it is very easy to determine the birefringence. Simply subtract the lowest R.I. reading from the highest R.I. reading and you have it. When using the loupe to examine any stone that has a birefringence over 0.020, you will easily see doubling of the back facet edges (as if you're "seeing double"). Checking the stone's birefringence offers a good way to double-check a stone's identity. A Birefringence Table is provided in the Appendix.

Troubleshooting

If you are unable to see a shaded zone on the refractometer and cannot obtain a refractive index reading, it means one of the following:

a. The stone is not making contact with the drop of liquid.

b. The facet is badly scratched or inadequately polished.

c. The facet is not flat.

d. The facet is not making contact because the prong protrudes beyond the facet's surface.

e. The stone is tarnished and fails to give a reading. Emeralds that have soaked too long in jewelry cleaner often become tarnished, old amethyst can tarnish, and old glass can tarnish.

f. The stone being viewed has a very high refractive index—such as diamond, zircon, CZ, YAG, GGG, synthetic rutile, and some garnet varieties—and the refractometer cannot read it. As we mentioned earlier, most refractometers can't provide readings on stones that have an R.I. higher than 1.80.

Determining the R.I. on a Curved Surface: The Distant-Vision or Spot Method

The refractometer works best with stones that have a large, highly polished, flat surface, but it can also be used for very small or badly scratched stones, and stones with curved surfaces (cabochons). Using the refractometer for such stones, however, requires a technique called the *distant-vision* or *spot method.*

1. *Use white light.* Place a strong white light source in front of the refractometer opening. White light is preferred because it has more brilliance that enables you to see more easily what you're looking for.

2. *Place a very small drop of liquid on the glass hemicylinder.* It is very important to use as small a drop of liquid as you can, preferably the size of a pinhead. The smaller the better when using this method. Note, however, that the very small drop of liquid will evaporate after only several minutes. If you are still examining the stone, be sure you still have contact liquid between it and the hemicylinder. If there is no liquid, you will be unable to get a numerical reading.

3. *Place the stone carefully on the liquid.* Most stones that require the spot method are oval or round. If oval, be sure to place it so that the length of the oval runs parallel to the length of the hemicylinder.

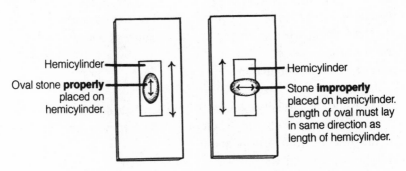

Proper placement of oval cabochon on hemicylinder

With very small stones set in jewelry it may be difficult to make contact with the drop of liquid. Once you do establish contact, it may be necessary to use a piece of Tacky-wax, chewing gum, or other sticky substance to secure it so that the stone can't move and lose contact with the liquid.

4. *Stand up.* While standing, move your head up and down slowly—and to the right and left—until you see an oval or football-shaped image on the refractometer scale. Now move your head up and down slowly until the football image is half light/half dark. Read the *midpoint* between the light and dark areas of the football—where the light portion meets the dark portion. Take the reading on the refractometer scale at that point.

The spot method gives only a single reading (even for double refracting stones), but one that is close to the R.I. of the stone. You should practice this several times on different stones (whose identity you already know) to get better experience. Jade can be fun to practice with—jadeite, for example, will probably read 1.65 and nephrite probably 1.62. Just be sure to take the reading at the spot that is half light/half dark, as in the diagram.

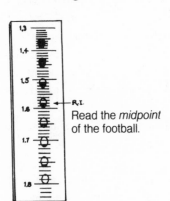

Taking a *spot reading*

Troubleshooting

If you are unable to obtain a refractive index reading using this method, it means one of the following:

a. The stone is not making contact with the drop of liquid. Be sure the liquid has not evaporated.
b. The surface is badly scratched or inadequately polished. Check it with the loupe because sometimes a cabochon surface appears shiny when it really has numerous, tiny scratches that prevent getting an R.I. reading.
c. The stone is tarnished (dulled from exposure to air, body fluids, chemicals) and fails to give a reading. Emeralds left too long in jewelry cleaner often tarnish. Old amethyst and old glass can also tarnish.
d. The stone being viewed has a very high refractive index—such as diamond, zircon, CZ, YAG, GGG, synthetic rutile, and some garnet varieties—so your refractometer cannot read it. As we mentioned earlier, most refractometers can't provide readings on stones that have an R.I. higher than 1.80. Note that with the spot method, you may still see a football-shaped shadow, but you will not observe a light-dark division giving you the necessary midpoint reading.

All you need now is a little practice, a little confidence, and you'll be ready to start using your refractometer on a daily basis.

CARING FOR YOUR REFRACTOMETER

When removing stones or placing them on the hemicylinder glass, exercise care. Remember, the hemicylinder scratches very easily.

If the contact liquid evaporates and hardens into little crystals on the hemicylinder, moisten the crystals by adding another drop of liquid and then wipe the glass gently. Don't try to wipe them off while dry because the crystals are abrasive and will scratch the glass hemicylinder.

If the stone you are examining becomes stuck to the hemicylinder, add another drop of liquid to the area to soften the hardened crystals. Then, gently remove the stone.

To help protect the hemicylinder, cover it with a thin layer of Vaseline when you store it for any length of time. This will prevent tarnishing, which can affect the refractometer's reliability. When you wish to use it again, the Vaseline can be easily and quickly wiped off with a little nail-polish remover.

Gently clean both the hemicylinder and the stone after using the refractometer, making sure to remove all traces of the liquid.

If the hemicylinder glass becomes too scratched or pitted, replace it or get it repolished ($50.00).

Check the calibration of the refractometer occasionally. To do this, simply take a stone you know, such as amethyst or citrine, and obtain a reading with the refractometer. If it gives you the correct reading, it is accurate. If not, it will need to be recalibrated (follow the manufacturer's instructions).

Always be sure to gently remove any excess liquid from the hemicylinder before putting your refractometer away. If it has a cover use it.

WHAT THE REFRACTOMETER WILL SHOW

As we've already explained, the refractometer will give you numerical readings of a stone's Refractive Index (R.I.), which is simply a measurement of the extent to which a light ray is bent (refracted) when it strikes its surface. Most gemstones are doubly refracting, and it is easy to obtain the two R.I. readings and then refer to the Refractive Index Table in the Appendix to determine the identity of a stone from those numerical readings. The singly refracting stones are not so numerous, however, and we would like to make some special comments on them.

It's important for you to understand that while a singly refracting stone will show only one reading on the refractometer scale, that reading may not be the same for all members of a particular gem family. Some singly refracting gem families that have more than one variety, such as garnet, may have different R.I. readings, depending on the variety. For example, pyrope garnet (a red variety of garnet) may have an R.I. reading of 1.746 while rhodolite garnet (another reddish variety of garnet) a reading of 1.76, and almandine (a purplish red variety of garnet) a reading of 1.79. Also, almandine can

Portable RosGem refractometer provides portability combined with unique lighting system shown here. Using a simple maglite for illumination, you can instantly convert white light to monochromatic with a simple slide; the slide contains a filter for whichever type of light you need.

have a reading higher than 1.80 and not be readable on the refractometer. However, when examining a particular singly refracting stone, no matter what variety, it will give only *one* R.I. reading.

Gemstones and other substances you might encounter that are singly refracting include spinel, opal, amber, glass, plastics, ivory, jet, and garnet. Diamonds, CZ, YAG, and GGG are also singly refracting, but their refractive indices are too high (over 1.80) to be read on the refractometer unless you are using a special type such as the Jemeter (a reflectivity meter which is no longer made).

One can really have fun with the refractometer but, as we've recommended, try to spend some time with someone who already knows how to use it. A few minutes with someone knowledgeable can provide the assurance you may need to be sure you're doing it right and seeing what you're supposed to be seeing. Once you master the refractometer, it's an instrument you will probably use every day.

This compact refractometer from Eickhorst has a built-in monochromatic filter, providing monochromatic lighting with whatever light source you use—even a maglite.

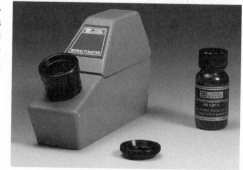

REFRACTIVE INDEX OF POPULAR SINGLE REFRACTING GEMSTONE MATERIALS

(See appendix for a more extensive list of singly refracting
and doubly refracting gems)

Gemstone	Approx. R.I.	Notations
Opal (genuine and synthetic)	1.40–1.46	In synthetic, colors are inside "boundaries" and lizard-skin-like markings are often seen. Beware synthetic Mexican fire opal; Has lower R.I. Lab testing recommended.
Sodalite	1.48	Looks like lapis lazuli, but the R.I. for lapis is 1.50.
Obsidian	1.48–1.51	Smoke from touching with hot needle produces a smell like burning cedar while plastic imitations produce disinfectant-like odor.
Plastics— many types: Casein Polystyrene Bakelite	1.49–1.66 1.55–1.56 1.59 1.61–1.66	All are soft and can be cut with a knife. Also warm to touch. Since they are soft, will show wear after minimal use.
Glass	1.50–1.65	Any transparent faceted stone having an R.I. within this range will be glass. Amber is an exception, but is seldom faceted and can be scratched with a knife. Note: Some glass can have an R.I. as low as 1.48 and, in rare cases, as high as 1.78.
Jet	1.64–1.68	A fossilized wood that has turned to coal. Used extensively in Victorian and mourning jewelry. Resembles black onyx, but much lighter.

Gemstone	Approx. R.I.	Notations
Spinel genuine, blues/reds genuine, some blues and other colors Synthetic	1.715–1.735 1.74–1.80 1.72–1.74	The R.I. is usually close to genuine, 1.72. Colorless spinel is very rare, so if it appears to be, it is probably synthetic. If so, it will glow a strong milky-white under shortwave ultraviolet examination (see Chapter 7). Also, strong ADR seen with polariscope proves synthetic (see Chapter 11).
Garnet Pyrope Rhodolite Grossularite	1.73–1.89 1.74–1.75 1.75–1.77	
Hessonite	1.742–1.748	"Cinnamon stone" is hessonite garnet.
Tsavorite	1.742–1.744	"Tsavorite" is an expensive emerald-green type.
Hydrogrossularite	1.73	Resembles jade and often sold as Transvaal jade. It is not jade.
Almandite	1.76–1.83	Medium to dark purple-red. Most common variety. Can be found in four- and six-rayed star type. Needle-like inclusions often can be seen with the loupe.
Spessartite	1.790–1.82	Reddish orange, brownish orange and yellow type. Very lively gem.
Andradite (Demantoid)	1.86–1.89	This green variety is called (Demantoid) demantoid and is expensive. The refractometer may not provide an R.I. reading because its R.I. is too high to be measured on most refractometers. It can be identified by the horse-tail inclusions that usually can be seen with the loupe. It is also very lively.

Gemstone	Approx. R.I.	Notations
Garnet-Topped False Doublets	1.77±	These are encountered in much older jewelry and were used before synthetics became available. They are constructed from a piece of garnet, usually almandite, fused to a piece of colored glass. Depending upon the color of the glass, one could "create" any gem—ruby, sapphire, emerald, etc. When examined with the refractometer, you will get the R.I. of the garnet rather than the R.I. of the stone being simulated.
Diamond	2.417	Most refractometers cannot provide readings for these gems because the R.I. is too high. Don't mistake a reading of 1.80 for that of the stone; it is the R.I. reading of the *liquid* used with the instrument.
Cubic Zirconia	2.15	See "diamond" notation.

NOTES

9 / The microscope

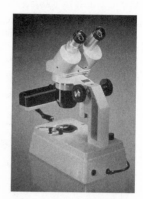

WHAT IS A MICROSCOPE?

The microscope has always been an important instrument for gem identification, but today it is indispensable because of its value in detecting new treatments and new-type synthetics.

The microscope, like the loupe, is a magnifier. The 10X loupe that we discussed in Chapter 4 is a low-powered magnifier, and the microscope is a high-powered magnifier that enables you to view things not visible with low magnification, and to see more clearly whatever is observed with the loupe. It is essential for distinguishing new-type synthetics from their natural counterparts, and for detecting various types of treatment. With slight modification, the microscope can also be adapted for use as a dichroscope, polariscope, refractometer, and spectroscope.

When we discuss microscopes, however, we are not referring to just any type. Those used by doctors, for example, are useless for the gemologist. For gem identification, one needs a binocular, stereoscopic microscope that offers a magnification range from 10X to at least 30X. This microscope has two eyepieces as opposed to a monocular microscope with only one. Monocular microscopes will give you a reversed image that can be very confusing when looking at gemstones. The stereoscopic binocular microscope does not reverse the image. Furthermore, it is constructed in a manner that creates a three-dimensional effect when you view the stone.

A good basic microscope for the gem identifier will cost between $990 to $3,700, depending on the features you select (see Chapter 2). It must provide both dark-field and bright-field illumination. A reflected-light source is also mandatory. If you plan to use it to examine the latest synthetics, you must have a magnification capability up to at least 60X. If you are working with diamond proportioning and measurements, a continuously variable zoom feature is also desirable, but is costlier ($1,995 and up) and is not essential if identification is the only goal.

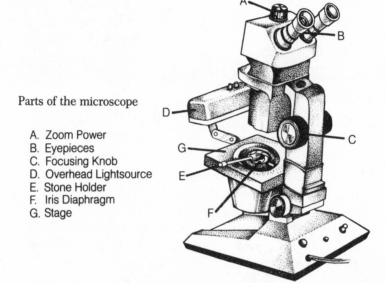

Parts of the microscope

A. Zoom Power
B. Eyepieces
C. Focusing Knob
D. Overhead Lightsource
E. Stone Holder
F. Iris Diaphragm
G. Stage

In addition to the microscope, we recommend purchasing a 2X adapter that fits onto the microscope lens to increase magnification twofold. With an adapter, a 30X microscope will magnify to 60X. We also recommend purchasing a stoneholder (tweezers) attachment if one is not included with the microscope (most models include them). The stoneholder will enable you to hold whatever is being examined more easily and steadily; it also improves your ability to carefully zero in on each area of the stone. As we discussed in Chapter 4, the higher the magnification, the more difficult it is to focus. Holding the item steady and examining it carefully in every area are essential to avoid missing something accidentally, especially when using very high magnification.

Mastering the microscope requires more time and practice than most other instruments. It takes time to become confident that you are using it properly, that the lighting is correct, that you are focusing it properly, and that you are seeing what you should be seeing. If possible, it is helpful to find a gemologist to work with for a few hours when you start out. But however long it takes, don't give up. Mastery will come, and it will pay off.

The microscope can open the door to some thrilling experiences—identifying a synthetic that by all other tests appears natural; determining that a stone has been treated; knowing absolutely what the origin of a fine gem may be (such as Burma ruby or Colombian emerald) by its own special telltale signs. All it takes is understanding how to use it, what to look for, a little guided practice, and patience.

Before we begin, we recommend obtaining a copy of *PhotoAtlas of Inclusions in Gemstones* by Edward Gubelin and John Koivula and *The Heat Treatment of Ruby and Sapphire* and *Mogok: Valley of Rubies and Sapphires,* both by Ted Themelis. In the color insert we provide some very good photographs of inclusions that you must learn to recognize, but the books above are encyclopedic in coverage and provide superb photographs. *PhotoAtlas* is the definitive work on the inclusions seen in virtually all gemstones, including synthetics and imitations, and the books by Themelis provide the most complete information currently available with regard to detecting treatments in corundum. Our book will get you started, but these books, while expensive, are essential references for anyone with a serious interest in gemology.

HOW TO USE THE MICROSCOPE

The first step in using the microscope is learning to adjust it to your eyes. Just follow these steps.

Focusing the Microscope

1. Tilt the microscope at its base so that when you look through it (from a sitting position) you feel comfortable and have no strain on your back.
2. Adjust the eyepieces so they comfortably accommodate the distance between your eyes. Binocular microscopes allow you to do this by pushing the eyepieces apart or pulling them together.

Adjust them until you are comfortable looking through both eye-pieces with both eyes.

3. Adjust the focus:

   a. Move the tip of the stoneholder attachment to the center of the opening through which the base light shines. Turn the knob that controls the magnification power to a high setting. Now close the left eye and, using the right eye only, look through the right eyepiece and focus on the tip of the stoneholder by carefully turning the focusing knob. Focus very, very slowly until the tip is clear and sharp.

   b. Without touching the focusing knob, close the right eye and use the left eye only. Looking through the left eyepiece, focus on the stoneholder by moving the top of the *eyepiece* itself, not the focusing knob. (The top of the left eyepiece is adjustable, the top of the right eyepiece is not.) Focus on the stoneholder sharply, as you did with the right eyepiece.

   c. Now, with both eyes open, look through the microscope at the tip of the stoneholder, which should be in sharp focus. Close one eye and look at the tip again with the open eye. Repeat using the other eye. Whichever eye is open, the tip should be in sharp focus. If not, repeat steps (a) and (b).

Examining Gems with the Microscope

Once you are comfortable focusing the microscope you are ready to examine a stone or piece of jewelry with it. Proceed in the following manner.

1. *Be sure the stone is clean.* Use a small brush (such as an artist's brush) dipped in rubbing alcohol (isopropyl) to carefully remove dirt and dust. Wipe the stone with a lint-free cloth. Use compressed air (see Chapter 2) to remove any remaining dust. This will eliminate the possibility of confusing dust with something in or on the stone.

   Caution: If you have an ultrasonic cleaner, *never* use it for opals, pearls, aventurine, sunstone, malachite, tanzanite, and most emeralds. It can damage these stones and any stone that has cleavage cracks, numerous inclusions, or fractures.

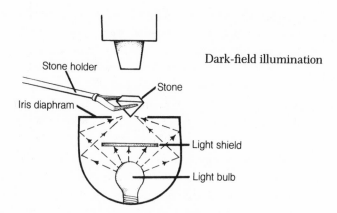

2. *Examine the stone using dark-field illumination.* Dark-field illumination is the type most often used for gem identification. To
use dark-field illumination, cover the light bulb with the flat,
non-reflective black shield provided under the iris diaphragm
(the lever to adjust the shield is normally on top of the microscope stage, near the stoneholder). This blocks direct light from
going through the stone (bright-field). Place the stone in the
stoneholder and position it just above the iris diaphragm so
that light is simultaneously entering the stone through its sides
(lateral lighting). You must be sure not to position the stone too
high above the light source or you will not get lateral lighting.
With dark-field illumination, the lateral lighting combined with
the blackened background from the light shield causes inclusions to stand out more clearly and makes them easier to see
and identify.

3. *Examine the stone under low power magnification.* Using dark-
field illumination as explained above, begin to examine the stone,
looking through both eyepieces with both eyes open. Start with
low power magnification (7X–10X) because lower power gives
a wider area of observation—the size of the area that will be
in focus at a given point—making it easier to spot inclusions.
Carefully examine each area of the stone, turning the focusing
knob slowly and focusing into the stone at different depths. Turn
the stone to a different position and examine it again so that you
view different portions of it, from different angles.

4. *Gradually increase the magnification.* Try to remember the position of anything you have seen under lower magnification so you can find it to view more carefully under higher magnification. Something you have seen under lower magnification may seem to disappear at higher magnification. This happens because the field of observation becomes smaller as magnification is increased. Since the area actually in view becomes smaller as the power at which you examine an object goes up, the object seen at lower magnification may no longer be inside the area in view. By slowly and carefully moving the stone you will be able to find it again.

Look for inclusions not visible under lower power. Be sure to turn the stone to examine it from different directions and angles following each increase in magnification.

Higher magnification enables you to spot internal characteristics and inclusions not visible at lower magnification. It also enables you to examine more clearly what you see under lower magnification. This is particularly important for inclusions that look like bubbles at low power. Bubbles usually indicate glass. An inclusion that appears bubble-like at 10X, however, may turn out to be something else—such as a rounded crystal—when viewed under higher magnification. Higher power examination of bubble-like inclusions may prevent the embarrassment of identifying as glass something that isn't!

5. *Examine with bright-field illumination.* Bright-field illumination is accomplished by placing the stone over the light source so that it is illuminated from behind. The shield used to create dark-field illumination is not used here. Bright-field illumination highlights

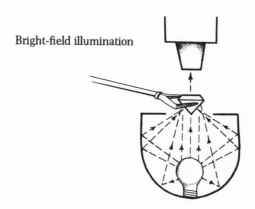

Bright-field illumination

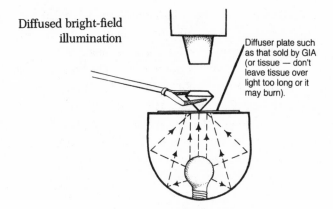

Diffused bright-field illumination

Diffuser plate such as that sold by GIA (or tissue — don't leave tissue over light too long or it may burn).

certain types of inclusions, particularly in emerald. It is also useful to observe twin planes, and to examine more carefully fractures or cleavage lines seen with dark-field. Again, remember to
turn the stone, and view it from every angle.

6. *Examine with diffused bright-field illumination.* In this method the
   light enters the stone from behind as in bright-field, but it has been
   diffused. To diffuse the light, simply place a white facial tissue or
   a thin sheet of white paper over the light-source opening. Diffused
   light will permit easier observation of weak curved striae and weak
   color-zoning or banding difficult to see in pale colored stones.

7. *Examine with vertical (overhead) illumination.* This method calls
   for shining the light directly on top of the stone so that light might
   reflect off inclusions within the stone. This method may enable you
   to see fine, needlelike inclusions such as those found in Burmese
   rubies and sapphires because these inclusions will reflect the light
   back to you. With sapphire it can also help you see reflections that
   will reveal halos or flat platinum crystals (shaped like triangles
   or little hexagons) indicating synthetic, and disc-like inclusions

Overhead (vertical) illumination—Light shines directly on
top of stone (from overhead light
attached to microscope, fiberoptic
or other stong light).

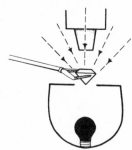

indicating heat-treating. For black opal, it may reveal the telltale flat, disc-like air bubbles often difficult to detect by any other method, proving the stone is a *doublet* and not genuine black opal.

8. *Examine with horizontal illumination.* This method calls for using a narrow beam of light (a fiber optic light source or penlight), directed through the stone *from the side* while the stone is being viewed through the microscope from the top. Pinpoint crystals and tiny bubbles are more easily seen this way because they stand out more brightly.

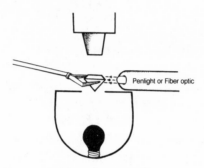

Horizontal illumination

9. *Examine with pinpoint illumination.* This method calls for light coming from directly behind the stone, *through a narrowed opening* obtained by closing the iris diaphragm to the desired degree. It is especially useful for observing curved striae more easily.

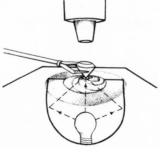

Pinpoint illumination—Note that the iris diaphragm is almost fully closed.

Now all it takes is practice. Experiment with stones you already have. Try looking at the same stone using different types of lighting techniques. Try to become familiar with certain types of inclusions such as those we will discuss now.

WHAT THE MICROSCOPE WILL SHOW

The real excitement of gem identification begins with competent use of the microscope. The microscope gives you a significant edge by enabling you to identify many of the new-type synthetics that, using all other tests, might otherwise appear to be natural. It can often tell you whether the color of a fine gem is natural or enhanced, whether cracks have been filled, and, in many cases, the probable origin of a gem.

We recently had an interesting experience that shows how valuable the microscope can be. At the Tucson Gem Show, one of the most important gatherings of colored-stone sellers in the country, a dealer was selling precious topaz at a very attractive price. Like other gem buyers, we are always looking for good value. We always become suspicious, however, when the price seems *too* good. We assumed the stones had been treated to enhance the color but the dealer assured us the color was natural. When we pressed further and asked how he could sell such fine color, natural topaz at such an attractive price, he said he obtained rough material at the mines and cut it himself.

We weren't convinced. He agreed to accompany us to examine one of his stones under the microscope. Using immersion (examining the stone while it's submerged in a special liquid) the microscope told us immediately that the color was not natural. We knew it had been treated because we saw something never present in a natural-color stone—a bright pink halo-like border encircling it. The dealer admitted to bombarding the material (with radiation) in an attempt to create "pink" topaz. He failed to create pink but did create a more beautiful color. Unfortunately, such color is not permanent.

It isn't always so easy to detect treatment. We are still unable to tell in some cases. We don't yet know how to separate naturally blue topaz, for example, from topaz that has been irradiated to make it blue (in the case of blue topaz, the resulting color appears to be permanent). But great progress has been made in revealing various types of gem treatment, synthesis, and simulation, and every day we make important new discoveries.

In most cases, inclusions offer the key. The microscope's importance for gem-identification purposes lies in its ability to provide more precise information about the inclusions present in a gem material.

What Is an Inclusion?

The term inclusion applies to any foreign body enclosed within a gemstone. An inclusion can be a gas, liquid, or solid enclosed within the stone. In gemstones, the term also applies to cleavage cracks, fractures, growth lines, color zoning, and crystals (of the same composition as the host gemstone, or some altogether different substance).

Inclusions provide valuable information because no gem material—whether made by humans or by nature—is entirely free of inclusions. They may not be visible to the unaided eye, or under 10X magnification, or even under 30X. It may be necessary to use 60X magnification to find them, but inclusions are always present.

Some inclusions are quite beautiful and make a stone more interesting, as in a specimen of ordinary quartz that can become quite *extra*ordinary when it is contains lovely thin, golden, needlelike crystals of the mineral rutile (rutilated quartz). Some inclusions are so large and ugly they destroy both the beauty and value of a stone that might otherwise have been a gem. Some are so small they don't detract from the stone's beauty or value at all, and, in fact, may add to it by proving country of origin or whether or not color is natural.

The key is knowing what types of inclusions to look for, what they look like and where they should or should not appear. We'll begin by describing the different types of inclusions found in gemstones.

NOTE: See the color section at the center of this book for photographic illustrations of the inclusions described here.

Common Types of Inclusions Found in Gems

Bubbles. These inclusions look like little bubbles of various shapes and sizes. Nice round bubbles usually indicate a synthetic or glass, though they can be found in natural amber. In synthetic ruby or sapphire, they can be round, profilated (a string of bubbles with a large bubble at the center and progressively smaller bubbles on each side), pear-shaped, or tadpole-shaped. In the last two, the tail always points in the same direction.

Clouds. Groups of fine bubbles or cavities.

Color Zoning. A term referring to uneven distribution of color. Inclusions often appear as whitish or colorless parallel planes. Zoning is frequently observed in ruby, sapphire, amethyst and citrine.

Dark Ball. Dark, opaque ball-shaped inclusion surrounded by an irregularly shaped, wispy, brown cloudlike formation. These are found exclusively in Thai rubies and are never seen in Burmese rubies.

Dendritic. Rootlike or beelike inclusions such as those seen in moss-agate.

Feather. Another term for an internal crack. Sometimes they resemble a feather, hence the use of this term.

Fiberlike or Needlelike. Inclusions of long, thin crystals that resemble needles or thin fibers. Often long thin crystals of rutile, as in rutilated quartz, or tourmaline, as in tourmalinated quartz. Can be seen in garnet, sapphire, and ruby.

Fingerprint. Small crystal inclusions arranged in curved rows in such a way as to resemble a fingerprint or maze. Seen in quartz and topaz. They closely resemble the healing-feathers seen in sapphires.

Halo or Disc-like. A halo is an inclusion resembling small, flat disc-like wings with a small zircon crystal in the center. They are stress cracks caused by radioactivity or strain associated with the growth of the zircon crystals. The zircon crystal often appears as a small dark dot at the center of the disc. Another type of disc-like inclusion, usually difficult for the novice to distinguish from a halo, provides an indication of *heating*. Unlike most halos, it is mirror-like and exhibits *multiple breaks around the border* of the "halo." Note: it takes great skill to tell by inclusions whether or not a gem is enhanced. A gem-testing lab specializing in enhancement (such as AGL or GIA—see Appendix) should be used.

Healing-Feather (Liquid Filled). An inclusion consisting of a maze-like arrangement of tubes. Often seen in sapphire.

Laser Path. A microscopic path created by a laser beam penetrating into a diamond to reduce the visibility of flaws and thus improve appearance. A visible black flaw, for example, can be vaporized and practically disappear. The laser path can be seen, however. In most cases it appears as a fine straight line resembling a white thread, going from the outer surface of the stone into the center. There will be a small, dot-like break at the surface of a facet where the laser beam entered. A new lasering technique—*internal laser drilling*—may be harder to detect, but the process leaves a glassy, transparent feather, and the drilling leaves irregular corkscrew or worm-like tunnels. These tunnels may appear dark when viewed with transmitted light.

Lath-like. Long, thin, flat (like a lath) crystals.

Negative Crystal. A cavity with a distinctive crystal shape. These are interesting because what you see is really just an outline (since it is not solid). However, the outline will always show the same shape as that of the crystal-form of the host material. If you are examining a piece of quartz with a negative-crystal inclusion, for example, the negative-crystal will have a hexagonal outline because the shape of a quartz crystal is hexagonal. Often seen in quartz and topaz.

Profilated Bubbles. A string of round bubbles in a straight row with the largest in the center, getting progressively smaller toward each end of the row. Often seen in synthetic corundum and synthetic spinel.

Rain. A type of inclusion that looks like dashed lines resembling falling rain. They are seen in flux grown synthetic rubies, such as the Kashan synthetic.

Sheaves. An inclusion of the mineral cacoxenite, found in amethyst. It gets its name because it looks like the top half of a sheaf of wheat, coming to a point at the bottom.

Silk. Thin intersecting needlelike crystals that exhibit a sheen similar to that of silk fabric when examined with reflected light. Often seen in ruby and sapphire.

Solid. A solid crystal or mineral fragment present in the host.

Striae. Curved concentric lines seen in old Verneuil synthetic ruby and sapphire.

Swirl Marks. Found in glass, these are curved lines and curlicues, swirling through the stone, usually in a darker color than the host substance. Can also be called striae, but unlike that described above, these will not be *concentric*.

Tabular. Tabular, solid metallic inclusions seen in synthetic diamonds.

Three-Phase. Cavities that contain liquid, a gas bubble, and a solid (usually a crystal). They may look like irregularly shaped pea pods, usually pointed at both ends. Within the pod (which is liquid filled) there is a bubble (gas) and, adjacent to the bubble, a cube or rhomboid-shaped crystal (solid). All matter is in either a gas, liquid, or solid state, but this type of inclusion contains all three states, hence its name. In emerald, the presence of a three-phase inclusion containing a cube or rhomboid-shaped solid proves the stone is natural and not synthetic.

Twinning. Resembles parallel lines, but are actually planes, like panes of glass lying in parallel planes. Often found in rubies and sapphires, and occasionally in some feldspar gems like moonstone. When present, twinning can prove genuineness for ruby or sapphire but, if too numerous, may weaken a stone and reduce its brilliance.

Two-Phase. Inclusions that usually have a "frankfurter" outline with an enclosed bubble that may (or may not) actually move as the "frank" is tilted from end to end. These are seen in topaz, quartz, synthetic emerald, and some tourmaline.

Veils. Small bubblelike inclusions arranged in layer formations that can be wispy, flat or curvaceous, broad or narrow, long or short. These may be easily observed in some synthetic emeralds.

Venetian Blinds. An inclusion occurring in green, yellow, and brown zircon. We call these "venetian blind" inclusions because they look like venetian blinds that are slightly closed, slightly turned down. Find photos of these inclusions in the center color insert and try to become familiar with what they look like. See if you can spot some in stones from your own inventory. Have fun.

SOME POPULAR GEMS UNDER THE MICROSCOPE

We have put together the following guidelines to assist you, stone by stone. In addition, refer to pages 58–66. Many commonly encountered inclusions seen when examining popular gems under the microscope are included, but there are too many inclusions to try to cover them all. You must also remember that new discoveries may make information here obsolete. It is important to keep up to date by reading gemological journals and trade publications. Persistent practice is also essential for learning to recognize particular inclusions and avoid confusing those that are similar. Where possible, we encourage you to try to locate a skilled gemologist to assist you at the beginning. And don't hesitate to keep books handy for reference.

Diamond

Colorless Diamond Crystal. A small diamond crystal that has grown within the host diamond. It can look like a dot or bubble with a loupe, but by using the microscope you can see clearly it is a crystal with an octahedral shape (like two pyramids placed base-to-base).

Zircon Crystal. A crystal of zircon that has grown inside the host diamond, "frankfurter" shaped with a more-or-less square cross-section.

Garnet Crystal. Transparent red crystals, well-formed or distorted, inside the diamond.

Diopside Crystal. Dull opaque (not transparent) green or transparent emerald-green crystals of diopside are sometimes observed inside a diamond.

Small Black Spot. Often erroneously referred to as "carbon spots," black inclusions are usually the black mineral called magnetite, or sometimes hematite or chromite. Black carbon inclusions are usually wispy and veil-like and are very rare.

Chrome Spinel Crystals. Deep, cherry-red, opaque crystals that are probably crystals of chrome spinel. Sometimes they may appear black in larger pieces and may be confused with magnetite.

Cleavage. This is a crack or break that has a flat plane and usually starts at the girdle. It is straight, not jagged. It may be very small or quite noticeable. If it is very pronounced and the stone is placed in an ultrasonic cleaner, the cleavage may become larger.

Feather. Another name for a crack. Differs from cleavage because it does not occur on a plane, but is jagged in appearance (sometimes resembling a feather). If pronounced, it can weaken the stone.

Laser Path. Stones with visible inclusions may be improved by laser techniques. One technique involves lasering from the stone's surface into the diamond, through which hydrochloric acid can be introduced to bleach out the black color and, in some cases, dissolve the inclusion altogether. Under magnification you can spot the laser path. You will see a fine straight line (like a thread) penetrating the stone, beginning at the surface of a facet as a small dot-like break.

Laser Drilling, Internal. A new lasering technique—*internal laser drilling*—may be harder to detect than the process above, but it leaves a glassy, transparent feather and irregular corkscrew or worm-like tunnels. These tunnels may appear dark when viewed with transmitted light.

Synthetic Diamond

Whitish Dust-like Particles. Many synthetic diamonds contain numerous small, white dust-like particles randomly dispersed throughout the stone. Some may resemble breadcrumbs.

Rod or Lath-like Inclusions. Metallic inclusions resembling a lath or small rod.

Black or Silvery Flux Inclusions. Dark, metallic, needle-like, elongated or tabular-shaped inclusions, often of iron, indicate synthetic.

Pinpoints. Small metallic flux inclusions that appear as isolated pin-head dots can be seen in synthetic yellow diamonds and near-colorless diamonds.

Cube-Shaped. Metallic cube-like shapes can appear, large or small.

Dust Clouds. Metallic dust clouds can occur, which have a distinctive character resulting from their reflecting the color of the diamond in which they occur.

Tabular. Tabular, solid metallic inclusions, often oblong and in groups, are frequently seen. These are remnants of the metallic solvent used as a catalyst for synthetic diamond growth.

Zoning. In fancy-color synthetic diamonds, you will notice distinctive color zoning (see Color Insert). In particular, sharply defined borders delineating the zones indicates synthetic. This is often seen in synthetic blue diamonds.

"Hourglass" or "Stop Sign" Graining Pattern. Is immediately indicative of synthetic.

Emerald

Three-Phase Inclusion. Seen in Colombian and Afghan emeralds. In Colombian stones, they resemble a Chinese snow-pea or a pointed pea pod; in Afghan stones, they resemble a finger. A three-phase inclusion that contains a square- or rectangular-shaped solid is positive proof that the emerald is natural and not synthetic.

Iron Pyrite. Emeralds from Chivor (Colombia) and some from Zambian (Africa) often contain beautifully formed crystals of iron pyrite. Iron pyrite, also known as "fool's gold," is easily recognizable by its brassy, metallic luster. It is often cubic in shape.

Mica. Small, thin, flat, hexagonally shaped black mica platelets are often seen in emeralds from Pakistan, Transvaal, Zambia and Tanzania. They are usually black. *Note:* mica can also be seen in another green gem, peridot.

Rutile Needles. Inclusions of rutile needles (long, straight, parallel needles) provide definitive, positive confirmation of Hiddenite, North Carolina, origin. They are not always present, but when they are, it is conclusive.

Tremolite. Fiberlike tubes, sometimes slightly curved, and often jumbled like a randomly tossed box of soda-pop straws, often seen in small (under one carat) fine, deep green emeralds from Sandawana.

Rectangular Cavity with Bubble. Two-phase inclusion that is a more-or-less rectangular shaped cavity with a bubble at one end, often seen in emerald. It can be L-shaped, with the bubble at the base of the "L."

Lath-like. Long, thin, flat inclusions of the mineral actinolite. This inclusion is often seen in Siberian emerald.

Synthetic Emerald

Crazing. This is crack-like webbing resembling a fish net. It is seen on the surface of Lechleitner synthetic emerald coated beryl.

Flux Fingerprints. Whitish "fingerprints" of flux used in the process (see Color Insert).

Nail-Head. Regency synthetic emeralds (formerly Linde) will exhibit thin rodlike crystals, all pointing in the same direction. Some have an enlargement at the end of the crystal resembling the head of a nail, hence this name. (These emeralds will exhibit a very strong red fluorescence when viewed under the ultraviolet lamp.)

Wispy Veils. Wispy, undulating ribbonlike veils are a common inclusion seen in Chatham synthetic emerald, and are also often seen in Gilson synthetic emerald.

Internal Growth Patterns. Some hydrothermally grown emeralds reveal an unusual internal growth pattern resembling a mountain range with pointed mountains. A roiled appearance also indicates synthetic.

Ruby

Silk. These are intersecting needlelike crystals that intersect each other, often at 60 degree and 120 degree angles. When examined with reflected light, they exhibit a sheen similar to the sheen of silk fabric, hence the name. Sometimes they can be seen with the loupe, but often the microscope is required. It is important to examine the stone with reflected light to see these needles clearly. When viewed this way, they can exhibit many colors. Silk is often seen in Burma ruby, occasionally in rubies from Kenya, but never in Thai rubies or synthetics. The presence of silk proves genuineness.

Ball-like. These are inclusions of pyrrhotite crystals. These crystals are ball-like in appearance and are surrounded by a yellowish-brown cloudlike veil. They are typical of Thai stones and are never seen in Burma stones. Some Thai stones have more than one ball.

Halo. These inclusions look like discs or haloes encircling a dark spot. They are actually tension cracks radiating from a zircon crystal, which is the dark spot in the center. The tension that produces these cracks results in one of two ways: either the zircon has expanded from heat and the expansion creates stress that creates cracks; or the zircon was radioactive and the radiation being produced creates stress, which creates cracks. *Important*: Don't confuse with disc-like inclusions seen in gems that have been heated to enhance color. *Haloes will always have a dark spot at the center.* Disc-like inclusions seen in heat-treated gems won't.

Pyrite Crystals. Metallic reflective inclusions, often showing cubic shape, characteristic of ruby from Kashmir, Pakistan.

Twinning Planes. These are more common in Thai rubies than Burmese. They are never present in synthetics so their presence proves genuineness. They may resemble fiberlike or needlelike inclusions when seen from certain directions, but they are actually planes—if you tilt the stone slightly and can observe planes going through the stone from one side to the other, you are observing twinning planes.

Healing-Feather (also called Liquid Feather). These inclusions are frequently seen in rubies from Cambodia and Sri Lanka (Ceylon). They resemble numerous slim, elongated tubes. Some are longer, some shorter, but all tend to point in the same direction and lie in a plane. The plane can be twisted and/or wavy.

Bubblelike Webbing. This type of inclusion is seen in natural and synthetic. If the bubbles are filled, the stone is synthetic; if hollow (open or unfilled), the stone is natural. You must use high-power magnification (at least 45X to 60X power) to tell whether or not the bubbles (holes) are filled.

Synthetic Ruby

Profilated Bubbles. Bubbles or clouds of small bubbles, sometimes stacked in a row with a larger bubble at the center and progressively smaller bubbles on each end. These will only be seen in old-type synthetics (Verneuil).

Curved Striae. Concentric curved lines (sometimes the curve is so slight they can appear almost straight) seen in old-type (Verneuil) synthetic ruby and sapphire. Positive proof of synthetic material when clearly observed.

Bubblelike Webbing. (See above.)

Rain. These are dashed lines that resemble rain. They are seen in flux grown synthetic rubies, such as the Kashan.

Growth Zoning. Roiled growth zoning is indicative of synthetic.

Blue Sapphire and Synthetic Blue Sapphire

Sapphires have all the inclusions described above for ruby except ball-like inclusions. Also, in addition to curved striae seen in Verneuil synthetic, they may show *curved color zoning.*

Pastel-Colored Ceylon Sapphire

These stones are usually highly included and will exhibit haloes, healing feathers, inclusions containing inclusions, and so on.

OTHER POPULAR GEMS
UNDER THE MICROSCOPE

Aquamarine

Rods. Very thin visible parallel tubes that seem to enclose a fine light-brown powder. These are often seen in aquamarine. There can be many or few, but too many will affect the stone's beauty and value.

Ghost Lines. Parallel lines that are visible one moment and disappear the next. If you examine your stones carefully, you'll find ghost lines present in over 90% of all aquamarines. When examining aquamarines, turn the stone very slowly and focus very carefully. When you see one or more parallel lines that seem to disappear simply by tilting the stone a speck, you are viewing ghost lines. They may be in only one section of the stone, or several.

Almandine (Garnet)

Rutile Needle Inclusions. Any purple-red garnet with long, thin needlelike inclusions of rutile will be almandine. The needles can be randomly oriented or crisscross at 90 degrees or at 70 and 110 degrees. Those that produce numerous needles intersecting at 90 degrees can produce a four-rayed star; those intersecting at 70 and 110 degrees, a six-rayed star.

Haloes. Seen in almandine garnets from Sri Lanka.

Tsavorite (Garnet)

Lath-like Inclusions. This lovely green variety of garnet may contain long, thin, flat (lath-like) crystals of the mineral actinolite.

Demantoid (Garnet)

Horse-Tails. Rare green demantoid garnet (much more expensive than tsavorite) contains fine fiberlike inclusions of the mineral byssolite. These inclusions are often tufted and resemble a horse's tail. They can be swirled or randomly located.

Quartz (All Varieties)

In all varieties of quartz, negative crystals, needlelike (crystals of rutile, tourmaline) or lath-like (long, thin, flat crystals of actinolite), can be seen.

Amethyst (Quartz)

Snakes. Fine, long, thin, ruby-red snake-shaped crystals (hematite or goethite). Often seen in genuine amethyst.

Multiple Twinning. Also called "zebra stripes" (Gubelin), these look like the teeth on a wood saw. They are usually stacked in fairly parallel rows.

Color Zoning. Color is seen in parallel planes or layers.

Sheaves. An inclusion of the mineral cacoxenite. It gets its name because it looks like the top half of a sheaf of wheat, coming to a point at the bottom.

Fingerprint. Numerous small crystal inclusions arranged in a pattern that resembles a fingerprint or maze.

Synthetic Amethyst (Quartz)

Fine Crumbs. Very small whitish crumblike inclusions. When present in a fine-colored amethyst that shows no other inclusions they indicate synthetic material.

Citrine (Quartz)

Color Zoning. Similar to zoning seen in amethyst.

Praseolite (Quartz)

Twinning. Zigzag, parallel lines showing multiple twinning is often visible on a polished facet.

Rose Quartz

Needlelike. Small needles of rutile are seen under high magnification in 95% of all rose quartz. The cloudiness associated with most rose quartz results from the presence of these rutile needles.

Spinel

Octahedra. Spinels often exhibit small octahedral crystal inclusions (of the mineral hercynite). An octahedron resembles two pyramids with their bases placed together. If present, they prove the spinel is genuine. Sometimes, if very small, they can look like small dots. Examination with the microscope at higher magnification will reveal whether or not they are really octahedra.

Frankfurters. Some hazy blue spinels may contain crystal inclusions that resemble a frankfurter.

Zircon Crystals. Often seen in blue and lavender spinel.

Topaz

Same as in quartz.

Tourmaline

Cracks. Tourmaline exhibits an odd-shaped, mirrorlike crack typical only of tourmaline. It is flat and broad with jagged points at the ends. Once you see them, you'll always be able to recognize them.

Copper Crystals. The presence of wiry-looking copper crystals in tourmaline indicates rare "cuprian" tourmaline and may indicate "Paraiba" origin.

Zircon

Venetian Blinds. An effect that resembles a partly closed venetian blind is often seen in green, yellow, and brown zircons.

AN IMPORTANT TIP: Any gemstone showing a rust-colored crack is genuine (as in some rubies). Attempts at introducing a "rusty" look into synthetic stones haven't been successful.

NOTES

PART 4

OPTIONAL INSTRUMENTS— WHEN AND HOW TO USE THEM

10 / The spectroscope

A spectroscope with
digital readout

WHAT IS A SPECTROSCOPE?

The spectroscope is a relatively small instrument that analyzes light
passing through a stone. It has never really been appreciated until
recently. For whatever reasons, many gemologists have ignored
it, preferring other instruments. However, the rapid growth in the
fancy-color diamond market is changing attitudes about its value. We
believe it is indispensable, one of the most interesting instruments to
use, and one that should be added sooner or later to complete your
gem-identification laboratory.

For those experienced in using it, a spectroscope provides one of
the quickest ways for identifying mounted or unset stones, including
rough material (material that has not been cut and polished). It is
especially useful with stones for which the refractometer (see Chapter
8) is ineffective—unpolished stones or stones with a very poor polish,
stones with a very high Refractive Index, any stone mounted in such
a way that it is impossible to place it on a refractometer, and cabochons that may be difficult to read on a refractometer. *It is the only
instrument widely available for separating natural-color diamonds
from those that have obtained their color by irradiation or heating.*
It is also particularly useful for distinguishing natural-color green
jadeite jade from dyed, some varieties of natural sapphire (especially
blue) from synthetics and look-alikes, and natural alexandrite from
synthetic color-change corundum and synthetic color-change spinel.

Two types of spectroscope are in common use: the "prism type"
and the "diffraction-grating type." For gem identification, either type
is acceptable. The standard diffraction type is less expensive, but the

175

prism type has two advantages: it admits more light into the instrument; and it's easier to read in the dark blue end of the spectrum. However, there are several new diffraction models—with fiber optic lighting and digital readout—that have essentially overcome these limitations. While somewhat more expensive, they're becoming increasingly popular.

We do not recommend most portable or hand-held types because they are usually more difficult to read and some models cannot provide readings in the dark blue portion of the spectrum. Many models also limit your ability to adjust the light entering the instrument.

A prism type spectroscope   A diffraction-grating spectroscope

In this chapter we'll explain how to use the standard prism type spectroscope unit, equipped with a good light source and stand. While the actual operation may differ slightly between this type and the diffraction or digital types, the basic principles will still apply and you should be able to easily adjust the technique described here to your instrument.

The prism spectroscope resembles two connected tubes, one next to the other—a taller "tube" which is the spectroscope proper, and a shorter tube that contains an illuminated scale. It has an adjustable slit at the end, through which light passes. Simply stated, this instrument divides white light into the spectral colors and analyzes it as it passes through a gem substance. It is really an easy instrument to use, and can be very interesting from a visual point of view. If you like rainbows, you'll love it!

As we discussed in the chapter on lighting, when all the colors of the visible spectrum are present (red, orange, yellow, green, blue, indigo, and violet) we get white light. To understand the spectroscope, all you need to realize is that *when white light travels through a gem material, one or more of the wavelengths that produce color are ABSORBED by the gem.*

This is not something we see with the naked eye, but if we could watch as light travels through a stone, if we could observe all the colors making up the white light as it enters, we would see that certain colors simply disappear as the light passes through it. This phenomenon— called selective absorption—provides a very useful clue to gem identity.

What the spectroscope actually does is enable us to see this phenomenon in many gems—to know what color has been absorbed—by producing a vertical black line or bar in the space where the spectral color that disappeared should be. By seeing what has disappeared, what is missing from the full spectrum, we get a distinct spectral picture for that gem. This picture is its "characteristic absorption spectrum"—the pattern of color seen, and the placement of the black bars, that is *characteristic* for a particular gem.

Since no two gem materials absorb the same wavelengths (color) in the same way, we can identify characteristic spectra for many gems. Unfortunately, not all gems exhibit a clear, distinct pattern, but when they do, these characteristic absorption spectra provide a quick, positive identification of the substance being examined, and, in some cases, tell whether or not the color is natural.

USING THE SPECTROSCOPE

First, before using the spectroscope to examine a gem, take a look though the eyepiece. Place a strong light in front of the instrument, shining up through the slit at the end. If you are using a diffraction type, be sure to use as strong a light as possible (fiber optic is recommended). As you look through the eyepiece you will see the full visible spectrum—a rainbow of seven colors—proceeding in a horizontal line from red on one end to violet on the other. If you are using a diffraction type, the spectral colors will be equally spaced. If you're using a prism type, the blue/violet end will look a little "spread-out" relative to the other colors, and the red/orange end will look a little compressed. That is, the orange and red colors seem crowded together, and the violet and indigo colors look spread apart.

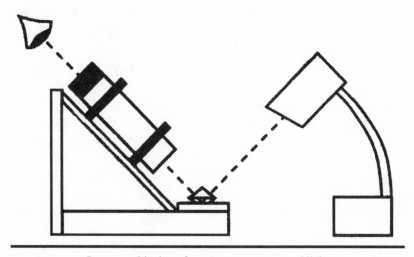

Proper positioning of spectroscope, stone, and light
in order to observe the absorption spectra

Note: In the new digital spectroscopes, the spectrum is viewed vertically rather than horizontally.

When you examine a stone with the spectroscope, you will continue to see the spectrum, but with a noticeable difference—a vertical black bar will appear at one or more places within the spectrum (some gems can have 10 or more lines!). Sometimes the bar is a very broad bar with hazy edges; sometimes it is a very narrow line and hard to see. *These black lines or bars occur wherever color has been absorbed by the gem material.* In other words, you are seeing black because the color that should be present at those same points has been absorbed by the gem.

You will also see a series of numbers along the top of the spectral display. These numbers go from 400 to 700 (in the older models the numbers go from 4000 to 7000). The sequence of numbers begins with 400 at the violet end of the spectrum and progresses through the spectrum to 700 at the red end. By noting where the black bars appear, at what numerical reading, you can easily check a chart and often identify a gemstone immediately.

Let's take a look at demantoid garnet (a variety of green garnet) as an example of how fast and easy the spectroscope can be to use. The refractometer can't be used for this gem because of its very high

R.I. But it's easy to identify with the spectroscope. When you look through the eyepiece you will see a lovely, colorful rainbowlike spectrum—and something more. In most demantoid you will observe a very strong bar in the violet end of the spectrum (see absorption spectra at end of chapter) at about 440 (4400). This is because the gem has absorbed some of the violet wavelength as the white light travelled through the stone, so we no longer see it. We see a black bar in place of the missing wavelength. If the demantoid is a rich, deep green, you will also note in the extreme red portion, at about 700, two very distinct black bars, very close together like railroad tracks (we call this a doublet). Again, as the white light travelled through the stone, some of the red wavelengths were absorbed, so we see black bars in place of where the red should be. When this pattern is present, the gem can only be demantoid garnet. It is the only green gem exhibiting this particular spectral (absorption) pattern.

Now let's examine blue sapphire. As you look through the eyepiece at the spectral display, you will see, in addition to the colors of the rainbow, a vertical black bar at the 450 (4500) mark, in the violet end of the spectrum. The deeper the color of the sapphire (or any gem), the more distinct the bar. Sometimes it is very easy to see, sometimes a little difficult, but if the stone is a rich blue sapphire, THERE WILL ALWAYS BE A BLACK BAR AT 450 (see absorption spectra). If the stone is another gem, such as blue spinel or tanzanite, you will not see it.

The spectroscope can also be helpful in distinguishing natural blue sapphire from synthetic. In most synthetic blue sapphire you will not see any bar at 450. So, if the color is a nice rich blue, and other tests suggest sapphire, you will know that the stone is synthetic if there is no line at 450. In some synthetics, you may see a *faint* blue line at 450. But if the material is a rich, *deep* blue, genuine sapphire it will exhibit a *distinct* line. A faint line in a rich blue stone should immediately suggest synthetic.

In the past, the spectroscope could immediately provide positive identification of genuine blue sapphire. Unfortunately, this is no longer true. Today there is an exception. One synthetic blue sapphire cannot be detected with the spectroscope—the Chatham synthetic. This synthetic exhibits almost the same absorption spectra as natural blue sapphire. While there are not many in circulation, you must be aware of them. If you have a very fine sapphire, and believe it to be genuine, to be absolutely sure you must examine it carefully with the microscope (which will reveal triangular or hexagonal platelets of platinum in the *synthetic*), or send it to a professional gem-testing lab.

HOW TO USE THE SPECTROSCOPE

1. *Be sure to use a good, strong light.* Having proper light is the key to successful use of this instrument. The stone must be intensely illuminated. Most spectroscope units contain their own light source. If you are using one that does not, it is important to have a very strong light that can be positioned to provide both trans-mitted and reflected light. A fiber optic light, or the intense light produced by a movie or slide projector can do the job.

2. *Be sure that only light that has been transmitted through the gem being examined, or reflected from it, enters the slit on the spectroscope.* Try to position the light and the spectroscope so that the slit in the spectroscope is as close as possible to the stone being examined, and the light is being transmitted or reflected directly into the slit. Try to prevent extraneous light from entering the slit.

3. *Use the spectroscope in a darkened room.* When examining a gem with the spectroscope, it is helpful to do it in a darkened room both to reduce extraneous light and so the eyes adjust more easily to what they are seeing in the spectroscope.

4. *Use transmitted light when examining transparent or translu-cent stones.* When using the spectroscope for transparent stones (stones you can see through clearly) or translucent stones (stones you can see through, but not clearly, as in "frosted glass"), simply place the stone in front of the spectroscope, *between* the spectro-scope and the light source. This way, the light will travel from behind the stone, *through it*, up into the spectroscope.

5. *Use reflected light to examine opaque stones.* With an opaque stone (one you cannot see through, such as turquoise), position the stone in front of the spectroscope, with the light positioned *above* it so that it hits the surface of the stone and the rays bounce off the surface into the spectroscope opening.

6. *With very dark stones, use a fiber optic illuminator or the pinpoint setting on a utility lamp.* A very strong light beam is required for dark stones to make sure they are adequately illuminated. If you have difficulty transmitting sufficient light, try using reflected light instead of transmitted.

7. *Adjust the slit at the base of the spectroscope, through which the light travels.* If the black bar or line is difficult to see, try adjusting the slit opening. Sometimes, by opening or closing it slightly, making it wider or narrower, the black bar can be more easily observed. (We do not recommend models without an adjustable slit.) Bars in the violet/blue end of the spectrum can be particularly difficult to see. Here the prism type instrument offers an advantage because the space given to the violet/blue end of the spectrum is spread out so the bars can be more easily seen.

8. *Make sure the instrument is steady.* The spectroscope must be steady or you will not be successful using it. This is another reason we do not recommend hand-held models. Use a stand to hold the spectroscope.

9. *Examine the stone from more than one direction.* If you cannot detect any distinct absorption bars, if you can pick up no distinct pattern, try examining the stone from several different directions. Sometimes you will be able to produce the pattern from one direction, but not from another. Or, try changing the angle at which the light is positioned.

10. *Avoid overheating the stone with prolonged exposure to the light.* The intense light required for proper illumination may cause the stone to get hot. Overheating can both damage a stone and reduce the spectroscope's effectiveness. Characteristic lines are especially difficult to detect in a treated diamond that has become overly hot from the intense lamp necessary to illuminate it. When heated, some stones lose their absorption spectra totally; others can lose it partially. Don't keep the stone being examined in the heat of the light for longer than necessary. Prior to examining, we recommend spraying the stone with a can of compressed air while holding the can upside down—this will produce the cooling agent, freon. It may give the stone a whitish appearance momentarily, but this will quickly evaporate. It will not hurt the

stone or your reading. *Caution:* to cool a stone that is already hot, allow it to cool somewhat prior to spraying (to prevent possible damage from thermoshock).

WHAT THE SPECTROSCOPE WILL SHOW YOU

As we discussed earlier in the chapter, the spectroscope will show you the "characteristic spectra" of many gems—a characteristic pattern created by vertical black lines or bars occurring in a particular portion of the color spectrum where color has been absorbed by the gem. Charts have been produced showing these patterns, the "absorption spectra" for different gem materials. Simply by using these charts, and comparing them to what you are seeing with the spectroscope, you can determine the identity of many stones. However, remember that it does not always separate natural from synthetic, and you must always keep up to date on the production of new synthetic material that may react differently with the spectroscope than previous synthetics.

Absorption Patterns Are Not Exact Reproductions

The spectra you will find here (and in other books) are not exact reproductions of what you will see. There is always some degree of variation. Don't expect them to match perfectly. If the pattern is close, that's usually enough.

More important, note that the pattern of the absorption spectra seen with a prism type spectroscope will look different from that seen with a diffraction type.

Prism Type. As we've mentioned, in the spectrum produced by the prism type spectroscope you will notice that the colors seen at the violet/blue end are spread out over a wider space than the other colors, while those at the red end are crowded together into a narrower space. The spreading of the colors at the violet/blue end provides an advantage because normally it is more difficult to see the bars in the violet/indigo portion. Spreading out the colors here makes them easier to see.

Diffraction Type. In the spectrum produced by the diffraction type spectroscope, you will notice that the colors are equally spaced.

Since the spacing of the spectral colors is different, the pattern produced by the black bars seen with a prism spectroscope may look very different from what is seen with the diffraction type. However, the numerical display will correspond even if the pattern looks different visually.

A FEW OF THE MOST IMPORTANT ABSORPTION SPECTRA TO KNOW

The spectroscope is especially important today for the following gems.

Alexandrite

Both natural and synthetic alexandrite show a pronounced doublet (two bars close together) in the red portion of the spectrum. The first is at about 680 (6800); the second at about 678 (6780). They may also exhibit a weak doublet at around 640 and 650. Neither synthetic color-change spinel nor synthetic color-change corundum, two gems often misrepresented as alexandrite, will exhibit this pattern or show the doublet in the red portion of the spectrum.

Fancy-Color Diamond

It will be extremely difficult to see the lines in diamonds unless they are kept cool. Spray the stone with an upside-down can of compressed air to coat it with freon prior to examination. If you live near an ice cream store, see if you can get a piece of dry ice on which to place the diamond (remember to use gloves when handling dry ice). Try opening the slit to its widest position to see the lines more easily.

In general, treated diamonds will exhibit more lines than natural. Also, if the red/orange portion of the spectrum is more or less blocked-out and appears blackish or grayish, suspect treatment.

Yellow. In the case of an intense, bright yellow diamond, the presence of a distinct line in the dark violet area of the spectrum at about 415 usually indicates treatment. A line at 415 is characteristic of off-color yellowish diamonds (cape stones). A colorless diamond will have no bar or line at this point. However, stones with an off-white, yellowish color will have a line at this point. The more pronounced the line, the more off-white or yellowish the diamond. Natural-color bright fancy yellow diamonds do not exhibit this line. The presence of a *faint* line at 415 in an *intense* "fancy" yellow is immediately indicative of an off-white diamond that has been irradiated to enhance the yellow.

Brown. Exhibits a weak line at 498, a stronger line at 504, and a weak line at 533.

Green. May exhibit a strong 504 and very faint 498.

Some Characteristic Lines in Artificial Colored Diamonds

Brown—592, 504, 498, 465, 451, 435, 423, 415
Green—741, 504, 498, 465, 451, 435, 423, 415
Yellow—592, 504, 498 (will appear stronger than the line at 504), 478, 465, 451, 435, 423, 415.
Pink (with orange fluorescence)—A strong line at 480 and a bright (not black) fluorescent line at 570.

IMPORTANT NOTE: The presence of a line at 592 is positive proof of treatment. When absent, search for lines at *both* 498 and 504, with the line at 498 being the stronger of the two. While lines at 498 and 504 may be present in natural stones, when they are both present in a stone, with the 498 line stronger, they provide positive proof of treatment.

Synthetic Diamond

Most natural diamonds—about 95%—exhibit a sharp absorption band at the 415 line, in the violet portion of the spectrum seen with the spectroscope. So far, this line has been absent in all synthetic diamonds. Synthetic "near-colorless" diamonds also lack other sharp optical absorption bands typical of most natural near-colorless diamonds.

Blue Sapphire

All natural blue sapphire will show a black bar in the violet/blue end of the spectrum, at 450 (4500). It may be difficult to see, especially in very pale blue Ceylon stones. The deeper the color, the more distinct the line will be. A *faint* line in a *deep blue* sapphire indicates *synthetic*. Most synthetic blue sapphire will not show the 450 line, nor will blue spinel, tanzanite, and glass. *The exception:* a new synthetic blue sapphire made today by Chatham will exhibit essentially the same spectrum as natural blue sapphire. When you see the line at 450, other tests must be conducted to be sure it is genuine and not one of the Chatham synthetics.

Demantoid Garnet

As we discussed earlier, since the Refractive Index of demantoid garnet is so high, the refractometer cannot be used to identify the stone. Therefore, the spectroscope is especially useful for this gem. Rich, deep green stones show a doublet at the extreme red end, at about 700; sometimes they also exhibit two weak bars in the orange/red area at about 625 and 645. Ordinary yellow green stones exhibit a very strong band in the violet, at about 440.

Natural Green Jadeite

Rich green jadeite always exhibits an unusual pattern in the red/orange portion of the spectrum. You will see a triplet—three bars—with each bar stronger than the one adjacent to it. The strongest bar will be at about 685; the next bar is weaker and appears at about 660; the third bar is the weakest and appears at about 630 (the 630 bar may be too weak to see).

Very fine green jadeite may exhibit bars that resemble three steps leading into each other, with each step a distinctively deeper shade of color (the most deeply shaded step beginning at the farthest end of the visible red and continuing to about 685, the next step beginning at about 685 and continuing to 660, and the most lightly shaded step beginning at 660 and continuing to 630). This pattern is never exhibited by dyed green jadeite, or other materials dyed to look like it.

Note: When the Chelsea filter suggests jadeite might be naturally green, be sure to use the spectroscope for positive proof.

ABSORPTION SPECTRA FOR POPULAR GEMS

In the color insert section at the center of this book we have provided absorption spectra to assist you in recognizing characteristic spectra for several popular gems. Note that these patterns are seen using a DIFFRACTION spectroscope rather than prism. For a much more comprehensive reference book, we highly recommend *The Spectroscope and Gemmology* (edited by R. Keith Mitchell). The *Handbook of Gem Identification* (Richard T. Liddicoat) also provides excellent photographs of spectra seen using the prism type. Since many of our readers may already have Liddicoat's book, and more people are choosing diffraction types today than previously, we decided to provide diffraction type for comparison.

If you are using a prism spectroscope, these spectra will still be useful to you, as long as you recognize that the pattern of the bars and colors may have a different appearance than what you are actually seeing with your instrument. If you are using the prism type, rely on the numerical scale rather than the visual pattern.

In addition to Liddicoat's book, characteristic spectra for the prism type may also be found in *Gems* by Robert Webster and for characteristic diamond spectra we recommend *Diamonds* by Eric Bruton (see Appendix).

With practice, you can become very quick at recognizing the most familiar absorption spectra. But beginners should not rely entirely on the spectroscope unless the pattern is so distinct there is no doubt. Don't expect too much at first. Practice on stones with distinct patterns and build your skill slowly.

NOTES

11 / The polariscope

A polariscope and
immersion cell

WHAT IS THE POLARISCOPE?

The polariscope is another instrument being employed increasingly
by those interested in gem identification today, primarily because of
its use in separating genuine from synthetic amethyst. The polariscope is a simple instrument, consisting of two round polarizing filters, one directly above the other, with a good light shining up from
the bottom.

The upper filter can be rotated. It is usually about three inches
above the lower piece, which is stationary.

HOW TO USE THE POLARISCOPE

We will discuss how to use the polariscope step by step, depending
on your purpose for using it. First we'll see how to use it to determine whether a gem is single or double refracting (see Chapter 6).
Next we'll discuss how to use it to separate natural from synthetic
amethyst. In addition, we will mention how to use it to separate jade
and chalcedony from glass or other single-refracting gems that might
try to imitate it.

Using the Polariscope to Determine Whether a Gem Is Single- or Double-Refracting

Until we learned of its use with amethyst, the primary purpose of the
polariscope was to separate single- and double-refracting gems. To
use it for this purpose is easy.

1. *Find the dark position.* First, before putting the stone in the polariscope, look through the top filter and turn it slowly. As you turn the filter, the light will become brighter and darker. In a complete rotation, it will go "bright" twice and "dark" twice. Turn the filter until you find the darkest position (this is called "crossed polars" or "crossed polarization"). Now stop.

2. *Place the stone in the polariscope between the two filters.* Place the stone in the polariscope between the two filters. We find it helpful to put the piece being examined in a small immersion cell or beaker filled with rubbing alcohol or water.

3. *Rotate the stone.* Rotate the stone laterally, approximately 1/4 turn. Does it go brighter? Turn the stone another 1/4 turn. Does it now go darker? If the stone is double-refracting, it will go bright, then dark again, then bright again, and dark again as you rotate the stone a full 360 degrees. In a full rotation, it will go bright twice, and dark twice. A stone that is single-refracting will remain dark continuously.

REMEMBER: After placing the stone in the polariscope, *turn the stone,* not the top filter.

AN IMPORTANT EXCEPTION: Now that you've learned how easy it is to use the polariscope, we must explain that there is an exception to the rule. We have just said that a single-refracting gem will stay dark continuously. This is true most of the time, but not in single-refracting gems that exhibit what is called "anomalous double refraction" (ADR), which means *false* double refraction.

How to Check for Anomalous Double Refraction. False double refraction is exhibited by all synthetic spinel and many garnets. If the stone you are examining appears to be one of these you must check for ADR. If you aren't sure, you must use other tests to be sure.

In Garnet. Garnet will behave in one of three ways as you rotate the stone:

1. It may behave as a normal single-refracting gem and remain dark during a full 360 degree rotation. In this case, you know the gem is single-refracting.

2. It may show *wiggly dark lines* going across the stone at random as you rotate it. This is a sure indication of ADR, of *false* double refraction. You know when you see these lines that the stone is single-refracting.
3. It may show typical bright-dark, bright-dark behavior just as in a normal double-refracting gem. In such cases, you must use other tests to be sure.

Anomalous double refraction in synthetic spinel—looks wiggly, cross-hatched

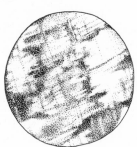

In Synthetic Spinel. With synthetic spinel you will always see wiggly black lines going across the stone at random as you rotate it. This is definite proof that the stone is not double-refracting, but single-refracting.

The polariscope can be invaluable in separating diamond from many other gemstones that occur in a colorless variety and which might be mistaken for diamond by the inexperienced. These include colorless corundum (sapphire), colorless topaz, colorless beryl, colorless quartz, colorless zircon, and the new diamond imitation, synthetic moissanite. These stones are all *double-refracting*, and can be quickly distinguished from diamond—which is single-refracting—using the polariscope (see previous section). The polariscope won't tell you the identity of these stones, but it will confirm that they are double-refracting, and thus *not* diamond, nor any other gem that is *single*-refracting.

Using the Polariscope to Separate Natural Amethyst from Synthetic

Using the polariscope for amethyst requires a slightly different technique.

1. *Find the optic axis.* One must first find the optic axis of the stone being examined. You don't need to understand what the optic axis is, but you do need to know how to find it.

   Again, before placing the stone in the polariscope, rotate the top filter until you find the darkest position and stop.

   Place a small immersion cell or beaker on top of the lower filter. Pour in a little benzyl benzoate (just enough to cover the amethyst being examined). This is a refractive index liquid, available from schools such as GIA and many jewelry and chemical supply houses. It makes it easier to see what you're looking for. If none is available, use rubbing alcohol.

   Place the amethyst in the liquid (you may need to use tweezers or a stone holder). Now, looking through the top filter, we'll find the optic axis of the amethyst. To do this, hold or place the stone in one position, for example, on its table facet (covered by the liquid), and then rotate it laterally while looking through the top filter. Be sure to *look through* the top filter only—*do not turn it.* Turn only the stone at this time.

   If the stone stays dark as you rotate it a full 360 degrees, you've found the optic axis. If it goes bright and dark, you are not viewing it through the optic axis and must try again viewing the stone through a different direction. You might try holding it on end next. Repeat the procedure. Keep changing the direction in which you view the stone until you find the direction that stays dark as you turn it. When it stays dark, you are looking at the stone through its optic axis.
2. *View the amethyst through its optic axis.* Once you find its optic axis, *be sure to keep the stone in that position as you continue to view it.*
3. *Rotate the top filter.* Look through the top filter, and, *holding the stone still,* turn the filter until you find the bright position. What you see now will tell you whether or not the amethyst is genuine or synthetic.

   If the stone looks smooth, even when viewed in this bright position, it is synthetic. If you see irregular lines (due to twinning, characteristic of all natural amethyst) you probably have a genuine stone.

We must caution you, however, that there is now a new synthetic amethyst that may also show the irregular lines resembling the twinning expected in natural amethyst. It usually has a more striated appearance than natural amethyst, but only someone very experienced in identifying amethyst would probably detect the difference. So, knowing for sure whether it is genuine may still pose a problem. *You can be sure it is synthetic if it has a nice smooth, even appearance. But you can't be sure it's genuine, even if it shows the characteristic irregular lines, the twinning, that indicates natural.*

The biggest mistake most people make in using the polariscope to separate synthetic and natural amethyst is not finding the optic axis of the amethyst first. In this case, one will not see the irregular lines observed in natural amethyst, and may erroneously conclude the stone is a synthetic when it may be genuine.

Using the Polariscope to Separate Jade and Chalcedony from Glass

Jade is a polycrystalline substance. This means it is made up of numerous, small interwoven crystals. Chalcedony is cryptocrystalline (made up of numerous submicroscopic crystals). All polycrystalline and cryptocrystalline substances will stay "bright" when examined with the polariscope (using the procedure described in checking for single- and double-refraction). When rotated a full 360 degrees, these gems will not go dark/bright, dark/bright as in double-refracting stones. Nor will they stay dark, as in single-refracting gems and glass. They will remain bright.

Therefore, the polariscope can provide a very fast, simple test to separate stones such as carnelian or sard from glass imitations. If the stone goes dark, it is glass or some other imitation; if it stays bright, it's genuine. This can be especially useful when examining antique pieces that may be intricately carved and set, such as a Roman or Greek ring where one might as easily find glass as genuine.

The same holds true for jade. Jade will stay bright when examined with the polariscope. Anything that looks like jade *but goes dark with the polariscope* cannot be jade.

NOTES

12 / The SSEF Diamond-Type Spotter and SSEF Blue Diamond Tester—essential tools for diamond buyers

Today, an increasing number of *synthetic colorless diamonds* are being produced. (Note: when the term "colorless" is used here, we are referring to diamonds in the D–Z category as opposed to fancy colors.)

Photo: Prof. H. Hänni, SSEF

As you know, synthetic diamonds have essentially the same physical and optical properties as diamond, but they are created in factories or laboratories rather than having formed naturally within the earth. Colorless synthetics are now commercially available in a variety of sizes. There is nothing wrong with the product, and it has its place in the jewelry market, but these "new" colorless synthetics are making headlines because of the increasing number being sold as "natural" diamonds. To complicate matters further from a gemological perspective, many *naturally occurring* diamonds are also being *treated* by ever-more sophisticated HPHT techniques to *transform* them from tinted or undesirable colors into more desirable colors; HPHT-treated stones include *colorless* stones—by far the largest segment of the diamond market—as well as a variety of lovely colors. Here again, there is nothing wrong with the product itself, but with people failing to disclose the treatment and selling them as natural-color diamonds, at higher prices it is important to be able to distinguish them from one another.

Today, we also have HPHT techniques used in conjunction with other techniques, such as irradiation, to create a wider range of colors, including higher grades in colorless diamonds as well as more "fancy" colors (some much more "natural" looking in appearance).

These developments have caused tremendous fear in today's marketplace because some of the synthetic diamonds and HPHT-treated diamonds have overlapping identification features that make positive identification more difficult.

A Short History of the HPHT Process and Diamond Synthesis

About a decade ago, the technique that has come to be referred to as *HPHT* (for "high pressure/high temperature") was introduced to transform very tinted or off-color diamonds into colorless and near-colorless stones, as well as a range of fancy colors. HPHT techniques can also—albeit this is very rare—transform "brown" diamonds into extremely rare blue and pink colors, as well as *improve* the color of natural-color blue and fancy pink diamonds by removing detrimental brownish undertones and, thus, intensifying the color. The HPHT process created widespread alarm because determining for sure whether or not any diamond of fine color had been treated by HPHT requires sophisticated testing available only at major gem-testing laboratories.

Simultaneously, HPHT technology was having an impact on the feasibility of synthesizing diamonds. By the 1980s, synthetic diamonds were commercially available in various shades of "fancy" yellow, and by the 1990s, synthetic pink and blue diamonds began to enter the market. Where fancy colors are concerned, most can be identified with standard gemological testing (fluorescence, inclusions, spectroscopic examination, and so on). Furthermore, for diamonds in the rarest colors, even in very small sizes, laboratory reports usually accompany the stone. So where fancy colors were concerned, there was less anxiety about them in the trade.

Colorless synthetic diamonds posed greater technological challenges. While colorless synthetic diamonds produced by single-crystal chemical vapor deposition (CVD) entered the market over a decade ago, initial production was limited to small sizes (most under ½ carat), fairly tinted colors (J–M), and sold at high prices, so there weren't many in the marketplace. Recent technological advances have changed this. Today we find much better colors and clarities (E–F color/VS–SI clarity) and a good supply of cut and polished stones in one-carat sizes; labs are also beginning to see cut and polished colorless synthetic diamonds weighing over 2 carats.

It is easy to see why anyone buying and selling diamonds today is concerned about the challenges presented by synthetic and HPHT-treated diamonds in terms of identification since most gemologists can't afford the equipment necessary to know for sure. Thus, everyone thought they would need to send *all diamonds* to a major laboratory.

Fortunately, this is not the case. Where colorless diamonds are concerned—which account for approximately 80% of all diamond sales—*all* **synthetic** *diamonds, and all* **HPHT-treated** *diamonds are a very rare diamond type, known as* **Type II**. This distinction is of major importance because it means that with a pre-screening tool, you have the ability to know—most of the time—when the diamond you're examining is *not* a synthetic or HPHT-treated colorless/near-colorless diamond. This greatly reduces dependency on major gem-testing laboratories.

Pre-Screening Made Easy with Tools Such as the SSEF Diamond Type-Spotter

Pre-screening colorless diamonds (as well as pink and blue diamonds) to determine whether or not they are Type I or Type II is essential today. Where colorless diamonds are concerned, if it is *not* a Type II diamond, *then it cannot have been whitened by HPHT to create a colorless stone, nor can it be a colorless synthetic diamond!*

This is significant because experts estimate that only *about 2% of all diamonds are Type II*. This means that, when examining *colorless* diamonds, a simple pre-screening device will enable you to know—for sure—about 98% of the time whether or not the stone being examined is synthetic or a type that *could* have been enhanced by HPHT. (This percentage drops as size increases, but it still provides reassurance approximately 80–90% of the time, even for large diamonds.) Only in a small percentage of cases will you need to submit a colorless diamond to a major laboratory for confirmation as to whether it is a natural or treated Type II diamond, or one of the new colorless synthetic diamonds.

Thus, by pre-screening to determine whether or not a diamond is a Type I or Type II, you can reassure yourself *most of the time* about what you are buying and selling when it comes to colorless diamonds. This is where tools such as the SSEF Diamond-Type Spotter provide an invaluable aid and greatly reduces dependency on laboratories. Only when a diamond is found to be a Type II is a major laboratory needed to know for sure.

In addition, many seek out brown-tinted diamonds today in the hope they can be transformed into much rarer, more desirable colors, and the spotter is invaluable as a tool to determine whether or not this can be done.

USING THE SSEF DIAMOND-TYPE SPOTTER TO SCREEN FOR COLORLESS SYNTHETIC DIAMONDS AND HPHT-ENHANCED DIAMONDS

The Swiss Gemmological Institute (SSEF) developed a simple tool to separate Type I from Type II diamonds. It is called the SSEF Diamond-Type Spotter, and its use greatly reduces anxiety and risk. We are going to discuss only this instrument here because it was the first instrument to distinguish between diamond types, and we are familiar with it. Today there is a similar instrument from HRD in Belgium.

In the case of *colorless* diamonds, the SSEF Diamond-Type Spotter makes it easy for *anyone* to quickly determine whether a diamond is one of the rare types that *could* be synthetic or treated. (NOTE: *all colorless synthetic diamonds produced today are Type II.*) If you discover the diamond is *not* a Type II, you do not have to worry about it being synthetic, nor worry that its color has been enhanced by HPHT. If, however, you discover the diamond *is* Type II, then you'll know you *must* send the stone to a lab to know for sure. In the case of brownish diamonds, it will tell you whether or not the color is improvable; that is, if it is a type that can be de-colorized by HPHT. In the case of *fancy-color* diamonds, the spotter has a more limited use—and we recommend that *all* fancy-color diamonds be submitted to a major lab for a current report confirming color origin—but it is a useful tool nonetheless, especially where blue diamonds are concerned.

DISTINGUISHING TYPE I DIAMONDS FROM TYPE II DIAMONDS

Since diamonds are in such high demand and represent such an important percentage of all jewelry sales, there is growing concern today about the number of "colorless" diamonds (that is, those in the D–Z category, rather than "fancy-color" diamonds) being sold without proper identification or disclosure. Of immediate concern is how to identify naturally colorless, natural diamonds from colorless *synthetic* diamonds and those that have been enhanced by HPHT methods. Fortunately, in the case of colorless synthetic diamonds and those transformed by HPHT into colorless stones, the process requires a rare diamond type, *Type IIa* (see diamond-type chart on page 203). Type IIa diamonds can also occur naturally in colorless to near-colorless grades, *but most colorless diamonds are Type Ia.* As mentioned earlier, it has been estimated by diamond producers that Type IIa diamonds represent less than 2% of *all* diamonds mined. (Note: the percentage is higher among larger diamonds with high clarity grades—over three carats—and Type II diamonds may be as high as 20% of stones over ten carats with clarity grades of VS and better.)

As mentioned earlier, distinguishing between natural and synthetic colorless diamonds, and detecting the use of HPHT methods to remove the tint to create a whiter diamond, can only be done with sophisticated testing available at major gem-testing laboratories. From a practical standpoint, however, it is not always possible to send a stone to a lab before making a buying decision, nor can anyone afford to send *every* diamond to a gem-testing lab. *However, in the case of colorless and near-colorless diamonds, it isn't necessary to send every stone to a lab, because the SSEF Diamond-Type Spotter enables you to know whether or not the diamond is a Type IIa. If it is not, no lab is needed!*

If the SSEF spotter shows you that a colorless diamond in question is *not* a Type IIa—which will be *most* of the time—then you know *it is not a synthetic* diamond and it *could not have been HPHT-treated*, so no lab is needed and you can rest assured that the stone is a natural diamond and not HPHT-enhanced. Conversely, if it *is* a Type IIa, then you will know that you *must* send the stone to a lab in order for the lab to determine whether it is a natural Type IIa diamond, a synthetic diamond, or one that has been HPHT-treated.

Note: **In cases where diamonds are accompanied by a diamond grading report issued prior to the year 2000, we recommend that it be resubmitted to a lab for confirmation. Prior to 2000, laboratories had not yet compiled sufficient data to know how to separate HPHT-treated colorless and near-colorless diamonds from the natural.**

HPHT-Treated "Fancy-Color" Diamonds

In addition to colorless diamonds, HPHT techniques can also be used to transform undesirable shades into much more desirable "fancy" colors. The fancy colors produced by HPHT currently include some of the more common colors, such as yellow to yellow-green shades, but also pink and blue shades, colors which are very rare and very costly when they occur naturally. The greatest risk occurs when considering rare fancy blue and fancy pink diamonds. Both natural-color pink and blue diamonds and those that have been HPHT-enhanced are extremely rare and costly, but HPHT-treated stones should sell for much less than the natural. In the case of *all pink and most blue diamonds,* it is essential to obtain *current* laboratory confirmation, and we recommend it for costly fancy-color diamonds, in all colors.

In the case of blue diamonds, the spotter *may* enable you to know immediately whether a diamond was HPHT-treated. In the case of blue diamonds, there are two diamond types: those containing boron (Type IIb) and those containing hydrogen (as found in some blue diamonds mined in Australia). The hydrogen type "blue" diamonds are very rare, and are typically a grayish blue or violet-blue, so they are usually not confused with those that are Type IIb. It is easy to separate them using the diamond type-spotter. With the spotter, the boron type will show the same reaction as Type IIa; the hydrogen type will show the same reaction you see for Type Ia. So, if you are checking a blue diamond using the SSEF spotter as explained below, and you do *not* get the reaction indicated below for a Type IIb diamond and the color has a definite grayish or violet hue, *then* you know the diamond is probably a natural color, hydrogen-type blue diamond. But this is the only case where we would rely on the result of the spotter when it comes to fancy-color diamonds. Also, do not forget that diamonds can be color-altered by irradiation techniques, with blue being one of the most popular irradiated colors; the color of the hydrogen-type blue diamond, however, is not produced by irradiation. A Type IIb diamond is also electrically conductive, but irradiated blue diamonds are not, so if you have the SSEF Blue Diamond Tester, or an electrical conductivity meter, it will enable you to identify Type IIb blue diamonds even without the SSEF Diamond-Type Spotter.

In the case of yellow and greenish-yellow diamonds, the spotter is *not* useful, so *all* diamonds in these hues must be sent to a lab.

If checking a brown or brownish diamond, the SSEF Diamond-Type Spotter will tell you whether or not you have a Type II, which could be improved by HPHT treatment, and the SSEF Blue Diamond Tester, or other electrical conductivity meter, will then tell you if the diamond is the rare Type IIb that will become *blue* when HPHT-treated.

We advise anyone buying any fancy-color diamond, or piece of jewelry containing fancy-color melee, to submit the stone to a major gem-testing laboratory for confirmation that they are natural and not synthetic, and whether or not the color is natural.

USING THE SSEF DIAMOND-TYPE SPOTTER

Below we will explain what the diamond-type spotter is, what it is showing, and how to use it. In addition, we will explain how HPHT methods can reveal pink and blue diamonds, or improve the purity of color in naturally pink and blue diamonds. All pink diamonds and most blue diamonds, whether they are natural-color or the result of HPHT techniques, will give the same reaction with the spotter and *must* be sent to a lab for confirmation.

What Is the SSEF Diamond-Type Spotter?

The spotter is a cylindrical, pocket-size instrument that is used in conjunction with a shortwave ultraviolet lamp. It has an opening on the top, surrounded by a ring of plasticine (silly putty), and an opening at the front. At the base of the front opening, you will notice a white coating. This special coating *fluoresces green when exposed to shortwave ultraviolet light.* If the coating fluoresces when testing a colorless, pink, or blue diamond, you'll know you have a diamond type that might be a synthetic diamond, or one that may have been HPHT-treated to create the color you are seeing. As you begin using the spotter to test diamonds, you will soon see that most of the time the diamonds are *not* a type that would indicate "synthetic" or "HPHT processing," and you'll know you don't have to worry or incur the costs of laboratory testing. In those cases where a diamond *is* a type that could be either of these, you will know you *must* send the stone to a major laboratory in order to know for sure. But since the spotter will usually indicate the diamond is not one of the rare types that might be synthetic or improvable by HPHT techniques, this simple screening test will save you lots of time, money, and needless concern.

What Is the Spotter Actually Testing?

When you test a stone with the SSEF spotter, you are actually testing the *shortwave transparency* of the stone; that is, whether or not it *transmits* shortwave radiation. There are basically four diamond "types"; some of these types transmit shortwave and others do not. The rare types that *can* be transformed by HPHT techniques to create colorless, near-colorless, pink, and blue diamonds *do transmit* shortwave, and other diamond types do *not.*

Diamond Types* and Their Response to HPHT Techniques

Type I Diamonds

Type IaA and Type IaA/B diamonds do *not* transmit shortwave ultraviolet light (they *absorb* it). Most diamonds are this type ("Cape" diamonds). There is also a very rare gray-blue to violet-blue diamond that is Type IaA. Type IaA/B stones may be HPHT-treated, but they do not produce colorless, near-colorless, pink, or blue stones.

Type Ib diamonds also do *not* transmit shortwave ultraviolet light. (These belong to the "Canary" series.)

Type IaB diamonds *do* transmit shortwave ultraviolet light. Diamonds of this type are the rarest of all diamonds and are reportedly being treated with HPHT techniques. This type will not produce colorless or near-colorless stones.

Type II Diamonds

Type IIa and IIb diamonds *do* transmit shortwave ultraviolet light; they cannot absorb it so they *transmit it through the stone.* Type IIa and IIb diamonds *can* be enhanced by HPHT techniques; they can also be *synthetic*:
- *Type IIa diamonds* occur naturally in colorless, near-colorless, brown, and pink shades. In addition, synthetic colorless and near-colorless diamonds are always Type II. Brown-tinted stones of this type can also be transformed into colorless, near-colorless, and fancy pink shades using HPHT techniques. The HPHT treatment removes the brown. As a result, brownish Type IIa diamonds—even those that are extremely tinted—can be trans-formed into colorless and near-colorless stones. In addition, some brownish diamonds have a pink component that is not visible because the brown tint masks it; in such stones, the HPHT process makes the pink visible by eliminating the brown tint, result-ing in a pink diamond. In the same way, naturally pink diamonds with a brownish undertone can be transformed into a purer, more

vivid pink. (*Note:* HPHT treatment does not add any pink but simply makes the pink more visible by eliminating the brownish undertone that masks the stone's inherent pink color.)

- *Type IIb diamonds* contain traces of boron and occur naturally in shades of brown or blue. *Synthetic* blue diamonds are also Type IIb. In naturally occurring diamonds, in rare instances when the boron concentration is extremely low, they may even appear colorless or near-colorless. In addition to the colors they exhibit naturally, the color of Type IIb stones can be enhanced by HPHT techniques. Type IIb diamonds that appear brownish (or near-colorless with a hint of brown) can be transformed by HPHT techniques into *blue* diamonds. Type IIb diamonds that are blue naturally, but exhibit an undesirable brownish undertone, can be transformed into purer, more vivid blues.

When an HPHT enhanced Type IIb diamond becomes blue, its original color was a mixture of blue and brown, but the blue hue was masked by the brown and, thus, diluted or undetectable. Since the HPHT treatment removes the brown color, the result is a much purer, more desirable blue. As was the case with the pink Type IIa diamonds described above, the HPHT treatment does not add any color, but simply makes the blue more visible by eliminating the brownish undertone that was masking the stone's inherent blue color. **NOTE: HPHT methods resulting in a blue diamond is extremely rare.**

* *Capital letters are used to name aggregates of Type Ia (A and/or B aggregates), small letters for subdivision of Type I and Type II (Type Ia, Type Ib, Type IIa, Type IIb).*

What Does the Spotter Tell You?

The spotter tells you whether the diamond is transmitting shortwave and, thus, enables you to place any diamond into one of two categories: those that *do* transmit shortwave versus those that *do not.* As you can see from the chart on pages 203–204, most diamonds belong to the category that does *not* transmit shortwave. Colorless and blue synthetic diamonds, and diamonds that can be transformed into colorless, near-colorless, pink, and blue diamonds by the HPHT process, belong to a category that *does* transmit shortwave. Therefore, by using this simple tool, you can determine whether or not the stone transmits shortwave and, thus, whether or not you need the services of a major laboratory for positive determination. In addition, if checking brownish diamonds, if the SSEF Diamond-Type Spotter indicates you have a Type II diamond, you know the color can be improved; then, if you check the stone with the SSEF Blue Diamond Tester (or electrical conductivity meter), and the indicator shows the stone *is* electrically conductive, you'll know you have a Type IIb, which will yield a rare *blue* diamond when HPHT techniques are used to remove the brown (although it is *extremely* rare to find a brown diamond that is Type IIb and would yield a blue diamond)!

NOTE: *All naturally pink* diamonds, whether they are natural, synthetic, or HPHT-treated, will show a green reaction in the spotter. If checking a "pink" diamond and the reaction is *not* green, you have a stone that is *definitely treated,* but by a different process, such as surface coating.

Where colorless, near-colorless, and blue diamonds are concerned, if the stone does *not* transmit shortwave, you know you don't have to worry or send it to a lab. If it *does,* you know immediately that it *could* be a synthetic diamond or one that has been treated by HPHT techniques, and you *must* submit the stone to a major gem-testing laboratory to know for sure.

Without this handy spotter, everyone without gemological expertise would need to send virtually *every* stone to a lab. Since this is not practical, this simple tool provides a great service by letting you know when a laboratory is needed and when it is not. For gemologists, it is also an invaluable timesaver, because the diamond can be categorized much more quickly by using this tool rather than a microscope.

The spotter will not indicate whether or not you have a Type IaAB diamond, on which HPHT techniques are also being used, but HPHT-treated diamonds of this type will not be colorless, near-colorless, pink, or blue.

HOW TO USE THE SPOTTER

Make sure you have a *shortwave* ultraviolet lamp to use in conjunction with the SSEF Diamond-Type Spotter. The shortwave output from a standard ultraviolet lamp (be sure it provides both longwave and shortwave) including portable models. We use a portable model most of the time because it is easier to control the direction of the short-wave output and can be used with very large diamonds mounted in jewelry. However, for anyone who expects to make frequent use of the spotter to test loose diamonds, we recommend the SSEF Shortwave Illuminator because it is the most powerful shortwave UV light source available for gemological purposes, and it protects against harmful shortwave rays. *WARNING:* USE CAUTION WHEN USING SHORTWAVE: PROTECT YOUR EYES AND SKIN FROM EXPOSURE TO SHORTWAVE AND **NEVER** LOOK INTO THE LAMP. BE SURE THE LIGHT IS DIRECTED AWAY FROM YOUR EYES OR SKIN! With a portable UV lamp, be sure the spotter is placed on a dark, non-reflective surface to prevent reflection of shortwave radiation from the surface toward the user's eyes. For additional eye protection, UV-protective glasses and goggles are available. We recommend using them when working with shortwave ultraviolet.

Be sure to use the spotter in a dark environment (turn off lights or use an ultraviolet viewing cabinet).

IMPORTANT: DO NOT TOUCH THE SMALL WHITE SCREEN BENEATH THE OPENING AT THE TOP OF THE SPOTTER. The screen has been coated with a powdery substance. Touching it, or inadvertently scratching it with tweezers, will destroy it and render the spotter unworkable.

To use the spotter, you simply place the diamond over the opening at the top (see below for directions on how to position the diamond), insert the spotter into the shortwave illuminator, and observe the white-coated area to see whether it fluoresces when you turn on the shortwave lamp. If using a hand-held shortwave ultraviolet lamp, hold the lamp over the stone, turn on the lamp, and note whether or not the coating fluoresces. IMPORTANT NOTE: When using a hand-held ultraviolet lamp, be sure the spotter is placed on a dark surface to prevent shortwave radiation from being reflected from a light colored surface back toward the user's eyes.

Here's how to use it correctly:

1. Remove the cover of the spotter by twisting it gently and pulling up. Before testing a diamond, observe what happens when you turn on the ultraviolet lamp, without a diamond. Notice that at the opening at the top, there is a ring of blue tack (plasticine, also called silly putty) encircling the round opening; lined up directly beneath the opening at the top of the spotter you will see a white screen. The white screen beneath the opening has been coated with a special substance that fluoresces green when exposed to shortwave ultraviolet light. Before testing your first stone, hold your shortwave UV lamp over the round opening at the top, turn it on, and note the color of the "white" surface—it glows green. The shortwave UV light passes through the open hole and strikes the white background, triggering the green fluorescent response. (If using the SSEF Illuminator, just turn the spotter upside down, insert it into the opening on top of the illuminator, press the button to turn on the shortwave illumination, and look at the specially-coated area of the spotter; it now glows green.)

2. Place the diamond over the opening, positioning it properly. Ideally, the stone should be placed on its side over the opening so that light is transmitted through the girdle of the stone (with the girdle perpendicular to the opening). If this isn't possible, place the stone over the opening with the table-facet facing down and the pavilion pointing up into the air. Make sure you **do not** place the diamond in a face-up position with the pavilion pointing down into the opening.

3. Mold the blue tack carefully around the stone to create a tight seal. This is very important to avoid leakage of the UV light through any opening or gap that might exist alongside the stone. Leakage creates a false green reaction resulting from UV light passing around the stone rather than having been transmitted through it. When the seal is tight, turn on the UV lamp and check the color of the coated white surface under the opening on which the diamond

is resting. If using a hand-held shortwave lamp, be sure to hold the lamp away from the front edge of the spotter so that you avoid any spillover of shortwave onto the coated white surface from the front of the unit. This would also create a false reaction simply because you held the lamp too far forward.

4. Check the white screen. Does it remain white, or is it now green? If it is white, you have a diamond that does not transmit shortwave, and you don't have to be concerned about whether or not the color is natural. If it is green, you know that you need a lab to do further testing. The stone may be natural, but it may also be HPHT-treated.

All colorless and near-colorless HPHT-processed diamonds are in the category of diamond types that do transmit shortwave. Most of them are reported to be Type IIa stones, which account for less than 2% of all diamonds. Keep in mind, however, that Type IIa diamonds account for a disproportionately high percentage of large diamonds—over three carats—with high clarity. This means the percentage of treated stones among larger diamonds with high clarity grades may be significantly higher than 2%. Also, keep in mind that all natural-color pink (Type IIa) and most blue (Type IIb) diamonds are extremely rare and valuable, and both natural-color and HPHT-treated stones will transmit shortwave. So it is imperative to confirm whether or not the color is natural when considering any pink diamond and most blue diamonds.

THE SSEF BLUE DIAMOND TESTER

The SSEF Blue Diamond Tester can be invaluable when testing "blue" diamonds as well as brown or brown-tinted diamonds. Natural diamonds that have been treated by radiation techniques, or by surface coating 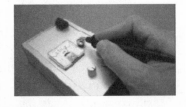 techniques, can be quickly separated from those with natural color. Natural-color blue diamonds (except the very rare Australian blue-gray/violet blue diamonds, which we've already discussed on p. 200) obtain their color from the presence of boron, and all boron-containing diamonds are *electro-conductive* (capable of passing an electrical current when a voltage is applied). This is not the case with blue diamonds that have been transformed into blue by irradiation or coating techniques. *So by using the SSEF Blue Diamond Tester—which indicates whether or not the diamond is electro-conductive—one can quickly and easily separate the natural-color from those that have been treated by irradiation or surface coatings.* (Note: it will *not* separate natural blue diamonds from *synthetic* blue diamonds, which also contain boron, but other tests such as fluorescence and phosphorescence can make this distinction). *If the needle on the tester does not move (see instructions below), this is positive confirmation of artificial color.* If the needle does move, you know it is electro-conductive and contains boron, so it may be a natural blue diamond, a blue synthetic diamond, or an HPHT-altered blue diamond. Fluorescence will separate the natural from the synthetic blue diamond, but if a natural diamond, you'll need a major lab to determine whether or not the diamond has been subjected to HPHT treatment.

The SSEF Blue Diamond Tester also provides a very useful tool that shows whether HPHT methods can produce a *blue* diamond from one that appears *brown*. HPHT techniques can remove, to varying degrees, the brown tint from Type II diamonds. When the brown is removed, Type IIa diamonds may become colorless, or, in rare cases, pink. Unfortunately, with Type IIa diamonds, there is no way to know which color will be seen following the HPHT treatment until after the treatment. But just the reverse is true with Type IIb diamonds; all Type IIb diamonds contain boron, and therefore, if you know in advance that the stone is IIb, you know even before the HPHT treatment that the resulting color will be some shade of blue!

Type II diamonds—both IIa and IIb—transmit shortwave radiation that can be easily determined using the SSEF Diamond-Type Spotter as described above. But when looking at brown diamonds, knowing whether it is Type IIa or IIb can be invaluable. For this, you must now use the blue diamond tester. We know that Type IIb diamonds contain boron, but, more importantly, they are also *electro-conductive* as mentioned above. So if we can determine whether or not the Type II diamond in question is electro-conductive, we will know whether or not it is IIa or IIb. If the diamond is electrically conductive, you know you have the rare Type IIb, and that when the brown is removed, the color of the diamond *will* be **blue**.

So the SSEF Blue Diamond Tester, used in conjunction with the SSEF Diamond-Type Spotter, is especially valuable in testing brown diamonds and blue diamonds. The SSEF Diamond-Type Spotter will tell you when you have a Type II diamond, and, if so, the blue diamond tester will separate Type IIa from IIb!

The SSEF Blue Diamond Tester is easy to use. It is a simple, portable, battery-operated electrical conductivity meter. As you look at the instrument, you'll notice there is a probe that resembles a pen situated along the right side of the unit. There is a gauge, with a needle that indicates varying degrees of electrical conductivity, beneath which is a dial that can be turned clockwise or counter-clockwise (this can provide an indication of the stone's electro-conductive strength, which could indicate how blue the stone may become). There is also a metal stone-holder for use with unmounted stones (the diamond being tested must be in contact with metal). The tip of the probe has been carefully inserted into a protective casing; to remove it, gently pull the probe toward the lower end of the instrument (and be sure to re-insert it for protection when you have finished testing the diamond). Turn the dial beneath the gauge in the clockwise direction, as far as it will go. Now, take the diamond in question and press the tip of the probe against its table facet (if unmounted, be sure the stone is placed on the metal stone holder in order to establish an electrical circuit). Note whether or not the needle moves. If the needle *moves*, the stone *is electrically conductive;* if it does not move, it is not electrically conductive. If the tester indicates the diamond is electrically conductive, you know you have a Type IIb, and that the color of the diamond following HPHT treatment will be some shade of blue. To determine how electro-conductive it is, and how "blue" the stone might become, turn the dial beneath the gauge slowly counter-clockwise and test again, and repeat this process until the needle stops moving—if the needle still moves when the dial has been turned all the way to the counter-clockwise position, this tells you the stone has significant electro-conductivity and should produce a stronger blue color.

SUMMARY

In summary, when checking *colorless* and *near-colorless* diamonds with the spotter, *no* green reaction with the spotter means it is *not synthetic* and it is *not HPHT-treated*. A green reaction indicates the diamond is a type that *might be synthetic or HPHT- treated* and *requires laboratory verification*.

Remember: *All naturally pink* diamonds, whether they are natural, synthetic, or HPHT-treated, will show a green reaction in the spotter. If checking a "pink" diamond and the reaction is *not* green, you have a stone that is *definitely treated,* but by a different process such as surface coating. The spotter is not useful for fancy-color yellow or greenish yellow diamonds. All diamonds in these colors must be sent to a lab for confirmation, or be accompanied by a current laboratory report. Given the fact that all synthetic colorless diamonds, and those that can be transformed into colorless/near-colorless, stones are Type II, and the fact that Type II diamonds are so rare, the spotter will usually provide reassurance that the stone is natural and its color is natural! So with it, your anxiety, as well as your dependence on laboratories, will be greatly reduced. NOTE: MAKE SURE THE STONE YOU ARE TESTING IS A DIAMOND. Natural colorless corundum (sapphire) will *not* transmit shortwave (same reaction with spotter as Type IaA, IaA/B, Ib), but Verneuil synthetics *do* transmit (same reaction with spotter as Type IIa, IIb, IaB).

If you know a stone is sapphire, but aren't sure if it is natural or synthetic, the spotter can be used to distinguish between the two!

Diamond Reactions to the SSEF Diamond-Type Spotter

Diamond Color	NATURAL COLOR DIAMONDS		HPHT-TREATED DIAMONDS	
	Diamond Type	Spotter Reaction	Diamond Type	Spotter Reaction
Colorless* (D–Z color, not *fancy* color)	Most are Ia	No green	Ia—tinted stones transformed into various fancy-colors	No Green
	Type IIa (very rare)	Green**	IIa—tinted stones transformed into colorless	Green**
Pink	Type IIa	Green**	IIa—tinted stones transformed into pink or into purer, more vivid pink	Green**
Blue	Most are IIb	Green**	IIb—tinted stones transformed into blue or into purer, more vivid blue	Green**
	Ia (hydrogen present—very rare)	No green		

All colorless synthetic diamonds now in the marketplace are type IIa and will give a green reaction with the spotter.
**Further testing is required at a major gem testing laboratory.

NOTES

13 / The immersion cell

Examining a gemstone while it is immersed in liquid can be invaluable to the gemologist. It makes it much easier to see certain characteristics and inclusions that are difficult, if not impossible, to see otherwise. Immersion can quickly enable one to spot doublets, see telltale inclusions such as the curved striae in flame-fusion synthetic rubies or sapphires, and see more clearly exactly where and how the color is distributed in a stone.

Today using immersion to examine stones has become especially important for anyone buying rubies and sapphires, because immersion can reveal whether or not a sapphire or ruby has obtained its color by diffusion methods—a technique used for *very pale* or *near-colorless* corundum to alter or improve color. Early diffusion techniques deposited a layer of color *on the surface only.* More recent techniques—using various chemical additives in conjunction with heat, sometimes called *bulk-diffusion*—can create "color centers" within the stone as well as on the surface. Viewing a ruby or sapphire while immersed will reveal whether the color is on the surface only, and it may also reveal unusual color centers indicative of color enhancement by heat combined with chemical additives. For ruby buyers, examining the stone while immersed may reveal where fractures have been filled, especially when a red-tinted filler has been used.

It is really easy to understand why immersion makes it so much easier to see inclusions and other growth features if you understand why they are normally not easy to see. The primary reason it is difficult to see inclusions and other important characteristics, especially in cut and polished gems, is because it is very difficult to illuminate the stone's interior. This is because so much of the light directed at the stone is reflected back from the stone's surface. Depending upon the R.I. of the stone being examined, however, and the R.I. of the liquid used, reflectivity can be dramatically reduced, and the approaching light, instead of being reflected back, can now enter the stone, thus illuminating its interior in a way that would otherwise be impossible. The closer the R.I. of the liquid to the R.I. of the stone, the greater the reduction of reflectivity; if they are the same, or close to it, the stone will actually seem to "disappear" when immersed. But not the inclusions! Most inclusions will have an R.I. that is different from the host stone, so with the host having disappeared, the inclusions will now be the only things visible, standing out in much sharper relief.

Today *horizontal immersion microscopes* are gaining in popularity because of the increased visibility immersion provides; this, coupled with the power provided by the microscope, is invaluable to a serious gemologist. But one doesn't need an immersion microscope to view gems using immersion techniques (although we encourage you to consider an immersion microscope as you gain greater confidence and proficiency with basic gemological skills!).

Immersing a stone for basic gem testing purposes can be accomplished very easily, without any sophisticated or costly instruments. Quite simply, all you need is a container large enough to hold the stone or piece of jewelry you need to examine, into which liquid can be poured. It can really be almost anything—a water glass, an ashtray, or a glass beaker—as long as it is deep enough that the liquid won't overflow when the stone or jewelry piece is placed in it, and large enough to accommodate the entire stone, totally immersed; you want to be sure that the stone is completely covered by the liquid. We recommend using something that will allow you to see the stone clearly when examining it from several different directions. In addition, the bottom of the container should be transparent so that lighting can be used when necessary; diffused light, positioned underneath the stone being examined, often facilitates examination.

We recommend using a clear, colorless glass container, or a metal-glass combination, because you may be using any one of several different liquids for immersing the stone, including water, alcohol, glycerin oil, or methylene iodide, and you don't want the liquid to react with the container. For example, if you were to use a styrofoam cup and fill it with methylene iodide, the methylene iodide would quickly eat through the styrofoam and you would have a very noxious mess to clean up!

WHAT IS AN IMMERSION CELL?

The "immersion cell" we want to discuss is not the clear glass "beaker" type used in most labs or with the immersion microscope, but a handy new compact instrument that makes it much more convenient to have everything you need—proper container, diffused lighting, liquid—readily available, whenever and wherever immersion techniques are called for. It is a sturdily constructed container designed to hold a gem within a liquid environment for easier examination. Some immersion cells provide see-through covers to eliminate exposure to the noxious odors produced by some of the liquids you might be using; some screw on and off so you can keep the liquid in the cell, even when carrying it from one place to another. Some immersion cells also have a built-in magnifying element to make it easier to see important diagnostic characteristics.

The GIA Immersion Cell ($45) can be used with GIA's polariscope and microscope and is a very convenient unit to use anywhere. The immersion cell provided in RosGem's Gem Analyzer, a combination dark-field loupe, polariscope and immersion cell ($285), provides diffused light from underneath, and offers a unique, focusable 10X magnifying element, the extra power being a valuable feature in a portable unit. It also provides the ability to examine a stone with the polariscope, while immersed, another important feature. Its smaller size, however, makes it difficult to use for a large piece of jewelry. Hanneman also offers an immersion unit, but it is difficult to use if the stones are mounted. If you find yourself without an immersion cell, however, and you need to examine a stone using immersion techniques, just remember what we said earlier: all you need is a glass, a flashlight, and a white cover of some type (such as a handkerchief, paper towel, napkin, etc.). Lay the white cover over the light (now you have diffused light), and set the glass on top. You now have an "immersion cell." Just pour in the liquid, and immerse the stone!

HOW TO USE AN IMMERSION CELL

Immersion cells are very easy to use.

1. Simply pour in sufficient liquid to completely cover the stone you wish to examine. We normally use methylene iodide because it has a refractive index (R.I.) that works in virtually every situation for which we use immersion. However, in many cases you need nothing more than water, glycerin oil (baby oil), or isopropyl (rubbing) alcohol.

2. Gently place the stone or piece of jewelry being examined into the liquid, taking care not to splash the liquid out of the container (you don't want to waste the liquid, or stain or damage the surface on which you are working).

3. Place the stone *table-down* in the immersion cell to begin. We also suggest using tweezers to immerse the stone, and to remove it; if a piece of jewelry is being examined, it is often possible to hold the shank, but tweezers usually make it easier. Always be careful to avoid getting chemicals on your skin (if you do, wash it off immediately).

4. Turn on the light, if built-in, or set the immersion cell over a diffused light source (or make your own, as we discussed above).

5. Examine the stone. First look with the unaided eye. What do you see? Next, examine the stone with magnification, first using the loupe. What do you see? Finally, if possible, position your immersion cell in a way that permits microscopic examination. What do you see? You may need to check the stone from several different positions, using tweezers to hold it. After examining it table-down, we always examine the stone through the side as well, with the tweezers grasping the stone by the table and culet.

To decide what liquid is most appropriate to use with a given gemstone to better see inclusions and other growth features, just select the one that has an R.I. that comes closest to the R.I. of the stone being examined. Keep in mind, however, that even water can make a big difference in what you see, and that you don't need to have a matching R.I., or make the stone "disappear," to be able to see important characteristics.

Liquids* Used to Immerse Gems for Better Examination

Liquid	R.I.
Water	1.33
Alcohol	1.36
Turpentine	1.47
Olive oil	1.47
Glycerin oil (glycerol)	1.47
Clove oil	1.54
Benzyl benzoate	1.57
Cinnamon oil	1.59
Methylene iodide	1.74

*One word of caution: Do not immerse porous stones such as opal and turquoise in any liquid except water because the liquids can be absorbed into the stones and cause discoloration. Also be careful when using strong solvents (such as benzyl benzoate) which may weaken the cement layer found in some doublets or triplets.

Separating Natural *Sapphire* *and Ruby from* Diffused

Everyone buying sapphire and ruby must be on guard against inadvertently buying stones that have been diffusion treated.

Today, very pale to colorless corundum can be specially treated to create rarer, more desirable colors, including red, blue, yellow, orange, and padparadscha (a rare pink-orange variety). These stones are called "diffused" sapphire or ruby or "bulk diffused," but both terms are currently under scrutiny. Surface-only diffused blue sapphire has been produced since the early 1990s; diffused ruby is less common but production has been increasing. Early diffusion techniques involved treating the surface of the stone with chemicals and then heating it for a prolonged period of time in a controlled environment. In the case of blue sapphire, diffusion treatment involved introducing chemicals (titanium and iron, the same coloring agents present in natural blue sapphire) into the surface of the stone and then heating it slowly over a period of time, during which the surface absorbs the titanium oxide and is transformed into "blue." The color penetration, however, was only about 0.4 millimeters deep, or less. This treatment also made stones somewhat more brittle and prone to chipping. In the case of diffused stones where color is confined to the surface, you may end up with a colorless stone should the stone ever need to be recut or repolished.

More recent techniques involving additives such as beryllium have enabled treaters to create color centers within the stone as well as on the surface. The use of additives is now so widespread that traditional heating is almost obsolete.

There is nothing wrong with anyone buying or selling diffused sapphire, as long as both the buyer and the seller know that it is diffused, and pay the right price. But this is not always the case. A friend saw us at one of the major international gem shows and rushed over to show us the large, beautiful, "blue" sapphire he had purchased the day before "at an unbelievable price" from a "miner." When he told us what he'd paid, we kiddingly suggested it must be "diffused." To our surprise, and his, it was! Unfortunately, since he was away from his lab, he didn't have the means to check for diffusion; we pulled out our portable immersion cell, immersed the stone, and it was obvious immediately.

The easiest and most reliable way to know whether or not a stone is surface-diffused is to immerse it and examine the girdle and facet joins.

- Put sufficient liquid in the immersion cell to cover the stone. For testing corundum (sapphire or ruby), we recommend using *glycerin oil* or *methylene iodide.*
- Place the sapphire or ruby in the liquid, *table-down.*
- Place the cell over a diffused light (or use one of the units which provide diffused light).
- Now examine the stone and LOOK FOR A SPIDERWEB EFFECT. Some magnification may be helpful. If the unit doesn't provide any magnification, try using your own loupe (but you will have to be about an inch away from the stone. If the unit has a lid or cover over the cell, this won't be a problem; if not, try not to breathe the fumes if you are using methylene iodide). Examine the stone, paying close attention to the facet joins and the girdle edge. *Surface-diffused stones will show a darker concentration of color along parts of the girdle and along portions of the facet edges.* Sometimes this darkening of parts of the facet edges and

girdles creates a pattern that looks something like a spiderweb as you view it table down. (See Color Section.)

When examining a sapphire or ruby using immersion techniques, the presence of darker and lighter concentrations of color along the girdle edge or facet joins provides positive confirmation that the sapphire or ruby is *diffused*. In addition, unusual color centers that are distinctly different from the typical color zoning of corundum (typically, zoning in corundum occurs in parallel, alternating zones, sometimes following the hexagonal growth structure of the crystal) may indicate heating with additives. In rare cases, you may not have positive identification without advanced spectroscopic examination at a major lab. NOTE: All other standard tests for sapphire or ruby will be the same for both natural and diffused stones, and this telltale effect seen when immersed will *not* be seen with normal examination with a loupe or microscope. It *must* be immersed and examined over diffused light.

Spotting Cobalt-Coated Tanzanite and Sapphire

Surface coatings are being applied to an ever-increasing number of gemstones. "Blue" sapphire and tanzanite are the latest to be treated in this way. Numerous stones have recently been found to be treated with a very thin surface coating of cobalt. In the case of tanzanite, this is particularly troublesome because many weigh ⅓-carat or *less*. Although cobalt-treated tanzanites in large sizes have been detected, there is a scarcity of fine material in small sizes and thus, an unusually large number of small stones are being treated in this manner. As a result, greater care must be taken when buying smaller stones.

Coated tanzanites and sapphires are also more difficult to detect than many other coated stones. For example, surface-coated topaz in virtually any color—such as "mystic topaz" or "Signity Blue Topaz"—are easy to spot because of an unusual iridescence that can be easily seen on the pavilion while tilting the stone back and forth under strong light. However, with tanzanite and sapphire this test is of little use; sapphire shows no surface iridescence on the pavilion, and in the case of tanzanite, it is often so subtle that one doesn't see it. In the case of sapphire, the Chelsea filter will immediately indicate something is wrong (see page 87), but the Chelsea filter is of no use with cobalt-coated tanzanite since many tanzanites show a reddish reaction through the Chelsea filter.

In the case of tanzanite, examining the stone using immersion techniques provides the best means to detect a surface-coating. In the case of sapphire, immersion is also an excellent way to spot the presence of a coating and it is also valuable as a means to confirm the presence of a coating on a stone that showed a pink or red reaction through the Chelsea filter. The cobalt coating applied to the surface of tanzanite and sapphire is very thin, so it can flake off fairly easily, revealing the lighter color below. When immersed, evidence of this can be seen, especially when magnification is used to examine the stone while it is immersed. When using magnification, place the stone *table-down* in the immersion cell, and place the immersion cell over a diffused light. For tanzanite, we recommend using simple isopropyl rubbing alcohol or glycerin oil (baby oil) as the immersion liquid; for sapphire, we recommend glycerin oil.

When examining a stone that is coated, you will see areas where the coating has flaked off or did not adhere properly during the coating process. It is easiest to see evidence of this along the facet joins or at the culet, where the thin coating will usually flake off more quickly, but it can also be seen on the flat faces of the facets. Look for whitish "scratches" or splotchy areas on facet faces, and areas of lighter color at the culet or along facet joins—these lighter-color areas are actually showing the true body color of the stone, the color *beneath* the coating. Occasionally you may also see what look like very tiny "dots" of color across the surface, barely larger than a pin head. These are all telltale indicators of surface coating. **Be sure to examine *all* surface areas on the pavilion—even though the color may appear *uniformly* blue, *some are coated on only one-half of the pavilion.***

DETECTING DOUBLETS AND TRIPLETS QUICKLY AND EASILY

Doublets and triplets have been around for centuries and continue to present problems today. We've discussed them earlier, and they are discussed in great detail in Chapter 16. There are two types that need to be mentioned here, however, because immersion is the fastest and easiest way to spot them. One type is called a "soudé" and is made of two pieces of colorless material (usually colorless synthetic spinel) joined together with an appropriately colored layer of cement or glue. This thin layer of colored cement creates the impression of color throughout the entire stone. Most people are amazed when they learn the top and bottom are colorless.

The other type is a much more serious problem: ruby and sapphire doublets. Thousands of ruby and sapphire doublets are being made by using a thin section of *genuine* corundum on the crown, fused to a *synthetic* ruby or sapphire bottom. Luckily, the genuine corundum is not actually the same color as the rest of the stone; in the case of the "blue" sapphire doublet, the bottom portion is blue (synthetic blue sapphire) and the color is carried through to the top. But the top is a cheap, brownish-greenish corundum. It is the same thing with the ruby doublet: synthetic ruby bottom, with a light brownish or near-colorless top. The result is very convincing and they are being sold worldwide, and mixed in with parcels of genuine rubies and sapphires. More important, unlike the soudé type, which can be separated with routine gemological tests, this type of doublet will pass all routine gemological testing except careful examination with the loupe or microscope viewing the stone through the side. When properly examined with the loupe, with proper lighting, one can see the color demarcation.

Fortunately, both of these types can be quickly and easily detected with immersion, even when mounted. Immersion will not hurt the stone, or the piece of jewelry, and can be done more quickly than checking with a loupe or microscope.

To determine whether or not the stone is a doublet, simply immerse it; in the case of the soudé, the top and bottom will "disappear" when in the liquid, leaving only a thin plane of colored cement. In the case of the ruby and sapphire doublets, the stone will still be visible, but as you turn it slightly in the liquid, you will see the distinct difference in color where the thin sliver of genuine corundum is fused to the synthetic bottom.

OTHER USES FOR THE IMMERSION CELL

The most important reasons for using the immersion cell today may be for identifying diffused sapphires and rubies and for spotting doublets, but it has many other important applications as well. As we mentioned earlier, the immersion cell makes it easier to see many telltale inclusions; with practice, you will see how important immersion is for examination of inclusions. It is much easier to see the telltale curved striae indicative of many synthetics, such as sapphire and ruby; diagnostic color zoning such as the characteristic hexagonal zoning seen in corundum; and distribution of color, which can be very helpful when examining rough gemstones to determine where the color is prior to cutting. And perhaps most important, immersion techniques may become invaluable as a quick and easy way to examine rubies to determine whether or not they are fracture-filled. And much more. You will clearly see things you might easily miss otherwise.

In some cases you need only the immersion cell and your unaided eye to see an important diagnostic characteristic; in other cases, magnification may be helpful. The important thing is to start using immersion techniques. Once you do, you'll understand how useful immersion can be. And you'll also understand how convenient a compact, portable immersion cell can be!

The *Gem Analyzer,* a recently introduced instrument made by RosGem, is a very handy tool that incorporates a focusable dark-field loupe, polariscope, and immersion cell into one small, portable unit that works simply by placing it on top of a maglite. It is one of the cleverest and most useful tools we now keep in our "basic kit."

NOTES

14 / The electronic diamond tester

More and more, people who are buying and selling diamonds are coming to depend on electronic diamond testers to determine genuineness. Many models are available today (see Chapter 2). Since they require no gemological skill, they make diamond testing both fast and easy—for anyone. They won't tell you what the stone is if it isn't a diamond, but, used properly, they can be very helpful, especially for the untrained. But they are not foolproof.

Electronic diamond testers are especially useful in checking diamond imitations that have high refractive indices such as cubic zirconia (CZ), strontium titanite, or zircon. Such imitations look more like diamond than those with lower refractive indices, such as glass, because the higher the refractive index, the greater the brilliance. In other words, imitations with a high refractive index have more "sparkle" and, thus, look more like a real diamond. Beginners often find it difficult to identify these imitations because standard instruments normally used to positively identify other stones, such as the refractometer, can't be used on stones with such high refractive indices. In such cases, the electronic diamond tester can be very helpful and reliable.

WHAT IS AN ELECTRONIC DIAMOND TESTER?

Most testers are small instruments that operate simply by reading the instructions, plugging them into the nearest electrical socket, and turning them on. Some also operate for a limited time by battery. They work by pressing a metal point against one of the stone's facets. The tester will then give a signal that indicates genuine or not genuine.

HOW TO USE THE DIAMOND TESTER

As we mentioned, using the electronic diamond tester is mostly a matter of reading and following instructions. But we've included a few pointers here that we feel will help optimize your use of the instrument. Some of these pointers are not included in the instructions accompanying most diamond testers, so it is critical that you read this section very carefully.

1. *Stones must be cool.* The most important thing to understand about using electronic diamond testers is that the stone being tested must be cool. Even one's body temperature can warm a diamond sufficiently, just by wearing it. This will affect the reliability of the test. If a genuine diamond is too warm when tested, it may test not genuine. We recommend cooling the stone before testing by spraying it with an upside-down can of compressed air (to get freon), or placing it under cold water and wiping it dry prior to testing.

2. *Adjacent stones cannot be tested immediately.* It is important to understand that you cannot get a reliable reading if you consecutively test stones that are adjacent to one another (as in pieces using pavé or pieces such as wedding bands where stones are set closely together). Few realize that when the electrical charge goes through the pointer touching the stone, it heats the point. The heat from the point is then transmitted into the stone. The stone then transmits heat to the stones adjoining it. Therefore, since the adjacent stones are now warm, the tester may give a false reading. The adjacent stones may read not genuine when they are genuine because the temperature of the stones being tested is too high.

   After testing the first stone, be sure to test stones that are not adjacent to it.

3. *Stones cannot be retested immediately.* If for some reason you immediately retest a diamond, you may get a different reading the second time for the same reason—overheating. After using the pointer to conduct the first test, the diamond will now be too warm and give a false reading for the second test.

4. *Be sure the pointer is not touching metal.* Electronic diamond testers will not work properly if the point is touching any metal,

such as a bezel edge or a prong. Be sure the point is not in contact with metal. Some models have a "metal alert," to warn you of this problem.

5. *Keep the battery well charged.* If you are using a model that operates by battery as well as with a cord, be sure to check the battery and keep it properly charged so that you get a proper reading when not using the cord. It must be well charged or it will not work. Most now have an indicator that tells you if the battery is insufficiently charged, but remember to check.

BEWARE OF IMITATIONS THAT CAN FOOL THE TESTER!

As we stated earlier, electronic diamond testers can be very helpful when it comes to separating the diamond from imitations such as CZ, strontium titanite, and other "look-alikes" that closely resemble diamond because of their very high refractive indices, but they are not foolproof.

While we have found electronic diamond testers to be reliable in the *negative*—that is, when they indicate the stone is *not* diamond—we have found in that some electronic diamond testers **erroneously indicate that a stone *is* "diamond" when it is *not*.** Below we provide specific examples of where additional testing is required to know for sure whether or not the stone in question is really diamond. We also recommend specific tests that you can use quickly and easily in combination with the diamond tester to avoid a costly mistake.

Beware of synthetic diamond. As we discuss in other chapters of the book, technological advances have resulted in successful synthesis of gem quality yellow and near-colorless diamonds. Synthetic diamond is virtually identical to natural diamond in its various properties. **Electronic diamond testers will indicate "genuine diamond" for all *synthetic* diamonds. Other tests—fluorescence, magnetism, inclusions—must be performed** to separate diamond from its synthetic counterpart (refer to Index).

Beware of true diamond doublets. This is a situation in which the diamond tester will always give you a false diagnosis—when testing a true diamond doublet (see Chapter 16). While we haven't seen many of these lately, they still pop up from time to time, especially in antique and estate jewelry. A true diamond doublet is made by taking a genuine diamond top (crown) and gluing it to a genuine diamond bottom (pavilion). The diamond tester will indicate that the stone is genuine because the material being tested is diamond. This is why it's called a true doublet—it is actually made from genuine pieces of the stone it is imitating. The diamond tester cannot tell you it's a doublet. Again, review the section on doublets so you can make this determination yourself.

Beware of false positive readings on colorless corundum (sapphire) and synthetic colorless corundum, and colorless zircon. While usually reliable in separating diamond from convincing imitations that closely resemble diamond because of their very high refractive indices (such as CZ), some electronic diamond testers are failing to distinguish between diamond, colorless sapphire, and natural zircon, providing a false "positive": that is, **the tester may erroneously indicate "*diamond*."**

Colorless zircon can usually be quickly separated from diamond using only a loupe since it is so strongly double-refracting. As a result, when you look at the stone with the loupe, looking down at the back facet edges from the top, through the table, the edges show *doubling.* In other words, instead of seeing a single, sharp edge, it will be as though you are looking at closely laid "railroad tracks." Take a stone you know to be a diamond and look at it in this way, and then do the same thing with a stone you know to be zircon, and you'll see what we mean.

Colorless sapphire has a much lower refractive index and, thus, lacks the "sparkle" and "brilliance" of diamond. With experience, your eye will probably recognize the difference. If you are unsure, the ultraviolet lamp is probably the fastest way to know the stone is not diamond, and the polariscope or refractometer will also quickly tell you whether or not you have diamond. With the ultraviolet lamp, sapphire will fluoresce strong whitish or milky blue-white under *short*wave and exhibit little if any fluorescence under longwave—just the reverse of diamond. Diamond may not show any fluorescence, but when it does, it fluoresces under *long*wave and its fluorescence becomes *weaker under shortwave.*

Since sapphire is double-refracting and has a refractive index that can be read on any standard refractometer, it can also be quickly separated from diamond with the refractometer or polariscope. With the polariscope, sapphire will "blink" while diamond won't (see Chapter 11). With the refractometer, corundum will give you a clear reading (1.76–1.77) whereas diamond will give no reading at all because its R.I. is higher than the scale on the refractometer (see Chapter 8).

When the electronic diamond tester indicates "diamond," check further. When properly used, a negative response is usually reliable. However, when the tester indicates the stone *is* diamond, we recommend additional testing. In addition to colorless sapphire and zircon, the new diamond imitation, *synthetic moissanite*, is reported to "fool electronic diamond testers."

ELECTRONIC DUAL TESTER SEPARATES SYNTHETIC MOISSANITE FROM DIAMOND

A new diamond imitation sold today under the name moissanite or synthetic moissanite has created new challenges in the jewelry marketplace. Found increasingly in antique and estate jewelry, misrepresented as diamond, its physical characteristics result in a false positive when tested with standard electronic thermal conductivity diamond testers.

Synthetic moissanite is silicon carbide, named after Dr. Moissan, the French scientist who discovered it. Before the introduction of synthetic moissanite, the standard electronic tester, which is based on thermal conductivity (how it conducts heat), could separate CZ and other diamond imitations from diamond. But when testing synthetic moissanite, thermal conductivity testers are unable to distinguish between diamond and synthetic moissanite and indicate "diamond." Because of this, many people initially concluded that moissanite was indistinguishable from diamond, but this is far from the case.

Gemologists can quickly and easily separate diamond from synthetic moissanite with simple tests, in most cases using only a 10x loupe. Viewing the facet joins of the pavilion with the loupe, examining them through the table, on a diagonal, you will notice strong doubling because moissanite is so strongly double-refracting. With the loupe you may also see long, white, needle-like inclusions never seen in diamond. Synthetic moissanite is lighter than diamond, so weighing it is a quick way to separate it from diamond if the stone is unmounted. It also has even greater brilliance, and much more dispersion (fire), than either diamond or CZ, and so it may not look quite right to the discerning eye. And, despite efforts to create a truly colorless imitation, most synthetic moissanite will exhibit a slight grayish/greenish cast when viewed against flat white.

For the novice, however, especially when stones are mounted in intricate settings or when examining stones in less-than-ideal conditions, synthetic moissanite might pose a problem. So a new type of electronic diamond tester was created: the *dual tester*. Diamond and synthetic moissanite cannot be separated by standard electronic testers measuring thermal conductivity, but they can be separated by *electrical* conductivity. The dual tester performs two separate tests, in a matter of seconds: one for thermal conductivity (which separates diamond from CZ and other diamond imitations except synthetic moissanite), followed immediately by a test for *electrical conductivity* (which then separates synthetic moissanite from diamond).

Dual testers operate in essentially the same way as the standard electronic tester, but reactions may vary between manufacturers so you must read the manufacturers' instructions to make sure you understand how to interpret the results.

When using electronic diamond testers, just keep in mind that colorless sapphire, zircon, and synthetic moissanite may not be the only gems to receive a false positive. As we have said repeatedly, where positive gem identification is concerned, relying on the results of a single test can result in a costly mistake and this is certainly true with some electronic diamond testers.

DiamondNite Dual Tester

NOTES

A Foil-backed "Pink" Topaz Necklace

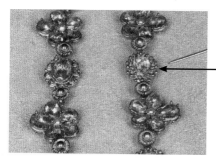

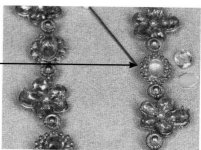

Foil-backed pink topaz necklace

Notice the pink foil that has been removed and the *colorless* topaz alongside.

Notice the back of the necklace is *closed*—the gold completely conceals the backs of the stones themselves. Also, notice the gold on the back of the left-hand stone is smooth and unbroken while the gold on the back of the other stone has a V-shaped crack. The crack allows air to enter, which oxidizes the foil and causes it to change color.

Notice the stone on the left is a distinctly different shade of color from other stones in the necklace. This has resulted from oxidation.

PHOTOS: E. MORGAN

Lead-Glass Composite Rubies

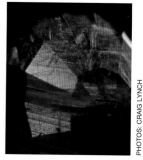

PHOTOS: CRAIG LYNCH

Rounded bubbles in lead-glass ruby. Usually seen throughout the stone.

Surface crazing seen in reflected light.

Blue flashes seen in intense transmitted light.

ANGSTROM UNITS

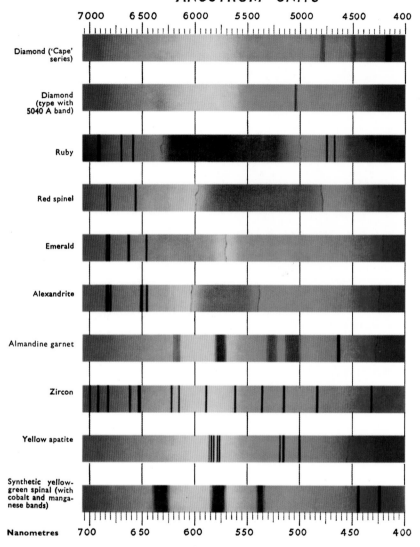

Absorption spectra of gemstones.
Note that the scales are shown linear, as with a diffraction-grating spectroscope.

ANGSTROM UNITS

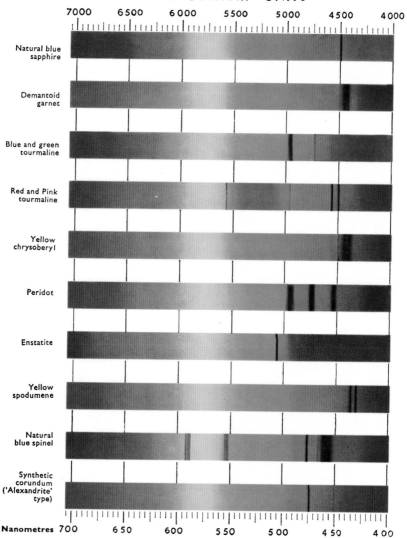

Absorption spectra of gemstones.
The scales here are linear, not condensed toward the red end as with a
prism-type spectroscope.

Reproduced from *Gemmologists' Compendium* by Robert Webster, FGA
(N.A.G. Press Ltd., England).

Some Diamond Inclusions & Blemishes Seen with Magnification
INCLUSIONS

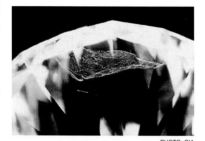

PHOTO: GIA

A cloud-like inclusion in a diamond

PHOTO: RON YEHUDA, YEHUDA DIAMOND CO.

"Flash effect" in a fracture-filled diamond, seen with dark-field illumination

PHOTO: GIA

"Reflector" inclusions, showing same inclusions reflected many times

PHOTO: D. JAFFE, AMERICAN GEMOLOGICAL LABORATORIES

A feather

PHOTO: GIA

Cleavage

PHOTO: GIA

Bearded girdle or girdle fringe

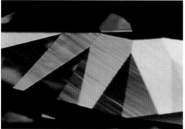

PHOTO: B. KANE, GIA

Graining

PHOTO: GIA

Surface graining

Laser drill holes

A knaat in table facet

Inclusions before laser drilling

Inclusions after laser drilling

BLEMISHES

Natural on the girdle

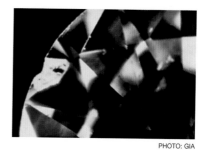

Nick or chip on girdle

Twinning

Scratch on table facet

Some Inclusions Seen in Colored Gems with Magnification

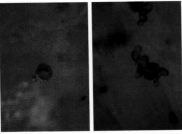

L: Pyrite crystal characteristic of ruby from Kashmir (Asad Kashmir).
R: Crystal cluster, probably apatite, in Kashmir ruby

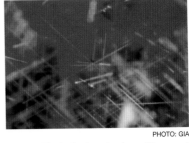

Needle-like inclusions in almandite garnet

Growth tubes in aquamarine

Needle-like inclusions of rutile in quartz

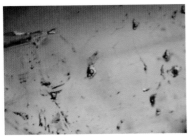

Two-phase inclusions (liquid & gas) in tourmaline

Three-phase inclusions in beryl

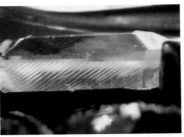

"Venetian-blind" inclusion. Seen in green, yellow and brown zircon

Fingerprint inclusion in almandite garnet

Inclusions in Colored Gems continued

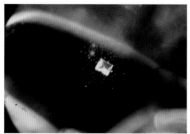

PHOTO: J. KOIVULA, GIA

One large and many tiny octahedra in spinel

PHOTO: R. BUCY, COLUMBIA SCHOOL OF GEMOLOGY

Curved striae in synthetic sapphire

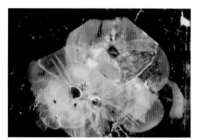

PHOTO: GIA

Halos in natural Thai ruby

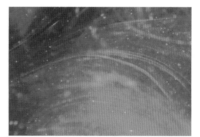

PHOTO: GIA

Swirl lines in glass

PHOTO: R. BUCY, COLUMBIA SCHOOL OF GEMOLOGY

Halo inclusion seen in peridot, resembling a lilypad

PHOTO: AMERICAN GEMOLOGICAL LABORATORIES

Disc-like inclusion in sapphire

PHOTO: GIA

"Rain" seen in Kashan synthetic ruby

PHOTO: R. BUCY, COLUMBIA SCHOOL OF GEMOLOGY

Profilated bubbles in synthetic ruby

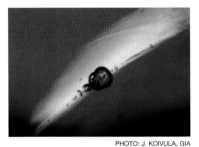

PHOTO: J. KOIVULA, GIA

Gas bubbles in man-made glass

PHOTO: GIA

Bubble with tail in YAG

PHOTO: B. KANE, GIA

White, wispy veils in flux-grown Chatham synthetic sapphire

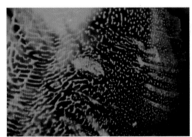

PHOTO: GIA

Flux fingerprint in synthetic emerald

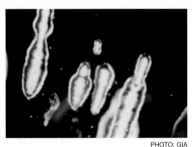

PHOTO: GIA

Semi-profilated gas bubbles in synthetic spinel

PHOTO: GIA

Color zoning in amethyst

PHOTO: R. BUCY, COLUMBIA SCHOOL OF GEMOLOGY

Zoning in sapphire

PHOTO: R. BUCY, COLUMBIA SCHOOL OF GEMOLOGY

Two-phase inclusion in beryl

PHOTO: D. JAFFE, AMERICAN GEMOLOGICAL LABORATORIES
Two-phase inclusions in emerald

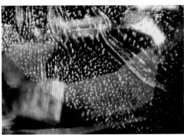

PHOTO: J. KOIVULA, GIA
Fingerprint inclusion in chrysoberyl (60X)

PHOTO: J. KOIVULA, GIA
Lilypad-shaped halos with negative crystal at center, in peridot (45X)

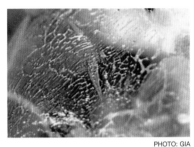

PHOTO: GIA
Healing-feather or liquid-filled inclusion in sapphire

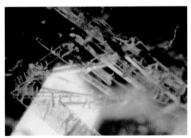

PHOTO: J. KOIVULA, GIA
Lath-like crystals of actinolite in emerald

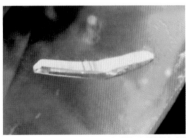

PHOTO: J. KOIVULA, GIA
Rare negative crystal in sapphire

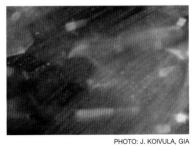

PHOTO: J. KOIVULA, GIA
"Rain" seen in Kashan synthetic ruby (40X)

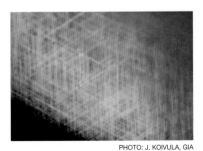

PHOTO: J. KOIVULA, GIA
"Silk" in natural sapphire. Notice needles intersecting at 60 degrees

PHOTO: R. BUCY, COLUMBIA SCHOOL OF GEMOLOGY

Solid crystal inclusion of pyrite in emerald

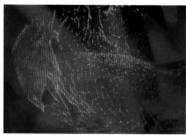

PHOTO: GIA

Flux fingerprint in Chatham synthetic ruby (50X)

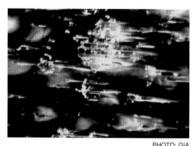

PHOTO: GIA

Nail-head inclusions in Linde synthetic emerald

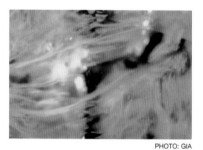

PHOTO: GIA

Veins seen in flux-grown synthetic emerald

PHOTO: R. BUCY, COLUMBIA SCHOOL OF GEMOLOGY

Three-phase inclusions in natural Colombian emerald

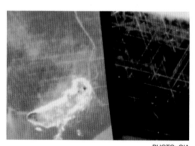

PHOTO: GIA

Needle-like inclusions in two natural rubies

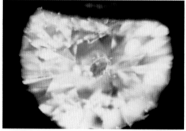

PHOTO: R. WELDON, GIA

Red garnet crystal in diamond

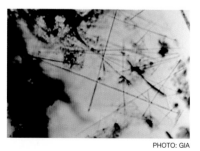

PHOTO: GIA

Tremolite needles in emerald from Sandewana

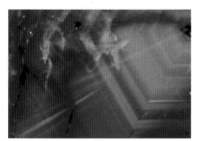

PHOTO: B. KANE, GIA

Zoning in sapphire

PHOTO: J. KOIVULA, GIA

Flux-grown inclusion, occasionally seen in pink sapphire

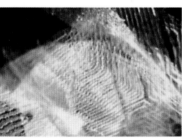

PHOTO: R. BUCY, COLUMBIA SCHOOL OF GEMOLOGY

Inclusions of byssolite in demantoid (andradite) garnet. Typical "horse-tail" inclusion

PHOTO: GIA

Snakes in amethyst

PHOTO: R. BUCY, COLUMBIA SCHOOL OF GEMOLOGY

"Zebra stripes" in amethyst caused by micro-twinning

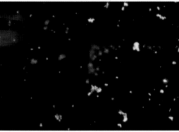

PHOTO: D. HARGETT, GIA

Fine crumbs, like breadcrumbs, in synthetic amethyst (45X)

PHOTO: J. KOIVULA, GIA

Mica in emerald

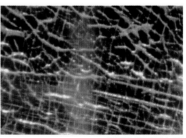

PHOTO: J. KOIVULA, GIA

Crazing seen on surface in Lechleitner synthetic emerald-coated beryl

Other Identifying Features

Fracture-filled emerald where *filler* is *fluorescing* when examined with an ultraviolet lamp, showing extent of treatment—only one small fissure

Left: Natural sapphire showing typical color zones. Right: Darkened girdle edges and facet joins create "web" effect in diffused sapphire

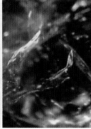

Orangey-yellow flash seen in epoxy-resin-filled emerald. Blue flash is also indicative of epoxy resin

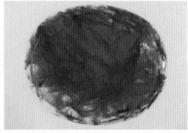

Corundum that has been artifically *stained* red

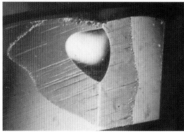

Ruby with a glass-filled chip. Note the difference in the surface luster where the glass is present

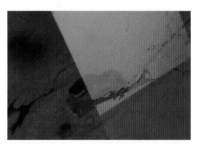

Fracture-filled ruby. Note difference in surface luster where glass reaches surface; also, tubes and channels from fracture are visible behind glass filler

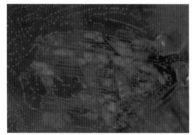

Heat- and glass-treated ruby showing groups of radiating whitish crystals in the glassy substance

Distinctive pattern of fluorescence typical of synthetic diamonds

15 / The carbide scriber—
An essential *tool for diamond buyers*

"Colorless diamonds" in the D–H color range are more costly today than ever before, and fancy-color diamonds are all the rage, in every color. Natural-color yellow and brown diamonds are in high demand, and demand is growing for rare, costly colors such as pink and blue. Such stones in larger sizes may be too costly for most people, but the market is hot for natural-color melee, not only in black, brown, and yellow, but also in rarer, costlier colors. But as in all things, as popularity, demand, and value rise, so does the need to be extra cautious to avoid buying something that isn't what it appears to be. While most diamonds today have laboratory documentation if they are ¾-carat or larger (and in the rarest colors, even in ¼-carat sizes you will find lab documentation), this is not the case with less rare colors or in melee sizes. So the risk is much greater.

When buying any colorless or fancy-color diamond, especially in smaller sizes, extreme caution must be used today because many "colorless" and "fancy-color" diamonds are being *created* through the application of *surface coatings* and sometimes sold without disclosure. **These surface coatings do not produce permanent results and the color can be removed or change over time.** The situation is further complicated because people are aware of "treated color" diamonds, and they are an accepted and attractive alternative for many. However, most people—consumers and those in the trade alike—assume that fancy-color diamond treatments can be grouped together in terms of "permanence" and "value" and this is not the case; coated diamonds sell for less than diamonds treated by other techniques that produce permanent results. So when buying treated-color diamonds, buyers need to know *what type of treatment has been used.* This, however, poses a dilemma because many dealers do not know themselves, and retailers are often misinformed by their vendors. So it is essential that *you* know how to detect surface coatings, or if not, that you retain the services of a gemologist.

There are numerous tests a gemologist can perform in a laboratory, such as boiling in sulphuric acid (which will remove the coating quickly and reveal the true color), but this is not practical in a retail environment, and other tests for detecting coatings require gemological training and a well-equipped lab. It is not feasible to send every small diamond to a lab, or diamonds in affordable champagne or pale yellow colors, but fortunately, there is an easy, quick, and affordable technique that anyone can master: using a carbide scriber. By taking a carbide scriber—a simple tool that looks like a pen—and dragging its carbide point across one of the facets, the point will scratch through the coating. A carbide scriber will *not scratch the diamond* but it will scratch through the coatings used to alter the color, and the scratch can then be seen immediately, often with the unaided eye, but certainly with a 10X loupe. (Note: It must be a *"tungsten carbide"* scriber which is much harder than scribers made from steel or other materials—see page 29.)

In the case of the fancy-colored diamonds, the surface-coated diamonds are coated *on the pavilion only* (the bottom portion of the stone) and so only the pavilion needs to be checked. Most colorless diamonds (once referred to as "painted" diamonds) have surface coatings that have been applied to the entire stone, or to the pavilion or crown, and the carbide scriber is ideal for detecting them as well as surface-coated fancy-color diamonds, but you must check the crown (top portion of the stone) as well as the pavilion. In some rare cases, colorless diamonds have been "painted" only around the girdle, but in this case, examination with a loupe or microscope will reveal "brush strokes" in the area of the girdle.

We recommend using a carbide scriber to check *any* diamond being bought or sold without laboratory documentation. We also recommend buying diamonds only from a reputable source in order to reduce the risk of buying a diamond accompanied by a counterfeit report from GIA or other respected lab.

Using a carbide scriber to test a crown facet and pavilion facet is not difficult or time-consuming. If the scriber scratches the surface of the diamond, it is definitely coated. (Note: In the case of colorless diamonds, we recommend checking facets on the crown and pavilion as the first step, and, if no evidence of coating is seen, then examine the girdle area with magnification—if the stone is one that has a painted girdle, you will see brush strokes around the girdle, from the actual brush used to paint the girdle. However, if the coating has been applied to the entire stone, or across the pavilion or crown, you will *not* see any brush strokes with magnification because a different technique is used to apply coatings to the larger crown/pavilion areas. Be sure to test with the scriber first).

HOW TO USE THE CARBIDE SCRIBER

Testing with a carbide scriber requires no gemological training. It is quick and easy. Here's how to do it:

1. You must make sure you are testing a diamond and not a diamond imitation such as CZ.
2. The scriber must be a *carbide scriber* (see page 29). There are different types of "scribers" available, depending upon the type of material you are testing. Make sure that the scriber you use is not stainless steel; only a tungsten carbide scriber will scratch through the surface coatings used to enhance diamonds.
3. If using a scriber with a fixed point, be especially careful when handling the scriber to avoid dropping it; carbide is very hard, but it is also brittle and the point can break if you drop it and it lands point-first on a hard surface. If using a scriber with a "replaceable point" the point is usually stored inside the shaft of the scriber to protect it; remove the point and follow the instructions that come with the scriber for inserting and securing it.
4. Hold the diamond, or piece of jewelry, in a way to ensure a firm grip and then drag the carbide point across a facet with a fair degree of pressure. Start with a facet on the pavilion.
   a. Examine the facet. Does it appear to have a scratch where you just dragged the scriber across the surface? If so, the stone is coated.

b. If there was no scratch, repeat the process on a table facet. If there is a scratch, the stone is coated.

5. Where colored diamonds are concerned, no scratch on the pavilion or table indicates it is not surface-coated. (NOTE: This indicates the color is not the result of surface coating, but the color may be the result of a more stable type of treatment such as radiation—this test does not confirm natural color. To confirm that color is natural usually requires testing with sophisticated equipment available only at a major gem testing laboratory.)

6. If testing a colorless diamond, if there are no scratches on the pavilion or table, examine the girdle area with the microscope to search for brush strokes. If there are no brush strokes, the diamond is not coated.

CAUTION: DO NOT USE A CARBIDE SCRIBER ON ANY GEMSTONE EXCEPT DIAMOND. THE CARBIDE POINT IS EXTREMELY HARD AND WILL SCRATCH ALL OTHER GEMSTONES.

NOTES

16 / The "synthetic diamond detectors"

Photo: Prof. H. Hänni, SSEF

Synthetic diamonds are not new, but the availability of gem-quality synthetic diamonds on a commercial scale, at an affordable cost, *is* new. Synthetic diamonds were first produced by General Electric in the 1950s, but technology was not available then to make production feasible. Today that has changed and numerous companies such as Sumitomo Electric Industries in Japan, DeBeers Research Laboratory, several Russian laboratories, and General Electric are actively involved in synthesizing gem-quality diamonds.

Synthetic diamonds in "gem" quality (as opposed to "industrial" quality, which have been synthesized on a large scale for years) are soon going to be a much larger factor in the jewelry marketplace than ever before, or ever expected. Synthetic diamonds are now available not only in shades of yellow or tinted white, but in fancy blue and pink, and colorless and near-colorless. We have seen the greatest progress in the near-colorless to colorless ranges, and diamonds that compare to a GIA color grade of "E" color have been seen, with clarity in GIA's VS range in sizes over 3/4 carat. New techniques could produce more stones in the colorless range, including D-color. In terms of size, most are small (under 1/2 carat), but crystals up to two carats have been produced so polished diamonds of one carat or more are possible.

With synthetic diamonds entering the market, anyone buying or selling diamonds must be able to separate the synthetic from the natural. All synthetic diamonds can be identified using routine gemological tests, and we have already mentioned some of the distinguishing characteristics using the loupe, microscope or ultra-violet lamp. With regard to colorless and near-colorless diamonds, as discussed in Chapter 12, pre-screening for Type I versus Type II will normally reassure you that a colorless diamond is *not* synthetic and will red-flag stones that need to be submitted to a major lab to know for sure. Being able to spot them quickly and easily, however, will become increasingly important.

Several very sophisticated pieces of equipment have been produced by DeBeers, *DiamondSure* and *DiamondView*, and other laboratories are working on other equipment that will aid in synthetic diamond detection. With these latest two, the DiamondSure is used first. It uses a specially designed probe to seek the 415 absorption band we look for with the spectroscope (as we mentioned earlier, this band is seen in 95% of natural diamonds, but *never* in synthetic); the DiamondSure can check 10–15 stones per minute. If a diamond is natural, it will read "pass"; if it doesn't "pass," it will say "refer to other tests." If you are referred to further tests, you proceed to the DiamondView. The DiamondView examines the fluorescence pattern, and has been tested on stones made by Russian labs, DeBeers, Sumitomo, and GE. The test has proven 100% accurate with all diamonds tested to date—including yellow, colorless, and even blue.

The cost of these new instruments is not known, but they are likely to be expensive. Nonetheless, for those who must frequently sort through large quantities of diamonds, quickly, they may prove to be a very worthwhile investment.

MAGNETISM CAN BE A TELLTALE SIGN OF SYNTHETIC

For most people, however, these sophisticated synthetic diamond detectors are costly and lack of portability makes them impractical in many cases. Furthermore, in many cases they are not necessary. In fact, one distinguishing characteristic of many synthetic diamonds (except blue)—*magnetism*—can provide a very simple, fast, and con-clusive identification technique. This characteristic, being attracted to a strong magnet, gives us one of the most reliable tests for a synthetic diamond *when magnetism is present*. Many of the earliest synthetic diamonds had a magnetic property, although today this is not the case. Nonetheless, if present, it is immediately diagnostic.

The magnet required for testing diamonds, however, is not your normal magnet. As mentioned earlier, it is a neodymium boron iron magnet (known as a "rare earth" magnet) which is notable for its incredible magnetic strength. Because of its strength, you need only a very tiny magnet, such as Hanneman's "Magnetic Synthetic Diamond Wand" (a match-size wooden stick with a rare-earth magnet attached to one end). *It should be noted, however, that these tiny magnets can pose a serious risk to anyone wearing a PACEMAKER or other similar life-saving device, and should not be used by, or near, anyone wearing such devices. One should also not use this type of magnet near computer equipment or disks.*

To use the rare earth magnet, place the diamond so that it is *pavilion down* on a slippery surface, such as a glossy magazine cover (do *not* place the diamond *table*-down). Simply hold the magnet near the diamond at about a 30° angle and watch what happens. *If the diamond is drawn to the magnet, it IS synthetic.* In some cases, the diamond will actually jump up to the magnet! In other cases where the diamond is less magnetic, the stone may not jump up to the magnet, but you may be able to *drag it* along the slippery surface using the magnetic pull of the wand.

[NOTE: This applies to "gem" diamonds only, that is, diamonds above I-3 clarity. Heavily included, industrial quality *natural* diamonds may be drawn to the magnet because the *inclusions* themselves may be magnetic.]

Checking a Mounted Diamond for Magnetism

It is very easy to check for magnetism when a diamond is unmounted, but often this is not the case. When the stone is mounted, it may be a little more difficult to check, but not impossible. If the mounted stone is strongly magnetic, placing the magnet close to the diamond and using it as a "pull" may cause the jewelry to move across the slippery surface; if it does, you know it is highly magnetic, and synthetic. Another technique is to place the piece of jewelry on a small piece of thin styrofoam, about 2 inches in diameter, and set the styrofoam "island" in a small basin of water (the water should be just deep enough to support the piece and keep it afloat). Now use the magnet. If you can pull the styrofoam island around the basin, the diamond is magnetic, and synthetic.

With the exception of industrial quality diamonds, whenever a diamond is drawn to the magnet, it is positive confirmation that the stone is synthetic.

Some of the newer synthetic diamonds do *not* possess magnetic properties. This means that if the diamond you are examining does *not* react to the magnet, this test is inconclusive; you cannot draw any conclusion without further testing. If the diamond does *not* react to the magnet you must examine it carefully with the loupe, microscope, spectroscope and ultraviolet lamp to be sure (see earlier chapters on these instruments and what they will show when testing diamonds and synthetic diamonds). If still in doubt, submit the stone to a gem testing laboratory.

Despite the fact that most synthetic diamonds today do not possess magnetic properties, testing for magnetism is a valuable and useful test because some do, and this test is reliable when the diamond *does* respond; it is confirmation of synthetic.

A longwave/shortwave ultraviolet lamp and "rare earth magnetic wand"—tools for quick and easy detection of some colorless synthetic diamonds

NOTES

PART 5
ANTIQUE AND ESTATE JEWELRY

17 / Antique and estate jewelry—the true test of gem identification skill

More and more, jewelry lovers have begun to focus on antique and estate jewelry. It has become an important new profit center for many jewelry firms, as well as a growing passion for jewelry collectors. Retailers and gem enthusiasts alike are travelling greater distances and paying higher prices so they can add that unique piece to their collection.

Recent record-breaking sales at auction houses such as Christie's and Sotheby's reflect the trend. We have also noticed an increase in the number of retailers offering antique and estate jewelry, as well as more exhibitors of antique and estate pieces at international gem and jewelry exhibitions, antique shows, and flea markets.

We share the current enthusiasm for antique and period jewelry. But as we examine many of these pieces, we are reminded of the ingenuity of our predecessors—ingenuity not only in design, but in the art of creating pieces that *appear to be something they are not.*

For the gem "detective," antique and estate jewelry offers a real testing ground for your skill. Don't be surprised to find imitation stones in beautiful gold or platinum settings, and synthetic stones in pieces made prior to the production of synthetic gems. Never assume that because something is old, or belonged to the best of families or most endeared of relatives, that it is what it appears to be. As you will see, often this is not the case.

In this chapter we will discuss some of the imitation and alteration techniques frequently encountered in antique and period jewelry. Anyone identifying stones in old jewelry should be on the lookout for them.

ENHANCEMENT TECHNIQUES

Dyeing

Dyeing is one of the oldest techniques used to enhance stones for jewelry. It has been practiced since earliest times, particularly with the less expensive gemstone called chalcedony (a variety of quartz). Other stones frequently dyed are jade, opal, coral, lapis, and, to a lesser extent, poor-quality star rubies, star sapphires, and emeralds.

What follows is a list of stones often found dyed in antique jewelry (some of these stones have been subjected to dyeing for hundreds of years; others are of more recent vintage but find their way into antique pieces to replace lost or damaged stones).

Chalcedony. Dyed to produce stones that look like black onyx, banded agate, carnelian, and chrysoprase (which was often mistaken for jade). It is often found in antique jewelry.

Jade (Jadeite). Dyed to improve the color so that it resembles the beautiful emerald-green of imperial jade. It is also dyed colors other than green.

Coral and Lapis. Dyed to deepen the color or create more uniform color.

Jasper. Dyed blue to resemble lapis and often sold as lapis, Swiss lapis, or German lapis.

Blackening

Blackening is a technique also used to alter color. It is done by starting a sugar-acid chemical reaction that produces carbon to blacken the color. This technique was used primarily with opal, to blacken it so it more closely resembled valuable black opal. This technique was also used on chalcedony to create "black onyx." Blackening of opal can be detected with the loupe or microscope because magnification reveals fine pinholes on the polished surface. With black onyx, however, there is no way to detect this treatment.

Smoking

Smoking is a technique used only for opal. An opal is wrapped in brown paper that is then charred. The charred paper deposits a thin dark brown coating on the opal to intensify its fire (the play of color that makes opal so desirable). This thin coating, however, eventually wears off. Normally such opals are easy to spot because they have a chocolate brown appearance not common to opal. If you suspect smoking, it can be detected simply by wetting the stone and observing the fire. In smoked opals the fire is diminished when wet, but returns when dry. Natural opals show essentially the same brilliance wet or dry.

Waxing

Waxing is a process used to enhance poor quality star rubies and, occasionally, star sapphires. It involves rubbing the stone with a tinted waxlike substance to hide surface cracks and blemishes and to improve color.

Waxing is detectable with a loupe or microscope.

Foil Backing and Diamond Jewelry

Foil backing is one of the most clever techniques from the olden days and, occasionally, even today. It was often used with stones that were set in closed-back settings (where you can't see the back of the stone). The technique simply involved lining the setting with a piece of colored metallic foil, and was used both for transparent cabochon stones and faceted stones. The foil was used to add brilliance and enhance or change the color.

Early diamond jewelry was sometimes foil backed to enhance the brilliance of the stones. Before diamond cutters perfected their art, diamonds lacked the brilliance we see today. By adding foil to the setting, the jeweler could add greater sparkle to the stones. Silver-foil backing was also used to mask the yellow in a diamond's body color, making the stone appear whiter.

In such pieces, the stones are genuine and the foil backing was used simply to enhance their beauty and desirability. When it comes to some of these early antique pieces, the diamond value is usually minimal, although it is really impossible to evaluate them properly without removing them from the setting. In most cases, however, removing them isn't advised because damage to the setting might reduce the value of the piece as a work of art. Careful consideration should always be given prior to removing stones from foil-backed settings.

Foil backing was not restricted to enhancement of genuine diamonds. It was more commonly used (and is still occasionally encountered in new jewelry) to create attractive imitations. When foil was placed behind glass or some other less valuable stone (such as colorless sapphire or topaz), it produced a clever imitation of diamond.

Several years ago, a young woman brought us a diamond ring inherited from her great-grandmother. It turned out, unfortunately, to be an excellent example of foil backing. As she unwrapped the ring from the handkerchief in which it was placed, she mentioned that one of its two diamonds had fallen out of the setting as she was cleaning it. Inside the setting she saw what she described as pieces of "tiny, mirror-like" fragments. She commented on how strange this was, but, unfortunately, it isn't as strange as most people think.

When we saw the ring we could immediately understand why she thought it was a fine heirloom. The ring was beautiful. Its design was classic. It held two "diamonds" appearing to be approximately one carat each. The ring mounting was finely worked platinum. But, alas, the stones were glass. The mirror-like fragments were pieces of silver foil. The foil acted as a mirror to reflect light back from the glass to the eye of the observer, causing the glass to appear brilliant enough to pass for genuine diamond!

Piggy-Backing—The Foil-Backing Master's Art.

Sometimes the foil backing had a special touch—the addition of a genuine diamond table and culet. The cleverest fake of all used foil backing in combination with a genuine diamond top and bottom—*with nothing but foil in between the two parts.* This is called piggy-backing. It is a very ingenious device to create the illusion that a diamond is larger than it really is. There are two types of piggy-backing.

In the first type, a small genuine diamond is set into the top portion of a ring. The mounting is constructed with a wide box-like bezel or rim that begins at the girdle and follows what should be the contour of the diamond down the pavilion to a small opening through which the culet can be observed. The top portion of the diamond is genuine and the culet is also genuine. But there is nothing between the top piece of diamond and the bottom piece except foil lining the setting. It is hollow!

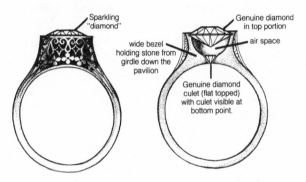

"Piggy back" diamond ring. As you can see from the cross-section, a *small* diamond sits in the very top, and a *small* diamond sits in the bottom, with only air in-between. Sometimes foil lines the inside of the bezel as well. An ingenious way to create a large diamond look!

The second method is often seen in jewelry using rose-cut diamonds and is also intended to make the stones appear deeper and heavier than they are. This method involves stamping the back of a closed-back setting with a *perfectly symmetrical facet pattern*. The back is painted with silver gilt. The diamond is mounted into the top of the setting—with nothing but air between it and the stamped back.

We recently examined an antique piece containing eight rose-cut diamonds. Keep in mind that there are different types of rose-cuts— some have a flat bottom (single-rose-cut); others have a bottom portion cut like the top portion (double-rose-cut). When we viewed this antique piece from the top, the diamonds all appeared to be lovely, large, *double-rose-cut* stones. However, they were not. What appeared to be depth—a bottom portion—was actually an optical illusion created by the gilt-covered, stamped back.

This latter method is easy to detect with a loupe. The first clue is the completely closed back. On careful examination of both the back facets and the top facets you will see something very curious. You will notice that *all* the back facets are *perfectly* symmetrical while the top facets are more or less *asymmetrical*. This occurs because the back facets aren't really facets, but a gilt imprint resulting from the precise machine-stamping. This is why it's so perfectly uniform. The top facets, however, are done very sloppily (they didn't merit careful cutting). In the antique piece we examined, we could see that all the back facets, in each of the eight rose-cuts, were perfectly symmetrical while the top facets weren't symmetrical at all. In such pieces, this is always the case—sloppy symmetry on the top facets and perfect symmetry on the bottom facets.

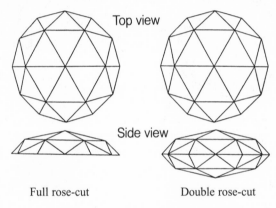

Top view

Side view

Full rose-cut   Double rose-cut

Foil Backing and Colored Gems

Foil backing was not restricted to diamond jewelry. It was frequently used with colored gems (and occasionally still is). We actually see more examples of foil backing in colored gemstone jewelry than in diamond jewelry. It served essentially the same purpose—to enhance brilliance and color, and to create clever imitations.

Sometimes foil was used (silver and gold were both common) simply to increase the brilliance and sparkle of the stones, or, in some cases, to lighten the appearance of stones that looked too dark in the setting. But more often than not, in colored gemstone jewelry the foil itself was *colored*. Coloring the foil added greater depth of color to a stone that was too light, and, when used with a colorless gem, could create any color gemstone desired. In antique jewelry one can find examples of colored foil used with glass; colored foil used with pale stones to deepen color; and colored foil used with colorless stones to add color.

Several years ago we purchased an antique necklace from a New York auction gallery (see color photos in center of this book). The necklace was described in bold print as an "antique 22 karat gold and topaz necklace." In the further description of the piece, provided in small print, it stated the necklace dated about 1810 and contained "pink topaz."

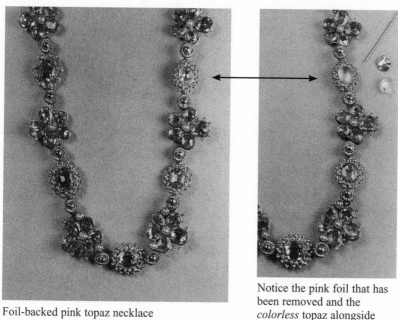

Foil-backed pink topaz necklace

Notice the pink foil that has been removed and the *colorless* topaz alongside

In examining the stone, it gave all the indicators of genuine topaz. It was also obvious (as you will understand in a moment) that the piece was foil backed. The unanswered question was, What is the true color of the topaz? Of course, there was no way to answer the question without removing the stones, which was not possible under the circumstances. We purchased the necklace at a price we felt reflected the value of the gold, pearls, and workmanship and discounted the stones altogether.

After purchasing the necklace we removed one of the stones. The stones were topaz, but not rare, valuable "pink" topaz. They were common, very inexpensive, colorless topaz that appeared pink because pink foil had been placed behind each stone.

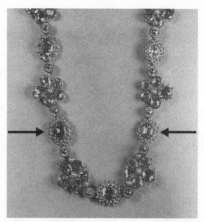

Notice the back of the necklace is *closed*—the gold completely conceals the backs of the stones themselves. Also, notice the gold on the back of the left-hand stone is smooth and unbroken while the gold on the back of the other stone has a "V"-shaped crack. The crack allows air to enter, which oxidizes the foil and causes it to change color.

Notice the stone on the left is a distinctly different shade of color than other stones in the necklace. This has resulted from oxidation.

This is not always the case. We've seen magnificent closed-back pieces that contain rich, deeply colored pink topazes (and other gems as well) that are indeed natural color. The golden reflections from the closed backs sometimes brighten the stones, but often the setting simply reflects the style of the day.

Spotting a Foil-Backed Stone

This usually requires only a good eye. The first clue will be the fact that the back of the setting will be closed. While not all closed-back settings conceal some form of deception, many do. One should always examine stones set in closed-back settings with extreme care. While gently tilting the setting back and forth, carefully look through the stone at the back facets. Use a strong, direct light such as a fiber-optic light or penlight. It is usually easy to spot the light reflecting off the foil—it will look different from a stone's natural reflectivity. Also, where colored foil has been used, you may be able to observe slight variations in the color of the foil itself. Discoloration will take place if for some reason air has reached the foil and caused it to oxidize (if, for example, there is a hairline crack in the backing or in the bezel holding the stone). With a loupe, one can usually spot the foil immediately, as well as the reflectivity differences and color inconsistencies. However, sometimes it is necessary to use a microscope.

Once you determine the presence of foil backing, you must use your other gemological skills to determine whether the stone in question is glass or genuine, and, if genuine, whether it is the stone it appears to be or one from another gem family. Finally, you must determine whether the color has been enhanced by the foil. If the stone can't be removed without damage to the setting, this may pose a problem. A dichroscope can be useful in this situation (see Chapter 6). In the case of our pink topaz necklace, for example, the dichroscope could have told us immediately that it didn't contain pink topaz. Pink topaz will show two distinctly different shades of pink when examined with the dichroscope; colorless topaz will show only one.

The depth of color seen with the dichroscope can also be helpful. For example, if "emerald" is created by using *pale* emerald and deep green foil to enhance its color and value, the dichroism—the colors seen in the windows of the dichroscope—will be *weak*. However, genuine deep green emerald would have a strong dichroism—the colors seen in the dichroscope will be deeper. The depth of color seen with the dichroscope reflects the depth of the color in the gem being viewed. So, if the color seen in the piece is deep, but the colors seen with the dichroscope are weak, you should be immediately suspicious.

No one interested in buying and selling antique and estate jewelry can afford to make an assumption based on appearance and superficial examination!

COMPOSITE STONES— DOUBLETS AND TRIPLETS

Composite stones were used extensively prior to the introduction of synthetic material. Simply stated, a composite stone is exactly what its name implies, a stone composed or made up of more than one part. A composite stone is any stone created by the fusing or cementing together of two or more pieces of material. When two main pieces are joined together we call them "doublets," and when three pieces are joined together we call them "triplets."

There are, however, some differences in terminology. The soudé type composite is called a "doublet" in Europe and a "triplet" in

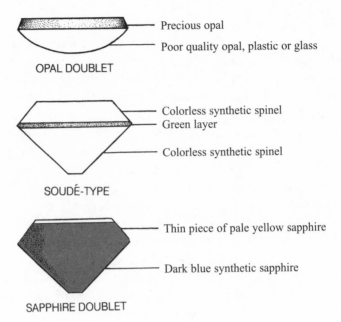

OPAL DOUBLET
— Precious opal
— Poor quality opal, plastic or glass

SOUDÉ-TYPE
— Colorless synthetic spinel
— Green layer
— Colorless synthetic spinel

SAPPHIRE DOUBLET
— Thin piece of pale yellow sapphire
— Dark blue synthetic sapphire

Composite stones (also called assembled stones)

America, probably because there is disagreement over whether or not the layer of colored gelatin or glass that lays across the girdle plane constitutes another part. Today the term "doublet" is generally applied to stones created by joining two pieces of material with a *colorless* bonding agent and the term "triplet" to stones created by joining together three pieces, or two pieces that are joined by a *colored* bonding agent.

Composites have been around for a long time. Doublets have been made since Roman times and used extensively through the Victorian period (until about 1900). They are also being made and sold today. Therefore, one must check for doublets not only in antique jewelry, but in new jewelry as well.

Beware of a *new type* of composite stone being sold extensively— even by honest, reliable jewelers—as a genuine ruby (see Chapter 18). These are also showing up in *antique* jewelry, cut in "old styles," and are very convincing. The GIA and other labs have encountered them in very fine, genuine, well-made antique pieces submitted to the lab for "ruby" reports. One was even surrounded by lovely, rare, natural pearls!

Two years ago, we met a young man in the diplomatic corps who thought he could make some extra money importing stones for which his country was famous. He had a "friend" in one of the mining districts who sent him a shipment of very fine aquamarine. He brought them to a local jeweler who brought them to us to examine because the price seemed too attractive. All were composites.

These "aquamarines" were made by taking colorless quartz tops and gluing them with blue glue to colorless quartz bottoms. It was easy to determine they were not aquamarine because they didn't exhibit the dichroism typical of aquamarine (see Chapter 6). Examination with the dichroscope told us immediately that there was something wrong—there was no dichroism.

Doublets and triplets should never be referred to as "genuine" stones (even if their respective parts are, in fact, genuine pieces of the stone they appear to be). Doublets and triplets generally were made for one of three reasons—to enhance the appearance of poor quality stones, to assemble small stones to create a larger stone, or to imitate more desirable, valuable gems. In the case of opal, the backing provided in a doublet or triplet serves to provide support for very thin opal that would break without such a backing.

Types of Composite Stones

There are many different types of composite stones. We will discuss some of the more common types.

Doublets. Doublets are the most frequently encountered type of composite stone. In antique jewelry the most commonly encountered doublet is a garnet-topped doublet, often referred to as a false doublet. The garnet-topped doublet consists of a thin portion of red garnet fused to glass. With the right combination, any gem could be simulated by this method, even diamond.

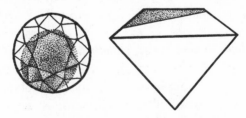

Garnet-topped doublet from top and side. Notice the garnet fused to the glass is not uniform in size or shape.

Garnets were used for the top portion of these doublets because of their high luster, excellent durability, and easy availability. They wouldn't crack when fused with the glass, and, perhaps most important (and very difficult for anyone unfamiliar with these doublets to believe), even though red garnet was used, the red in its natural color did not affect the color seen in the final product. When one looks at a garnet-topped-glass "sapphire," for example, there will be no trace of red.

Garnet-topped glass doublets made excellent imitations of topaz, sapphire, emerald, ruby, and amethyst, and were used extensively in antique jewelry in the era prior to the availability of synthetic stones (the Verneuil process, the first commercial method for synthesizing gem material, was announced in 1902). Doublets are encountered extensively in Victorian jewelry as well as jewelry from earlier periods.

Another type of doublet is made by taking two parts of a gemlike material, usually colorless, and cementing or fusing it together in the middle with an appropriately colored glue. For example, a colorless synthetic spinel top and bottom held together in the middle (at the girdle) by red, green, or blue glue will make an excellent "ruby," "emerald," or "sapphire."

True Doublets. There are also doublets that are referred to as true doublets because they are made from two pieces of the genuine stone they are trying to create. Blue sapphire doublets are true doublets, composed of two parts of genuine sapphire. But the pieces are usually inexpensive, common *pale yellow* sapphire. The top and bottom are cemented with blue glue, so the resulting product is a "blue sapphire." These are especially convincing.

Another type of doublet is even more cleverly constructed and is particularly difficult to detect. This type is composed of a thin, *genuine pale-yellow or brownish sapphire top fused to a synthetic blue sapphire or a synthetic ruby bottom.* The result is a stone that appears to be a very fine *genuine blue sapphire or ruby.*

These can fool even a good gemologist because three different tests will all indicate that the stone is genuine when it is not. Normally the loupe, dichroscope, and refractometer would provide sufficient information to know what you have, but with this type of doublet they aren't enough. More important, if you stop after only these tests the information they provide may lead you to erroneously conclude such a doublet is genuine. Here's how. First, both the dichroscope and refractometer will give readings that indicate blue sapphire. A good gemologist, however, understands that these instruments can't separate natural sapphire from synthetic, so the next step would be examination with the loupe. With the loupe one can be easily misled by the inclusions *in the natural pale-yellow sapphire top*. The inclusions seen in the genuine, natural sapphire are indicative of natural rather than synthetic because the top portion *is* natural. So, in this case, the inclusions in the top portion of the doublet will lead one to conclude that the whole stone is genuine—genuine, fine *blue* sapphire.

Sometimes you can see the difference in color between the top and bottom if you are able to look across the stone, through the girdle. If the stone is set in a way that prevents this, the spectroscope can immediately tell you something is wrong. The microscope will also reveal telltale signs at the girdle. And, finally, if immersed in methylene iodide you will see immediately that you have a doublet because the entire top portion of the stone seems to disappear while in the liquid.

True-emerald-doublets and true-ruby-doublets are also encountered (although ruby doublets don't look as convincing). These are usually made by cementing together two pieces of pale or colorless beryl (for emerald) or corundum (for ruby) with the appropriate color glue. We've also seen true-emerald-doublets made from a piece of overly dark green emerald glued to a piece of pale or colorless beryl to create a larger "emerald."

Soudé-Type. The soudé-type is often used to imitate emerald (and other stones less frequently). Here the "emerald" is created from two pieces of colorless stone, such as quartz or, today, synthetic colorless spinel, fused with a layer of green-colored gelatin (old type) or green glass (new type). Flawed stones are sometimes used to imitate emerald-like flaws. Colorless synthetic spinel also is used, and the spinel can be given a crackled effect to create a similar emerald-inclusion look.

We have a beautiful, large antique soudé-emerald ring that we use in lectures. Everyone says "ooh" and "aah" the moment they see it. We then submerge it in methylene iodide and everyone gasps as the top and bottom portions of the stone *totally disappear* (after all, they are really colorless) leaving only a thin plane of dark green glue visible (which appears across the plane of the girdle)!

Sometimes pale genuine pieces of the stone being created are used, but the colored layer improves the color significantly. For example, a stone made with a crown and pavilion of *pale green* beryl with a layer of deep green glass or gelatin can make a very convincing fine, large deep-green emerald.

Diamond Doublets. One must also be attentive to the existence of diamond doublets, although they don't appear often. They are made by gluing together two pieces of diamond to create the appearance of one larger diamond. Sometimes the crown is a re-cut "old mine" or "old European" stone, glued to a pavilion made from another piece of diamond. Occasionally one may see a diamond doublet composed of a genuine diamond crown glued to another material such as synthetic sapphire or synthetic spinel. You might

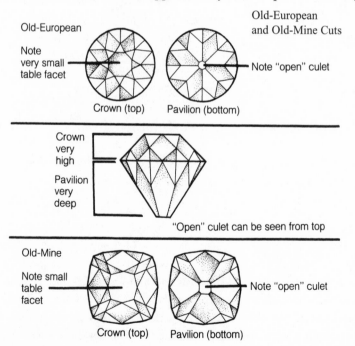

Side profile is similar in both. The Old-Mine cut has a higher crown and deeper pavilion than the Old-European, and usually "cushion" shaped as illustrated here.

also encounter a stone with a genuine diamond crown, a genuine diamond culet, and, as we discussed with foil-backs, nothing but metallic foil in between (see page 252).

Opal Doublets and Triplets. There are also opal doublets. These usually consist of a thin top layer of genuine opal cemented to a base of poor quality opal or some other substance altogether.

The most commonly encountered opal doublets are those made to resemble the precious black opal. These are usually composed of a translucent or transparent top cemented with black cement to a bottom portion of cheap opal or other material that acts as a support. The top of these "black opal" doublets is seldom genuine black opal, though they certainly do look like it.

Opal doublets can also be made by cementing a piece of fine opal to a larger piece of less fine opal to create a larger overall appearance. If the girdle can be observed, these doublets can be detected by noting the dark line where the cement joins the two pieces (the cement is usually black).

Triplets are frequently encountered in the opal market and have essentially replaced the opal doublet. These are similar to the opal doublet except a cabochon cap of colorless quartz (the third part) has been placed over the entire doublet, adding brightness and giving the delicate doublet greater protection from breakage.

Jadeite Triplets. Sometimes encountered, these are made by joining together three pieces of common white jadeite with a green cement that resembles mint jelly. They usually have a hollowed-out cabochon that is fitted onto another cabochon. A layer of green glue is inserted between the two, giving a green color to the whole stone. These can be very difficult to detect when set, but the abnormal pattern seen with the spectroscope can tell you immediately that you don't have natural green jadeite.

Composite Star Sapphire. This is a stone that has only recently entered the market. An excellent imitation of grayish-blue star sapphire, it is made by assembling star rose quartz, blue glass with a mirror on its underside, and dyed blue chalcedony to form the back. Some have also been made by "sputtering" a mirror-like substance to the back of star rose quartz.

The doublets and triplets we've covered here represent those that are most commonly encountered. Any stone can be imitated by doublets or triplets. Amethyst, topaz, even garnet itself can be created with composite stones. It is important to check for them particularly in antique jewelry, but never forget they are still being made today.

Detecting Doublets

Sometimes it is difficult to detect a well-made doublet or triplet, but most can be fairly quickly detected with a few simple tests, especially if the girdle and pavilion can be easily examined.

Examine with a Loupe.

1. *From the top* (Opals and Diamonds). When examining opals, first examine them from the top with the loupe, looking for the presence of any small telltale bubbles. Opal doublets and triplets usually reveal small bubbles when examined carefully with a loupe or higher magnification, evidence of more than one part being glued together (the bubbles in doublets or triplets are *flattened* air bubbles trapped in the cement between the two layers and will look more like flat discs than round bubbles). It is particularly important to examine opals carefully. Opal doublets and triplets are usually bezel-set so that the girdle can't be examined and, therefore, the line at the girdle where the parts are glued together can't be seen. When opals are bezel-set, one should be particularly cautious and alert to the possibility of a composite stone.

   With black opals, also examine the stone from the back. Genuine black opals usually have a black or grayish-black back, whereas black opal doublets or triplets will not.

   When examining diamonds, the use of a loupe with a strong light shining down on top of the stone will usually expose a diamond doublet. As we mentioned, diamond doublets may be made by gluing two pieces of genuine diamond (true doublets)—one piece forming the crown portion, one forming the pavilion portion—to make a larger diamond. Such stones are easy to detect. Examine the stone with the loupe, looking through the table at a slight angle, slowly tilting it back and forth. If the stone is a doublet, you will see a reflection of the table on the plane where the two parts are glued together. A normal diamond will not exhibit any such reflection.

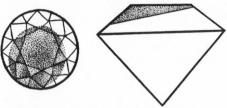
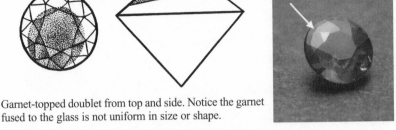

Garnet-topped doublet from top and side. Notice the garnet
fused to the glass is not uniform in size or shape.

Right: A garnet-topped doublet examined with reflected light. Note the difference in
the shininess (see arrow) where the garnet and glass appear side-by-side. This results
from differences in reflectivity (the way they reflect light).

2. *From the side of the crown* (Colored Gems). First, examine the
   stone focusing on the side of the crown portion with a strong light
   shining from above. In garnet-topped doublets you should be able
   to see a difference in the reflectivity of the light where the garnet
   portion and the glass are joined. The garnet portion will be much
   shinier than the glass. You can easily spot the contrast between
   the two with a little practice. You should be able to observe this
   in any garnet-topped doublet. *Note*: The garnet top seldom constitutes the entire crown of the stone. It is usually an irregular
   section that includes the table and only a portion of the top part
   of the crown. Therefore, to detect this telltale contrast, you must
   rotate the stone, always keeping the light shining on the sloping
   area, to make sure you find where the glass and garnet are joined.
3. *From the girdle.* If the girdle is visible, examine it carefully
   and you will see where the stone has been fused or cemented
   together. If you can't see the girdle, examine the stone from the
   top and look for the characteristic disc-like inclusions (flattened
   air bubbles, all on the same plane, trapped where the parts have
   been fused together).

Examine with Liquid. This is the easiest and most positive way
to detect many doublets or triplets. Immerse the stone or piece of
jewelry in rubbing alcohol, using tweezers. Once immersed, many
doublets will exhibit a strange phenomenon—instead of seeing one
stone, you will see two or three distinct parts. One or more of the
parts may even seem to disappear (because they may actually be

When some composite stones are immersed in *liquid* (such as alcohol or methylene iodide) one can often see two or three distinct parts. With soudé emeralds, the top and bottom may seem to disappear, leaving only a green plane visible across the girdle area. (Note: Immersion will not reveal garnet-topped doublets.)

colorless). You can actually see the lines of demarcation showing where the parts have been fused or cemented together. *Note:* you will not see this phenomenon with garnet-topped doublets. If alcohol doesn't reveal anything, you may want to try immersing the piece in methylene iodide (diiodomethane). Methylene iodide often makes it easier to see. We frequently use it and have never had a negative reaction, but be careful not to leave the stone in the liquid for any extended length of time. The chemical may attack the glue or cement, weaken it, and alter the appearance of the stone.

Examine with a Dichroscope. Since most colored gems are dichroic, it is often possible to separate a doublet or triplet from the gem it is trying to imitate by using the dichroscope. This will work with all garnet-topped glass doublets and some false doublets. It will not be conclusive for true doublets or doublets such as the sapphire doublet we mentioned earlier (with the genuine pale yellow sapphire top and synthetic blue sapphire bottom).

With the dichroscope, one can usually tell in seconds if the stone is not what it appears to be. If the stone appears to be emerald, but is a false doublet, the dichroscope will not exhibit the colors that are appropriate for emerald. For example, a soudé-type emerald made with a synthetic white spinel or colorless quartz top and bottom, cemented with a layer of green glass or gelatin, will not exhibit the dichroic colors that would be exhibited by emerald. If it were emerald, green would be seen in one window of the dichroscope and bluish-green or yellowish-green in the second window. With the doublet, one will see only green; you will not be able to pick up a second color. The dichroscope may not tell you the stone is a doublet, but it will inform you it is not an emerald.

If you get only one color with the dichroscope, and the stone you're examining is supposed to show two colors, you will know that something is wrong, that the stone must be something else. In this case, other tests should tell you what you really have.

A word of warning is needed here. The dichroscope provides an immediate signal that a stone is not what it may appear to be only when you *DON'T see what you should*. The converse is not true. If you do see what you should see, you could still have a doublet—a true doublet. Other tests are required to know for sure.

Examine against a White Surface. This is a simple test to use on unmounted stones. It will quickly reveal garnet-topped glass doublets if the stone it is imitating is *any color other than red*. Place the stone, table down, on a piece of white paper or other white background. Placing it table down on top of a few drops of water on a white ceramic surface works especially well, but simply placing it on any white background will also work. Look straight down on the stone. If you have a garnet-topped doublet you will see a red ring around the girdle. It may be weak or it may be distinct, but if it's there you have a doublet. Just remember, this test is only reliable for stones that are not red.

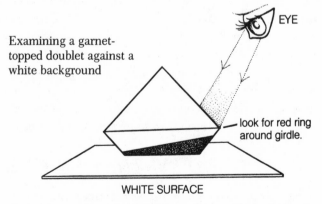

Examining a garnet-topped doublet against a white background

EYE

look for red ring around girdle.

WHITE SURFACE

Examining a garnet-topped doublet against a white background

Examine with a Spectroscope. Abnormal absorption spectra provide an immediate indicator that a stone is not what it appears to be. As in the case of jadeite triplets, the dye used in the green jelly causes an inappropriate spectral pattern to be seen. For stones that are set, the spectroscope can be fast and effective.

Failure to Be Thorough Can Cause Error

It is especially important to understand that you will not succeed in detecting certain types of doublets if you rely exclusively on inclusions, refractive index, or dichroism alone for positive ID. These tests can lead you to an erroneous conclusion.

For example, in the case of the sapphire doublet we mentioned earlier, the type made with a genuine pale yellow sapphire top and a dark blue synthetic sapphire bottom, these tests alone would lead you to conclude you were examining a genuine blue sapphire. Since the top is genuine sapphire (being yellow won't make any difference), you will see typical sapphire inclusions and since the bottom is dark blue (being synthetic won't make any difference) you would get the correct dichroism for blue sapphire. Also, because of the yellow sapphire top, you will also get the correct refractive index reading for sapphire.

When other tests indicate genuine, always be sure to examine carefully with the loupe or higher magnification for join lines, bubbles where the stone could be fused or cemented together, and differences in reflectivity between the different portions of a composite stone.

With a little practice one can learn to spot many doublets or triplets very quickly. As with all gem identification, however, it is usually easier to grasp if you spend a little time with a gemologist, focusing exclusively on composite stones. If there is a school that teaches gemology in your area (see Appendix), it might be possible to arrange to spend an hour or two studying composite stones from their teaching collection. If you can't locate anyone in your community, please write to us and we'll be happy to try to put you in touch with someone who might be helpful.

IMITATIONS AND SYNTHETICS ABOUND

We've already discussed numerous techniques used over the centuries to alter or enhance color and to imitate various stones, such as foil backing, piggy-backing, and the creation of composite stones. Now we will discuss imitations and synthetics to guard against whenever buying antique and estate jewelry.

Few realize how long humans have been imitating rare and beautiful gems. One of the earliest known imitations was turquoise. Highly prized by the Egyptians for both its beauty and magical powers, the Egyptians succeeded over 7,000 years ago in making a turquoise-colored ceramic material called faience that was used to make beads, amulets, pendants, and rings. They are also known to have produced beautiful glass, such as the lovely blue glass gems discovered in King Tut's tomb.

A very clever medieval sapphire imitation was discovered in the beautiful medieval Ardennes cross, a wooden gem-studded cross measuring 73 cm by 45 cm that is on display at the German National Museum in Nuremburg. It contains red garnets, rock crystal, green glass, and numerous "sapphires." Upon gemological examination (with dichroscope, Chelsea filter, UV lamp, and in some cases refractometer), it was found that fifteen large "sapphires" were quartz pebbles that had been dipped in molten blue glass!

Glass has been used as a simulant for thousands of years. Most of us are aware of these fakes. We are also acutely aware of the use of synthetics today. But few think about synthetics when they examine old jewelry—especially very old jewelry. Few realize how long synthetics have been produced commercially. And fewer still are alert to the fact that often the original stones in a very old or antique piece have been damaged or lost and then replaced with a synthetic. Making assumptions because something is old can be very costly.

How Is a *Simulant* Different from a *Synthetic*?

The terms "simulant" and "imitation" mean the same thing for our purposes, and can be used interchangeably. However, synthetic has a different, and very specific, meaning. These terms are confusing to many so, before we begin, we'd like to explain what each means.

A simulated gem is made by man. It's important to understand, however, that *a simulant has no counterpart found in nature*. For example, a brilliant green stone such as green YAG may have an emerald-green color and resemble an emerald, but it won't have any of the physical properties of real emerald. Nor will it have any physical properties of any other green gem that occurs in nature. It was not intended to duplicate a natural stone. YAG is a simulant or imitation. Glass is a simulant. Simulants are easy to distinguish from genuine gems of the same color since they are very different physically. Color is usually the only thing they have in common. The eye alone can often tell a simulant from the genuine—too much brilliance, not enough brilliance, etc. A few simple tests (often just the loupe) will quickly separate the simulant from the genuine.

A synthetic gem, however, while also made by man, has been scientifically developed *to duplicate a gem that occurs naturally*. It will, therefore, have virtually the same physical and chemical properties of the stone it appears to be. A synthetic stone may be easily confused with the genuine if one does not examine it carefully. Chatham emeralds are synthetic—they duplicate a substance found in nature and possess essentially the same physical and chemical characteristics. The Kashan ruby is a synthetic ruby, and was so close to the genuine that when it was first introduced it was mistaken by many for the genuine.

Synthetic gems have been produced commercially since the beginning of this century—synthetic ruby was being produced commercially in 1905 (although it was available earlier), synthetic blue spinel was introduced in 1908 (widely available after 1925), and synthetic blue sapphire in 1911.

In fact, many pieces of jewelry from the early part of the 20th century contained small synthetic gems to add color and accent other genuine gems. We have a beautiful natural seed pearl bracelet accentuated with genuine diamonds and *synthetic* blue sapphires. The sapphires are small, calibre-cut stones used to provide color. Given their small size, the fact that they're synthetic rather than genuine doesn't really affect the overall value of this beautiful piece. Nonetheless, it's important to know they're synthetic. If I sold this bracelet and neglected to point out that the sapphires are not genuine, my credibility and overall reputation would be seriously damaged if the buyer were to learn of it later.

Synthetic Stones in Antique Jewelry

One must also be alert to the fact that synthetic stones may also appear in jewelry made long before synthetics were being produced—jewelry in which missing stones have been replaced.

We can't overemphasize the importance of carefully examining any stone that appears to be a fine gem. One cannot make assumptions based on the age of a jewelry piece, the reputation of the family to which it belonged, the beauty and detail in the workmanship, or the quality of diamonds used to enhance the main stone. In Geneva, Switzerland, at the auction of the magnificent jewels of the Duchess of Windsor, you may remember there was a strand of pearls that belonged to the Duchess. These pearls were listed in the catalogue as genuine, cultured pearls. They were not. They were fake! A serious mistake was made because someone *assumed*, given who the owner was, that they could only have been genuine. After all, who could have imagined the Duchess with a strand of fake pearls! Be careful not to make similar assumptions. (The auction house did announce the error prior to the start of bidding.)

We've seen examples of synthetic ruby, emerald, and sapphire used in magnificent, diamond-studded jewelry from the early part of this century. And we've seen much earlier jewelry that contains synthetic center stones, some complete with 18th- or 19th-century hallmarks, even enhanced by antique-cut diamonds appropriate to the age of the piece.

Even though synthetics may not yet have been produced at the time a given piece of jewelry was made, one must always be alert to the possibility of an original stone having been replaced with a synthetic. It is not unusual for a stone to be lost or damaged and then replaced with something less valuable than the original. Sad, but true.

Tremendous progress has been made in the area of synthesizing gems in recent decades. Synthetic emerald came on the scene in the 1930s, star ruby in the 1940s. In the 1970s, synthetic turquoise entered the market, as well as synthetic amethyst, synthetic alexandrite, and synthetic opal. In the 1980s, we find synthetic jadeite jade being produced (not yet commercially), and, most recently, the seemingly impossible has been achieved—gem-quality synthetic diamond has been produced (although currently only very small fancy-color yellow stones are being manufactured in any quantity).

Detecting Synthetics

Synthetic gems offer affordable alternatives to natural gems today. However, they also pose problems for today's jeweler and gem enthusiast because they are so difficult to distinguish from genuine. Although we've discussed how to identify synthetic stones in earlier chapters, we'd like to make a few additional comments here.

Today's synthetics present a real challenge. Some appear to be flawless when examined with the 10X loupe, and require very high magnification—sometimes up to 60X or more—to spot inclusions indicating synthetic. Others are being produced with visible inclusions to more closely imitate what one normally sees in the natural. We recommend very careful examination of any fine gem.

1. *Examine with a microscope.* Most gem enthusiasts today realize that flawless, gem-quality emeralds, sapphires, or rubies are so rare that such a stone is most likely synthetic. When a gem has typical looking inclusions, however, one is normally less suspicious. Yet inclusions now found in synthetic stones have been developed to better simulate the natural stone. Remember, careful examination with the microscope (with at least 60X magnification) is essential for any gem that appears to be genuine.

2. *Examine with the spectroscope.* Old-type synthetics such as the Verneuil synthetic sapphire are also posing problems today: they are being heated to remove their telltale signs. Heat treatment of the Verneuil type synthetic blue sapphire can successfully remove the curved striae (curved lines) and color zoning. Even with the microscope it might be difficult to determine that one of these stones is synthetic. So, when examining blue sapphire with fine color—not too dark, not too light—it is essential to examine also with the spectroscope (see Chapter 10). If the stone is an old-type synthetic, no absorption line will be observed at 450 (4500). *Note: very dark* blue synthetic material may show a weak band at 450 (4500) and *very pale* natural blue sapphire may exhibit nothing.

3. *Examine with a polariscope.* There is a tremendous amount of synthetic amethyst currently on the market. Most of it is being properly represented as synthetic but some is being sold as

genuine. So, careful examination with the polariscope is essential when examining fine, exceptionally clean, deep purple amethyst (see Chapter 11).
4. *Examine with a balance.* Synthetic lapis is a surprise to many. Lapis should also be tested, and there's an easy way to test it if you use a delicate balance. Weigh the piece of jewelry or unmounted stone and record the exact weight. Immerse it in clean water for about two minutes. Remove it and carefully wipe dry. Weigh it again. If it weighs more, it is synthetic. Synthetic lapis is very porous and readily absorbs water. Genuine lapis does not.

A Word about Turquoise

Turquoise is a gem that requires particular attention today. One must be alert to the presence of numerous materials that look like turquoise—natural turquoise, synthetic turquoise, reconstituted (reconstructed) turquoise, and imitation turquoise. We are seeing tremendous misrepresentation of turquoise throughout the marketplace. Fine natural turquoise is very difficult to obtain. However, there is an abundance of reconstituted turquoise, often represented as natural. It is not. Also, reconstituted turquoise should not be confused with the synthetic turquoise now being produced. Reconstituted turquoise is not synthetic. Reconstituted turquoise is a product made by taking turquoise powder (made by pulverizing poor quality genuine stone) and mixing it with a binding agent (plastic) to form into solid pieces. It is something anyone dealing in turquoise should be aware of and on guard against.

Today's Synthetics

Manufacturers of synthetic gems have come a long way. Their products are beautiful. And they are, indeed, so good that they may easily be mistaken for the real thing.

Gemologists have also come a long way in learning how to identify and separate the natural from the synthetic and imitation. (See chart on the following pages.) Nonetheless, there are still some stones that, to be absolutely positive, require sophisticated testing and equipment not available to most. Infrared spectroscopy offers tremendous promise for the future ... and for staying one step ahead of those who continue in their efforts to perfect the art of synthesizing. GIA is currently experimenting with the infrared spectroscope, and preliminary results lead them to believe this piece of equipment may well provide the means to separate, without question, any synthetic from the natural.

The world of gemstone synthesis is a dynamic one. The 20th century has seen the introduction and perfection of many synthetic gems. New developments are occurring constantly. Keeping on top of new developments may be the ultimate challenge to the jeweler and gem lover over the next few decades.

Fracture-Filled Diamonds in Antique and Period Jewelry

One of the newest treatments for diamond enhancement, the filling of fractures in diamonds to improve their appearance, is little more than a decade old. The jewels in which this treatment is being found, however, can be hundreds of years old!

We want to caution you to check the diamonds in old jewelry very carefully to be sure they are not fracture-filled (see Chapter 4). We have seen fracture-filled diamonds in antique rings and other jewelry at well-known establishments, even at well-known auction houses, being sold without disclosure of this treatment. We have seen them in antique pieces, in beautiful "period" jewelry; we have seen them in pawnshops and in flea markets. How they got there is pure speculation. But one thing is certain: Where old pieces are concerned, never let your guard down. Old stones can be removed from an old setting, the fractures filled, and the stone reset in the original setting following treatment. "New" stones can also be mounted in "old" or "antique" settings. There is nothing wrong with the owner of a badly fractured diamond wanting to have it filled; there is nothing wrong with anyone buying or selling a filled diamond. But if you are buying one, you want to know it; and if you are selling one, you must know what you are selling so that you can disclose the treatment to a potential buyer.

Synthetic Moissanite Substituted for Diamond in Antique and Estate Jewelry

As we mentioned in the section on electronic diamond testers, synthetic moissanite has been found in numerous pieces of antique and estate jewelry, misrepresented as diamond. Gem-testing laboratories around the world have reported incidents and warn against assuming that any stone in an antique or old mounting is a genuine diamond. Keep in mind also that standard electronic diamond testers, which operate solely on thermal conductivity, will indicate "diamond" when testing synthetic moissanite; if using an electronic diamond tester, be sure it is a dual tester, testing both thermal conductivity and electrical conductivity (see page 231).

A Final Word about Antique and Estate Jewelry—Enjoy

We hope that we have not intimidated you with this discussion but, instead, enlightened you so that you can be more aware and less likely to inadvertently buy something that is not what it appears to be. We hope the information here has armed you in a way to give you greater confidence about what you are seeing, buying, and selling. No doubt you'll encounter many of the techniques we've discussed here. We think they add interest to many pieces and can be fascinating in their own way. We hope you'll agree that the key to enjoying them is understanding and appreciating what you have.

Synthetic Gemstones and Man-Made Imitations

Color	Commercially Available	Method of Growth or Synthesis	Comments and Identification Characteristics
SYNTHETIC TYPES			
COLORLESS			
Diamond (exact date difficult to ascertain)	1990s	Flux grown	1. All can be distinguished by routine gemological testing. 2. Most are slightly tinted or near-colorless but colorless also being produced. 3. Shows distinctive zoning. 4. Differing from natural, many are magnetic. Magnetism is always indicative of synthetic. 5. Most fluoresce and exhibit very distinctive fluorescence pattern. 6. May exhibit telltale "hourglass" or "stop sign" graining. 7. Also produced in rich yellow hues that exhibit characteristics similar to colorless.
Sapphire	1910	Verneuil	1. No curved striae or coloration observed because stone is colorless. 2. Identifiable by exposure to shortwave ultraviolet radiation, which will produce a dull, deep blue fluorescence.
Spinel	1910	Verneuil	1. Can be easily identified by exposure to shortwave ultraviolet, under which it will fluoresce or glow a strong bluish-white. Inert under longwave U. V. Also can be identified by the anomalous double refraction seen with the polariscope.
Rutile	1948	Verneuil	1. Too much "fire" or dispersion (seven times more than diamond). 2. Soft—can be scratched by a quartz gem such as amethyst, etc. The hardness on Mohs scale is 6 to 6.5. 3. Cloudy appearance if cut wrong (due to the strong doubling effect of its high birefringence—0.287). 4. Can be cut quite shallow without "leaking" light, due to its very high refractive index—2.616–2.903.
*Cubic Zirconia (CZ)	1973 (commercially 1976)	Skull furnace	1. Higher "fire" or dispersion than diamond—.060 versus .044 diamond. 2. Higher specific gravity. When compared to a one-carat round diamond, the CZ will weigh approximately 1.75 carats.

			3. Hardness about 8.5 on Mohs scale. Can be easily scratched by a tungsten carbide pen.
			4. Fluoresce orangish-yellow under longwave and stronger under shortwave ultraviolet though there are some that react just the opposite.
			5. Negative reaction to diamond testing probes, needles or reflectometers.
			6. Girdle reflections are slightly more "glassy" looking than that of diamond.
			7. The readability test. In an unmounted CZ, placed table-facet down over a fine pen line or black print, you will be able to see some of the black line or print when viewed from above at a slight angle. With a well cut diamond you will not be able to read any print or see the black line.
Moissanite	1990s	Flux grown	1. Synthetic silicon carbide; strongly double-refracting and shows "doubling."
			2. Much higher dispersion than diamond; exhibits too much "fire."
			3. Has a grayish or greenish cast that is seen when viewed against a flat white background.
			4. May show long, white "needle" inclusions never seen in diamond.

* We have listed cubic zirconia as a synthetic since it has been *found in nature* as an inclusion. We consider it a simulant, however, since the stone it is imitating is diamond, the properties of which differ significantly from CZ.

BLUE

Sapphire	1911	Verneuil flame-fusion	1. Curved growth lines (curved striae) and color zoning.
			2. Small spherical or pear-shaped bubbles.
			3. Bluish-green to dull green usually exhibited by synthetic blue sapphire under shortwave ultraviolet radiation.
			4. Heat treatment of synthetic blue sapphire can successfully eradicate the curved striations and color zoning. Therefore, examine with the spectroscope (see Chapter 10).
			5. The dichroscope will *not* differentiate between natural and synthetic.
Spinel	1908 (in wide use after 1925)	Verneuil flame-fusion	1. Easily identified by observing the red coloration when examined with the (in wide use Chelsea filter under incandescent light.
			2. Anomalous double refraction seen under cross-polars when using the polariscope.
			3. Profilated bubble inclusions.
			4. Most fluoresce red under longwave ultraviolet and most fluoresce orange, red or bluish-white under shortwave ultraviolet.

Synthetic Gemstones and Man-Made Imitations *(continued)*

Color	Commercially Available	Method of Growth or Synthesis	Comments and Identification Characteristics
SYNTHETIC TYPES			
Blue continued			
Turquoise	1972 (Gilson)	Methodology not revealed	1. Weak dull blue under long- and shortwave ultraviolet radiation.
			2. Under microscopic examination seems to exhibit small angular crystalline pieces in a whitish groundmass.
			3. With a loupe, one can sometimes see evenly distributed, small, whitish "cotton puffs."
			4. Synthetic turquoise can be even-colored or exhibit "spiderweb" matrix design.
Lapis-lazuli (Gilson)	mid 1970s	Methodology not revealed	1. Easy to identify if you use a delicate balance. Weigh the jewelry piece or stone carefully on the balance and record the weight. Immerse in clean water for about two minutes and then carefully wipe dry. Weigh again. If it is synthetic it will weigh more. Synthetic lapis lazuli is porous and readily absorbs water.
			2. If examined with a strong pen-light you will note that genuine lapis is slightly translucent and the Gilson synthetic is not
			3. It may or may not have pyrite inclusions.
GREEN			
Emerald	1934	Flux grown (I. G. Farben)	1. Very few were produced.
			2. Wispy veils.
	1935	Flux grown (Chatham)	1. Wispy or veil-like feathery inclusions, liquid filled.
			2. Phenacite crystal inclusions.
			3. Gas bubbles.
			4. Platinum crystal platelets, usually triangular shaped, but may be hexagonally shaped.
			5. Strong red under Chelsea filter examination in incandescent light.
			6. Red fluorescence under longwave ultraviolet radiation.
			7. Pink reaction to synthetic emerald filter.

early 1960s	Flux grown (Gilson)	1. Veil-like inclusions. 2. Strong red under Chelsea filter. 3. Red under longwave ultraviolet. 4. One (type N) does not fluoresce but has an absorption spectra at 4270 (427). 5. Pink reaction to synthetic emerald filter.
1961 to 1970	Hydrothermal (Linde) Continued to be produced by Vacuum Ventures, Inc. of California and New Jersey. (Under license rom Union Carbide)	1. Long, thin crystals that all point one way. Many are capped with a small ball and referred to as "nail-head" inclusions. 2. Some of the lower grades made by Vacuum Ventures will show whispy inclusions. 3. Strong red fluorescence under longwave ultraviolet radiation.
1960	Hydrothermal (Lechleitner)	1. A faceted beryl (aqua, emerald, etc.) on which a layer of hydrothermally grown synthetic emerald has been deposited. With a loupe, you can see easily that the surface of the facets are criss-crossed with a series of fine "fish-net" type cracks. The specific gravity of this type of stone will vary slightly, depending on the type of beryl coated.
1986	Hydrothermal (Biron)	1. Can have "nail-head" type inclusions as seen in Linde synthetic. 2. Two-phase inclusions. 3. Gold platelets. 4. Ghost lines—lines you see one moment, but which disappear when slightly tilted. 5. Small whitish specks. 6. Good red under the Chelsea filter. 7. Non-fluorescent under ultraviolet (unusual for synthetic emerald). 8. Exhibits a 4270 (427) absorption spectra like the synthetic Gilson "N" Type II.
1984	Flux grown (Seiko, Japan)	1. Fluoresces green under ultraviolet. 2. Can exhibit thin parallel inclusions that look like lines. 3. Reasonably "clean" of inclusions.

Synthetic Gemstones and Man-Made Imitations *(continued)*

Color	Commercially Available	Method of Growth or Synthesis	Comments and Identification Characteristics
SYNTHETIC TYPES			
Green continued			
Spinel	1925	Verneuil	1. Tourmaline-green in color. 2. Synthetic spinels all exhibit anomalous double refraction under the polariscope. 3. They will not exhibit any dichroism. 4. Colorless spinel is used to make emerald colored doublets. The top and bottom will be colorless spinel, the two sections cemented together with green glue (see Chapter 16).
Jadeite Jade	1984	High pressure vice or belt (made by General Electric)	1. Jadeite jade (including green and lavender) are not at this time being produced for commercial use. 2. These jades have a slightly higher hardness, 7.5 to 8, versus 7 for natural. 3. They appear to have a more granular texture and the colors are made blotchy or spotty. 4. The fluorescence, refractive indices and specific gravities are similar to natural jadeite. 5. The spectroscope is useful for separating from natural—the 4370 absorption line seen with natural stones is not seen in the fancy colored synthetic. 6. The Suwa Seikosha Co., Ltd. of Japan obtained a patent in 1985 for the production of synthetic jadeite. Who knows what the future for synthetic jadeite will hold.
Sapphire	1910	Verneuil	1. Same inclusions as seen in synthetic blue sapphire. 2. Shows reddish through the Chelsea filter (natural green stays dark).
RED			
Ruby*	Commercially 1905	Verneuil flame-fusion	1. Curved growth striations, curved color banding. 2. Small spherical, pear-shaped or tad-pole shaped bubbles. 3. Profilated gas bubble (a row of bubbles which, together, have a sausage-shaped outline). 4. Small black "dots" (excessive chromium oxide that did not melt or absorb during the synthesis). This is often observed in old ruby synthetics. 5. Strong red fluorescence when observed under longwave ultra violet radiation. Burmese rubies also fluoresce strong red, but weaker than the synthetic.

	Date	Method	Characteristics
	after 1920	Czochralski pulling method Can produce very large crystal.	1. Very "clean" flaw-wise. May exhibit a weak layered or parallel color zoning. 2. Strong red fluorescence like the Verneuil.
	mid 1960's	Flux grown or diffusion	1. Small irregular-shaped, elongated bubbles. 2. A meshed net or veil in which the droplets are filled. Natural rubies could look similar but the droplets are not filled. The mesh holes are often hexagonally shaped in the Chatham synthetics. 3. In some of the Kashan rubies you can observe irregular-shaped forms consisting of flux residues. 4. Some Kashans are slightly cloudy from the presence of inclusions that resemble falling rain. They exhibit faint, light-colored straight lines that traverse the stone— you may think you are looking at a facet edge on the opposite side. 5. Flux grown Kashans do not fluoresce as strong a red under the ultraviolet as those that are grown using the Verneuil growth method. 6. Chatham synthetics may contain small, usually triangular shaped, platinum platelets. 7. In some Ramaura synthetic rubies, you may see nearly straight parallel growth bands that disappear as you tilt the stone slightly. 8. Ramaura may show bluish under shortwave ultraviolet and also may fluoresce slightly yellow.
Star Ruby	1947	Verneuil flame-fusion	1. Star is perfect, all 6 rays perfectly aligned. 2. Linde-type will often show a poorly etched letter "L" on the back side of the cabochon. 3. Many European grown will be more translucent and if examined carefully will exhibit curved striae or color zoning. 4. A natural star stone will exhibit, to some degree, hexagonal cross-hatching visible on the back side of the cabochon. This will not be observed in the synthetic stone. 5. Some European stones will exhibit fine concentric circles on the back side of the cabochon.

*Synthetic rubies were being produced as early as 1885 (Geneva), but were not really commercially available until after 1900.

Synthetic Gemstones and Man-Made Imitations *(continued)*

Color	Commercially Available	Method of Growth or Synthesis	Comments and Identification Characteristics
SYNTHETIC TYPES			
Red continued			
Red Spinel	1930s	Verneuil flame-fusion	1. The refractive index of these spinels is slightly higher than that of naturaal red spinels. Recently, however, some are being synthesized that have refractive indices comparable to natural stones.
			2. Under crossed-polars in the polariscope, these stones will exhibit anomalous double refraction (ADR).
			3. Natural and synthetic red spinels will fluoresce strong red under longwave ultraviolet, though slightly weaker than the natural or synthetic rubies having the same shade of red.
			4. Ruby has good dichroism but red spinel and glass have none.
			5. Genuine red spinel usually will show under magnification some small octagonally-shaped crystal inclusions not seen in synthetic.
			6. Synthetic red spinel is often internally fractured (particularly earlier stones).
PURPLE			
Amethyst	1975	Hydrothermal autoclave	1. Fine deep purple, exceptionally "clean" synthetics are quite plentiful.
			2. They can be identified by carefully examining with the polariscope (see Chapter 11). The synthetic may not exhibit twinning lines seen in 99% of natural amethysts.
ALEXANDRITE TYPES			
Alexandrite	1973	Flux grown (Creative Crystals of California)	1. Veil-like patterns of interconnecting canals (healing feather types).
			2. String-like arrangement of small bubbles.
			3. Small brownish hexagonal platelets.
			4. Flux type inclusions.
			5. Platinum crystals, hexagonal or triangular in shape.
			6. Strong red fluorescence under longwave and shortwave ultraviolet.
Synthetic Spinel—		Verneuil	1. No Dichroism. Spinel is single-refracting while alexandrite is triple-refracting.

Alexandrite type

2. Very good color change, green to red.
3. Gas bubbles.
4. Anomalous double refraction under polariscope not seen in natural.
5. Refractive index = 1.73.

Synthetic Corundum— Alexandrite type   Verneuil

1. Refractive index = 1.762–1.770.
2. Strong red fluorescence longwave and shortwave ultraviolet.
3. Some fluoresce orange under longwave and shortwave ultraviolet.
4. Color change grayish-green to purple.
5. With the dichroscope this synthetic will show two colors while genuine or synthetic alexandrite will show three. The trichroism in genuine alexandrite varies slightly, depending on country of origin.

NOTE: Synthetic sapphires and spinels have been produced in many colors for experimental and scientific studies. We have not listed them all since most are not encountered in the trade.

SIMULANTS AND IMITATION GEMSTONES (Simulants are not found naturally—synthetics duplicate gems that occur naturally.)

COLORLESS

Strontium titanate   1955   Verneuil

1. Very high "fire" or dispersion—more than four times that of diamond.
2. Very high specific gravity, (5.13), approximately 1.5 times higher than diamond (3.52).
3. Very soft, 6 to 6.5, and brittle.
4. Non-fluorescent.
5. To make the stone more durable and reduce the dispersion, it is made into a doublet with either a synthetic sapphire or spinel crown.
6. Sold as Wellington and Fabulite.

YAG (Yttrium Aluminum Garnet)   1969   Czochalski "pulling"

1. Dispersion is low (.028), nearly half that of diamond.
2. Has a good hardness, about 8.5 on Mohs scale.
3. Sold under the name "Diamonair" and "Diamonique."
4. Like strontium titanate, it has an R.I. that cannot be read on the normal refractometer.
5. Some fluoresce yellow under long- and weaker under shortwave ultraviolet. Some will fluoresce weak pink under longwave ultraviolet. Some will not fluoresce under either longwave or shortwave ultraviolet.
6. Since the R.I. is low, you can read print easily through the stone when trying the readability test.
7. Twisted drop-like inclusions, black square or triangular shaped crystals.

Synthetic Gemstones and Man-Made Imitations *(continued)*

SIMULANTS AND IMITATION GEMSTONES (Simulants are not found naturally—synthetics duplicate gems that occur naturally.)

Color	Commercially Available	Method of Growth or Synthesis	Comments and Identification Characteristics
Colorless continued			
GGG (Gadolinium Gallium Garnet)	1975	Czochalski "pulling"	1. Dispersion nearly the same as diamond. 2. Specific gravity practically twice that of diamond, 7.02. 3. Hardness (7, same as the quartz gems) much lower than diamond, but durable. 4. Exposure to ultraviolet or sunlight will eventually turn GGG brown. The more exposure, the deeper the shade of brown. 5. Yellow fluorescence under longwave and weaker under shortwave ultraviolet.
YELLOW-ORANGE Langasite	1990s	Czochalski and others	1. This recent imitation can be mistaken for several gemstones, but the high R.I. separates it from sapphire and spinel. 2. Double-refraction and dichroism (indicated by polariscope and dichroscope) separate it from CZ, YAG, GGG, or fancy-color diamonds. 3. A desk-model spectroscope can separate it from zircon, for which it could otherwise be mistaken.
GREEN YAG (Yttrium Aluminum "Garnet")	1969	Czochalski "pulling"	1. Some fluoresce strong red under ultraviolet and are red under the Chelsea filter. Those that get their coloration from praseodymium are very weak under ultraviolet or Chelsea. 2. Looks like emerald but it is extremely "clean." 3. You can measure the R.I. of emerald but you cannot read the R.I. of YAG on your refractometer.
BLUE Imitation Lapis	1954	Germany	1. This was made from coarsely ground synthetic blue spinel, heated (but not melted) to form a solid mass. Sometimes gold specks were added. 2. Identifiable with the Chelsea filter (it exhibits a red coloration not seen in genuine). 3. Not many have been seen since 1954.

Chortanite/Coranite (synthetic corundum imitating *tanzanite*)	mid-1990s	Verneuil	1. Being mixed with tanzanite, but doesn't really look like it. 2. Dichroic (tanzanite is trichroic). 3. Internal inclusions typical of other Verneuil synthetics (see page 162).

PURPLE/VIOLET

YAG (tanzanite color) Also sold as "Coranite."	1995	Czochalski "pulling"	1. Visually difficult to distinguish from natural *tanzanite*, but easy to separate with standard gem tests. 2. Singly refracting; high R.I. (1.83). 3. Most distinctive characteristic is unique fluorescence; fluoresces moderate reddish-orange under longwave; intense orange under shortwave (reaction can be seen using even a low-intensity, portable UV lamp, but it must have shortwave as well as longwave.

MULTICOLORED

Opal	1972	Methodology kept secret. (Gilson)	1. Color patches are within boundaries and do not "blend" into the adjoining color patches. 2. Examination of stone's surface with 10X loupe will show patterns resembling "snakeskin," "chicken-wire," "honeycomb," or fine "wrinkles." 3. Immersed in chloroform, they will develop a colorless or clear envelope, a few millimeters thick, around the whole stone. When lifted out of the chloroform, clear envelope disappears. Make sure you do not inhale much chloroform!! 4. Gilson has stopped making opal and has turned over the synthesis to the Japanese.
Opal	1977	Glass having a controlled precipitation. (J. L. Slocum)	1. Can be easily distinguished as imitation when examined with a 10X magnifier. Though there are many types of color configurations in Slocum opals, none resemble the genuine opal. 2. The specific gravity (2.40 to 2.50) is higher than that of natural opal (1.25 to 2.23). 3. The R.I. (1.49 to 1.50) is higher than natural (about 1.45). 4. The hardness is near 6 on Mohs scale.

Synthetic Gemstones and Man-Made Imitations *(continued)*

Color	Commercially Available	Method of Growth or Synthesis	Comments and Identification Characteristics

SIMULANTS AND IMITATION GEMSTONES (Simulants are not found naturally—synthetics duplicate gems that occur naturally.)

Opal continued

Opal	1983	Japanese (methodology complicated)	1. A plastic imitation that looks very realistic.
			2. The specific gravity is low—1.18 to 1.20.
			3. The R.I. is a little higher—1.48 to 1.53.
			4. The hardness is very low, about 2.5.
			5. You can cut it with a sharp knife.
			6. Mounted in a ring, it could fool you by resembling a precious opal that has a white groundmass.

NEW TYPE OF LEAD-GLASS COMPOSITE (Low-quality corundum infused throughout with lead-glass.)

Ruby and Sapphire (in all colors)	mid-2000s		1. Surface crazing.
			2. Blue flash seen while moving intense maglite/pen-light around/through stone.
			3. Rounded gas bubbles.
			4. Yellow "pools" are sometimes seen in these composite rubies which is actually yellow-tinted lead-glass.

YAG, GGG, and CUBIC ZIRCONIA can be produced in many colors—blue, yellow, red, etc. though not commonly seen. Recently a synthetic blue Russian sapphire turned out to be a blue CZ. None of these stones will exhibit dichroism and none are readable on the normal refractometer. Fluorescence and inclusions may help identify these "gems."

Glass is made in many colors to imitate many stones. The facet edges are usually not sharp. Any single reading on the refractometer from 1.50 to as much as 1.65 usually indicates the gem is glass. (Cryptocrystalline quartz such as chalcedony, amber and a few very rare gems are exceptions.) Glass imitations will not exhibit any dichroism. The stones they are trying to imitate will usually have two readings on the refractometer.

NOTES

18 / A new type of "composite" imitation

As we discussed in Chapter 17, "composite" stones have been around for a very long time. The standard definition is exactly what its name implies: a stone that is a *composition* produced by combining two or more parts. Historically, composites were made by joining together two or three *layers* of whatever material was used; stones comprised of two layers were called *doublets*; those with three layers, *triplets*. The layers could be genuine or artificial, or a combination of the two.

Composites are more convincing imitations than other types of artificial products and, as you learned in Chapter 17, those composed of genuine parts of the gem being imitated (known as "true" doublets or triplets) are especially convincing. We've seen quite a few "true" emerald doublets over the years, with very pale genuine emerald on the top and bottom portions, with a deep green layer between the two, resulting in a "gem" that looks like a much larger, much "finer," and much costlier emerald. Furthermore, with "true" doublets, certain gemological tests also indicate "genuine emerald." Nonetheless, whether genuine, partly genuine, or wholly artificial, it is deceptive to sell *any* composite as a genuine stone.

Today we are seeing a new type of composite that has been formed in an entirely new way; the parts are not layers, and do not form distinct "planes" that are joined by a bonding agent of some type or by fusing. These new composites are combined in an altogether different method, but like the "true" doublets discussed earlier, they have a "genuine component" that makes them much more difficult to detect unless you are aware of their existence and are checking for the telltale indicators. As a result, we now have a major international problem, accompanied by widespread confusion and deception.

Initially the problem was limited to rubies. Horror stories from bench jewelers—those who actually make jewelry or repair, re-size, and remount stones—revealed that there was something very wrong with these "rubies" because they didn't behave at all like rubies should, treated or otherwise; these were quickly and *irreparably* damaged by jewelers using techniques they'd always used when working with ruby. One jeweler described how a "ruby" turned to a molten glob when he performed routine work with the torch; another described how a ruby was totally destroyed while immersed in the "jeweler's pickle" for final cleaning, something that was unheard of previously. Today, more and more jewelers are experiencing the horror of removing a piece of ruby jewelry from a cleaning solvent only to see numerous deep, whitish etch lines throughout the entire stone, destroying the stone's beautiful appearance (as my students saw after we immersed one in an acid as mild as lemon juice)!

A NEW *TYPE* OF COMPOSITE FOOLS THE JEWELRY INDUSTRY

The gemological community learned that these "rubies" were not rubies that had been treated by some new and more extreme process. Instead, they discovered that these rubies were an entirely different product, a new type of composite. As we mentioned earlier, a composite is a product made by combining two or more materials—which is certainly the case here—but they were blending the two different materials (very *low-quality corundum* and quantities of *lead-glass)* in a way that had never been seen before.

Gemological examination of the stones revealed unprecedented quantities of glass—a highly refractive *lead*-glass not previously used in gems—combined with some unknown quantity of corundum. In short, a blend of two materials that were *altogether different* in terms of physical properties and *not visible* without knowing what to look for in this new product.

Subsequent research revealed that the lead-glass becomes an integral part of the blended product and *cannot be removed without* destroying the entire "gem." Furthermore, the *properties associated with "ruby" are no longer the same* since the properties associated with lead-glass are also present and inseparable. These are two critical differences between this product and treated rubie*s*.

Without the lead-glass, there is no "ruby" in terms of color and transparency, but *with* the lead-glass, the physical properties are so altered that the resulting "ruby" lacks the characteristics that make "ruby" a ruby. The fusion of these two very different materials creates something that is neither ruby nor glass, but a new type of composite that combines properties of both, each of which is inseparable from the other.

To better understand the confusion, it's important to understand the allure of ruby and how its treatment history unfolds. Only then will you understand why it took so long to clearly distinguish between treated rubies and these new composites, why there are now so many being sold at inflated prices without disclosure as to what they really are, and why extreme care is needed when wearing or handling them.

A BRIEF HISTORY ON RUBY TREATMENTS

Ruby is the most valuable variety of the gem species corundum. It is one of the most sought-after gemstones throughout the world. Prices range from several hundred dollars per carat for low quality, treated commercial grade stones, to over $80,000 per carat for the highest quality, rarest rubies in sizes over five carats, and even more for the rarest, natural (untreated) "gem" quality rubies.

Ruby is the second hardest natural gemstone (only diamond is harder) and is also one of the toughest of gemstones—it doesn't easily crack, chip, or break; it can take extremely high heat as well as extremely low temperatures, and can withstand significant pressure.

Improving the appearance of rubies—as well as sapphires and many other gemstones—using one or more of a variety of techniques is common practice; some have been used routinely for over fifty years and have been accepted by the trade. Treated rubies are valued depending upon the type and extent of treatment used. Where ruby is concerned, acceptable treatments include heating techniques to improve color and transparency, and use of fillers (oil or common "silica" glass) to reduce the visibility of internal fractures or to reduce their reflectivity. Almost all rubies and sapphires are heated and, at the lower end of the market, fracture-filling is common. Some are heated *and* filled.

A much more extreme type of treatment entered the market about 12 years ago using extremely high heat and a surface coating of borax, which melts and leaves minor residues of glass in surface-reaching fractures. Some stones treated in this manner are also filled with glass or oil in order to reduce the visibility of larger internal cracks. This is considered an extreme treatment and rubies treated in this manner sell for much less than most other treatments, but they are, nonetheless, accurately identified as "treated" ruby.

The most recent ruby-like product—the "new type composite"—began to enter the market in the mid-2000s. It was very different from anything seen before, but no one understood this in the beginning. In addition, the moment anyone examining one of these composites saw indications of glass, they immediately assumed it was one of the less expensive stones that was treated by more extreme methods. It was assumed the stone was one of the inexpensive "heavily treated" rubies with glass fillings that had been in the market for years. Thus, they were erroneously identified. It didn't take long, however, to realize there was something significantly different about these stones.

The new treatment was directly connected to the discovery of a new source of very low-quality corundum (which, as mentioned earlier, is the mineral we know as "ruby" only when it occurs in a transparent, red variety, which is rare). This particular material was ideal for a new, two-step process. The corundum was entwined with other minerals and "debris" that could be easily leached out chemically, but what remained after the chemical leaching was very porous because of the voids and pits now present where the debris had once been. So step one was chemical leaching; step two required filling those voids, pits, and other openings. The ideal material for filling was *tinted molten lead-glass* because the high R.I. lead-glass made it impossible to see what was glass and what was ruby. When the glass cooled, it solidified, and the result was a beautiful, bright, red "ruby."

It began to show up at gem shows around the world, selling for $1–$4 per carat. No one questioned what they really were because they were cheap and it was assumed they were just the latest generation of "extreme" ruby treatments. When articles appeared about a new generation of "glass-filled" rubies, most people thought this was old news—glass-filled rubies had been around for years—and couldn't understand what the fuss was about. Most were excited to have such an attractive and affordable ruby alternative.

So, countless jewelers bought these stones as "treated" ruby and sold them to customers as such, never realizing they were actually a type of composite. When anyone took one to an appraiser, the moment that evidence of "glass" was seen (such as tiny rounded gas bubbles often seen in glass) they immediately identified them as the inexpensive rubies that had been subjected to extreme heating techniques and glass filling—and valued them accordingly—at "only a few *hundred* dollars" per carat. But had they been accurately identified, they *should have been* valued at only *a couple of dollars* per carat!

The problems presented by the erroneous identification of these composites were soon understood to be much worse than a matter of pricing. It was soon apparent that there was something significantly different about these new "treated" rubies.

The lead glass present in these rubies results in significant detrimental changes to the ruby's natural physical characteristics, which is why they cannot be considered "treated" rubies, and must be considered an artificial product.

An increasing number of experts and organizations in the United States and around the world agree that these stones are imitations; many identify them as "composite ruby" or by other similar names such as "glass-ruby composition" or "ruby with glass /glass with ruby." Whatever you call them, they are artificial. Personally, we prefer to call them "composites" and think this term best describes them. While the parts are not fused or glued together in flat "planes," they are nonetheless made from two different materials, artificially joined together, to create the appearance of a finer, rarer gem. Furthermore, the term "composite" already exists in the gemological literature and is understood to be an artificial product.

Unfortunately, there continues to be extensive confusion among jewelers about these new ruby composites, which puts everyone buying any ruby at risk. Many jewelers buy them without understanding what they are really buying and then inadvertently misrepresent what they are selling. They fail to disclose the need for extreme care when wearing or cleaning them, and whenever having work done on a piece of jewelry containing one. In addition, bench jewelers are at great risk of being accused of damaging one when the fault is not with the jeweler but with the product itself.

Perhaps most important, since they can easily chip or crack, they can more easily come out of settings without the wearer realizing it, or knowing where or how it was lost. This can put young children at risk of lead poisoning if they should find one on the floor and swallow it; the stomach acid will quickly dissolve the glass and release the lead! While no incidence of this has been reported, it is a very real possibility given the nature of the stone and the fact that they are also often set in cheap mountings in which prongs holding a stone in its setting can move or break off, causing the stone to fall out.

The use of lead-glass makes them more vulnerable to damage because lead-glass is softer than other types of glass, and more easily damaged by chemicals. This product requires a glass with a high R.I. however, which is why the glass used is *lead*-glass; the R.I. of the lead-glass is almost identical to ruby, which is why no one can see where one begins and the other ends. This is also why the treatment is much more effective in creating the appearance of fine ruby, and why the refractometer indicates "ruby."

These composite rubies look great—in fact, they often look like very fine rubies, of fine color—but they do not have the same hardness and durability of ruby, they do not have the same value as ruby, and a significant percentage of the stone is an altogether different material: lead-glass.

Note: While a "new" type of product, these are showing up in antique jewelry pieces around the world. When set in a very fine, genuine "period" piece—such as the one that turned up at the GIA lab, surrounded by fine diamonds and very fine, rare *natural* pearls— they are particularly convincing. Who would ever suspect that the large, red center stone in such a wonderful setting would be anything but a genuine ruby ... and given the age of the jewelry piece, possibly a "natural" ruby!

"COMPOSITE" RUBIES: A FEW FACTS TO SET THE RECORD STRAIGHT

The following is provided to help eliminate the confusion about these products—whatever they are being called—and help provide some clarity on how they differ from ruby or "treated" ruby. Here we will refer to them as "composite" ruby.

1. *What is "composite" ruby?*

   "Composite" rubies are created by using chemicals on very low-quality corundum to leach out extraneous minerals and debris. This step is followed by infusing molten lead-glass into the spaces and voids created by the removal of the unwanted material from the corundum.

2. *How do these compare to the value of natural or treated?*

   These are much cheaper than any "natural" or "treated" ruby, even rubies treated by extreme methods. Three years ago, most could be purchased at prices between $2–$5 per carat in sizes up to three carats; two years ago, prices were $4–$8 per carat; today prices are 3–4 times the original price, reflecting the dramatic rise in demand by buyers who still do not understand what they are actually buying.

3. *How much lead-glass is in a "composite" ruby?*

   The percentage of lead-glass present typically varies from about 15% to over 50%, but any stone that contains *any* amount of lead-glass must be identified as a "composite" ruby, even in cases where the amount of lead-glass appears to be minimal. This is because the refractive index (R.I.) of lead-glass is very high—and very close to that of ruby. This means that as light moves through the stone, *you cannot see where one substance ends and the other begins.* For this reason, in lead-glass products, one *can't see the fractures clearly* and can't accurately evaluate the stone's durability. It is virtually impossible to determine how deep or wide—how dangerous—any fracture(s) or void(s) might be. *Even a single fracture can be extremely dangerous and make the stone much more fragile and vulnerable to breaking, depending on where it is located and how far it penetrates into the stone.*

4. Does the presence of lead-glass affect color and clarity grading?

Since the lead glass is tinted and cannot be removed from the stone, it is not possible to accurately and reliably grade the *color*. With regard to clarity, the very high R.I. of the lead-glass, which is virtually a match to the R.I. of corundum, also makes it impossible to grade the stone's clarity.

The R.I. of a stone relates to how the light moves through, and between, different media—in the case of these composites, ruby and glass. The greater the difference between the R.I. of each substance, the more easily you can see important internal characteristics; the closer the R.I., the more difficult it is to see them. If the R.I. is essentially the same for both substances, you cannot distinguish where one ends and the other begins. This is why other types of glass sometimes seen in ruby and sapphire (usually silica glass) are different; they have lower R.I.s so you can actually see where the fracture is and properly grade the stone's clarity.

Since the R.I. of lead-glass is almost a perfect match to that of ruby, this is why these lead-glass products look clean and bright ... because you can't see the fractures or planes between the two substances. It is also impossible to determine how deep or wide—and how dangerous—any fracture(s) might be.

5. Does the presence of lead-glass affect the weight indicated for "composite" rubies? How do they compare to "treated" rubies that contain glass?

The "represented weight" for "composite" rubies and sapphires does not represent the weight of the ruby but, rather, the *combined* weight of the ruby *plus however much glass is present*. To make matters worse, lead-glass weighs approximately 1.5 times more than ruby or sapphire. So the actual weight of the ruby or sapphire in any of these new composites will always be less than the indicated weight and depending on the percentage of lead-glass in the stone, the actual weight might be significantly less than what is indicated.

By comparison, "treated" rubies contain *normal* glass, and only minimal amounts of glass are present, either as residue in surface reaching fissures as a result of very high heat techniques requiring that the stone be coated with borax for protection, (which melts and forms the glass residues) or in fractures that have been filled with glass to reduce their visibility or reflectivity (called "fracture-filled" or "in-filled" ruby).

Traditionally "treated" rubies containing glass have *much* less glass than lead-glass added to the low-quality corundum used to create "composite" ruby. As a result, the glass present in traditionally treated rubies has very little, if any, impact on a stone's weight.

6. *Are lead-glass ruby composites more fragile than "natural" or "treated" rubies?*

Yes. Coming into contact with a variety of common household substances and various types of surfaces that pose no threat to "natural ruby," or rubies treated by routine techniques, have proved disastrous for composite rubies.

Substances such as lemon juice and other solutions commonly found in households or on a jeweler's bench can quickly, easily, and irreparably damage these stones. Even lemon juice that accidentally gets splattered onto one of these stones while squeezing a lemon into iced tea or onto a salad or fish can etch the glass if not quickly removed, creating an ugly and undesirable stone that cannot be repaired.

Lead-glass is softer than other types of glass, and much softer than corundum, so these "composite" rubies are much more vulnerable to chipping and scratching from contact with any harder surface. Lead-glass hides cracks from view so they are more prone to being broken if accidentally knocked where the fracture reaches the surface of the stone. Facet edges are more easily abraided, becoming dull and unattractive

7. *Is damage to a "composite" ruby permanent and irreparable?*

Yes, which is not the case with natural and traditionally treated rubies; in the later, jewelry repairs or settings are much less likely to be damaged in the normal course of wear. But, should there be any damage, it is normally easy to repair with minimal loss of weight or value.

8. *These composites contain glass that is high in lead-content.* Below you can see how the quantity of lead present in the glass

itself affects the R.I.—the more lead, the higher the R.I. This also shows that the percentage of lead present in the glass used to create these new "composite" rubies and sapphires is very high since it matches the R.I. for ruby/sapphire which is approx. 1.76–1.77: This may pose health risks yet to be discovered.

R.I.'s for Various Glasses

Glass, Fused Silica -	RI 1.459
Glass, Pyrex -	RI 1.474
Glass, Flint, 29% lead -	RI 1.569
Glass, Flint, *55% lead -*	*RI 1.669*
Glass, Flint, *71% lead -*	*RI 1.805*

HOW TO DISTINGUISH "COMPOSITE" RUBY FROM TREATED OR NATURAL RUBY

It's not at all difficult to detect most rubies that are infused with lead-glass. The information and photographs here will show you some important indicators of lead-glass infusion. We recommend that you also take a hands-on workshop to gain an opportunity to see these features first hand and to gain confidence in spotting them.

Anyone buying rubies really only needs a couple simple, basic tools to be able to spot a composite: 1) a very small, very bright penlight; 2) a 10X loupe; and 3) a good dark-field loupe. For those who have the expertise, a good gemological microscope with dark-field and fiber optic lighting is also very useful if you have the luxury of being able to examine the piece in the comfort of your lab. An inexpensive, pocket-size 45X "binocular microscope," such as those offered all over the internet from $5–$10, is also very useful for seeing telltale surface crazing more quickly and easily. I now carry one with me everywhere!

It is essential that the entire stone be illuminated. It is also important to move the light source around the stone; you will need to light the stone from the top, side, and bottom, while observing carefully. Essentially you really have to *LIGHT IT UP!* See figures 2–4

Figure 1. Recommended lights include inexpensive intense lights such as a mini-maglite or other intense small light. Using a loupe with overhead lighting, or one of the lighted loupes like a lumi-light, are not as effective as using a tiny, intense light that is independent of the loupe. Using a loupe *alone* is inadequate to show you the telltale indicators.

Figure 2

Figure 3

Figure 4

THREE BASIC FEATURES ARE INDICATORS OF LEAD-GLASS "COMPOSITE" RUBY

Now that you're ready to carefully examine the ruby, there are three basic features to look for with the loupe/pen-light, dark-field loupe, or microscope using fiber optic light:

- Irregular surface features—*crazing*—on the surface of the stone. Compare figure 5 (the surface of a normal ruby) with figures 6–7, which show crazing typically seen in "composite" ruby.
- Blue flash-effects (see bluish areas in figure 4)
- Gas bubbles (see rounded "bubbles" in figures 3–4 and 11–12)

These three features are typical in most "composite" rubies. While it may not be easy to see all three in a single stone without a good gemological microscope with proper lighting and a little experience, most lead-glass infused rubies show at least two of these features using only a loupe and intense light.

1. Irregular Surface Features (crazed surface)

Lead-glass "composite" rubies show *crazing* from the many filled-cracks and voids present in this type of ruby. These can be seen with the loupe as you examine the *surface* of the ruby in *reflected* light (lighting the stone so the surface is "glassy"—like the surface seen on a lake with the sun reflecting off the water).

Below (figure 5) is the table facet of a *normal* ruby which has been processed in the traditional manner; you might see some tiny pin-point "dots" or a single line or two resulting from a minute amount of glass residue resulting from accepted heating techniques, or the filling of a fracture with common glass which is sometimes done in addition to the heating of a ruby (the material previously known as "glass-filled ruby"). Traditionally "treated" ruby with glass residues or glass-filled cracks are quite stable and account for most commercially priced ruby that has been sold until the introduction of these new lead-glass infused rubies.

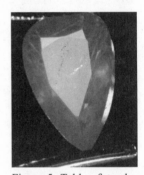

Figure 5. Table of a ruby seen in reflected light.

The images to the right (figures 6–7) show the typical surface of a composite when examined in reflected light. Note the crazed effect—lots of lines often criss-crossing each other; each of which is a surface-reaching crack or small opening filled with glass.

Figures 6 and 7 showing crazing in composite ruby.

2. Flash Effects

Most composites show a blue "flash effect" (figures 8–10) quite similar in appearance to fracture-filled diamonds. Traditionally treated ruby *does not* show this feature. (See photos in color insert.)

Figure 8

Figure 9

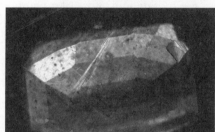

Figure 10

3. Gas Bubbles

Often, "composite" rubies contain so much lead-glass that gas bubbles can be seen throughout the stone; sometimes, entire "voids" can be seen (as yellowish blobs within the stone). This is not seen in traditionally "treated" ruby (see figures 11–12).

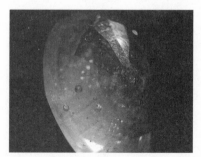

Figure 11

Figure 12

In summary, it really takes no time at all to become proficient in identifying "composite" ruby. This same process is also now used to create sapphire composites; we have seen green and yellow "composite" sapphires that were sold on eBay as genuine "treated" sapphires, without special care warnings. The telltale indictors remain the same.

We highly recommend getting a copy of a booklet entitled *IS THAT REALLY A RUBY?*, by Craig Lynch, GG. Copies are available from the Accredited Gemologists Association (www.accreditedgemologists.org) or directly from the author (craig@ouellet-lynch.com). It is a brief booklet, with minimal text and many superb color photos of the telltale indicators of a composite. At approximately $18.00, it is a must-have for anyone buying rubies or sapphires today.

NOTES

APPENDICES

GEMSTONE PROPERTY TABLES

Frequently Encountered Transparent Gems

RED AND PINK GEMSTONES AND THEIR LOOK-ALIKES

Almandite garnet
Beryl (pink–morganite;
  red–called red beryl or
  "red emerald")
Chrysoberyl (alexandrite)
Corundum (ruby &
  pink sapphire)
Diamond
Glass
Plastics
Pyrope garnet
Quartz (rose quartz)

Rhodolite garnet
Spinel
Spodumene (kunzite)
Synthetic corundum
Synthetic spinel
Topaz
Tourmaline
Zircon

Doublets
Triplets
Foil backs

BROWN AND ORANGE GEMSTONES AND THEIR LOOK-ALIKES

Amber and pressed amber
Beryl
Chrysoberyl
Copal (and other natural resins)
Corundum
Diamond
Glass
Grossularite garnet
  (hessonite)
Opal (fire opal)
Plastics
Quartz
Chalcedony (carnelian and sard)

Sinhalite
Spessartite garnet ("mandarin"
  or "kashmirene")
Spinel
Synthetic corundum
Synthetic rutile
Synthetic spinel
Topaz
Tourmaline
Zircon

Doublets
Triplets

YELLOW GEMSTONES AND THEIR LOOK-ALIKES

Amber

Beryl

Chrysoberyl

Corundum

Diamond

Glass

Grossularite garnet
  (hessonite)

Opal

Plastics

Quartz (citrine)

Spessartite garnet

Spodumene

Synthetic corundum

Synthetic diamond

Synthetic rutile

Synthetic spinel

Topaz

Tourmaline

Zircon

Doublets

Triplets

Foil backs

GREEN GEMSTONES AND THEIR LOOK-ALIKES

Andradite garnet (demantoid)

Beryl (emerald)

Chrysoberyl (including cat's
  eye and alexandrite)

Corundum (green sapphire)

Diamond

Glass

Grossularite garnet
  (tsavorite)

Peridot

Plastics

Quartz

Spinel

Synthetic corundum

Synthetic diamond

Synthetic garnet (YAG)

Synthetic emerald

Synthetic spinel

Topaz

Tourmaline

Zircon

Doublets

Triplets

BLUE GEMSTONES AND THEIR LOOK-ALIKES

Apatite

Beryl (aquamarine)

Corundum (sapphire)

Diamond

Synthetic corundum

Synthetic forsterite

Synthetic rutile

Synthetic spinel

Blue continued

Glass	YAG
Iolite (dichroite)	Zircon
Plastics	Zoisite (tanzanite)
Quartz (dyed)	
Opal	Doublets
Spinel	Triplets
Topaz	Foil backs
Tourmaline (indicolite)	

PURPLE AND VIOLET GEMSTONES AND THEIR LOOK-ALIKES

Almandite garnet	Synthetic corundum
Chrysoberyl (alexandrite)	Synthetic forsterite
Corundum (sapphire)	Synthetic spinel
Diamond	Topaz
Glass	Tourmaline
Plastics	YAG
Pyrope garnet	Zircon
Quartz (amethyst)	Zoisite (Tanzanite)
Rhodolite garnet	
Spinel	Doublets
Spodumene (kunzite)	

COLORLESS GEMSTONES AND THEIR LOOK-ALIKES

Beryl	Strontium titanate
Corundum (white sapphire)	Synthetic corundum
Diamond	Synthetic diamond
Glass	Synthetic rutile
Grossularite garnet	Synthetic spinel
Opal	Topaz
Feldspar (moonstone)	Tourmaline
Plastics	YAG
Quartz (rock crystal)	Zircon (jargoon)
Spinel	

Frequently Encountered Non-Transparent Gems

BLACK GEMSTONES AND THEIR LOOK-ALIKES

Andradite garnet (melanite)   Jet
Black coral   Nephrite jade
Chalcedony (black onyx)   Obsidian
Corundum (star sapphire)   Opal
Diopside (star)   Opal doublets
Diamond   Plastics
Glass   Psilomelane
Hematite   Tourmaline
Jadeite jade

GRAY GEMSTONES AND THEIR LOOK-ALIKES

Chalcedony (agate)   Jadeite jade
Corundum (star sapphire)   Labradorite feldspar
Hematite   Nephrite jade
Hemetine   Sintered synthetic corundum

WHITE GEMSTONES AND THEIR LOOK-ALIKES

Alabaster   Jadeite jade
Chalcedony (chalcedony   Nephrite jade
  moonstone)   Onyx marble
Coral   Opal
Corundum   Opal doublets
Glass   Feldspar (moonstone)
Grossularite   Plastics

Blue GEMSTONES AND THEIR LOOK-ALIKES

Corundum   Lapis
Chalcedony   Sodalite
Glass   Turquoise

Hardness of Popular Gems

Diamond & Syn.	10
Silicon carbide (syn. moissanite)	9 $1/4$
Corundum & Syn.	9
Chrysoberyl	8 $1/2$
YAG	8 $1/4$
Spinel & Syn.	8
Topaz	8
Beryl & syn. emerald	7 $1/2$–8
Zircon (high, medium)	7 $1/2$
Almandite garnet	7 $1/2$
Rhodolite garnet	7–7 $1/2$
Pyrope garnet	7–7 $1/2$
Spessartite garnet	7–7 $1/2$
Tourmaline	7–7 $1/2$
Andalusite	7–7 $1/2$
Iolite	7–7 $1/2$
Grossularite garnet	7
Quartz & Syn	7
Chalcedony	6 $1/2$–7
Peridot	6 $1/2$–7
Jadeite	6 $1/2$–7
Andradite garnet (Demantoid)	6 $1/2$–7
Diaspore	6 $1/2$–7
Idocrase	6 $1/2$
Scapolite	6 $1/2$
Kornerupine	6 $1/2$
Zircon (low)	6 $1/2$
Spodumene	6–7
Sinhalite	6–7
Epidote	6–7
Zoisite	6–7
Rutile & Syn.	6–6 $1/2$
Albite-Oligoclase	6–6 $1/2$
Orthoclase	6–6 $1/2$
Nephrite	6–6 $1/2$
Pyrite	6–6 $1/2$
Benitoite	6–6 $1/2$
Marcasite	6–6 $1/2$
Labradorite	6
Amblygonite	6
Hematite	5 $1/2$–6 $1/2$
Rhodonite	5 $1/2$–6 $1/2$
Opal	5–6 $1/2$
Diopside	5–6
Glass	5–6
Strontium titanate	5–6
Lazulite	5–6
Lazurite (lapis-lazuli)	5–6
Turquoise	5–6
Sodalite	5–6
Sphene	5–5 $1/2$
Obsidian	5–5 $1/2$
Bowenite (serpentine)	5–5 $1/2$
Apatite	5
Dioptase	5
Smithsonite	5
Syn. Turquoise	5
Syn. Opal	4 $1/2$
Fluorite	4
Rhodochrosite	3 $1/2$–4 $1/2$
Malachite	3 $1/2$–4
Azurite	3 $1/2$–4
Sphalerite	3 $1/2$–4
Coral	3 $1/2$–4
Conch Pearl	3 $1/2$
Calcite	3
Black Coral	3
Pearl	2 $1/2$–4 $1/2$
Jet	2 $1/2$–4
Serpentine	2–4
Amber	2–2 $1/2$
Copal	2
Alabaster	2
Steatite (soapstone)	1 $1/2$–2 $1/2$

Specific Gravity Table

Cassiterite..................	6.95 (±.08)	Kornerupine	3.30 (±.05)
Cubic Zirconia	5.80 (±.20)	Diopside....................	3.29 (±.03)
Strontium titanate......	5.13 (±.02)	Ekanite	3.28
Pyrite........................	5.00 (±.10)	Enstatite....................	3.25 (±.02)
Marcasite..................	4.85 (±.05)	Fluorite.....................	3.18 (±.01)
Langasite (lab-grown)	4.65	Apatite......................	3.18 (±.02)
Zircon		Spodumene................	3.18 (±.03)
(high)......................	4.70 (±.03)	Syn. Moissanite........	3.17 (±.03)
(medium)................	4.32 (±.25)	Andalusite	3.17 (±.04)
Gahnite......................	4.55	Euclase	3.10 (±.01)
YAG..........................	4.55	Lazulite	3.09 (±.05)
Smithsonite	4.30 (±.10)	Tourmaline................	3.06 (-.05, +.15)
Rutile & Syn.	4.26 (±.02)	Amblygonite	3.02
Spessartite	4.15 (±.03)	Danburite...................	3.00 (±.01)
Almandite.................	4.05 (±.12)	Nephrite....................	2.95 (±.05)
Sphalerite	4.05 (±.02)	Phenakite.................	2.95 (±.01)
Gahnospinel	4.01 (±.40)	Datolite....................	2.95
Zircon (low)	4.00 (±.07)	Brazilianite................	2.94
Corundum & Syn......	4.00 (±.03)	Pollucite	2.92
Malachite..................	3.95 (-.70, +.15)	Prehnite	2.88 (±.06)
Andradite..................	3.84 (±.03)	Beryllonite................	2.85 (±.02)
Rhodolite..................	3.84 (±.10)	Conch pearl	2.85
Azurite......................	3.80 (-.50, +.07)	Turquoise	2.76 (-.45, +.08)
Pyrope	3.78 (-.16, +.09)	Steatite......................	2.75
Chrysoberyl..............	3.73 (±.02)	Lazurite	
Rhodochrosite	3.70	(lapis-lazuli)...........	2.75 (±.25)
Syn. spinel................	3.64 (-.12, +.02)	Beryl........................	2.72 (-.05, +.12)
Benitoite	3.64 (±.03)	Labradorite................	2.70 (±.05)
Kyanite.....................	3.62 (±.06)	Calcite	2.70
Grossularite	3.61 (-.27, +.12)	Scapolite...................	2.68 (±.06)
Taaffeite	3.61	Syn. emerald	
Spinel	3.60 (-.03, +.30)	(hydroth.)	2.68 (±.02)
Topaz........................	3.53 (±.04)	(Gilson).................	2.67 (±.02)
Diamond...................	3.52 (±.01)	(flux)	2.66
Sphene......................	3.52 (±.02)	Quartz & Syn.	2.66 (±.01)
Rhodonite.................	3.50 (±.20)	Syn. Turquoise.........	2.66
Sinhalite	3.48	Albite-Oligoclae........	2.65 (±.02)
Idocrase	3.40 (±.10)	Coral........................	2.65 (±.02)
Epidote	3.40 (±.08)	Iolite	2.61 (±.05)
Diaspore	3.39	Chalcedony	2.60 (±.05)
Peridot......................	3.34 (-.03, +.14)	Serpentine	2.57 (±.06)
Jadeite	3.34 (±.04)	Orthoclase	2.56 (±.01)
Zoisite (tanzanite)	3.30 (±.10)	Microcline	2.56 (±.01)
Dioptase	3.30 (.05)	Variscite...................	2.50 (±.08)

Obsidian	2.45 (±.10)	Opal	2.15 (-.90, +.07)
Moldavite	2.40 (±.04)	Syn. Opal	2.05 (±.03)
Apophyllite	2.40 (±.10)	Coral (black)	1.37
Thomsonite	2.35 (±.05)	Jet	1.32 (±.02)
Alabaster	2.30	Plastics	1.30 (±.25)
Glass	2.3 to 4.5	Amber	1.08 (±.02)
Sodalite	2.24 (±.05)	Copal	1.06
Chrysocolla	2.20 (±.10)		

Refractive Index Tables
Single Refracting Gems

Gemstone	Refractive Index Reading
Diamond	2.417
Strontium titanate	2.409
Sphalerite	2.37
Cubic zirconia	2.15 (±.03)
Andradite garnet	1.875 (±.020)
YAG	1.833
Spessartite garnet	1.81 (±.010)
Gahnite (blue/blue green spinel)	1.80
Almandite garnet	1.79 (±.030)
Rhodolite garnet	1.76 (±.010)
Gahnospinel (blue spinel)	1.76 (±.02)
Pyrope garnet	1.746 (-.026, +.010)
Grossularite garnet	1.735 (+.015, -.035)
Synthetic Spinel	1.73 (±.01)
Spinel	1.718 (-.006, +.044)
Jet	1.66 (±.020)
Bakelite	1.61 (±.06)
Ekanite	1.597
Amber	1.540
Pollucite	1.525
Lazurite (lapis-lazuli)	1.500
Obsidian	1.500
Sodalite	1.483 (±.003)
Glass (normal)	1.48–1.70
(extreme)	1.44–1.77 (Most read between 1.45–1.65)
Moldavite	1.48
Opal	1.45 (-.080, +.020)
Synthetic opal	1.44
Fluorite	1.434

Refractive Index Tables
Double Refracting Gems

Gemstone	Low R.I. Reading	High R.I. Reading
Syn. Moissanite...........	2.65	2.69
Rutile & Syn.	2.616	2.903
Cassiterite....................	1.997	2.093
Zircon (high)...............	1.925	1.984
Scheelite......................	1.918	1.934
Langasite.....................	1.909	1.921
Sphene........................	1.900 (±.018)	2.034 (±.020)
Zircon (medium).........	1.875 (±.045)	1.905 (±.075)
Zircon (low)................	1.810 (±.030)	1.815 (+.030)
Corundum	1.762 (-.003, +.007)	1.770 (-.003, +.008)
Synthetic corundum	1.762	1.770
Benitoite......................	1.757	1.804
Chrysoberyl.................	1.746 (±.004)	1.755 (±.005)
Azurite.........................	1.73 (±.010)	1.84 (±.010)
Rhodonite....................	1.73	1.74
Epidote	1.729 (-.015, +.006)	1.768 (-.035, +.012)
Taaffeite	1.719	1.723
Kyanite........................	1.716 (±.004)	1.731 (±.004)
Idocrase......................	1.713 (±.012)	1.718 (±.014)
Diaspore (color-change)	1.702	1.750
Zoisite (Tanzanite)......	1.691 (±.002)	1.704 (±.003)
Axinite........................	1.678	1.688
Diopside	1.675 (-.010, +.027)	1.701 (-.077, +.029)
Sinhalite	1.668 (±.003)	1.707 (±.003)
Kornerupine	1.667 (±.002)	1.680 (±.003)
Jadeite	1.66 (±.007)	1.68 (±.009)
Malachite....................	1.66	1.91
Spodumene..................	1.660 (±.005)	1.676 (±.005)
Enstatite......................	1.658 (±.005)	1.668 (±.005)
Dioptase	1.655 (±.011)	1.708 (±.012)
Peridot........................	1.654 (±.020)	1.690 (±.020)
Euclase	1.654 (±.004)	1.673 (±.004)
Phenakite....................	1.654 (-.003, +.017)	1.670 (-.004, +.026)
Apatite........................	1.642 (-.012, +.003)	1.646 (-.014, +.005)
Synthetic Forsterite	1.635 (±.002)	1.670 (±.001)
Andalusite	1.634 (±.006)	1.643 (±.004)
Danburite....................	1.630 (±.003)	1.636 (±.003)
Datolite.......................	1.626	1.670
Tourmaline..................	1.624 (±.005)	1.644 (±.006)
Smithsonite	1.621	1.849

Double Refracting Gems—Continued

Gemstone	Low R.I. Reading	High R.I. Reading
Topaz	1.619 (±.010)	1.627 (±.010)
Natural pink	1.63	1.64
Prehnite	1.615	1.646
Turquoise	1.61	1.65
Lazulite	1.612	1.643
Amblygonite	1.612	1.636
Nephrite	1.606	1.632
Brazilianite	1.602	1.621
Rhodochrosite	1.597	1.817
Synthetic turquoise	1.59	1.60
Beryl	1.577 (±.016)	1.583 (±.017)
Synthetic emerald (New Gilson)	1.571	1.579
Synthetic emerald (hydrothermal)	1.568 (±.02)	1.573 (±.02)
Synthetic emerald (flux)	1.561	1.564
Variscite	1.56	1.59
Serpentine	1.56 (-.07)	1.570 (-.07)
Coral, black (akabar)	1.56	1.57
Labradorite and andesine feldspar	1.559 (±.01)	1.568 (±.01
Beryllonite	1.552	1.562
Agalmatolite (soapstone)	1.55	1.60
Scapolite	1.55	1.572
Quartz & Syn.	1.544 (±.000)	1.553 (±.000)
Iolite (dichroite)	1.542 (-.010, +.002)	1.551 (-.011,+.045)
Steatite (meerschaum)	1.54	1.590
Chalcedony	1.535	1.539
Apophyllite	1.535	1.537
Albite-oligoclase (moonstone)	1.532 (±.007)	1.542 (±.006)
Microcline (Amazonite)	1.522	1.530
Orthoclase (Moonstone)	1.518	1.526
Thomsonite	1.515	1.540
Calcite	1.486	1.658
Coral	1.486	1.658

Table of Dispersion

The following figures represent the difference in the gem's refractive index for red light and blue-violet light.

Fluorite	.007		
Silica glass	.010	Spinel	.020
Beryllonite	.010	Dioptase	.022
Kyanite	.011	Almandine garnet	.024
Orthoclase feldspar	.012	Rhodolite garnet	.026
Quartz	.013	Pyrope garnet	.027
Beryl	.014	Spessartite garnet	.027
Topaz	.014	Grossularite garnet	.028
Phenakite	.015	Epidote	.030
Chrysoberyl	.015	Zircon	.038
Euclase	.016	Benitoite	.044
Danburite	.016	Diamond	.044
Datolite	.016	Sphene	.051
Scapolite	.017	Andradite garnet	
Tourmaline	.017	(Demantoid)	.057
Spodumene	.017	Cassiterite	.071
Corundum	.018	Syn. Moissanite	.09
Kornerupine	.019	Sphalerite	.156
Idocrase	.019	Strontium titanate	.109
Peridot	.020	Synthetic rutile	.280

Table of Birefringence of Gemstones

Apatite	.002–.006	Tourmaline	.018–.02+
Syn. emerald		Euclase	.019
(flux melt)	.003	Brazilianite	.019
Zircon (low)	about .005	Diopside	.026
Beryl	.005–.009	Peridot	.036
Andalusite	.008–.013	Epidote	.039
Corundum	.008	Sinhalite	.039
Topaz	.008–.010	Syn. Moissanite	.043
Zoisite (tanzanite)	.008	Datolite	.044
Chrysoberyl	.009	Benitoite	.047
Quartz	.009	Diaspore	.048
Beryllonite	.010	Dioptase	.053
Enstatite	.010	Zircon	up to .059
Kornerupine	.013	Cassiterite	.096
Kyanite	.015	Sphene	.134
Phenakite	.015	Calcite	.172
Scheelite	.016	Syn. Rutile	.287
Spodumene	.016		

Glossary

absorption spectrum—A term referring to the rainbow-like spectral picture of a gem produced by the spectroscope, characterized by dark lines or bars where some wavelengths of light have been absorbed by the gemstone as light passes through it. The areas of absorption appear in characteristic patterns for many gems and provide useful data for identification.

ADR (anomalous double refraction)—An optical effect resembling wiggly dark lines observed when using the polariscope with certain cubic or amorphous gems. It is caused by strain during crystal growth (see Chapter 11).

AGL—American Gemological Laboratory, a New York–based laboratory specializing in colored gemstone testing and detection of treatments. AGL also provides internationally recognized reports on colored gems.

amorphous—A term referring to substances that do not have crystalline properties, such as glass, amber, and opal.

anisotropic—Another term for gems that are double refracting.

antique jewelry—Jewelry that is at least 100 years old.

Art Deco jewelry—Jewelry exhibiting a decorative style popular from about 1920 to 1930. Derived from cubism, it is characterized by strong geometric design.

Art Modern (Retro)—Jewelry from about 1940, characterized by wide use of rose gold with both natural and synthetic ruby. Affordable colored stones such as citrine and aquamarine were popular. The style is typically large and bold.

Art Nouveau jewelry—A style of jewelry popular from the early 1890s until about 1915, frequently mixing gemstones with more common materials (such as jet) regardless of intrinsic value. The style was flowing, with heavy use of enamelling. Baroque pearls with interesting shapes were often used. Themes evolved around nature, whimsical subjects, and mythology.

asterism—A star effect exhibited by some gems (natural and synthetic) when viewed under strong light. The star can be four- or six-rayed.

bezel facet—The facets in a brilliant-cut stone that slant upward from the girdle to the table (kite shaped).

bezel setting—A setting in which the stones are held along the girdle by a rim of metal rather than prongs.

birefringence—A measurement of the strength of a gem's double refraction; a value obtained for double-refracting gems that reflects the difference in its highest and lowest refractive index (see Chapter 8).

blackening—a technique using a sugar-acid chemical reaction to introduce carbon into a stone to blacken it. Most "black onyx" and some "black opal" is created by this technique.

brilliance—The intensity or vividness of color, or the degree of brightness, resulting from the reflection of light from the back facets back to the eye.

bubble—A type of inclusion that resembles a bubble. Bubbles provide important clues to gem identification (see Chapters 4 and 9).

bulk diffusion—enhancement technique to create blue sapphire, ruby, or fancy-color sapphire from near-colorless stones, using heat and chemical additives such as beryllium.

carat—A unit of weight (one-fifth of a gram) by which gemstones are weighed.

cabochon—A cutting style that produces a stone with a smooth, polished, rounded, or convex surface. It lacks the tiny, flat faces (facets) seen in most gems, such as diamond, to enhance their brilliance.

CG or **CGA**—Certified Gemologist or Certified Gemologist Appraiser, highly respected titles awarded by the American Gem Society to those who pass stringent examinations. One of the most prestigious titles awarded to gemologists and gemologist appraisers in the U.S.

chatoyancy—An optical phenomenon exhibited by some gems such as "cat's-eye chrysoberyl," whereby an "eye" effect is seen as the stone is tilted under a strong light.

clarity—The term that refers to a stone's freedom from inclusions. Sometimes referred to as the "flaw grade."

cleavage—A plane of weakness along which some gems will split apart, leaving a fairly smooth surface where it has split rather than a jagged edge (as seen in most cracks or fractures). Cleavage planes occur in certain definite directions, and some gems have a tendency to break along these planes.

closed back setting—A type of setting that completely encloses the back of the stone so that it can't be seen from the back side. Used often in antique jewelry to add brilliance, this type of setting was also used to deceive (see Chapter 14).

composite stone—a) A stone created by gluing or fusing together two or three parts (see Chapter 14), or b) a stone created by chemically leeching out extraneous minerals and debris from low-quality material and infusing it throughout with molten glass, in which the glass and stone components are inseparable. The new glass *infused* type composite can be easily mistaken for a single stone (see Chapter 18).

crown—The top portion of any faceted stone; the part above the girdle.

cryptocrystalline—A gemstone composed of innumerable small crystals that are so small they can't even be detected with most high power microscopes (they are visible with the powerful, highly sophisticated electron microscope).

cubic system—A crystal system (also called isometric) in which several gems crystallize. These gems are single refracting and their properties do not change when examined from various directions.

culet—A tiny flat facet that runs parallel to the girdle and is located at the very tip of the pavilion of a faceted stone (it is so small that to most people it looks like a "point").

dendritic—A pattern having a root- or branch-like design.

density—The weight of a substance compared to the weight of an equal volume of water; or, how many times heavier a substance is than the same amount of water. The term "density" is usually used for liquids and the term "specific gravity" for solids.

depth of field—The limited distance or range in which objects are in focus while being viewed under a magnifier such as a loupe or microscope (see Chapters 4 and 9).

dichroism—The property of a stone that causes two colors or shades of the same color to be visible when examined with the dichroscope. These are called dichroic stones (see Chapter 6).

diffusion—a treatment process used to add surface-color to sapphire and ruby using chemical coatings with controlled heat (see "bulk diffusion").

dispersion—The extent to which a transparent gem splits white light into the seven colors of the spectrum and displays "fire"—the flashes of color reflected from the internal facets of the cut stone. Diamond has a high dispersion and synthetic rutile has the highest.

doublet—A stone created by man by fusing or cementing two pieces of material together (doublet); when three pieces are used, it is called a "triplet."

doubling—A phenomenon that resembles "seeing double" when looking through some stones to the back facet edges with a magnifier. When viewing certain stones with a loupe or microscope from different directions, through at least one direction the edges of the back facets will appear doubled, like railroad tracks.

double refracting—A property found in most gems whereby single rays of light entering the stone are split into two rays (see Chapters 6 and 8).

emerald filter—Another name used for the Chelsea color filter since it was originally used to separate genuine emeralds from their lookalikes.

facet—A polished, flat plane on the surface of a cut gem.

faceted—A cutting style that consists of placing small, flat, polished "faces" around a stone at varying angles to one another, usually in a repeated, geometric pattern. It is normally used for transparent gems, to influence the way light travels through the stone so that maximum brilliance and fire are obtained. Faceting is an art form that has only been fully developed in the 20th century.

fancy—(1) A colored diamond; (2) an unusual cut or cutting style. A diamond dealer specializing in "fancies" either specializes in natural colored diamonds or in diamonds cut in special or unusual cuts/shapes.

FGA—Fellow of the Gemmological Association of Great Britain, a designation awarded to individuals who have passed examinations given by this association. The FGA title is considered one of the most prestigious titles awarded to gemologists anywhere in the world.

fire—The variety and intensity of rainbow colors seen in a gem. Another word for "dispersion."

fluorescence—A property found in some diamonds and colored gems that causes them to appear one color when viewed in normal light and to glow a different color when exposed to radiation, such as that provided by an ultraviolet lamp. As a result of fluorescence, in certain lights some diamonds can appear whiter than they actually are. Whether or not a stone fluoresces, and the particular color it may fluoresce, provides an important clue in diamond and colored gemstone identification (see Chapter 7).

fluorescent light—Light produced by the fluorescence of phosphors inside a glass tube (these are what you have in a fluorescent lamp).

foil backing—A technique used for jewelry in which the setting is lined with a sheet of metallic foil. Foil backing was used for both transparent faceted stones and cabochons to add brilliance and enhance or change the color (see Chapter 14).

GG—Graduate Gemologist, the highest title awarded by the Gemological Institute of America, to persons who have passed the required examinations administered by the GIA. Internationally recognized.

GIA—Gemological Institute of America, an organization that offers educational programs in gemology and related fields; also operates the Gem Testing Laboratory (New York and Carlsbad) that issues reports on diamonds, colored gems and pearls.

girdle—The edge of the stone that forms its perimeter; the point (border) at which the top portion meets the bottom portion of the stone—its "dividing line." The portion usually grasped by the setting.

HPHT—high-pressure/high-temperature annealing techniques used to transform tinted diamonds into colorless, near-colorless, and fancy-color diamonds, or to intensify or purify fancy colors; also, a technique used to create synthetic diamonds.

immersion microscopy—Microscopic examination of a stone that is immersed in a liquid (normally with a high refractive index). This often enables one to more easily see inclusions, color banding, striae, twin lines, and other phenomena.

incandescent light—Light such as that produced by an ordinary light bulb or candle (see Chapter 3).

imitation stone—Materials such as glass or plastic that resemble a genuine stone in appearance but do not possess the chemical, physical, or crystal properties of the stone it is trying to imitate.

inclusion—Something that is "included" inside the gemstone—any foreign body enclosed within it. It can be a gas, liquid, or solid. Inclusions provide important clues for gem identification (see Chapters 4 and 9).

inert—A gem that shows no change under testing procedures. For example, a stone that shows no color change when examined with the Chelsea filter is inert; a stone that shows no color change when examined under the ultraviolet lamp is inert.

iridescence—A rainbow-like effect that usually occurs when light hits a fracture (crack) in a stone (especially noticeable when the crack breaks the surface).

irradiation—The bombardment of gems by atomic particles or exposure to radioactive radiation to change or enhance their color.

isotropic—Amorphous materials (opal, amber, glass, plastic) and gems that crystallize in the cubic system. Such gem materials are single refracting and will exhibit the same optical properties from any direction.

luster—The intensity and quality of reflected light from the surface of a stone. Luster varies among different gemstone families as a result of different physical characteristics and can be described as adamantine (bright luster as seen in diamond), vitreous (shiny or glassy), resinous, and pearly. Most gems have vitreous luster.

Master Gemologist Appraiser (MGA)—The highest title awarded to gemologist appraisers of the American Society of Appraisers, to those passing very stringent examinations given by the Accredited Gemologists Association. One of the most prestigious gemologist appraiser titles available in the United States.

monochromatic light—A light source that produces only one color of the visible spectrum. Monochromatic yellow light is often used for gem testing (see Chapter 3).

metamict—A gemstone (such as zircon) that has had its internal structure disrupted by radioactive exposure causing it to lose its original crystal structure and become amorphous.

Mohs hardness scale—A scale ranging from 1 to 10 that is used to indicate relative hardness. The value of 1 indicates the softest (talc) and 10 indicates the hardest (diamond).

oiling—A gem enhancement technique used to hide or seal cracks in a stone and, in some cases, to improve a stone's color.

Old European cut—a round, brilliant-cut developed in the 1880s and characterized by its small table facet, high crown, and large (open) culet. It was replaced by the modern brilliant-cut, after 1919.

Old mine cut—an early brilliant-cut that evolved from the rose cut, probably in the 18th century, and continued into the 19th century until the development of the old European cut. It can be either round or cushion-shape (roundish, but slightly squared or rectangular), has an even higher crown than the old European, and, usually an even larger culet and smaller table.

opaque—A term used for gemstones such as lapis or malachite through which light cannot travel; stones through which you can't see any light at all.

paste—A term loosely applied to all glass imitation gemstones.

pavilion—The bottom portion of a stone; the portion below the girdle.

phosphorescence—The property of some gems that have been exposed to radiation such as ultraviolet to continue to glow after the radiation has been turned off (see Chapter 7).

pleochroism—A general term embracing dichroism and trichroism (see Chapter 6).

polycrystalline—A term describing gems that are made up of aggregates of very small crystals. Jadeite is a very good example.

reflected light—Light shining off a polished surface is reflected light. Gems having a high refractive index tend to reflect light more strongly than those with a lower refractive index.

refraction—The amount a light ray bends as it passes through a gem.

refractive index—A measurement of the angle at which light is bent as it travels through a stone (see Chapter 8).

rough—Uncut gem material.

sheen—An effect resembling luster that is caused by the reflection of light from fine inclusions or structural texture inside a gem. Luster is light reflected from the surface of a gem and sheen is light reflected from something within the gem.

silk—Fine, intersecting, needlelike crystal inclusions that exhibit a silky sheen in reflected light.

simulant—A gem material that is manmade and has not been found to occur naturally.

single refracting—A gem material that allows a single ray of light to enter it and continue through as a single ray (see Chapter 8).

soudé-type composite—A stone created by fusing together two pieces of gem material such as colorless quartz or synthetic colorless spinel with an appropriate coloring agent in the center. There are many soudé-type emerald doublets.

specific gravity—See *density*.

species—A term used to designate a gem family. Quartz is a species that has varieties called rose quartz, amethyst, citrine, smoky quartz, praseolite, aventurine, chalcedony, jasper, and so on; beryl is a species that has varieties called emerald, aquamarine, heliodor, and morganite.

synthetic—A manmade stone that has essentially the same physical, chemical, and optical properties of the genuine stone it is trying to imitate. Some of the newest synthetics are extremely difficult to distinguish from the genuine. Care must be taken to verify that a gem is genuine and not synthetic. Do not confuse with "imitation," a term that refers to man-made stones that may look like something they aren't but are very easily distinguished from the genuine because their physical and chemical properties are completely different.

table—The large, flat, horizontal facet at the very top of a faceted stone. The table is the largest facet.

transmitted light—Light shining through a stone from the bottom or sides.

translucent—Transmitting light imperfectly so that one cannot see through the material clearly. With the exception of translucent material such as star ruby, star sapphire, or precious cats-eye, most is suitable only for cabochons, beads, or carvings.

treated stone—A stone that has been dyed, stained, heated, and/or irradiated to enhance color or improve clarity; also, gems that have had cracks filled with glass to conceal them or to enhance color.

trichroism—A property exhibited by some stones that causes three colors or shades of the same color to be visible—two at a time—when viewed with the dichroscope. These are called trichroic gems (see Chapter 6).

triplet—A stone created by joining together three pieces of some gemlike material; a type of composite stone like the doublet but composed of three pieces rather than two (see Chapter 14).

variety—Different types and colors of a gem within a species. See species.

Verneuil—The name of the first commercial method for making synthetic gems. Starting in 1902, this flame-fusion method was used to produce synthetic ruby and spinel.

Victorian jewelry—Jewelry made from about 1837 to 1901.

waxing—A process in which the stone is rubbed with a tinted waxlike substance to hide surface cracks or blemishes and improve color.

vitreous luster—Luster with a shiny, glassy appearance. Most gems exhibit this glass-like luster.

zoned—A term used to describe uneven distribution of color. In such stones, zoning usually occurs in parallel planes (zones) with a zone of color laying parallel to a colorless zone. When viewed from the top, the stone may appear to have uniform color. Zoning can be most easily seen viewing the stone through the side (against a flat white background, if possible) rather than from the top.

Recommended Reading

Books

Anderson, B. W. *GEM TESTING*. 10th ed. Oxford: Butterworth-Heinemann, 1990.

Fully updated and revised. Essential for the serious gemologist.

Anderson, Basil, and James Payne. *THE SPECTROSCOPE AND GEMMOLOGY*. Edited by R. Keith Mitchell. Woodstock, Vt.: GemStone Press, 2006.

Important resource for anyone using a spectroscope. Comprehensive photo library of absorption spectra for gemstones.

Arem, Joel E. *COLOR ENCYCLOPEDIA OF GEMSTONES*. 2nd ed. New York: Springer, 1987.

Excellent color photography makes this book interesting for anyone, but it is of particular value for the gemologist.

Ball, S. H. *A ROMAN BOOK ON PRECIOUS STONES*. Los Angeles: Gemological Institute of America, 1950.

Very interesting from a historical perspective, especially for the knowledgeable student of gemology.

Bruton, E. *DIAMONDS*. 2nd ed. Radnor, Penn.: Chilton Book Co., 1979.

An excellent, encyclopedic, well-illustrated book, good for both amateur and professional gemologists.

Cavenago-Bignami Moneta, S. *GEMMOLOGIA*. Milan: Heopli, 1980.

One of the most extensive works on gems available. Excellent photography. Available in the Italian language only. Recommended for advanced students.

Fernandes, Shyamala, and Gagan Choudhary. UNDERSTANDING ROUGH GEMSTONES. Mumbai: Indian Institute of Jewellery, 2010.

Valuable information pertaining to identifying and grading gemstones in their rough form with insights into characteristics also applicable to cut and polished gems.

Gubelin, Edward, and J. L. Koivula. *PHOTOATLAS OF INCLUSIONS IN GEMSTONES*. 3 vols. Carlsbad, Calif.: Gemological Institute of America, 2004–2008.

All are recommended for the serious student of gemology. Best and most comprehensive collection of photographs of inclusions ever assembled. Important for learning to recognize the indicators of treatments and synthetics—especially new-type synthetics.

Hurlbut, Cornelius S., and Robert C. Kammerling. *GEMOLOGY.* 2nd ed. New York: Wiley-Interscience, 1991.

Liddicoat, R. T. *HANDBOOK OF GEM IDENTIFICATION.* 12th ed. Los Angeles: Gemological Institute of America, 1993.

Excellent textbook for the student of gemology.

Matlins, Antoinette. *COLORED GEMSTONES,* 3rd Edition: *THE ANTOINETTE MATLINS BUYING GUIDE—How to Select, Buy, Care for & Enjoy Sapphires, Emeralds, Rubies and Other Colored Gems with Confidence and Knowledge.* Woodstock, Vt.: GemStone Press, 2010.

Easy-to-read yet comprehensive information including the latest on treatments, new cutting styles, and new gemstones. Includes price guides.

———. *DIAMONDS,* 3rd Edition: *THE ANTOINETTE MATLINS BUYING GUIDE—How to Select, Buy, Care for & Enjoy Diamonds with Confidence and Knowledge.* Woodstock, Vt.: GemStone Press, 2011.

The latest information on diamonds, including an in-depth explanation of the four Cs, important sections on fancy-color diamonds, new enhancement techniques, and price guides.

———. *JEWELRY & GEMS AT AUCTION: THE DEFINITIVE GUIDE TO BUYING & SELLING AT THE AUCTION HOUSE & ON INTERNET AUCTION SITES.* Woodstock, Vt.: GemStone Press, 2002.

Only book available that covers everything you need to know about the auction process *and* buying diamonds, pearls, and colored gemstones at auction.

———. *THE PEARL BOOK,* 4th Edition: *THE DEFINITIVE BUYING GUIDE—How to Select, Buy, Care for & Enjoy Pearls.* Woodstock, Vt.: GemStone Press, 2008.

In addition to its wealth of fascinating information on all types of pearls, it includes invaluable information on tests for identifying pearls and treatments.

Matlins, Antoinette, and Antonio Bonanno. *ENGAGEMENT & WEDDING RINGS,* 3rd Edition: *THE DEFINITIVE BUYING GUIDE FOR PEOPLE IN LOVE.* Woodstock, Vt.: GemStone Press, 2003.

Filled with romantic as well as practical advice, and important sections on judging quality and value, ring design, and jewelry care.

———. *JEWELRY & GEMS,* 7th Edition: *THE BUYING GUIDE—How to Buy Diamonds, Pearls, Colored Gemstones, Gold & Jewelry with Confidence and Knowledge.* Woodstock, Vt.: GemStone Press, 2009.

Well reviewed for its discussion of factors affecting quality and value, what to look for and look out for. Covers diamonds, pearls, and colored gemstones. Includes comparative price charts.

Miller, Anna M. *GEMS & JEWELRY APPRAISING,* 3rd Edition: *TECHNIQUES OF PROFESSIONAL PRACTICE.* Revised by Gail Brett Levine. Woodstock, Vt.: GemStone Press, 2008.

————. *ILLUSTRATED GUIDE TO JEWELRY APPRAISING,* 3rd Edition: *ANTIQUE, PERIOD AND MODERN.* Woodstock, Vt.: GemStone Press, 2003.

These two books provide a complete library for the appraiser: the first provides general appraising guidelines for the gem and jewelry field; the second provides excellent advice pertaining specifically to jewelry from all periods.

————. *CAMEOS OLD & NEW,* 4th Edition. Revised by Diana Jarret. Woodstock, Vt.: GemStone Press, 2008.

Nassau, Kurt. *GEMS MADE BY MAN.* Los Angeles: Gemological Institute of America, 1980.

Important work on synthetics. A primary reference source.

————. *GEMSTONE ENHANCEMENT.* 2nd ed. Oxford: Butterworth-Heinemann, 1994.

Possibly the most comprehensive, up-to-date, and understandable book available on gem enhancement.

Pagel-Theisen, V. *DIAMOND GRADING ABC HANDBOOK FOR DIAMOND GRADING.* 11th ed. New York: Rubin & Son, 1993.

Highly recommended for anyone in diamond sales.

Penney, D., ed. *BIODIVERSITY OF FOSSILS IN AMBER FROM THE MAJOR WORLD DEPOSITS.* Manchester: Siri Scientific Press, 2010.

Covers amber from around the world and is a must for anyone interested in amber and its inclusions. Superb photos.

Read, Peter G. *GEMMOLOGY.* 3rd ed. London: Robert Hale, 2008.

Especially good for students preparing for examinations to earn the title "Fellow of the Gemmological Association of Great Britain" (FGA).

Rygle, Kathy J., and Stephen F. Pedersen. *TREASURE HUNTER'S GEM & MINERAL GUIDE TO THE USA,* 5th Edition: *WHERE & HOW TO DIG, PAN AND MINE YOUR OWN GEMS & MINERALS.* 4 vols. Woodstock, Vt.: GemStone Press, 2011.

Schumann, W. *GEMSTONES OF THE WORLD: REVISED & EXPANDED EDITION.* 4th ed. Translated by E. Stern. New York: Sterling, 2009.

This book has superior color plates of all of the gem families and their different varieties and for this reason is valuable to anyone interested in gems.

Sinkankas, John. *GEMSTONE AND MINERAL DATA BOOK: A COMPILATION OF DATA, RECIPES, FORMULAS AND INSTRUCTIONS FOR THE MINERALOGIST, GEMOLOGIST, LAPIDARY, JEWELER, CRAFTSMAN.* Prescott, Ariz.: Geoscience Press, 1994.

A great collection of information for the serious gem enthusiast.

Spencer, L. J. *KEY TO PRECIOUS STONES*. London: Read, 2008.

Good for the beginning student of gemology.

Strack, Elisabeth. *PEARLS*. Germany: Rühle-Diebener-Verlag, 2006.

An exhaustive, scientific work that is an essential resource for gemologists and anyone who loves pearls.

Themelis, Theodore. *BERYLLIUM-TREATED RUBIES & SAPPHIRES*. Los Angeles: A&T Publications, 2003.

———. *FLUX ENHANCED RUBIES*. Los Angeles: A&T Publications, 2004.

Interesting insights into ruby treatment and identifying characteristics.

———. *THE HEAT TREATMENT OF RUBY AND SAPPHIRE*. 3rd ed. Los Angeles: A&T Publications, 2013.

A comprehensive book on ruby and sapphire treatment.

———. *MOGOK: VALLEY OF RUBIES, GEMS & MINES*, 2 vols. Los Angeles: A&T Publications, 2008.

A tour through the mysterious Mogok region of Burma (now Myanmar) as only an insider can provide, focusing on Burma's ancient place in the world of ruby and sapphire. An important contribution to understanding the geology of Burma and its gems.

Webster, R. *GEM IDENTIFICATION*. New York: Sterling Pub. Co., 1977.

———. *GEMOLOGIST'S COMPENDIUM*. 7th ed. Edited by E. A. Jobbins. London: Robert Hale, 1999.

———. *GEMS*. With Peter G. Read. 5th ed. Oxford: Butterworth-Heinemann, 1995.

———. *GEMS IN JEWELRY*. London: N.A.G. Press, 1975.

———. *PRACTICAL GEMOLOGY*. 6th ed. London: Robert Hale, 1993.

All of the above are highly recommended for the serious student of gemology, especially GEMS.

Computer Software Programs

These are just becoming available and can provide invaluable reference material. Each program must be evaluated in terms of your own need, but one program we like—especially its gemstone data tables—is *GT Pro* from www.gemologytools.com. For color communication, while no system is perfect, we do like Gem^{e}wizard™ (www.gemewizard.com).

Journals

ANTWERP FACETS. Published by Hoge Raad Voor Diamant Institute of Gemmology, Hoveniersstraat 22, B-2018, Antwerp, Belgium.

AUSTRALIAN GEMMOLOGIST. Published by the Gemmological Association of Australia, P.O. Box 1587, East Victoria Park, WA 6981, Australia.

CANADIAN GEMMOLOGIST. Published by the Canadian Gemmological Association, 1767 Avenue Rd., Toronto, Ontario, Canada M5M 3Y8.

GEMOLOGIA. Published by the Associacao Brasileira de Gemologia e Mineralogia, Departmento de Mineralogia e Petrografia, Sao Paulo University, Brasil.

GEMMOLOGY. Also entitled *JEMOROJI.* Published by Zenkoku Hoseigaku Kyokai, Tokyo, Japan.

GEMS & GEMOLOGY. Published by the Gemological Institute of America, 5345 Armada Drive, Carlsbad, CA, 92008. Quarterly; containing many technical articles on gems and gem treatments.

HOLLAND GEM. St. Annastraat 44, NL 6524 GE, Mijmegen, Holland (Tel./Fax 31-24-322-6979).

JOURNAL OF GEMMOLOGY. Published by the Gemmological Association of Great Britain, London. Quarterly; containing many technical articles on gems and gem treatments. One annual hardcopy.

JOURNAL OF THE GEMMOLOGICAL SOCIETY OF JAPAN. Also entitled *HOSEKI GAKKAISHI.* Published by the Society, Sendai, Tohoku University.

REVUE DE GEMMOLOGIE. Published by the Association Francaise de Gemmologie, 162 rue St. Honore, 75001 Paris, France.

ZEITSCHRIFT. Published by Deutsche Gemmologische Gesellschaft, Postfach 12 22 60, D-6580 Idar-Oberstein, FRG.

Magazines

ASIA PRECIOUS. Published by Publications Ltd., 22nd Fl., Yee Hing Loong Commercial Bldg., 151 Hollywood Rd., Hong Kong, China.

ASIAN JEWELRY. Published by Myer Publishing Ltd., 18/F, Flat B, Loyong Court, 212-220 Lockhard Rd., Wanchai, Hong Kong, China.

AURUM. Published by Aurum Editions S.A., Geneva, Switzerland.

BANGKOK GEMS & JEWELLERY MAGAZINE. Published by B.G. & J. Co. Ltd., Ste. 57, Bangkok Gems & Jewelry Tower, 322 Surawong Rd. 22F, 1H 10500 Bangkok, Thailand.

EUROPA STAR. Published by Miller Freeman, Inc., Rte. des Acacias 25, P.O. Box 1355, CH 1211 Geneva, Switzerland.

GZ (GOLDSCHMIEDE UND UHRMACHER ZEITUNG). Published by Ruhle-Diebener-Verlag GmbH & Co. KG, Stuttgart, West Germany.

HONG KONG WATCH & JEWELLERY REVIEW. Published quarterly by Brilliant-Art Publishing Ltd., Wanchai, Hong Kong, China.

JEWELERS' CIRCULAR-KEYSTONE (JCK). Published by Chilton, Radnor, PA. Monthly; readable, business oriented review of events within the U.S. jewelry industry.

JEWELLERY INTERNATIONAL. Published by Jewellery International Publishers, Mount Pleasant 31, London WC1X OAD, England.

JEWELLERY NEWS ASIA. Published by UBM Asia Ltd., 17/F, China Resources Building, 26 Harbour Rd., Wanchai, Hong Kong, China. Widely distributed throughout Asia; a readable, reliable publication.

JEWEL SIAM. Published by Jewel Siam, 919 Silom Rd., 10500 Bangkok, Thailand.

JOURNAL SUISSE D'HORLOGERIE ET DE BIJOUTERIE. (Swiss Journal of Clocks and Jewelry) Published by Editions Scriptar SA, Chernin du Creux-de-Corsy 25, CH 10931 Lausanne, Switzerland.

JQ (JEWELRY & GEM QUARTERLY). Published by JQ Magazine, 1-3- W. Higgins Rd., Ste. 218, Park Ridge, IL 60068.

KOMPASS DIAMONDS. Published by Kompass Diamonds, Quinten Matsijsleill-Box 3, 8th Fl., Rm. 8B, 2018 Antwerp, Belgium.

LAPIDARY JOURNAL. Published by Lapidary Journal, Inc., P.O. Box 469004, Escondido, CA 92046. Monthly; very readable magazine for gem cutters, collectors, and jewelers.

L'ORATO ITALIANO. Published by L'orato Italiano, Via Nerves 6, I-20139 Milano, Italy.

UHREN JUWELEN SCHMUCK. Published by Verlag GmbH Chmielorz, P.O. Box 2, 229, Wiesbaden 65012. Published monthly.

NATIONAL JEWELER. Published by Neilsen Expositions, 770 Broadway, 8th Fl., New York, NY 10003, 24 issues per year; readable, business oriented review of events and issues within the U.S. jewelry industry.

RETAIL JEWELLER. Published by EMAP Ltd., Greater London House, Hampstead Rd., London NW1 7EJ.

RIDGEVILLE LTD. HK JEWELLERY MAGAZINE. Published by Ridgeville Ltd., Flat A 12/F, Kaiser Estate, Phase 1 Man Yue St. 41, Hunghorn, Kowloon, Hong Kong.

Sources of Price Information

AUCTION MARKET RESOURCE. P.O. Box 18, Rego Park, NY 11374.

GEM^{E}PRICE and *GEM^{E}WIZARD.* Online diamond and gemstone pricing program. www.Gemewizard.com.

PALMIERI'S MARKET MONITOR. Gemological Appraisal Association, P.O. Box 5053, New York, NY 10185.

THE GUIDE. (Quarterly—diamonds and colored gems) Gemworld International, Inc., 650 Dundee Rd., Northbrook, IL 60062.

RAPAPORT DIAMOND REPORT. 1212 Avenue of the Americas, Ste. 1103, New York, NY 10036.

Where to Go for Additional Gemological Training

Some of the organizations listed below offer formal training; others offer short courses or workshops. The Gemological Institute of America (GIA) and Gem-A (The Gemmological Association of Great Britain) and its Gem-A Accredited Teaching Centres are located worldwide and also offer correspondence courses, extension courses, and workshops. For the most current listing of GIA locations, visit: http://www.gia.edu/nav/toolbar/find-locations/index. html. For the most current listing of Gem-A Accredited Teaching Centres, visit: http://www.gem-a.info/education/options-for-study/accredited-teaching-centres.aspx.

UNITED STATES

Arizona

International Gemological
   Services—Center for Training
   & Research
2933 N. Hayden Rd., Ste. 1A
Scottsdale, AZ 85251
Tel. (480) 947-5866
www.internationalgemservices.com

California

California Institute of Jewelry
   Training
4854 San Juan Ave.
Fair Oaks, CA 95628
Tel. (800) 731-1122
www.jewelrytraining.com

Gemological Institute of America
   (GIA) World Headquarters
Robert Mouawad Campus
5345 Armada Dr.
Carlsbad, CA 92008
Tel. (800) 421-7250
www.gia.edu

Revere Academy of Jewelry Arts
785 Market St., Ste. 900
San Francisco, CA 94103
Tel. (415) 391-4179
www.revereacademy.com

Florida

American School of Jewelry
2240 N. University Dr.
Sunrise, FL 33322
Tel. (954) 741-4555
www.jewelryschool.net

Karen Bonanno DeHaas, PG,
   FGA, MGA
7308 Ambleside Dr.
Land O'Lakes, FL 34637
Tel. (813) 406-5730
E-mail: karendehaas@gmail.com

Georgia

American Jewelry Institute
3455 Peachtree Rd.
Atlanta, GA 30326
Tel. (404) 271-3278
www.ajigroup.org

Art Institute of Atlanta
6600 Peachtree Dunwoody Rd. NE
100 Embassy Row
Atlanta, GA 30328
Tel. (770) 394-8300
www.artinstitutes.edu/atlanta

Emory University
201 Dowman Dr.
Atlanta, GA 30322
Tel. (404) 727-6123
www.emory.edu

Illinois

Parkland College
2400 W. Bradley Ave.
Champaign, IL 61821
Tel. (217) 351-2200
www.parkland.edu

Minnesota

Minneapolis Community and
  Technical College
1501 Hennepin Ave.
Minneapolis, MN 55403
Tel. (612) 659-6000
www.minneapolis.edu

Nevada

American Gem Society (AGS)
  Laboratories
8881 W. Sahara Ave.
Las Vegas, NV 89117
Tel. (702) 233-6120
www.agslab.com

New York

American Gemological
  Laboratories, Inc. (AGL)
Gem Sciences Research Ctr.
580 Fifth Ave., Ste. 706
New York, NY 10036
Tel. (212) 704-0727
www.aglgemlab.com

European Gemological Laboratory
  (EGL) USA
580 Fifth Ave., Ste. 2700
New York, NY 10036
Tel. (212) 730-7380
www.eglusa.com

Fashion Institute of Technology
7th Ave. at 27th St.
New York, NY 10001
Tel. (212) 217-7999
www.fitnyc.edu

Gemological Institute of America
  (GIA)
New York Campus
50 W. 47th St., Unit 800
New York, NY 10036
Tel. (800) 366-8519
www.gia.edu

National Association of Jewelry
  Appraisers
P.O. Box 18
Rego Park, NY 11374
Tel. (718) 896-1536
www.najaappraisers.com

Yeshiva University
500 W. 185th St.
New York, NY 10033
Tel. (212) 960-5400
www.yu.edu

Pennsylvania

Gary Smith, ASA, MGA
344 Broad St.
Montoursville, PA 17754
Tel. (570) 368-4436
E-mail: pagemlab@comcast.net

Tennessee

Diamond Council of America
3212 West End Ave., Ste. 400
Nashville, TN 37203
Tel. (615) 385-5301
www.diamondcouncil.org

Texas

Texas Institute of Jewelry
Technology
Paris Junior College
2400 Clarksville St.
Paris, TX 75460
Tel. (800) 232-5804
www.parisjc.edu/index.php/pjc2/
main/tijt

Vermont

GemStone Press
Antoinette Matlins' U.S. and
International Courses
Sunset Farm Offices, Rte. 4
P.O. Box 237
Woodstock, VT 05091
Tel. (802) 457-4000
www.gemstonepress.com

Virginia

American Society of Appraisers
11107 Sunset Hills Rd., Ste. 310
Reston, VA 20190
Tel. (703) 478-2228
www.appraisers.org

Bonanno Gemological Services
1027 Julian Dr.
Fredericksburg, VA 22401
Tel. (540) 373-1909

Washington

Northwest Gemological Institute
10801 Main St., Ste. 105
Bellevue, WA 98004
Tel. (425) 455-0985
www.nwgem.com

Wisconsin

Howard Academy for the Metal Arts
P.O. Box 472
Stoughton, WI 53589
Tel. (800) 843-9603
www.howard-academy.com

Milwaukee Area Technical
College
700 W. State St.
Milwaukee, WI 53233
Tel. (414) 297-6282
www.matc.edu

Northeast Wisconsin Technical
College
P.O. Box 19042
2740 W. Mason St.
Green Bay, WI 54307
Tel. (800) 422-6982
www.nwtc.edu

Correspondence Courses

Gem-A (The Gemmological
Association of Great Britain)
21 Ely Place
London EC1N 6TD
England
Tel. (44) 20-7404-3334
www.gem-a.com

Gemological Institute of America
(GIA) World Headquarters
Robert Mouawad Campus
5345 Armada Dr.
Carlsbad, CA 92008
Tel. (800) 421-7250
www.gia.edu

OTHER COUNTRIES

Armenia

Zang
North Ave. 1, Ste. 31
Yerevan 0001
Armenia
Tel. (374) 10-568-229
E-mail: zang@cornet.am

Australia

Canberra Institute of Technology
  Information Centre
G.P.O. Box 826
Canberra ACT 2601
Australia
Tel. (61) 2-6207-3100
www.cit.edu.au

Gemmological Association of
  Australia (NSW Division)
24 Wentworth Ave.
Darlinghurst NSW 2010
Australia
Tel. (61) 2-9264-5078
www.gem.org.au

Gemmological Association of
  Australia (Queensland Division)
P.O. Box 967
North Lakes QLD 4509
Australia
Tel. (61) 7-3481-2857
www.gem.org.au

Gemmological Association of
  Australia (South Australia
  Division)
P.O. Box 191
Adelaide SA 5001
Australia
Tel. (61) 8-8227-1377
www.gem.org.au

Gem Studies Laboratory
301 Pitt St.
Sydney NSW 2000
Australia
Tel. (61) 2-9264-8788
www.gsl.net.au

Austria

*Austrian Gemmological
  Association (Österreichische
  Gemmoligische
  Gesellschaft-OGEMG)
Goldschlagstrasse 10
A-1150 Vienna
Austria
Tel: (43) 1-231-2238
www.gemmologie.at

WIFI (Wirtschafts-Foerderungs-
  Institut) upper Austria
Gemmologenausbildung
Wiener Strasse No. 150
4021 Linz
Austria
Tel. (43) 732-333-2274

Belgium

European Gemological Laboratory
  and College of Gemology
Hovinierstraat 55
Antwerp
Belgium
Tel. (32) 3-233-24-58
www.egl.co.za

HRD Institute of Gemmology
Hoveniersstraat 22
BE-2018 Antwerp
Belgium
Tel. (32) 3-222-06-11
www.hrd.be

International Gemmological
  Institute (IGI)
Schupstraat 1
2018 Antwerp
Belgium
Tel. (32) 3-401-08-88
www.igiworldwide.com

State University Antwerp
(AIESEC RUCA)
Prinsstraat 13
2000 Antwerp
Belgium
Tel. (32) 3-265-41-11
www.uantwerpen.be

Brazil

Brazilian Association of
Gemologists & Jewelry
Appraisers (ABGA)
Rua Visconde de Pirajá, 540,
Ste. 211
Rio de Janeiro 22410-001
Brazil
Tel. (55) 21-2540-0059
www.gemsconsult.com.br

Gemological Laboratory of the
Center for Mineral Technology
(CETEM)
Av. Pedro Calmon, 900, Cidade
Universitária
Rio de Janeiro 21941-908
Brazil
Tel. (55) 21-3865-7222
www.cetem.gov.br

IBGM Gemological Laboratory
SCN Centro Empresarial A, Conj.
1105
Brasilia, DF 70712-903
Brazil
Tel. (55) 61-3326-3926
www.ibgm.com.br

Laboratório Gemológico Dr.
Hécliton Santini Henriques
Ave. Paulista, 688, 17th Fl.
Belavista 01310-100
Brazil
Tel. (55) 11-3016-5850
www.ajesp.com.br

Realgems—Laboratório Brasileiro
de Pesquisas Gemológicas
Rua Visconde de Pirajá, 540,
Ste. 210
Rio de Janeiro 22410-002
Brazil
Tel. (55) 21-2239-4078
www.realgemslab.com.br

Universidade Federal de Ouro
Preto Campus
Ouro Preto, MG 35400-000
Brazil
Tel. (55) 31-3599-1530
www.ufop.br

Canada

Canadian Gemmological
Association
55 Queen St. E, Lower Concourse,
Ste. 105
Toronto, ON
M5C 1R6
Canada
Tel. (647) 466-2436
www.canadiangemmological.com

Canadian Institute of Gemmology
P.O. Box 57010
Vancouver, BC
V5K 5G6
Canada
Tel. (604) 530-8569
www.cigem.ca

Carleton University
1125 Colonel By Dr.
Ottawa, ON
K1S 5B6
Canada
Tel. (613) 520-2600
www.carleton.ca

European Gemological Laboratory
55 Queen St., Ste. 500
Toronto, ON
M5C 1R6
Canada
Tel. (416) 368-1200
www.eglcanada.ca
Also at:
European Gemological Laboratory
United Kingdom Bldg.
736 Granville St., Ste. 622
Vancouver, BC
V6C 1G3
Canada
Tel. (604) 630-0464
www.eglcanada.ca

George Brown College of Applied
  Arts & Technology
Box 1015
Station B
Toronto, ON
M5T 2T9
Canada
Tel. (416) 415-2000
www.gbrownc.on.ca

Les Gemmologistes Associes
603-1255 Rue du Square
Montreal, QC
H3B 3G1
Canada
Tel. (514) 528-1828
www.gemmologistesassocies.com

Montreal School of Gemmology
  Ecole de gemmologie de
  Montréal
460, Rue Sainte Catherine Ouest, 913
Montréal, QC
H3B 1A7
Canada
Tel. (514) 844-0024
www.ecoledegemmologie.com

Saidye Bronfman Center for the
  Arts
5170 Cote Sainte Catherine Rd.
Montreal, QC
H3W 1M7
Canada
Tel. (514) 739-2301
www.segalcentre.org

China

Asian Gemmological Institute and
  Laboratory Ltd.
11 Lock Rd., 7th Fl.
Tsim Shat Sui
Kowloon
Hong Kong
China
Tel. (852) 2723-0429
www.agil.com.hk

*Hong Kong Gems Laboratory
4/F, Tung Hip Commercial Bldg.
248 Des Voeux Rd. Central
Hong Kong
China
Tel. (852) 2815-1880
www.hkgems.com.hk

Gemmological Association of
  Hong Kong (GAHK)
P.O. Box 97711, TST
Kowloon
Hong Kong
China
Tel. (852) 2366-6006
www.gahk.org

International Gemological Institute
(IGI)–Hong Kong
Ste. 501, Tower 1
The Gateway, Harbour City
25 Canton Rd.
Tsim Shat Sui
Hong Kong
China
Tel. (852) 2522-9880
www.igiworldwide.com

England

Department of Mineralogy
British Museum (Natural History)
Cromwell Rd.
London SW7 5BD
England
Tel. (44) 20-7942-5000
www.nhm.ac.uk

Gem-A (The Gemmological
Association of Great Britain)
21 Ely Place
London EC1N 6TD
England
Tel. (44) 20-7404-3334
www.gem-a.com

(For Accredited Teaching Centres:
www.gem-a.com/education/
study-options/accredited-
teaching-centres.aspx)

Huddlestone Gemmological
Consultants Ltd.
Edney House, Lower Ground Fl.
46 Hatton Garden
London EC1N 8EX
England
Tel. (44) 20-7404-5004

Precious Stone Laboratory
25A Hatton Garden
London EC1N 8BN
England
Tel. (44) 20-7320-1439

Finland

M&A Gemological Instruments
Alhotie 14
04430 Järvenpää
Finland
www.gemmoraman.com

France

European Gemological Laboratory
9 Rue Buffault
75009 Paris
France
Tel. (33) 1-4016-1635
www.egl.co.za

Laboratoire Français de
Gemmologie
30 Rue Notre Dame des Victoires
75002 Paris
France
Tel. (33) 4026-2545
www.laboratoire-francais-
gemmologie.fr

Germany

Deutsche Gemmologische
Gesellschaft
(German Gemmological
Association)
Prof.-Schlossmacher-Str. 1
D-55743 Idar-Oberstein
Germany
Tel. (49) 6781-50840
www.dgemg.com

Deutsche Stiftung
  Edelsteinforschung (DSEF)
(German Foundation for Gemstone
  Research)
Prof.-Schlossmacher Str. 1
D-55743 Idar-Oberstein
Germany
Tel. (49) 6781-50840
www.dsef.de

Institute of Gemstone Research,
  Idar-Oberstein
Centre of Gemstone Research
University of Mainz
Becherweg 21
D-55099 Mainz
Germany
Tel. (49) 6131-3924-365
www.uni-mainz.de/FB/Geo/
  mineralogie/gemstone/

Stiftung Deutsches Diamant
  Institut (DDI)
Poststrasse 1
D-75172 Pforzheim
Germany
Tel. (49) 7231-32211
E-mail: ddi.diamant@t-online.de

India

Gem Testing Laboratory
Rajasthan Chamber Bhawan
Mirza Ismail Rd., 3rd Fl.
Jaipur 302 003
India
Tel. (91) 141-2568-029/2574-074
www.gjepc.org

Gemological Institute of India
29 Gurukul Chambers
187–189 Mumbadevi Rd.
Mumbai 400 002
India
Tel. (91) 22-2342-0039

Indian Diamond Institute
Katargam, GIDC, Box 508
Sumul Dairy Rd.
Surat 395 008
Gujarat
India
Tel. (91) 26-1240-7847
www.diamondinstitute.net

International Gemological Institute
  (IGI)—India
Dr. Dadasaheb Bhadkamkar Marg
702, the Capitol, Bandra Kurla
  Complex, Bandra E.
Mumbai 400 051
India
Tel. (91) 22-4035-2550
www.igiworldwide.com

Israel

European Gemological College
  Ltd.
EGL Platinum Center
8 Shoham St.
Ramat Gan 52521006
Israel
Tel. (972) 3-612-1375
www.egl-platinum.com

Universal Gemological
  Laboratories (IGC)
Diamond Exchange
Maccabi Bldg., Ste. 1956
1 Jabotinsky St.
Ramat Gan 52520
Israel
Tel. (972) 3-751-4782
www.gci-gem.com

Italy

Alberto Scarani
Via di Santa Maria in Monticelli, 30
00186 Rome
Italy
Tel. (39) 06-686-4946

ARCOGEM S.r.l.
Dipartimento Geomineralogico
Università degli Studi di Bari
Via E. Orabona, 4
70125 Bari
Italy
Tel. (39) 080-544-2585
www.arcogem.it

Centro Analisi Gemmologiche
Viale Vicenza, 4/D
15048 Valenza
Italy
Tel. (39) 013-192-4557
www.analisigemme.com

Gemological Education
  Certification Institute
Via delle Asole 2
20123 Milano
Tel. (39) 02-8498-0022
www.geci-web.it

Istituto Gemmologico Italiano
Piazza San Sepolcro, 1
20123 Milano
Italy
Tel. (39) 02-8050-4991
www.igi.it/
  istitutogemmologicoitaliano

Istituto Gemmologico Nazionale
Via S. Sebastianello, 6 (Piazza di
  Spagna)
00187 Rome
Italy
Tel. (39) 06-678-3056
www.ignroma.it

Masterstones Centre for
  Gemological Analysis
Via Reberto Allesandri, 6/A
00151 Rome
Italy
Tel. (39) 06-5327-3434
www.masterstones.eu

Japan

AGT Gem Laboratory
Okachimachi Cy Bldg., 2F
5-14-14 Ueno
Taito-Ku, Tokyo 110-0005
Japan
Tel. (81) 3-3834-8586

Central Gem Laboratory
Miyagi Bldg., 2F
5-15-14 Ueno
Taito-Ku, Tokyo 110-0005
Japan
Tel. (81) 3-3836-1627
www.cgl.co.jp

Gem Research Japan Inc.
Nagahori Hall Bldg., 5F
1-3-10 Higashi-Shinsaibashi
Chuo-ku, Osaka 542-0083
Tel. (81) 6-6252-1222
www.grjapan.ddo.jp/index.html

Gemological Institute of America
Okachimachi, Cy Bldg. 2–3/F
5-15-14 Ueno
Taito-Ku, Tokyo 110-0005
Japan
Tel. (81) 3-3835-7046
www.giajpn.gr.jp

International Gemological Institute
  (IGI)—Japan
UT Bldg.
2-21-13 Higashi Ueno
Taito-Ku, Tokyo 110-0005
Japan
Tel. (81) 3-5807-2958
www.igiworldwide.com

Japan Gem Society
Aurum Building 207
1-26-2 Higashi Ueno
Taito-ku, Tokyo 110-0015
Tel: (81) 3-5812-4785
www.japangemsociety.org
"Allied Teaching Center of the
  Gem-A"

Madagascar

Institut de Gemmologie de
  Madagascar (IGM)
Rte. d'Andraisoro Ampandrianomby
Antananarivo 101
Madagascar
Tel. (261) 20-22-591-37
www.igm.mg

Netherlands

Netherlands Gemmological
  Laboratory
P.O. Box 9517
2300 RA Leiden
Netherlands
Tel. (31) 71-5687665
E-mail: hanco.zwaan@naturalis.nl

Pakistan

Gemming International Company
Flat #3-B, Gems Trade Plaza
Namak Mandi Khyber
  Pakhtunkhwa, Pakistan
Peshawar
Tel. (92) 091-2253174

National Center of Excellence
  in Geology
University of Peshawar
Peshawar 25120
Khyber Pakhtunkhawa, Pakistan
Tel. (92) 091-9216427
www.nceg.upesh.edu.pk

Portugal

LABGEM-Rui Galopim de
  Carvalho Gem Consulting
Apart. 2026, Colares 2706-909
Sintra
Portugal
Tel. (351) 21-924-2468
www.labgem.org

Russia

GCI Gemological Centers–Russia
Smolnaya St., 12, Office 250
125493 Moscow
Russia
Tel. (7) 495-452-22-78
www.igc-gem.ru

Gemological Center GEMEXIM
  Ltd.
Miclukho-Maklaya St., 23
117997 Moscow
Russia
Tel. (7) 495-280-04-38
www.gigia.ru

Smolensk Gemmological
  Certification Center
Shkadov St., 2
214031 Smolensk
Russia
Tel. (7) 481-231-69-00
www.smolgem.ru

Yakutian Gemmological
  Certification Center
Assay Chamber
Oktiabrskaya St., 30
677027 Yakutsk
Russia
Tel. (7) 411-235-38-35
www.assaygem.ru

Singapore

Far East Gem Institute
12 Arumugam Rd.
#04–02 Lion Industrial Bldg. B
Singapore 409958
Tel. (65) 6745-8542
www.gem.com.sg

Jewellery Design & Management
  International School
100 Beach Rd.
#02-50 to #02-57, Shaw Towers
  Gallery
Singapore 189702
Tel. (65) 6221-5253
www.jdmis.edu.sg

Nan Yang Gemological Institute
14 Scotts Rd.
#03-80, Far East Plaza
Singapore 228213
Tel. (65) 6333-6238
www.ngi.com.sg

South Africa

European Gemological Laboratory
225 Main St.
SA Diamond Ctr., Ste. 410, 4th Fl.
Johannesburg 2001
South Africa
Tel. (27) 11-334-4527
www.egl.co.za

Gem Education Centre
20 Drome Rd.
Lombardy
South Africa
Tel. (27) 11-346 1657
E-mail: gec@mweb.co.za

Independent Coloured Stone
  Laboratory
P.O. Box 177
Pinegowrie, Johannesburg 2125
South Africa
Tel. (27) 11-787-3326
E-mail: icamp@global.co.az

University of KwaZulu-Natal
University Road Westville
Private Bag X 54001
Durban 4000
South Africa
Tel. (27) 31-260-8596
www.ukzn.ac.za

University of Stellenbosch
Private Bag X1
Matieland 7602
South Africa
Tel. (27) 21-808-9111
www.sun.ac.za

South Korea

EGL Korea
701, 7th Fl., Shanho Bldg.
28 Jongro 3GA
Jongroku, Seoul
Republic of Korea
Tel. (82) 2-747-6978
www.egl-labs.com

Mi-Jo Gem Study Institute
244-39 Hooam-Dong
Youngsan-Ku
Seoul 140-190
Republic of Korea

Mirae Gem Laboratory Co., Ltd.
8F, Jewelry Department Store, 23
Bongik-dong, Jongro-gu
Seoul 110-390
Republic of Korea
Tel. (82) 2-766-3331
www.gem.or.kr

School of Gemology
7F, Hansung Bldg.
200 Myo-dong
Jongno-gu
Seoul 110-370
Republic of Korea
Tel. (82) 2-743-7990

Spain

Laboratorio Gemologico Gemior S.L.
Av. Baron De Carcer 48-6M
46001 Valencia
Spain
Tel. (34) 963-517-311

Laboratorio Gemológico
  MLLOPIS
Burriana, 42, 6, PTA
12-46005 Valencia
Spain
Tel. (34) 96-374-9078
www.mllopis.com

Laboratorio Oficial
Viladomat, 89–95, E-3
08015 Barcelona
Spain
Tel. (34) 93-292-4712
E-mail: as.gemmologia@sefes.es

Sri Lanka

Gemmologists Association of Sri
  Lanka
275/76, Stanley Wijesundara
  Mawatha
Colombo 7
Sri Lanka
Tel. (94) 11-2-590944
www.gemmology.lk

International Gemmological
  Academy
3A Darmaraja Mawatha
Colombo 3
Sri Lanka
Tel. (94) 72-2-948282
www.gemexpeditions.com

Petrological Laboratory
Geological Survey Dept.
569 Epitamulla Rd.
Pitakotte
Sri Lanka
Tel. (94) 11-2-886289

University of Moratuwa
Dept. of Earth Resources
Katubedda Campus
Moratuwa
Sri Lanka
Tel. (94) 11-2-650353
www.ere.mrt.ac.lk

Sweden

Rolf Krieger, Ltd.
Champinjonvagen 5
S-141/46 Huddinge
Sweden

Switzerland

Swiss Gemmological Institute (SSEF)
Falknerstrasse 9
CH-4001 Basel
Switzerland
Tel. (41) 61-262-0640
www.ssef.ch

Thailand

Asian Institute of Gemological
  Sciences
919/1 Silom Rd.
Jewelry Trade Center, 2nd Fl.,
  Unit. 214
Bangrak, Bangkok 10500
Thailand
Tel. (66) 2-267-4325
www.aigsthailand.com

Gem and Jewelry Institute of
Thailand
140/1–3, 5 Tower Bldg.
Silom Rd., Suriyawong
Bangrak, Bangkok 10500
Thailand
Tel: (66) 2-634-4999
www.git.or.th

International Gemological Institute
BGI Bldg., 9 Soi Charoen Krung
36 New Rd.
Bangkok 10500
Thailand
Tel. (66) 2-630-6726
www.igiworldwide.com

Themelis Treatment Center*
35/2 Soi Yommarat
Saladaeng, Silom
Bangkok 10500
Thailand
Tel. (66) 2-676-4851
www.themelis.com
*Program focuses on corundum
treatments and how to identify
them.

United Arab Emirates

Dubai Central Laboratory–Dubai
Gemstone Laboratory
Dubai Municipality
P.O. Box 67
Dubai
United Arab Emirates
Tel. (971) 4-302-7007
www.dcl.ae

International Gemological Institute
(IGI)—Dubai
Office Unit 27 A, B, C & G Almas
Tower, Plot No. LT-2
Jumeriah Lake Towers
Dubai
United Arab Emirates
Tel. (971) 4-450-8027
www.igiworldwide.com

Zimbabwe

Gem Education Centre of Zimbabwe
Faye March Jewelers, 1st Fl.,
Travel Plaza
Harare 707580
Zimbabwe
Tel. (263) 4-707-922
E-mail: fayemarch@zol.co.zw

**Correspondence Courses,
International Campuses, and
Allied Teaching and Tutorial
Centers**

Gemological Institute of America
(GIA) World Headquarters
Robert Mouawad Campus
5345 Armada Dr.
Carlsbad, CA 92008
Tel. (800) 421-7250
www.gia.edu
(For an updated list of GIA's international campuses and distance
education offerings, visit www.
gia.edu/gem-education/distance)

Gem-A (The Gemmological
Association of Great Britain)
21 Ely Place
London EC1N 6TD
England
Tel. (44) 20-7404-3334
www.gem-a.com
(For an updated list of Gem-A's
Accredited Teaching Centres
worldwide, visit www.gem-a.
com/education/study-options/
accredited-teaching-centres.aspx)

Gem Testing Laboratories and Gemologists in the USA

Below we show only the U.S. labs that provide internationally recognized reports. There are so many laboratories and gemologists in the United States that it is impossible to list them all. For an up-to-date listing of courses and gemologists accredited by the Certified Gemologist Appraisers (CGAs) in your area, contact the American Gem Society, 8881 W. Sahara Ave., Las Vegas, NV 89117 (Tel. 866-805-6500; www.ags.org), for a listing of Master Gemologist Appraisers, contact the American Society of Appraisers, 11107 Sunset Hills Rd., Ste. 310, Reston, VA 20190 (Tel. 703-478-2228; www.appraisers.org). For laboratories accredited by the Accredited Gemologists Association (AGA), contact the AGA, 3315 Juanita St., San Diego, CA 92105 (Tel. 619-501-5444; www.accreditedgemologists.org).

American Gemological
  Laboratory, Inc (AGL)
580 Fifth Ave., Ste. 706
New York, NY 10036
Tel. (212) 704-0727
www.aglgemlab.com

Gem Certification and Assurance
  Lab (*diamonds only*)
580 Fifth Ave, LL
New York, NY 10036
Tel. (212) 869-8985
www.gemfacts.com

Gemological Institute of America
  (GIA) World Headquarters
Robert Mouawad Campus
5345 Armada Dr.
Carlsbad, CA 92008
Tel. (800) 421-7250
www.gia.edu
Also at:
50 W. 47th St.
New York, NY 10036
Tel. (800) 421-7250
www.gia.edu

International List of Gem Testing Laboratories and Gemologists

The following has been compiled in part from the International Colored Gemstone Association membership. We hope it will aid you in locating laboratories and gemologists to assist you with gem identification or to offer guidance in developing your own proficiency. An asterisk has been placed by labs we know to be accredited or recognized by a respected gem or jewelry industry association. Please note that address and telephone information is frequently changed. Information provided here was current at the time this book went to press.

Armenia

Zang
North Ave. 1, Ste.31
Yerevan 0001
Armenia
Tel. (374) 10-568-229
E-mail: zang@cornet.am

Australia

Australian Gemmologist
P.O. Box 6055
Mitchelton QLD 4053
Australia
Tel. (61) 7-3355-5080

Bauer Gemmological Laboratories
330 Little Collins St., Level 6, Ste. 309
Melbourne Victoria 3000
Australia
Tel: (61) 3-9663-5548

Diamond Certification Laboratory
of Australia
Ste. 1, Level 1, Piccadilly Tower
133 Castlereagh St.
Sydney NSW 2000
Australia
Tel. (61) 2-9261-2104
www.dcla.com.au

Gemmological Association of
Australia (Queensland Division)
P.O. Box 967
North Lakes QLD 4509
Australia
Tel. (61) 7-3481-2875
www.gem.org.au

Gemmological Association of
Australia (South Australia
Division)
P.O. Box 191
Adelaide SA 5001
Australia
Tel. (61) 8-8227-1377
www.gem.org.au

Gemmological Association of
  Australia (Western Australia
  Division)
P.O. Box 431
Claremont WA 6910
Australia
Tel. (61) 8-9385-5489
www.gem.org.au

Gem Studies Laboratory
301 Pitt St.
Sydney NSW 2000
Australia
Tel. (61) 2-9264-8788
www.gsl.net.au

Austria

*Austrian Gemmological
  Association (Öster-
  reichische Gemmoligische
  Gesellschaft-OGEMG)
Goldschlagstrasse 10
A-1150 Vienna
Austria
Tel: (43) 1-231-2238
E-mail: office@gemmologie.at

Bahrain

Gem and Pearl Testing Laboratory
  of Bahrain
Ministry of Industry & Commerce
P.O. Box 5479, Manama
Kingdom of Bahrain
Tel: (973) 1757-4843
E-mail:
  metalgem@commerce.gov.bh

Belgium

European Gemological Laboratory
  and College of Gemology
Hovinierstraat 55
Antwerp
Belgium
Tel. (32) 3-233-24-58
www.egl.co.za

HRD Institute of Gemmology
Hoveniersstraat 22
BE-2018 Antwerp
Belgium
Tel. (32) 3-231-06-11
www.hrd.be

International Gemmological
  Institute (IGI)
Schupstraat 1
2018 Antwerp
Belgium
Tel. (32) 3-401-08-88
www.igiworldwide.com

Brazil

Brazilian Association of
  Gemologists & Jewelry
  Appraisers (ABGA)
Rua Visconde de Pirajá, 540,
  Ste. 211
Rio de Janeiro 22410-001
Brazil
Tel. (55) 21-2540-0059
www.gemsconsult.com.br

Centro Gemologico da Bahia
Ladeira do Carmo, 37
Santo Antonio (Centro Historico)
Salvador 40301-410
Brazil
Tel. (55) 71-3326-1747
www.cgb.ba.gov.br

GEMLAB-IGC-USP
Rua do Lago 562
Instituto de Geociencias da USP
Sao Paulo 01042-001
Brazil
Tel. (55) 11-3091-3958
www.igc.usp.br

Gemological Laboratory of the
Center for Mineral Technology
(CETEM)
Ave. Pedro Calmon, 900, Cidade
Universitária
Rio de Janeiro 21941-908
Brazil
Tel. (55) 21-3865-7222
www.cetem.gov.br

IBGM Gemological Laboratory
SCN Centro Empresarial A, Conj.
1105
Brasilia, DF 70712-903
Brazil
Tel. (55) 61-3326-3926
www.ibgm.com.br

Laboratório Gemológico AJORIO
Av. Graça Aranha
19 Gr. 404
Rio de Janeiro 20030-002
Brazil
Tel. (55) 21-2220 8004
www.ajorio.com.br

Laboratório Gemológico Dr.
Hécliton Santini Henriques
Ave. Paulista 688, 17th Fl.
Belavista 01310-100
Brazil
Tel. (55) 11-3016-5850
www.ajesp.com.br

Realgems-Laboratório Gemológico
Rua Visconde de Pirajá, 540,
Ste. 210
Rio de Janeiro
Brazil
Tel. (55) 21-2239-4078
www.realgemslab.com.br

Bulgaria

Laboratory of Gemology
New Bulgarian University
21 Montevideo St.
1618 Sofia
Bulgaria
Tel. (359) 2-811-0180
www.nbu.bg

Canada

Canadian Institute of Gemmology
P.O. Box 57010
Vancouver, BC
V5K 5G6
Canada
Tel. (604) 530-8569
www.cigem.ca

Centre de Gemmologie GEMS,
Inc.
620 Rue Cathcart, Ste. 821
Montreal, QC
H3B 1M1
Canada
Tel. (514) 393-1600

European Gemological Laboratory
55 Queen St., Ste. 500
Toronto, ON
M5C 1R6
Canada
Tel. (416) 368-1200
www.eglcanada.ca
Also at:
*European Gemological
Laboratory
United Kingdom Bldg.
736 Granville St., Ste. 456
Vancouver, BC
V6C 1T2
Canada
Tel. (604) 630-0464
www.eglcanada.ca

Gem Scan International, Inc.
27 Queen St. E., Ste. 406
Toronto, ON
M5C 2M6
Canada
Tel. (416) 868-6656
www.gemscan.com

*De Goutiere Jewellers, Ltd.
A. de Goutiere (CGA)
2542 Estevan Ave.
Victoria, BC
V8R 2S7
Canada
Tel. (250) 592-3224
www.degoutiere.com

*The Gold Shop
Ian M. Henderson (CGA)
374 Ouellette Ave. #302
Windsor, ON
N9A 6L7
Canada
Tel. (519) 258-8541
www.thegoldshop.ca

*Harold Weinsten Ltd.
55 Queen St. E., Ste. 1301
Toronto, ON
M5C 1R6
Canada
Tel. (416) 366-6518
www.hwgem.com

Kinnear d'Esterre Jewellers
Robern N. McAskil (CGA)
Florence Kimberly (CGA)
168 Princess St.
Kingston, ON
K7L 1B1
Canada
Tel. (613) 546-2261

*Nash Jewellers
John C. Nash (CGA)
182 Dundas St.
London, ON
N6A 1G7
Canada
Tel. (519) 672-7780
www.nashjewellers.com

Penner Fine Jewellers, Inc.
Ernest Penner (CGA)
10-436 Vansickle Rd.
St. Catharines, ON
L2S 0A4
Canada
Tel. (905) 688-0579
www.pennerjewellers.com

China

Asian Gemmological Institute and
    Laboratory Ltd.
7/F, 11 Lock Rd.
Tsim Shat Sui
Kowloon
Hong Kong
China
Tel. (852) 2815-0429
www.agil.com.hk

BG Gemological Institute
China Arts Bldg., 103 Jixiangli
Chaoyangmenwai
Beijing
China
Tel. (86) 10-6551-2259

China Gems Laboratory Limited
    (CGL)
25/F, Lok Fook Jewellery Center
No. 239 Temple St.
Jordan, Kowloon
Hong Kong
China
Tel. (852) 2783-2789
www.chinagemslab.com

Dabera Ltd.
Block M, 10/F, Phase 3
Kaiser Estate
11 Hok Yuen St.
Hungnon, Kowloon
Hong Kong
Tel. (852) 2527-7722
E-mail: dabera@omtis.com

*Hong Kong Gems Laboratory
4/F, Tung Hip Commercial Bldg.
248 Des Voeux Rd. Central
Hong Kong
China
Tel. (852) 2815-1880
www.hkgems.com.hk

Hong Kong Jade and Stone
  Laboratory Ltd.
Rm. 1401–2
Chow Sang Sang Bldg.
229 Nathan Rd.
Kowloon
Hong Kong
China
Tel. (852) 2388-9688
www.jadeitelaboratory.com.hk

International Gemological Institute
  (IGI)—Hong Kong
Ste. 501, Tower 1
The Gateway, Harbor City
25 Canton Rd.
Tsim Shat Sui
Hong Kong
China
Tel. (852) 2522-9880
www.igiworldwide.com

Jewelry Trade Laboratory Limited
13/F, Hong Kong Jewellery Bldg.
178–180 Queens Rd. Central
Hong Kong
China
Tel. (852) 2545-8848
www.hkjga.hk

National Gemstone Testing Centre
  (NGTC)
No.19 Xiaohuangzhuang Rd.
Andingmenwai Street
Beijing 100013
China
Tel. (86) 10-8427-4008
www.ngtc.gov.cn/ngtc

Sincere Overseas Jewellery Ltd.
  (Laboratory)
42 Hankow Rd.
7/F Howard Bldg., TST
Kowloon
Hong Kong
China
Tel. (852) 2356-1988

Valuation Services Ltd.
Flat 7, 6/F, On Wah Bldg.
40 Man Tai St.
Hunghom
Kowloon
Hong Kong
China
Tel. (852) 2869-4350
E-mail: ed@gemvaluation.com

Colombia

CDTEC
Calle 13, #6-82 P-11
Bogota
Colombia
Tel. (57) 001-243-8871
www.gemlabcdtec.com

Centro Gemologico Colombiano
Av. Jimenez N 5-43 OF 113
Colombia
Tel. (57) 001-248-4829
E-mail: colombiangemological@
  yahoo.com

Laboratorio de Certificacion de
Gemas R.G.
Av. Jimenez #5-43 Of.902
Bogota
Colombia
Tel. (57) 310-689-8392
E-mail: emerald_research@
yahoo.com

Czech Republic

General Directorate of Customs—
Customs Technical Laboratories
Budějovická 7
Prague 4, 14096
Czech Republic
Tel: (420) 261-333-841
www.celnisprava.cz

England

*AnchorCert
P.O. Box 151
Newhall Street
Birmingham B3 1SB
United Kingdom
Tel. (44) 087-1423-7922
www.anchorcert.co.uk

Department of Mineralogy
British Museum (Natural History)
Cromwell Rd.
London SW7 5BD
England
Tel. (44) 020-7942-5000
www.nhm.ac.uk

*Gem-A (The Gemmological
Association of Great Britain)
21 Ely Place
London EC1N 6TD
England
Tel. (44) 020-7404-3334
www.gem-a.com

*Huddlestone Gemmological
Consultants Ltd.
Edney House, Lower Ground Fl.
46 Hatton Garden
London EC1N 8EX
England
Tel. (44) 020-7404-5004

*Sunderland Polytechnic
Gemmological Laboratory
Dept. of Applied Geology
Benedict Bldg., St. George's Way
Stockton Rd.
Sunderland SR2 7BW
England
Tel. (44) 91-567-9316

Finland

M&A Gemological Instruments
Alhotie 14
04430 Järvenpää
Finland
www.gemmoraman.com

France

*European Gemological Laboratory
and College of Gemology
9 Rue Buffault
75009 Paris
France
Tel. (33) 1-4016-1635
www.eglinternational.org

Laboratoire Francais De
Gemmologie—CCIP (LFG)
30 rue Notre Dame des Victoires
75002 Paris
France
Tel. (33) 1-4026-2545
www.laboratoire-
francais-gemmologie.fr

Muséum National d'Histoire
  Naturelle-Minéralogie
36 Rue Geoffroy
  Saint Hilaire 75005 Paris
France
Tel: (33) 1-4079-5601
www.mnhn.fr

Germany

Bundesverband Edelstein-und
  Diamant Indusrie EV
Haptstrasse 161
55743 Idar-Oberstein
Germany
Tel. (49) 6781-944240
www.bv-edelsteine-diamanten.de

Department of Gemstone Research
Johannes Gutenberg—University
Becherweg 21
D-55099 Mainz
Germany
Tel. (49) 6131-3924-365
www.uni-mainz.de

*Deutsche Gemmologische
  Gesellschaft
(German Gemmological
  Association)
Prof.-Schlossmacher-Str. 1
D-55743 Idar-Oberstein
Germany
Tel. (49) 6781-50840
www.dgemg.com

Deutsche Stiftung
  Edelsteinforschung (DSEF)
(German Foundation for Gemstone
  Research)
Prof.-Schlossmacher Str. 1
D-55743 Idar-Oberstein
Germany
Tel. (49) 6781-50840
www.dsef.de

EPI-Institut für Edelsteinprüfung
Riesenwaldstr. 6
77797 Ohlsbach
Germany
Tel. (49) 7803-600-808
www.epigem.de

Elisabeth Strack Gemmologisches
  Institut Hamburg
Poststrasse 33
Business Center, 6th Fl.
20354 Hamburg
Germany
Tel. (49) 4035-2011
www.gemmologisches-
  institut-hamburg.de

*Stiftung Deutsches Diamant
  Institut (DDI)
Poststrasse 1
D-75172 Pforzheim
Germany
Tel. (49) 7231-32211
E-mail: ddi.diamant@t-online.de

India

Gem Identification Laboratory
S.C.O-105, 2nd Fl.
Sector-35C, Chandigarh-160 022
Chandigarh, India
Tel. (91) 172-260-0796

Gem Testing Laboratory
Rajasthan Chamber Bhawan
Mirza Ismail Rd., 3rd Fl.
Jaipur 302 003
India
Tel. (91) 141-256-8029
www.gjepc.org

Gemological Institute of India
29 Gurukul Chambers
187–189 Mumbadevi Rd.
Mumbai 400 002
Tel. (91) 22-2342-0039
www.giionline.com

Indian Diamond Institute
Katargam, GIDC, P.O. Box 508
Sumul Dairy Rd.
Surat 395 008
Gujarat, India
Tel. (91) 26-1240-7847
www.diamondinstitute.net

Indian Institute of Gemology
10980 East Park Rd.
Karol Bagh
New Delhi 110 005
India
Tel. (91) 11-2352-0924
www.iig.firm.in

International Gemological Institute
  (IGI)-India
702, the Capital Bandra Kurla
  Complex Bandra E.
Mumbai 400 051
India
Tel. (91) 22-4035-2550
www.igiworldwide.com

Universal Gemological
  Laboratories (IGC)-India
Sunville Bldg., Paper Mill Ln.
Opp-Greens Restaurant
Lamington Rd.
Mumbai 400 004
India
Tel. (91) 22-2388-2535
www.gci-gem.com

Israel

EGC European Gemological
  Center Ltd. and College
EGL Platinum Center
8 Shoham St.
Ramat Gan 5251006
Israel
Tel. (972) 3-612-1375
www.egl-platinum.com

European Gemological Laboratory
23 Tuval St.
Diamond Exchange, Noam Bldg.,
  Ste. 112
Ramat Gan 52522
Israel
Tel. (972) 3-752-8428

IDI Gemological Laboratories
  (Israel Diamond Institute)
54 Betzalel St.
Ramat Gan 52521
Israel
Tel. (972) 3-751-7845

*National Gemological Institute
  of Israel
52 Betzalel St.
Ramat Gan 52521
Israel
Tel. (972) 3-751-7845

Universal Gemological
  Laboratories (GCI)
Diamond Exchange
Maccabi Bldg., Ste. 1956
1 Jabotinsky St.
Ramat Gan 52520
Israel
Tel. (972) 3-751-4782
www.gci-gem.com

World Gemological Institute
21 Tuval St.
Ramat Gan 52522
Israel
Tel. (877) 944-5944

Italy

Alberto Scarani
Via di Santa Maria in Monticelli, 30
00186 Rome
Italy
Tel. (39) 0-6686-4946

ARCOGEM S.r.l.
Dipartimento Geomineralogico
Università degli Studi di Bari
Via E. Orabona, 4
70125 Bari
Italy
Tel. (39) 080-544-2585
www.arcogem.it

Centro Analisi Gemmologiche
Viale Vicenza, 4/D
15048 Valenza
Italy
Tel. (39) 0131-924-557
www.analisigemme.com

Gemological Education
  Certification Institute
Via delle Asole 2
20123 Milano
Tel. (39) 02-8498-0022
www.geci-web.it

Istituto Analisi Gemmologiche
Via Sassi, 44
15048 Valenza
Italy
Tel. (39) 01-3194-6586
www.tuttogemmologia.it

Istituto Gemmologico Italiano
Piazza San Sepolcro, 1
20123 Milano
Italy
Tel. (39) 02-8050-4991
www.igi.it/
  istitutogemmologicoitaliano

Istituto Gemmologico Nazionale
Via S. Sebastianello, 6 (Piazza di
  Spagna)
00187 Rome
Italy
Tel. (39) 06-678-3056
www.ignroma.it

*Laboratorio Scientifico
  Professionale di Controllo di
  Diamanti, Pietre Preziose e Perle
  della Confedorafi
Via Ugo Foscolo, 4
1-20121 Milano
Italy

Masterstones Centre for
  Gemological Analysis
Via Reberto Allesandri, 6/A
00151 Rome
Italy
Tel. (39) 06-5327-3434
www.masterstones.eu

RAG Ricerche e Analisi
  Gemmologiche
Corso San Maurizio, 52
Torino
Italy
Tel. (39) 011-887-166
www.raglabgem.com

Japan

AGT Gem Laboratory
Okachimachi Cy Bldg., 2F
5-15-14 Ueno
Taito-Ku, Tokyo 110-0005
Japan
Tel. (81) 3-3834-6586

Central Gem Laboratory
Miyagi Bldg., 2F
5-15-14 Ueno
Taito-Ku, Tokyo 110-0005
Japan
Tel. (81) 3-3836-3131
www.cgl.co.jp

CIBJO Institute of Japan
(*only diamonds*)
Tokyo-Bihokaikan 1-24
Akashi-Cho
Chuo-Ku, Tokyo
Japan
Tel. (81) 3-543-3821

Diamond Grading Laboratory
4F, Amano Bldg.
5-18-7 Ueno
Taito-Ku, Tokyo 110-0005
Japan
Tel. (81) 3-3832-2432
www.agl.jp

Diamond Grading Laboratory
5-30-12 Imaike Chikusa-ku
Aichi, Nagoya 464-0850
Japan
Tel. (81) 052-732-0580
www.agl.jp

Diamond Grading Laboratory Co.,
Ltd.
Ezebiru 4F, 3-3-10 Minami Senba
Chuo-Ku, Osaka 542-0081
Japan
Tel. (81) 6-6253-1436
www.agl.jp

Gemmological Association of All
Japan
Daiwa Ueno Bldg., 8F
5-25-11 Ueno
Taito-Ku, Tokyo 110-0005
Japan
Tel. (81) 3-3835-2466
www.gaaj-zenhokyo.co.jp

International Gemological Institute
(IGI)—Japan
UT Bldg.
2-21-13 Higashi Ueno
Taito-Ku, Tokyo 110-0005
Japan
Tel. (81) 3-5807-2958
www.igiworldwide.com

Japan Gem Testing Center
Nisshin Bldg., 5th Fl.
4-29-13 Taito
Taito-Ku, Tokyo 110-0016
Japan
Tel. (81) 3-3836-1388
E-mail: gtc@alpha.ocn.ne.jp
Also at:
1-9-24 Higashi Shinsaibashi
Chuo-Ku, Osaka 542-0083
Japan
Tel: (81) 6-6251-1571

Japan Technical Gem Laboratory
2F, Hanabusa Bldg., 2-3-5
Soto Kanda, Chiyoda-Ku
Tokyo 101-0021
Japan
Tel. (81) 3-3834-5491

Kokuhoren
2F, Sanko Higashi Shinsaibashi Bldg.
1-8-27 Higashi Shinsaibashi
Chuo-Ku, Osaka 542-0083
Japan
Tel. (81) 6-6252-8818

Kenya

Mr. P. Dougan
P.O. Box 14173
Nairobi
Kenya

Mines & Geology Department
Mandini House, Machakos Rd.
P.O. Box 30009-00100
Nairobi
Kenya
Tel. (254) 20-553-034
E-mail: cmg@mining.go.ke

*Ruby Center of Kenya, Ltd.
P.O. Box 47928, Fedha Tower 5,
2nd Fl.
Muindu Mbingu St.
Nairobi
Kenya

Liechtenstein

GGTL Laboratories
Gnetsch, 42
FL-9496 Balzers
Principality of Liechtenstein
Tel. (423) 262-24-64
www.ggtl-lab.org

Lithuania

A. Kleismantas Laboratory of
  Gemstones
"Du Safyrai"
Kurpiu St., 13
Kaunas 44287
Lithuania
Tel. (370) 37-227-780

Madagascar

Institut de Gemmologie de
  Madagascar (IGM)
Rte. d'Andraisoro Ampandrianomby
Antananarivo 101
Madagascar
Tel. (261) 20-22-591-37
www.igm.mg

Myanmar

FGA Gem Trading and Testing
  Laboratory
71 West C Block
Bogyoke Aung San Market
Yangon
Tel. (95) 9-504-2186

GGA-Genuine Gem Associates
  Co., Ltd.
474–476 Mahabandoola St.
Yangon
Tel. (95) 1-254-410

Macle Gem Trade Laboratory
98, 99 Level 3, FMI Center, Level 1
380 Bogyoke Aung San Rd.
Yangon
Tel. (95) 1-240-400/246-788/
240-376 ext. 1398
E-mail: macgems@baganmail.net.mm

Mandalay Gem Association
  Trading Co., Ltd.
91A, 77th St, Btn. 26th & 27th St.
Mandalay
Tel. (95) 02-31-248

New Aurora Gem Testing
  Laboratory
Co U Myo Chit and Daw Myint
  Myint Than
(Linn Family Jewelry)
Zay Thit
Mogok
Tel. (95) 9-697-0477

Stalwart Gem Lab
FMI Center, Rm. 33/34, Level 1
380 Bogyoke Aung San Rd.
Pabedan Tsp.
Yangon
Tel. (95) 1-240-400

Summit Gemological Laboratory
No. 23, Face Wing, 1st Fl.
Bogyoke Aung San Market
Yangon
Tel. (95) 1-253-508

The Netherlands

*Nederlands Edelsteen Laboratorium
(Dutch Precious Stone Laboratory)
  (*only gemstones*)
P.O. Box 9517
2300 RA Leiden
Tel. (31) 071-568-7596
www.naturalis.nl

*Stichting Nederlands Diamant
  Institut
  (*only diamonds*)
Van de Spiegelstraat 3
Postbus 29818
NL-2502LV's-Gravenhage
Netherlands
Tel. (31) 070-469-607

Pakistan

Al-Ahsan Jewellers & Gemologist
55 Shopping Mall, Regent Plaza
Sharah-e-Faisal, Karachi 75530
Pakistan
Tel. (92) 21-5631311
E-mail: al-ahsan@cyber.net.pk

National Center of Excellence in
  Geology
University of Peshawar
Peshawar 25120
Khyber Pakhtunkhawa, Pakistan
Tel. (92) 91-9216427
www.nceg.upesh.edu.pk

Gems Collection
No. 4, Block F, School Rd., Super
  Market
Sector F-6
Islamabad 44000
Pakistan
Tel. (92) 51-2820453
E-mail: gemscollection@gmail.com

Sagar Gems & Jewelers
Shop 10, Al Habib Arcade
Block 7, Clifton
Karachi
Pakistan
Tel. (92) 21-35863465
www.sagarjeweler.com

Portugal

LABGEM—Rui Galopim de
  Carvalho Gem Consulting
Apart. 2026, Colares 2706-909
Sintra
Portugal
Tel. (351) 21-924-2468
www.labgem.org

Russia

Expert Department of Gokran
Financial Ministry
1812 St., 14
121170 Moscow
Russia
Tel. (7) 495-148-46-67
E-mail: expgokhr@rinet.ru

Gemological Center GEMEXIM
  Ltd.
Miclukho-Maklaya St., 23
117997 Moscow
Russia
Tel. (7) 495-280-04-38
www.gigia.ru

Moscow University Main Bldg.,
  A-429
Gemological Center Testing Lab
Department of Geology
Leninskie Gory GSP-1
119991 Moscow
Russia
Tel. (7) 495-939-49-73
www.gemology.ru

Moscow Gemmological
  Certification Center
Malaya Bronnaya St., 18
103104 Moscow
Russia
Tel. (7) 495-650-72-53
www.assaygem.ru

Smolensk Gemmological
  Certification Center
Shkadova St., 2
214031 Smolensk
Russia
Tel. (7) 481-231-69-00
www.smolgem.ru

Yakutian Gemmological
  Certification Center
Assay Chamber
Oktiabrskaya St., 30
677027 Yakutsk
Russia
Tel. (7) 411-235-38-35
www.assay.ru

Singapore

Far East Gem Institute
12 Arumugam Rd.
#04-02 Lion Industrial Bldg. B
Singapore 409958
Tel. (65) 6745-8542
www.gem.com.sg

Nan Yang Gemological Institute
14 Scotts Rd.
#03-80, Far East Plaza
Singapore 228213
Tel. (65) 6333-6238
www.ngi.com.sg

South Africa

European Gemological Laboratory
225 Main St.
SA Diamond Ctr., Ste. 410, 4th Fl.
Johannesburg 2001
South Africa
Tel. (27) 11-334-4527
www.egl.co.za

*Gem Education Center
20 Drome Rd.
Lombardy
South Africa
Tel. (27) 11-346-1657
E-mail: gec@mweb.co.za

Independent Coloured Stone
  Laboratory
P.O. Box 177
Pinegowrie
Johannesburg 2123
South Africa
Tel. (27) 11-787-3326
E-mail: icamp@global.co.za

Jewellery Council of South Africa
  (JCSA)
The Hamlet
27 Ridge Rd.
Parktown, 7764
South Africa
Tel. (27) 11-484-5528
www.jewellery.org.za

South Korea

EGL Korea
701, 7th Fl., Shanho Bldg.
28 Jongro 3GA,
Jongro-gu, Seoul
Republic of Korea
Tel. (82) 2-747-6978
www.egl-labs.com

The First Gem Laboratory
37-7 Jongro 3GA
Jongro-gu, Seoul 110-390
Republic of Korea
Tel. (82) 2-3672-7592
www.firstgem.co.kr

Gemmological Association of All
 Korea
244-39 Hooam-dong Youngsan-ku
Seoul 140
Republic of Korea
Tel. (82) 2-754-5075/0642

Hanmi Gemological Institute
 Laboratory (HGI)
3F, 35-1, Sam Sam Bldg.
 Bongik-dong Jongro-gu
Seoul 110-390
Republic of Korea
Tel. (82) 2-3672-2803
www.hanmilab.co.kr

Mirae Gem Laboratory Co., Ltd.
8F, Jewelry Department Store,
 23 Bongik-dong, Jongro-gu
Seoul 110-390
Republic of Korea
Tel. (82) 2-766-3331
www.gem.or.kr

Virgin Gemological Laboratory
#501 Sanho B/D, 28 Jongro 3GA
Jongro-gu, Seoul 110-390
Republic of Korea
Tel. (82) 2-743-7100
www.virgindia.co.kr

Spain

Gemacyt Laboratorio Gemológico
C. Siena, 15. 1
28027 Madrid
Spain
Tel. (34) 91-700-0935
www.gemacyt-lab.com

*Instituto Gemologico Español
C. Alenza, 1
28003 Madrid
Spain
Tel. (34) 914-414-300
www.ige.org

Laboratorio Gemologico Gemior S.L.
Av. Baron De Carcer 48-6M
46001 Valencia
Spain
Tel. (34) 963-517-311

Laboratorio Gemológico
 MLLOPIS
Burriana, 42, 6, PTA
12-46005 Valencia
Spain
Tel. (34) 96-374-9078
www.mllopis.com

Laboratorio Oficial
Viladomat, 89–95, E-3
08015 Barcelona
Spain
Tel. (34) 93-292-4712
E-mail: as.gemmologia@sefes.es

Sri Lanka

Gemmologist Association of Sri
 Lanka
275/76 Stanley Wijesundara
 Mawatha
Colombo 7
Sri Lanka
Tel. (94) 11-2-590944
www.gemmology.lk

Lakshani Gem Testing Laboratory
52A, Galle Rd.
Colombo 3
Sri Lanka
Tel. (94) 11-2-337443

National Gem and Jewellery
  Authority
No. 25, Galle Face Terrace
Colombo 3
Sri Lanka
Tel. (94) 11-2-390658
www.srilankagemautho.com

Petrological Laboratory
Geological Survey Dept.
569 Epitamulla Rd.
Pitakotte
Sri Lanka
Tel. (94) 11-2-886289

Sheriff Abdul Rahuman
95A, Chatham St.
Colombo 1
Sri Lanka
Tel. (94) 11-2-502759
E-mail: sheriff@qtex.com

*University of Moratuwa
  Gemmology Laboratory/Dept. of
  Earth Resources
Katubedda Campus
Moratuwa
Sri Lanka
Tel. (94) 11-2-650353
www.ere.mrt.ac.lk

Sweden

Rolf Krieger Ltd.
S-141/46 Huddinge
Sweden

Swedish Institute for Gem Testing
Alsatravagen 120
S-12736 Skarholmen
Sweden

Switzerland

*Gemgrading
Rue Albert-Gos 4
1206 Geneva
Switzerland
Tel. (41) 22-346-6061

*Gemmologie Laboratoire
  Services
Rue de Bourg 3
CH-1002 Lausanne
Switzerland
Tel. (41) 32-721-4172
www.gls-gemmologie.ch

GGTL Laboratories
Rte. des Jeunes 4B
1227 Les Acacias
Geneva
Switzerland
Tel. (41) 22-731-5880
www.gemtechlab.ch

GRS Gemresearch Swisslab AG
P.O. Box 3628
6002 Lucerne
Switzerland
Tel. (41) 41-210-3131
www.gemresearch.ch

*Gübelin Gem Lab Ltd.
Maihofstrasse 102
6006 Lucerne
Switzerland
Tel. (41) 41-429-1717
www.gubelingemlab.com

*Swiss Gemmological Institute
  (SSEF)
Falknerstrasse 9
CH-4001 Basel
Switzerland
Tel. (41) 61-262-0640
www.ssef.ch

Thailand

*Asian Institute of Gemological
  Sciences
919/1 Silom Rd.
Jewelry Trade Center, 2nd Fl.,
  Unit. 214
Bangrak, Bangkok 10500
Thailand
Tel. (66) 2-267-4325
www.aigsthailand.com

Emil Gem Laboratory (Japan)
4F4 4th Fl., BIS Bldg.
119 Mahesak Rd.
Bangkok 10500
Thailand
Tel. (66) 2-234-8872
www.emil.co.th

Gem and Jewelry Institute of
  Thailand
140/1–3, 5 Tower Bldg.
Silom Rd., Sungawong
Bangrak, Bangkok 10500
Thailand
Tel. (66) 2-634-4999
www.git.or.th

GRS (Thailand) Co., Ltd.
Unit 501–506, Silom 9 Bldg.
Soi 19, Silom
Bangrak, Bangkok 10500
Thailand
Tel. (66) 2-237-5898
www.gemresearch.ch

International Gemological Institute
BGI Bldg., 9 Soi Charoen Krung
36 New Rd.
Bangkok 10500
Thailand
Tel. (66) 2-630-6728
www.igiworldwide.com

United Arab Emirates

Dubai Central Laboratory—Dubai
  Gemstone Laboratory
Dubai Municipality
P.O. Box 67
Dubai
United Arab Emirates
Tel. (971) 4-302-7007
www.dcl.ae

Dubai Gem Certification
  Convention Tower
World Trade Center Complex
  7th Fl., # 702
P.O. Box 48800
Dubai United Arab Emirates
Tel. (971) 4-329-2499
E-mail: laurent.grenier@dmcc.ae

International Gemological Institute
  (IGI)—Dubai
Office Unit 27 A, B, C, & G,
  Almas Tower, Plot LT-2
Jumeriah Lake Towers
Dubai
United Arab Emirates
Tel. (971) 4-450-8027
www.igiworldwide.com

Zimbabwe

Gem Education Centre of
  Zimbabwe
Faye March Jewelers
  1st Fl., Travel Plaza
29 Mazowe St.
Harare 707580
Zimbabwe
Tel. (263) 4-707-922
E-mail: fayemarch@zol.co.zw

International List of Associations

Australia

Gemmological Association of
  Australia (Queensland Division)
P.O. Box 967
North Lakes QLD 4509
Australia
Tel. (61) 7-3481-2857
www.gem.org.au

Gemmological Association of
  Australia (South Australia
  Division)
P.O. Box 191
Adelaide SA 5001
Australia
Tel. (61) 8-8227-1377
www.gem.org.au

Australian Gem Industry Association
31 Market St.
Sydney
NSW 2000
Australia
Tel. (02) 92-67-13-10

Austria

Bundesgremium Des Handels Mit
  Juwelen
Karl M. Heldwein
P.O. Box 440
A-1045 Vienna
Austria

Brazil

Brazilian Gemological and
  Mineralogical Association
Rue Barao de Itapetininga
Galeria California
No. 255, 12 Andar Conj.
  1213/1214
Sao Paolo 01042-001
Brazil
Tel. (55) 11-3231-0916
www.abgm.com.br

Ajorio-Sindicato National
Do. Com. Atacadista de Pedras
  Preciosas
Av. Graça Aranha, 19-404
  Group-Centro
Rio de Janeiro 20030-002
Brazil
Tel. (55) 21-2220-8004
www.sistemaajorio.com.br

Brazilian Association of
  Gemologists & Jewelry
  Appraisers (ABGA)
Rua Visconde de Pirajá 540,
  Ste. 211
Rio de Janeiro 22410-001
Brazil
Tel. (55) 21-2540-0059
www.gemsconsult.com.br

Centro Gemologico da Bahia
Ladeira do Carmo, 37
Santo Antonio (Centro Historico)
Salvador 40301-410
Brazil
Tel. (55) 71-3326-1747
www.cgb.ba.gov

GEMLAB-IGC-USP
Rua do Lago 562
Instituto de Geociencias da USP
Sao Paulo 01042-001
Brazil
Tel. (55) 11-3091-3958
www.usp.br

Gemological Laboratory of the
  Center for Mineral Technology
  (CETEM)
Ministry of Science, Technology
  and Innovation
Ave. Pedro Calmon, 900, Cidade
  Universitária
Rio de Janeiro 21941-908
Brazil
Tel. (55) 21-3865-7222
www.cetem.gov.br

IBGM Gemological Laboratory
SCN Centro Empresarial A,
  Conj. 1105
Brasilia, DF 70712-903
Brazil
Tel. (55) 61-3326-3926
www.ibgm.com.br

Laboratório Gemológico AJORIO
Av. Graça Aranha
19 Gr. 404
Rio de Janeiro 20030-002
Brazil
Tel. (55) 21-2220-8004
www.ajorio.com.br

Laboratório Gemológico Dr.
  Hécliton Santini Henriques
Ave. Paulista, 688, 17th Fl.
Belavista 01310-100
Brazil
Tel. (55) 11-3016-5850
www.ajesp.com.br

Sistema Sindijoias Ajomig
Goitacazes St., 10th Fl. Ste. 1003
Centro, Belo Horizonte,
  30190-050
Brazil
Tel. (55) 31-3214-3545
www.sindijoiasmg.com.br

Realgems-Laboratório Gemológico
Rua Visconde de Pirajá 540,
  Ste. 210
Rio de Janeiro
Brazil
Tel. (55) 21-2239-4078
www.realgemslab.com.br

Canada

Association Professionelle des
  Gemmologists du Quebec
6079 Boul. Monk
Montreal, QC
H4E 3H5
Canada
Tel. (514) 766-7327

Canadian Gemmological
  Association
55 Queen St. E, Lower Concourse,
  Ste. 105
Toronto, ON
M5C 1R6
Canada
Tel. (647) 466-2436
www.canadiangemmological.com

Canadian Jewellers Association
27 Queen St. E., Ste. 600
Toronto, ON
M5C 2M6
Canada
Tel. (416) 368-7616
www.canadianjewellers.com

China

Gemmological Association of
  China
Fl. 22, Bldg. C, Global Trade Ctr.
36 North Third Ring Rd.
Beijing 100013
China
Tel: (86) 10-5827-6081
www.jewellery.org.cn

Gemmological Association of
  Hong Kong (GAHK)
P.O. Box 97711, TST
Kowloon
Hong Kong
China
Tel. (852) 2366-6006
www.gahk.org

International Colored Gemstone
  Association
Unit No. 11, 8th Fl.
Heng Ngai Jewelry Centre
No. 4 Hok Yuen St. E.
Hung Hom, Kowloon
Hong Kong
China
Tel. (852) 2365-9318
www.gemstone.org

National Gemstone Testing Centre
  (NGTC)
No. 19 Xiaohuangzhuang Rd.
Andingmenwai St.
Beijing 100013
China
Tel. (86) 10-8427-4008
www.ngtc.gov.cn

England

De Beers UK Ltd.
17 Charthouse St.
London EC1N 6RA
England
Tel. (44) 20-7404-4444
www.debeersgroup.com

Gem-A (The Gemmological
  Association of Great Britain)
21 Ely Place
London EC1N 6TD
England
Tel. (44) 20-7407-3334
www.gem-a.com

Jewellery Information Centre
44 Fleet St.
London ECA
England

Finland

Gemmological Society of Finland
P.O. Box 6287
Helsinki
Finland

France

Association Francaise de
  Gemmologie
7 Rue Cadet
75009 Paris
France
Tel. (33) 1-4246-7846
www.afgemmologie-lyon.fr

Claude Varnier
Service Public du Controle
2 Place de la Bourse
75002 Paris
France

French Diamond Association
7 Rue du Chatesudun
75009 Paris
France

Syndicat des Maitres Artisans
  bijoutiers-joailliers
3 Rue Sainte-Elisabeth
75003 Paris
France

Germany

Deutsche Gemmologische
  Gesellschaft
(German Gemmological
  Association)
Prof.-Schlossmacher-Str. 1
D-55743 Idar-Oberstein
Germany
Tel. (49) 6781-50840
www.dgemg.com

Diamant-und Edelsteinbörse
  Idar-Oberstein EV
Hauptsrasse 161
55743 Idar-Oberstein
Germany
Tel. (49) 6781-94420
www.diamant-edelstein-boerse.de

India

The All India Jewellers
  Association
19 Connaught Pl.
New Delhi
India

Bangiya Swarna Silpi Samitee
82 Prem Chand Boral St.
Kolkata 700 012
India
Tel. (91) 33-2219-7878

Bombay Jewellers Association
308 Sheikh Memon St.
Mumbai 400 002
India

The Cultured and Natural Pearl
  Association
1st Agiary Ln., Dhanji St.
Mumbai 400 003
India

Gem and Jewellery Information
  Centre of India
A-95, Jana Colony
Journal House
Jaipur 302 004
Rajasthan
India
Tel. (91) 141-261-4398

Gold, Silver, Jewellery and
  Diamond Merchants Association
1-3-65 Dhan Bazar
Secunderabad
Telangana 500 003
India
Tel. (91) 40-2781-6433

Gujarat State Gold Dealers and
  Jewellers Association
2339-2, Manek Chowk
Ahmedabad, Gujarat
India

Jewellers Association
835/1 Sridevi Shopping Arcade
Nagarthpet, Bangalore
Karnataka 560 002
India
Tel. (91) 80-2221-1037

Tamil Nadu Jewellers Federation
  (also The Madras Jewellers
  & Diamond Merchants
  Association)
2/10 Car St.
NSC Bose Rd., Sowcarpet
Chennai 600 079
India
Tel. (91) 44-4216-7405
www.mjdma.org

Indonesia

Indonesian Gemstone & Jewelery
  Association
L.G. Tampubolon
JL Teuku Umar 53
Jakarta 10310
Indonesia

Israel

Gemmological Association of
  Israel
Diamon Exchange
Maccabi Bldg., Ste. 1956
1 Jabotinsky St.
Ramat Gan 52520
Israel
Tel. (972) 3-751-4782
www.gci-gem.com

Italy

CIBJO
Piazza G.G. Belli, 2
Roma 00153
Italy
Tel. (39) 06-58-661

Istituto Gemmologico Italiano
Piazza San Sepolcro, 1
Milano 20123
Italy
Tel. (39) 02-8050-4991
www.igi.it

Japan

CIBJO Institute of Japan
Tokyo-Bihokaikan 1-24
Akashi-Cho
Chuo-Ku, Tokyo
Japan
Tel. (81) 3-543-3821

Gemmological Association of All
  Japan
Daiwa Ueno Bldg., 8F
5-25-11, Ueno
Taito-Ku, Tokyo 110-0005
Japan
Tel. (81) 3-3835-2466
www.gaaj-zenhokyo.co.jp

Kenya

Kenya Gemstone Dealers
  Association
P.O. Box 47928
Nairobi
Kenya

Malaysia

Malaysian Institute of
  Gemmological Sciences
Wisma Stephens
Lot 3, 76-3, 78, 3rd Fl.
Jalan Caja Chulma
Kuala Lumpur
Malaysia

Myanmar

Gem and Jade Corporation
86, Kala Aye Pagoda Rd.
P.O. Box 1397
Rangoon
Myanmar

Pakistan

All Pakistan Gem Merchants and
  Jewellers Association
1st Fl., Gems & Jewellery Trade
  Centre
Blenken St., off Zaibunnisa St.
Saddar, Karachi 74400
Pakistan
Tel. (92) 21-35210400

Singapore

Singapore Gemologist Society
20 Maxwell Rd., #06–07/08,
  Maxwell House
69113
Singapore

South Africa

Gemological Association of South
  Africa
A. Thomas
P.O. Box 4216
Johannesburg 2000
South Africa

Sri Lanka

Gemmologists Association of Sri
  Lanka
Professional Centre
275/76 Stanley Wijesundera,
  Mawatha
Colombo 7
Sri Lanka
Tel. (94) 11-2-590944
www.gemmology.lk

Sweden

Swedish Association of
  Gemmologists
Birger Jarlsgatan 88
S-114 20 Stockholm
Sweden

Swedish Geological Society
Box 670
S-751 28 Uppsala
Sweden
Tel. (46) 018-179-000
www.geologiskaforeningen.se

Switzerland

CIBJO—The World Jewellery
  Confederation
Schmiedenplatz 5
Postfach 258
CH-3000 Bern 7
Switzerland
Tel. (41) 31-329-20-72
www.cibjo.org

Swiss Gemmological Society
Schmiedenplatz 5
Postfach 258
3000 Bernz
Switzerland
Tel. (41) 31-329-20-72
www.gemmologie.ch

Swiss Gem Trade Association
Nuschelerstrasse. 44
8001 Zurich
Switzerland

Thailand

Asian Institute of Gemological
  Sciences
919/1 Silom Rd.
Jewelry Trade Center, 2nd Fl.,
  Unit 214
Bangrak, Bangkok 10500
Thailand
Tel. (66) 2-267-4325
www.aigsthailand.com

Thai Gems and Jewelry Traders
  Association
919/119, 919/615–621 Jewelry
  Trade Center, 52nd Fl.
Silom Rd.
Bangrak, Bangkok 10500
Thailand
Tel. (66) 2-630-1390
www.thaigemjewelry.or.th

United Arab Emirates

Institute of Goldsmithing and
  Jewellery
Sikat Al Khail Rd.
P.O. Box 11489
Dubai, UAE

United States

Accredited Gemologists Association
3315 Juanita St.
San Diego, CA 92105
Tel. (619) 501-5444
www.accreditedgemologists.org

American Gem Society
8881 W. Sahara Ave.
Las Vegas, NV 89117
Tel. (866) 805-6500
www.americangemsociety.org

American Gem Trade Association
3030 LBJ Freeway, Ste. 840
Dallas, TX 75234
Tel. (800) 972-1162
www.agta.org

American Society of Appraisers
11170 Sunset Hills Rd., Ste. 310
Reston, VA 20190
Tel. (703) 478-2228
www.appraisers.org

Appraisers Association of America
212 W. 35th St., 11 Fl. S.
New York, NY 10001
Tel. (212) 889-5404
www.appraisersassoc.org

Diamond Council of America, Inc.
3212 West End Ave., Ste. 400
Nashville, TN 37203
Tel. (615) 385-5301
www.diamondcouncil.org

International Colored Gemstone
  Association
62 West 47th St., Ste. 905
New York, NY 10036
Tel. (212) 620-0900
www.gemstone.org

Jewelers of America, Inc.
120 Broadway, Ste. 2820
New York, NY 10271
Tel. (800) 223-0673
www.jewelers.org

National Association of Jewelry
  Appraisers
P.O. Box 18
Rego Park, NY 11374
Tel. (718) 896-1536
www.najaappraisers.com

New York Diamond Dealers Club
580 5th Ave. at 11 W. 47th St.,
  Fl. 580
New York, NY 10036
Tel. (212) 790-3600 ex 1113
www.nyddc.com

Zambia

Zambia Gemstone and Precious
  Metal Association
P.O. Box 31099, Rm. 17
Luangwa House
Cairo Rd., Lusaka
Zambia

Zimbabwe

Gem Education Centre of
  Zimbabwe
Faye Marsh Jewelers, 1st Fl.,
  Travel Plaza
29 Mazowe St.
Harare 707580
Zimbabwe
Tel. (263) 4-707-922
E-mail: fayemarch@zol.co.zu

Selected List of
Gem Identification Equipment Suppliers
in the United States and Canada

Bausch & Lomb, Inc.
1 Bausch & Lomb Pl.
Rochester, NY 14604
Tel. (585) 338-6000

Berco Company
29 E. Madison St., Ste. 550
Chicago, IL 60602
Tel. (800) 621-0668
www.bercojewelry.com

Bourget Bros.
1636 11th St.
Santa Monica, CA 90404
Tel. (310) 450-6556
www.bourgetbros.com

Carl Zeiss, Inc.
One Zeiss Dr.
Thornwood, NY 10594
Tel. (914) 747-1800
www.zeiss.com

Cas-Ker Co.
2550 Civic Ctr. Dr.
Cincinnati, OH 45231
Tel. (513) 674-7700
www.casker.com

The Contenti Co.
515 Narragansett Park Dr. 1
Pawtucket, RI 02861
Tel. (401) 305-3000
www.contenti.com

Dallas Jewelry Supply House
9979 Monroe Dr.
Dallas, TX 75220
Tel. (214) 351-2263

Ebersole's Lapidary Supply Inc.
5830 W. Hendryx Ave.
Wichita, KS 67209
Tel. (316) 945-4771

Esslinger & Co.
1165 Medallion Dr.
Saint Paul, MN 55120
Tel. (651) 452-7180
www.esslinger.com

Euro Tool, Inc.
14101 Botts Rd.
Grandview, MO 64030
Tel. (800) 552-3131
www.eurotool.com

FDJ On Time
1180 Solana Ave.
Winter Park, FL 32789
Tel. (800) 323-6091
www.fdjtool.com

Findco, Inc.
6222 Richmond Ave., Ste. 610
Houston, TX 77057
Tel. (888) 712-0093
www.findcoinc.com

Gemological Products Corporation
56771 Lunar Dr.
Sunriver, OR 97707
Tel. (541) 593-9663
www.gemproducts.com

GemStone Press
Sunset Farm Offices, Rte. 4
P.O. Box 237
Woodstock, VT 05091
Tel. (802) 457-4000
Tel. (800) 962-4544
www.gemstonepress.com

GIA Gem Instruments
Gemological Institute of America
5345 Armada Dr., Ste. 300
Carlsbad, CA 92008
Tel. (800) 421-7250
www.gia.edu
Also at:
W. 47th St. 50, Unit 800
New York, NY 10036
Tel. (212) 221-5858

Hanneman Gemological
  Instruments
P.O. Box 1944
Granbury, TX 76048
Tel. (817) 573-9552

Kassoy, Inc.
28 W 47th 2
New York, NY 10036
Tel. (212) 719-2291
www.kassoy.com

Sy Kessler Sales, Inc.
10455 Olympic Dr.
Dallas, TX 75220
Tel. (800) 527-0719
www.sykessler.com

Kingsley North, Inc.
910 Brown St.
Norway, MI 49870
Tel. (800) 338-9280
www.kingsleynorth.com

Linton Enterprises P/L
1 Sophie Court
Wellington Point, QLD 4160
Australia
Tel. (61) 7-3207-3782

Livesay's
456 W. Columbus Dr.
Tampa, FL 33602
Tel. (813) 229-2715
www.livesaysinc.com

J.F. McCaughin Co.
2628 N. River Ave.
Rosemead, CA 91770
Tel. (626) 573-3000

M&A Gemological Instruments
Alhotie 14
04430 Järvenpää
Finland
www.gemmoraman.com

Nikon, Inc., Instrument Division
1300 Walt Whitman Rd.
Melville, NY 11747
Tel. (631) 547-8500
www.nikoninstruments.com

Otto Frei and Jules Borel
P.O. Box 796
126 Second St.
Oakland, CA 94604
Tel. (510) 832-0355
www.ofrei.com

Page and Wilson, Ltd.
5608 Goring St.
Burnaby, BC
V5B 3A3
Canada
Tel. (604) 685-8257
www.pwltd.com

Raytech Industries
475 Smith St.
Middletown, CT 06457
Tel. (800) 243-7163
www.raytech-ind.com

Rio Grande
7500 Bluewater Rd. NW
Albuquerque, NM 87121
Tel. (800) 545-6566
www.riogrande.com

Roseco, Inc.
13740 Omega Rd.
Dallas, TX 75244
Tel. (800) 527-4490
www.roseco.com

Rosenthal Jewelers Supply Corp.
145 E. Flagler St.
Miami, FL 33131
Tel. (800) 327-5784
www.jewelerstoystore.com

Spectronics Corporation
956 Brush Hollow Rd.
Westbury, NY 11590
Tel. (800) 274-8888
www.spectroline.com

Stuller
P.O. Box 87777
Lafayette, LA 70598
Tel. (800) 877-7777
www.stuller.com

Transcontinental Tool Co.
55 Queen St. E.
Toronto, ON
M5C 1R6
Canada
Tel. (416) 363-2940

Tulper and Co.
2223 E. Colfax Ave.
Denver, CO 80206
Tel. (303) 399-9291

Vibrograf USA Corp.
504 Cherry Ln.
Floral Park, NY 11001
Tel. (516) 437-8700

INDEX

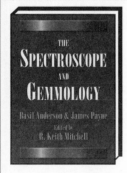

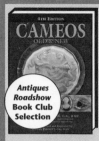
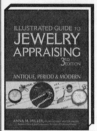

DIAMONDS, 3RD EDITION
THE ANTOINETTE MATLINS BUYING GUIDE
How to Select, Buy, Care for & Enjoy Diamonds with Confidence and Knowledge
by Antoinette Matlins, PG, FGA

Practical, comprehensive, and easy to understand, this book includes price guides for old and new cuts and for fancy-color, treated and synthetic diamonds. **Explains in detail** how to read diamond grading reports and offers important advice for after buying a diamond. **The "unofficial bible" for all diamond buyers who want to get the most for their money.**

6 x 9, 240 pp, 12 full-color pages, with over 150 color and b/w photos and illus.; index
Quality Paperback Original, 978-0-943763-73-6 **$18.99**

COLORED GEMSTONES, 3RD EDITION
THE ANTOINETTE MATLINS BUYING GUIDE
How to Select, Buy, Care for & Enjoy Sapphires, Emeralds, Rubies and Other Colored Gems with Confidence and Knowledge
by Antoinette Matlins, PG, FGA

This practical, comprehensive, easy-to-understand guide **provides in depth** all the information you need to buy colored gems with confidence. Includes price guides for popular gems, opals and synthetic stones. Provides examples of gemstone grading reports and offers important advice for after buying a gemstone. **Shows anyone shopping for colored gemstones how to get the most for their money.**

6 x 9, 256 pp, 24 full-color pages, with over 200 color and b/w photos and illus.; index
Quality Paperback Original, 978-0-943763-72-9 **$18.99**

THE PEARL BOOK, 4TH EDITION
THE DEFINITIVE BUYING GUIDE
How to Select, Buy, Care for & Enjoy Pearls
by Antoinette Matlins, PG, FGA
COMPREHENSIVE • EASY TO READ • PRACTICAL

This comprehensive, authoritative guide tells readers everything they need to know about pearls to fully understand and appreciate them, and avoid any unexpected—and costly—disappointments, now and in future generations.

- A journey into the rich history and romance surrounding pearls.
- The five factors that determine pearl value & judging pearl quality.
- What to look for, what to look out for: How to spot fakes. Treatments.
- Differences between natural, cultured and imitation pearls, and ways to separate them.
- Comparisons of all types of pearls, in every size and color, from every pearl-producing country.

6 x 9, 232 pp, 16 full-color pages, with over 250 color and b/w photos and illus.; index
Quality Paperback, 978-0-943763-54-5 **$19.99**

The "Unofficial Bible" for the Gem & Jewelry Buyer

AWARD WINNER

Book Club Selection

JEWELRY & GEMS
THE BUYING GUIDE, 7TH EDITION

How to Buy Diamonds, Pearls, Colored Gemstones, Gold & Jewelry with Confidence and Knowledge

by Antoinette Matlins, PG, FGA, *and* A. C. Bonanno, FGA, ASA, MGA

—over 400,000 copies in print—

Learn the tricks of the trade from *insiders:* How to buy diamonds, pearls, precious and other popular colored gems with confidence and knowledge. More than just a buying guide . . . discover what's available and what choices you have, what determines quality as well as cost, what questions to ask before you buy and what to get in writing. Easy to read and understand. Excellent for staff training.

6 x 9, 352 pp, 16 full-color pages, with over 200 color and b/w photos and illus.; index

Quality Paperback, 978-0-943763-71-2 **$19.99**

ENGAGEMENT & WEDDING RINGS, 3RD EDITION

by Antoinette Matlins, PG, FGA, *and* A. C. Bonanno, FGA, ASA, MGA

COMPREHENSIVE • EASY TO READ • PRACTICAL

Tells **everything you need to know to design, select, buy and enjoy that "perfect" ring** and to truly experience the wonder and excitement that should be part of it.

Updated, expanded, filled with valuable information.

Engagement & Wedding Rings, 3rd Ed., will help you make the *right* choice. You will discover romantic traditions behind engagement and wedding rings, how to select the right style and design for *you*, tricks to get what you want on a budget, ways to add new life to an "heirloom," what to do to protect yourself against fraud, and much more.

6 x 9, 320 pp, 16 full-color pages, with over 400 color and b/w photos and illus.; index

Quality Paperback Original, 978-0-943763-41-5 **$18.95**

JEWELRY & GEMS AT AUCTION
The Definitive Guide to Buying & Selling at the Auction House & on Internet Auction Sites

by Antoinette Matlins, PG, FGA

with contributions by Jill Newman

As buying and selling at auctions—both traditional auction houses and "virtual" Internet auctions—moves into the mainstream, **consumers need to know how to "play the game."** There are treasures to be had and money to be saved and made, but buying and selling at auction offers unique risks as well as unique opportunities. This book makes available—for the first time—detailed information on how to buy and sell jewelry and gems at auction without making costly mistakes.

6 x 9, 352 pp, 16 full-color pages, with over 150 color and b/w photos and illus.; index

Quality Paperback Original, 978-0-943763-29-3 **$19.95**

Buy Your *"Tools of the Trade ..."*

Gem Identification Instruments Directly from *GemStone Press*

Whatever instrument you need, GemStone Press can help.
Use our convenient order form, or contact us directly for assistance.

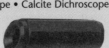
ITEM / QUANTITY	PRICE EA.*	TOTAL $
Pocket Instrument Set		
_____ With Bausch & Lomb 10X Loupe • EZview Dichroscope • Chelsea Filter	$179.95	_____
Loupes—Professional Jeweler's 10X Triplet Loupes		
_____ Bausch & Lomb 10X Triplet Loupe	$44.00	_____
_____ Standard 10X Triplet Loupe	$29.00	_____
_____ Dark-field Loupe	$58.95	_____
• Spot filled diamonds, identify inclusions in colored gemstones. Operates with Standard Mini Maglite (additional—see below).		
Calcite Dichroscope		
_____ Dichroscope (EZview)	$115.00	
Color Filters		
_____ Chelsea Filter	$44.95	_____
_____ Synthetic Emerald Filter Set (Hanneman)	$34.95	_____
_____ Tanzanite Filter (Hanneman)	$29.95	_____
_____ Bead Buyer's & Parcel Picker's Filter Set (Hanneman)	$24.00	_____
Diamond Testers and Tweezers		
_____ SSEF Blue Diamond Tester	$695.00	_____
_____ SSEF Diamond-Type Spotter	$150.00	_____
_____ DiamondNite Dual Tester	$269.00	_____
_____ Diamond Tweezers/Locking	$10.65	_____
_____ Diamond Tweezers/Non-Locking	$7.80	_____
Jewelry Cleaner		
_____ Speed Brite Ionic Jewelry Cleaner	$85.00	_____
_____ Ionic Solution—32 oz. bottle	$22.00	_____

Buy Your "Tools of the Trade ..."
Gem Identification Instruments Directly from *GemStone Press*
Whatever instrument you need, GemStone Press can help.
Use our convenient order form, or contact us directly for assistance.

ITEM / QUANTITY	PRICE EA.*	TOTAL $
Lamps—Ultraviolet & High Intensity		
_____ UV-Blocking Goggles	$24.95	_____
• Recommended for use with all UV lamps.		
_____ Portable Longwave/Shortwave (UVP)	$85.00	_____
_____ High Intensity Longwave/Shortwave (UVP)	$237.00	_____
_____ Viewing Cabinet for Large Lamp (UVP)	$195.00	_____
_____ **Purchase Large Lamp & Cabinet together**	$385.95	_____
and save over $45.00		
_____ SSEF High-Intensity Shortwave Illuminator	$499.00	_____
• Operates with SSEF Diamond-Type Spotter (additional—see above).		
Other Light Sources		
_____ Standard Mini Maglite	$15.00	_____
_____ Flex Light	$29.95	_____
Polariscope		
_____ Polariscope	$145.00	_____
Refractometer		
_____ Refractometer-Eickhorst	$649.00	_____
_____ Refractometer-Fable	$550.00	_____
_____ Refractive Index Liquid 1.81—10 grams	$69.95	_____
Scale		
_____ GemPro500 Precision Scale	$225.00	_____
Spectroscopes		
_____ Spectroscope—Pocket-sized model (OPL)	$98.00	_____
_____ Spectroscope—Desk model w/stand (OPL)	$235.00	_____
_____ Spectroscope—Prism	$115.00	_____

Shipping/Insurance per order in the U.S.: $10.95 first item, SHIPPING/INS. $_____
$3.95 each add'l item; $14.95 total for pocket instrument set.

Outside the U.S.: Please specify *insured* shipping method you prefer
and provide a credit card number for payment.
TOTAL $ _____ **

Check enclosed for $ _____ (Payable to: GEMSTONE PRESS)
Charge my credit card: ❏ Visa ❏ MasterCard
Name on Card _____ Phone (_____)_____
Cardholder Address: Street _____
City/State/Zip _____ E-mail _____
Credit Card # _____ Exp. Date _____
Signature _____ CID # _____
Please send to: ❏ Same as Above ❏ Address Below
Name _____
Street _____
City/State/Zip _____ Phone (_____)_____

Phone, mail, fax, or e-mail orders to:
GEMSTONE PRESS, P.O. Box 237, Woodstock, VT 05091
Tel: (802) 457-4000 • Fax: (802) 457-4004
Credit Card Orders: (800) 962-4544 (8:30AM–5:30PM EST Monday–Friday)
sales@gemstonepress.com • www.gemstonepress.com
Generous Discounts on Quantity Orders

TOTAL SATISFACTION GUARANTEE
If for any reason you're not completely delighted
with your purchase, return it in resellable condition
within 30 days for a full refund.

*Prices, manufacturing specifications and terms subject to change
without notice. Orders accepted subject to availability.

**All orders must be prepaid by credit card, money order or
check in U.S. funds drawn on a U.S. bank.

Please send me:

CAMEOS OLD & NEW, 4TH EDITION
_____ copies at $24.99 (Quality Paperback) *plus s/h**

COLORED GEMSTONES, 3RD EDITION: THE ANTOINETTE MATLINS BUYING GUIDE
_____ copies at $18.99 (Quality Paperback) *plus s/h**

DIAMONDS, 3RD EDITION: THE ANTOINETTE MATLINS BUYING GUIDE
_____ copies at $18.99 (Quality Paperback) *plus s/h**

ENGAGEMENT & WEDDING RINGS, 3RD EDITION: THE DEFINITIVE BUYING GUIDE
_____ copies at $18.95 (Quality Paperback) *plus s/h**

**GEM IDENTIFICATION MADE EASY, 5TH EDITION:
A HANDS-ON GUIDE TO MORE CONFIDENT BUYING & SELLING**
_____ copies at $38.99 (Hardcover) *plus s/h**

GEMS & JEWELRY APPRAISING, 3RD EDITION
_____ copies at $49.99 (Hardcover) *plus s/h**

ILLUSTRATED GUIDE TO JEWELRY APPRAISING, 3RD EDITION
_____ copies at $49.99 (Hardcover) *plus s/h**

**JEWELRY & GEMS AT AUCTION: THE DEFINITIVE GUIDE TO BUYING & SELLING
AT THE AUCTION HOUSE & ON INTERNET AUCTION SITES**
_____ copies at $19.95 (Quality Paperback) *plus s/h**

JEWELRY & GEMS, 7TH EDITION: THE BUYING GUIDE
_____ copies at $19.99 (Quality Paperback) *plus s/h**

THE PEARL BOOK, 4TH EDITION: THE DEFINITIVE BUYING GUIDE
_____ copies at $19.99 (Quality Paperback) *plus s/h**

THE SPECTROSCOPE AND GEMMOLOGY
_____ copies at $49.95 (Quality Paperback) *plus s/h**

**TREASURE HUNTER'S GEM & MINERAL GUIDES TO THE U.S.A., 5TH EDITION:
WHERE & HOW TO DIG, PAN AND MINE YOUR OWN GEMS & MINERALS
IN 4 REGIONAL VOLUMES** $14.99 per copy (Quality Paperback) *plus s/h**
_____ copies of NE States _____ copies of SE States _____ copies of NW States _____ copies of SW States

*In U.S.: Shipping/Handling: $3.95 for 1st book, $2.50 each additional book.
Outside U.S.: Specify shipping method (insured) and provide a credit card number for payment.

Check enclosed for $_____ (Payable to: GemStone Press)
Charge my credit card: ❏ Visa ❏ MasterCard
Name on Card (PRINT) _____ Phone (_____)_____
Cardholder Address: Street _____
City/State/Zip _____ E-mail _____
Credit Card # _____ Exp. Date _____
Signature _____ CID # _____
Please send to: ❏ Same as Above ❏ Address Below
Name (PRINT)_____
Street _____
City/State/Zip _____ Phone (_____)_____

**TOTAL
SATISFACTION
GUARANTEE**
If for any reason you're
not completely delight-
ed with your purchase,
return it in resellable
condition within 30
days for a full refund.

Phone, mail, fax, or e-mail orders to:
GEMSTONE PRESS, Sunset Farm Offices,
Rte. 4, P.O. Box 237, Woodstock, VT 05091
Tel: (802) 457-4000 • *Fax:* (802) 457-4004
Credit Card Orders: (800) 962-4544
(8:30AM–5:30PM EST Monday–Friday)
sales@gemstonepress.com • www.gemstonepress.com
Generous Discounts on Quantity Orders

Prices subject
to change

Try Your Bookstore First